DURABLE BY DESIGN?

Following the landmark Paris Agreement, policy makers are under pressure to adopt policies that rapidly deliver deep, society-wide decarbonisation. Deep decarbonisation requires more durable policies, but not enough is known about whether and how they actually emerge. This book provides the first systematic analysis of the determinants of policy durability in three high-profile areas: biofuel production, car transport and industrial emissions. It breaks new ground by exploring how key European Union climate policies have shaped their own durability and their ability to stimulate supportive political dynamics in society. It combines state-of-the-art policy theories with empirical accounts of landmark political events such as 'Dieselgate' and the campaign against 'dirty' biofuels, to offer a fresh understanding of how and why policy makers set about packaging together different elements of policy. By shining new light on an important area of contemporary policy making, it reveals a rich agenda for academic researchers and policy makers.

ANDREW J. JORDAN is Professor of Environmental Policy at the Tyndall Centre for Climate Change Research, University of East Anglia. He has published extensively on European Union (EU) and United Kingdom (UK) environmental policy and politics, and provided expert advice to both EU and UK institutions. He is a director of the Economic and Social Research Council (ESRC) Centre for Climate Change and Social Transformations (CAST), and a co-chair of the ESRC-funded Brexit & Environment network (a group of scholars providing independent research on how Brexit is affecting policy, governance and the environment). He is also a member of the Scientific Committee of the European Environment Agency and an elected Fellow of the Academy of Social Sciences.

BRENDAN MOORE is Senior Research Associate at the Centre for Climate Change and Social Transformations (CAST) and the Tyndall Centre for Climate Change Research, University of East Anglia. His research focuses on government-led decarbonisation transformations, EU climate change policy, the politics of emissions trading and the impact of Brexit on UK and EU environmental governance.

DURABLE BY DESIGN?

Policy Feedback in a Changing Climate

ANDREW J. JORDAN
University of East Anglia

BRENDAN MOORE
University of East Anglia

CAMBRIDGE
UNIVERSITY PRESS

University Printing House, Cambridge CB2 8BS, United Kingdom

One Liberty Plaza, 20th Floor, New York, NY 10006, USA

477 Williamstown Road, Port Melbourne, VIC 3207, Australia

314–321, 3rd Floor, Plot 3, Splendor Forum, Jasola District Centre, New Delhi – 110025, India

79 Anson Road, #06-04/06, Singapore 079906

Cambridge University Press is part of the University of Cambridge.

It furthers the University's mission by disseminating knowledge in the pursuit of education, learning, and research at the highest international levels of excellence.

www.cambridge.org
Information on this title: www.cambridge.org/9781108490016
DOI: 10.1017/9781108779869

© Cambridge University Press 2020

This publication is in copyright. Subject to statutory exception and to the provisions of relevant collective licensing agreements, no reproduction of any part may take place without the written permission of Cambridge University Press.

First published 2020

A catalogue record for this publication is available from the British Library.

Library of Congress Cataloging-in-Publication Data
Names: Jordan, Andrew, 1968– author. | Moore, Brendan (Brendan P.), author.
Title: Durable by design? : policy feedback in a changing climate / Andrew J Jordan, Brendan Moore.
Description: Cambridge ; New York, NY : Cambridge University Press, 2020. | Includes bibliographical references and index.
Identifiers: LCCN 2020007777 | ISBN 9781108490016 (hardback) | ISBN 9781108747929 (paperback)
Subjects: LCSH: European Union. | Climatic changes–Government policy–European Union countries. | Environmental policy–European Union countries. | European Union countries–Politics and government. | European Union countries–Environmental conditions.
Classification: LCC QC903.2.E85 J67 2020 | DDC 363.738/7456094–dc23
LC record available at https://lccn.loc.gov/2020007777

ISBN 978-1-108-49001-6 Hardback

Cambridge University Press has no responsibility for the persistence or accuracy of URLs for external or third-party internet websites referred to in this publication and does not guarantee that any content on such websites is, or will remain, accurate or appropriate.

Abstract

Following the landmark Paris Agreement, policy makers are under mounting political pressure to design more durable climate policies that rapidly deliver deep, society-wide decarbonisation. But while the political rationale for adopting such policies is regularly articulated, far less is known about whether and how they emerge in the real world and thus what differentiates them from fragile policies that are amended at the first sign of political opposition.

This book provides the first systematic analysis of the determinants of policy durability in three high-profile areas: biofuel production, car transport and industrial greenhouse gas emissions. It breaks new ground by going beyond the adoption of key European Union (EU) climate policies, to study the policy feedbacks they have triggered over time. This new approach creates a fuller understanding of how these policies have shaped both their own durability and, crucially, their ability to stimulate supportive political dynamics in society.

Across nine chapters, it combines state-of-the-art policy theories with new empirical evidence to explore how and why designers in the EU set about packaging together different elements of policy – including broad, long-term goals and increasingly complex policy instruments. It reveals that the most durable and effective policies have incorporated a subtle mix of design features that lock certain aspects into place, but provide sufficient flexibility to prevent policy drift and redundancy.

In making fresh theoretical and conceptual linkages between the debates on policy durability, policy feedback and policy design, it opens up a rich new agenda for both academic researchers and policy makers.

Contents

List of Figures	*page* ix
List of Tables	x
Preface	xi
List of Abbreviations	xiv

Part I Policy Durability

1 The Quest for Durability: When, Where and How Do Policies Feed Back into Politics? 3

2 Designing Durable Policies: An Instruments Perspective 29

Part II Designing Policy Durability

3 Designing Climate Policy in the European Union 57

4 Climate Policy Designs: Contexts, Choices, Settings and Sequences 80

5 Regulation: The Governance of Biofuels 106

6 Emissions Trading: The Governance of Large Stationary Emitters 133

7 Voluntary Action: The Governance of Car Emissions 158

Part III Climate Policy: Durable by Design?

8   Climate Policy Feedbacks: Significant Mechanisms, Effects
and Directions   187

9   Durable by Design? Policy Making in a Changing Climate   212

References   245
Index   272

Figures

8.1	Significant policy instrument changes: speed of adoption (in days)	*page* 209
8.2	Significant policy instrument changes: variation in adoption speed over time	209
8.3	Significant policy instrument changes: longevity (in days)	210
8.4	Significant policy instrument changes: variation in longevity over time	211
9.1	Biofuels: significant feedback directions	222
9.2	Emissions trading: significant feedback directions	223
9.3	Car emissions: significant feedback directions	225

Tables

1.1	The dimensions of policy feedback	*page* 13
2.1	The main directions of policy feedback: typical effects	40
2.2	The potential interaction between policy feedback mechanisms and policy feedback effects	41
2.3	Positive and negative policy feedbacks: changes in scope, stringency and time horizon	43
2.4	Designing policy: different durability and flexibility devices	47
2.5	A typology of the main policy instruments	51
3.1	EU climate policy: examples of policy durability and flexibility devices	77
3.2	EU climate policy: selected major instruments, 1992–2019	78
5.1	Biofuels: significant policy instrument changes, 2003–2019	131
6.1	Emissions trading: significant policy instrument changes, 2003–2019	156
7.1	Car emissions: significant policy instrument changes, 1998–2019	182
8.1	Policy instrument sequences in the three areas of governance, 2003–2019	208

Preface

Climate change is a grand societal challenge. The landmark 2015 Paris Agreement committed participating nations to limit warming to 'well below' 2°C above pre-industrial temperatures and to 'pursue efforts' to limit the rise to just 1.5°C. It is widely accepted that achieving these commitments will require an entirely new phase of decarbonisation which is both deeper – i.e. genuinely society-wide – and more rapid than anything that has been achieved until this point. The Agreement interpreted 'rapid' to mean countries peaking their emissions 'as soon as possible' so as to ensure no net greenhouse gas emissions ('net zero') by the second half of this century. Deep decarbonisation is therefore a uniquely long-term challenge: 2050 is well beyond the term of office of today's politicians, and the two temperature targets effectively apply forever.

Unfortunately, existing attempts to decarbonise are not deep or rapid enough. Globally, atmospheric concentrations and emissions continue to rise, and there is a significant gap between current mitigation efforts and the Paris commitments. Recent years have witnessed record heatwaves and fast-spreading wildfires, resonating with scientific warnings that the Earth is at grave risk of tipping into a hothouse state. The publication, in late 2018, of an international scientific report on the impacts of a 1.5°C temperature rise triggered fresh political demands for new sources of mitigation to achieve net zero emissions well before 2050. In many parts of the world, politicians are under mounting pressure both to establish very long-term net zero targets and, in the near term, to adopt the detailed policies in areas such as electricity generation, afforestation and car emissions, to ensure that they are eventually met.

Policy makers are not starting from a blank slate. In recent years, many new climate policies have been adopted, particularly in the industrialised countries. However, collectively, they are not delivering emission reductions rapidly enough to avert the risk of dangerous climate change. Often, it is not an absolute lack of understanding of the science of climate change or the unavailability of technological solutions that is holding back new policy efforts. More commonly, it is the *politics* of policy formulation, policy adoption and policy implementation that is preventing more countries from peaking and, ultimately, rapidly reducing their greenhouse gas emissions. Many existing policies are simply not stringent enough. Others are not durable enough – they are weakened in the face of political opposition and thus fail to entrench deep decarbonisation dynamics in broader society.

In this book we explore the durability of climate policy making. Durability's importance has been repeatedly underlined by influential international bodies such as the Intergovernmental Panel on Climate Change and eminent economists such as Nicholas Stern. Durable policies should nurture a society-wide expectation that deep decarbonisation has begun and will persist through to the end of the twenty-first century and beyond. The most durable policies are sustained by positive policy feedbacks that create a more supportive form of politics around them that, in time, drives the next round of policy making to a higher level of ambition. Consequently, key actors such as car producers and electricity generators become advocates of the policies. And crucially, over time they perceive the policies to be durable: once durable policies have been adopted, deep and rapid decarbonisation is inevitable.

The aim of this book is to move from these well-known and widely deployed policy prescriptions and explore how far they are actually applied by policy makers in the cut and thrust of everyday policy design situations in the European Union, an enthusiastic adopter of new climate policies since the 1990s. In particular, we attempt to understand whether policy designers in such situations seek to intentionally create durable climate policies that are supported by positive policy feedback and, if so, why, how and with what effects. In order to do so, we draw together and make fresh connections between several bodies of literature (on policy design, policy feedback, policy instruments and policy change) that, by and large, have not been connected together before.

We attempt to provide the first systematic analysis of the determinants of policy durability in three politically salient areas: biofuel production, car transport and industrial greenhouse gas emissions. We break new analytical ground by going beyond the adoption of key European Union climate policies to study the policy feedbacks they have created over time, in order to arrive at a fuller understanding of what shaped their own durability and, crucially, their ability to trigger deep decarbonisation dynamics across society. Across nine chapters, we combine state-of-the-art policy and political theories with new empirical evidence of decarbonisation to explore how and why designers in the EU set about packaging together different elements of policy – long-term goals, instruments and specific instrument-level settings.

In some respects, our central finding is uncontroversial: the most durable and effective climate policies incorporate a subtle mix of design features that lock certain aspects into place but provide sufficient flexibility to prevent policy drift and redundancy. However, the more complex question – which we also address – is in what circumstances do such policies emerge when politicians, businesses and voters are under pressure to address near-term concerns? Climate change is, of course, only one among many societal challenges. However, we hope that by building new theoretical and conceptual linkages between the debates on policy durability, policy feedback and policy design, we can open up a rich new agenda for both academic researchers and policy practitioners.

Like many books, this one has been a long time in the writing. Andy Jordan did some of the initial thinking during a Leverhulme Trust Major Research Fellowship (2010–2014) and the COST-funded Action Innovations in Climate Governance (INOGOV). He would also like to acknowledge the financial support provided by the ESRC CAST Centre (ES5012257/1). Funding from the INOGOV Action also supported fieldwork in Brussels during Brendan Moore's PhD research. This work directly informed the sections on emissions trading. A number of other individuals played an important part in the writing and publication of this book. At an early stage, three anonymous referees provided very helpful comments on an initial book proposal and preliminary drafts of some of the chapters. As the manuscript began to take shape, Dave Huitema, Tim Rayner and Sebastian Sewerin provided more detailed comments on revised versions of the chapters in Parts I and III. Of course, the responsibility for any remaining errors or mis-interpretations rests entirely with us. Alfie Kirk kindly turned a series of pencil drawings into the three summary figures that appear in Chapter 9. Finally, at Cambridge University Press, Matt Lloyd, Emma Kiddle and Sarah Lambert were very supportive from the early stages and helped us bring the book to fruition.

Last but not least, we would like to thank our families for their continuous support (and patience!) throughout the writing process.

Abbreviations

ACEA	European Automobile Manufacturers' Association
AEII	Alliance of Energy Intensive Industries
CARS 21	Competitive Automotive Regulatory System for the 21st Century
COP	Conference of the Parties
COPA-COGECA	Union of European Farmers and European Agri-Cooperatives
DG	Directorate-General of the European Commission
DG CLIMA	Directorate-General for Climate Action
DG Energy	Directorate-General for Energy
DG Environment	Directorate-General for the Environment
EBB	European Biodiesel Board
eBIO	European Bioethanol Fuel Association
EBTP	European Biofuels Technology Platform
ECCP	European Climate Change Programme
EEA	European Environment Agency
EEB	European Environmental Bureau
ENVI	European Parliament Committee on the Environment, Public Health and Food Safety
ePure	Renewable Ethanol Association
EU	European Union
EU ETS	European Union Emissions Trading System
Eurelectric	Union of the Electricity Industry
EUROPIA	European Petroleum Industry Association
FEDIOL	European Vegetable Oil and Proteinmeal Industry
IETA	International Emissions Trading Association
ILUC	Indirect Land Use Change
IPCC	Intergovernmental Panel on Climate Change

ITRE	European Parliament Committee on Industry, Research and Energy
MEP	Member of the European Parliament
MSR	Market Stability Reserve
MVEG	Motor Vehicle Emissions Group
NAP	National Allocation Plan
NGO	Non-Governmental Organisation
OECD	Organisation for Economic Co-operation and Development
RED	Renewable Energy Directive
T&E	European Federation for Transport and Environment
UNFCCC	United Nations Framework Convention on Climate Change

Part I
Policy Durability

1

The Quest for Durability

When, Where and How Do Policies Feed Back into Politics?

> ... governments stimulate [...] industries dependent on [...] legislation for their existence, and these industries form the fighting legions behind the policy. The [policy] likewise [...] [creates] [...] losers [who] adapt themselves to the new conditions imposed upon them, find themselves without the means to continue the struggle, or become discouraged and go out of business. *Is this not true, in varying degrees, of nearly all other policies also? New policies create a new politics.*
> (Schattschneider, 1935: 288, emphasis added)

1.1 The Quest for Durable Climate Policies

Climate change is often described as a wicked policy problem *par excellence*. The Intergovernmental Panel on Climate Change (IPCC) has made the scientific case for cutting greenhouse gas emissions to effectively zero by the middle of this century ('net zero' emissions), most recently in its 2018 special report on the most likely impacts of a temperature rise of 1.5°C (IPCC, 2018: 1). That report effectively underlined the need for 'rapid, far reaching and unprecedented changes in all aspects of society' (IPCC, 2018: 1). The economic rationale for adopting such a radically different trajectory of human development is well known. So why – to paraphrase Nicholas Stern (2015), one of the world's leading climate economists – is the world still waiting for deep and rapid decarbonisation to occur?

It is undeniably true that many new climate policies have been adopted by governments in the last decade or so (Averchenkova *et al.*, 2017). Indeed, climate change is arguably one of *the* most active areas of environmental policy making (Huitema *et al.*, 2011). However, the policies that have been adopted are collectively not delivering emission reductions rapidly enough to avert dangerous climate change (United Nations Environment Programme, 2018; van Renssen, 2018). To support deep and rapid decarbonisation, climate policies must certainly be sufficiently large in number and stringent in their ambitions; but they should also be politically durable (Rose, 1990: 274). The word 'durable' means persistent, steadfast and unyielding. Therefore, by definition, a policy that is durable *lasts*. Durable climate policies nurture a society-wide expectation that deep decarbonisation has begun and will persist through to the end of the twenty-first century and beyond. Above all, key actors should perceive such policies to be durable: because deep and rapid decarbonisation is inevitable there is no point opposing the policy.

The importance of establishing durable climate policies has been repeatedly underlined by Stern himself (2006: 368), by influential international bodies such as the IPCC (Parson and Karwat, 2011: 744) and economists working in the World Bank (2010: 339–40). There is also a growing strand of academic literature that identifies policy durability as a critical factor enabling decarbonisation (Eskridge and Ferejohn, 2001; Parson and Karwat, 2011: 751; Levin *et al.*, 2012: 1271; Rietig and Laing, 2017: 576; Iacobuta *et al.*, 2018: 10; Edmondson *et al.*, 2018), at international, national and regional levels (Compston and Bailey, 2008: 268; Webster, 2008: 60; Princen, 2009: 17; Keohane and Victor, 2011: 19). Borrowing from Schattschneider (1935: 288), who is quoted in the epigram above, durable climate policies will create and in turn be supported by 'a new politics' of deep decarbonisation. Politics and policy are, in other words, two sides of the same coin, and should be studied that way accordingly.

As a broad starting point, in this book we define a durable policy as one that endures and is influential over a particularly long period of time. Such a policy fosters and sustains its own political support base over time, triggering legacy effects 'that endure even after the waning of the political forces that generated the policy's original enactment' (Jenkins and Patashnik, 2012: 15). In the real world of politics, it is often immensely difficult to design and secure sufficient support to adopt such policies (Goodin, 1996: 29; Glazer and Rothenberg, 2001: 110; Sidney, 2005: 80–81; Peters, 2018: 7). Ensuring that they endure – that they have the capacity to ride out the inevitable political bumps in the road that lies ahead without diminishing their effectiveness – is an altogether more challenging task. In climate policy making, election-focused politicians often seek to persuade powerful societal actors to make long-term investments in what are often new, unproven technologies such as electric cars, carbon capture and storage facilities, and ultralow carbon transport fuels (Glazer and Rothenberg, 2001: 6; Liang and Fiorino, 2013: 109). Even if those actors agree to make such long-lasting investments, it does not necessarily mean that the accompanying policies (or the investments) will endure: circumstances could very easily change and politicians may opt to pursue different goals. The history of renewable energy deployment is littered with examples of ambitious policies that secured sufficient support to be adopted, but were subsequently revised and/or subjected to sudden cutbacks that significantly disrupted the innovation and diffusion of new green energy technologies

(Cointe, 2015; Meckling, Sterner and Wagner, 2017: 920; Michaelowa *et al.*, 2018: 279; Gürtler *et al.*, 2019). In the area of climate change, policies which were originally perceived to be ambitious and politically popular have also been scaled back and some have even been completely dismantled (van Renssen, 2018: 357; Rosenbloom *et al.*, 2019: 168). Policy retrenchment has occurred across the globe, including in Canada (Fankhauser, *et al.*, 2015: 55), Australia (Pearse, 2017), the United States (Rabe, 2016), Spain and Germany (Meckling, Sterner and Wagner, 2017: 920). The 'inconvenient truth' is that a surprisingly large number of existing climate change policies have been neither durable nor influential enough (van Renssen, 2018). Durable policies do not, in other words, appear to readily 'design themselves' (Howlett and Lejano, 2013: 11). This reality throws the contemporary challenge of using policy to trigger rapid decarbonisation into stark relief.

Yet the very idea that policy durability is somehow difficult for policy designers to achieve runs counter to a stream of work in public policy analysis. Schattschneider (1935: 288) expected new policies to create 'new' forms of politics. The 'new politics' that make some policies durable flow from the new coalitions of political support – comprising interest groups, businesses, policy makers and voters – that inevitably spring up around them after the adoption process is complete. Kaufman (1976) famously claimed that because of these dynamics, all public policies eventually achieve a state of immortality. In his widely cited work on welfare state policies, Pierson (1994) implied that durability in that area is relatively common; policy dismantling is the conspicuously rarer phenomenon, only occurring when policies fail to create sufficiently strong supportive coalitions or nurture new opponents.

The term 'policy feedback' refers to the variety of ways in which existing policies shape subsequent politics and policy-making dynamics in ways that affect their durability (Béland and Schlager, 2019: 184). Schattschneider's (1935) original observation greatly informed a growing literature that has sought to understand more precisely how, when and for whom 'new policies create a new politics' (Pierson, 1993: 595; see also Kumlin and Stadelmann-Steffen, 2014: 5). Pierson (1993) did much to popularise policy feedback, but the concept has deep intellectual roots. These were reviewed by Skocpol (1992: 58) who also argued that feedback should be the focus of a dedicated research programme:

Too often social scientists [...] forget that policies, once enacted, restructure subsequent political processes [...] *We must make [...] policies the starting points as well as the end points of analysis: As politics creates policies, policies also remake politics.*
(emphasis added).

She too emphasised that policy and politics are two sides of the same coin. Policy feedback and policy durability are thus interrelated concepts: a policy that fails to nurture a new and more supportive form of politics is less likely to be durable than one that does, and vice versa. With respect to decarbonisation, Meadowcroft (2011: 73) has made the same basic claim, arguing that more durable policies are needed at all levels of governance to 'create positive feedbacks driving further reform'.

However, since Skocpol's penetrating insight, the literatures on policy durability and policy feedback have generally gone their own way, greatly limiting our ability to understand the durability of climate change policies. First, a significant proportion of policy feedback studies have concentrated on the unfolding political effects of welfare state policies, which typically involve national governments distributing large quantities of public money via pensions, unemployment and disability support. Concentrated policy benefits are what most clearly differentiate these types of policy from others (Jacobs and Mettler, 2018: 347). Many climate change policies, on the other hand, are an example of a type of policy which Lowi (1972) would recognise as more regulatory, meaning that they often involve imposing concentrated costs on target groups to generate long-term, relatively diffuse benefits (in the case of climate change, via a more stable and habitable climate). In these conditions, relatively durable policies sustained by positive policy feedbacks and new, more supportive forms of politics, are arguably much less likely to appear than they are in some areas of social policy (Pierson, 1993; Weaver, 2010; Jacobs and Weaver, 2015). In fact, Lowi's work and that of others (Heidenheimer *et al.*, 1990: 309) suggests that regulatory policies are more likely to generate the forms of political opposition hypothesised by Schattschneider (1935), thus potentially rendering them significantly less, not more, durable. At first blush, this essential insight does appear to broadly correspond to the unfolding empirical patterns of climate policy making noted above.

Second, as academics we lack a sufficiently clear definition of policy durability (Thompson, 2012; Carlson and Fri, 2013; Rabe, 2016), to put alongside definitions of policy feedback. Often, policy durability is elided with other terms and concepts, including policy sustainability (Patashnik, 2003, 2008), policy stability (Rietig and Laing, 2017; Rosenbloom *et al.*, 2019: 168), policy consistency (Biber, Kelsey and Meckling, 2017: 628) and policy stickiness (Schmidt and Sewerin, 2017: 3; Schmidt *et al.*, 2018). Some academics have directly equated durability with stability, as when Jenkins and Patashnik (2012: 10) defined it as 'the longevity of a legislative product', i.e. how long a policy persists 'in its original form without significant change'. Thompson (2012: 17), equated durability with 'political strength that allows [policies] to resist retrenchment, erosion, or termination'. We will certainly incorporate these two interpretations into our own analysis, but we also suspect that durability has other important dimensions that also deserve to be considered, such as policy stringency. For example, some scholars have stretched their definition of durability to include a policy's ability not only to endure, but to expand and become more stringent through time (Rietig and Laing, 2017). Carlson and Fri (2013) have, however, noted that continual increases in stringency are not necessarily beneficial. In doing so, they have helpfully draw attention to another potentially important distinction between a policy's durability (stability) and its flexibility. Rabe (2016: 105–106) further distinguished between three components of climate policy durability, one of which focuses on stability (political resilience, 'does the policy survive intact?') and another which focuses on flexibility (design flexibility). In what follows, we shall explain why and how all these dimensions are pertinent. Indeed, there may often be an inherent tension between them both in principle and in practice. In Section 1.4 we will explore why and how the manner in which these dimensions interconnect is particularly salient in an area of particular long-term policy making such as climate change.

Third, there is a great deal of ambiguity about the most relevant analytical dimensions of policy durability. For us, three appear to be especially significant. The first relates to the *means* of policy, as expressed through specific implementing policy instruments. A particular policy instrument such as a tax or a regulation is not durable if it is rapidly amended or even completely dismantled (Lazarus, 2009: 1193; Thompson, 2012: 17; Carlson and Fri, 2013: 121). Although there is no accepted minimum time threshold that an instrument must pass to be counted as 'durable', it is often equated with at least one electoral cycle (Hacker and Pierson, 2014: 651; Rabe, 2016: 105–106).[1] The second dimension concerns the policy's overarching *goals*, which of course are an expression of its stringency. Some recalibration of a policy's implementing instruments is likely if the policy as a whole is to remain on course to achieve its goals (Hall, 1993), but a policy is unlikely to be durable if its goals are significantly changed (Patashnik, 2003: 207; Jenkins and Patashnik, 2012: 10; Chattopadhyay, 2015: 7). Finally, it is important to be mindful of a policy's *outcomes*, i.e. do the most durable policies actually produce the substantive effects that their designers originally expected (Patashnik, 2003: 207; Schneider and Ingram, 2019)?[2] Some policies may become so durable that designers struggle to 'keep up' as the world changes around it (Hacker and Pierson, 2014: 647). It has been argued that as they 'drift' (Béland, 2007), such policies may become progressively less effective over time. For example, welfare state policies drift when the value of benefits fails to adjust to rising levels of inflation (Hacker, 2004: 246; van der Heijden, 2011). In the rest of this book, we shall explore whether unpacking these three dimensions and applying them to the case of climate change differentiates policy durability from some of the similar terms and concepts outlined above.

Fourth, while the defining characteristics of durable policies have been relatively well established,[3] as noted above the determinants and unfolding effects of durability continue to be black-boxed in the existing literatures (Clemens and Cook, 1999).

Crucially, how do the most durable policies – and the 'new' politics that they supposedly trigger and benefit from – actually come about (Levin *et al.*, 2012)? In many ways, this is the key question exercising climate policy makers today. One reason why the existing literatures have struggled to provide answers is that they often adopt a particular research design, which involves focusing only on the most durable and/or most successful policies and tracing them back to their origins (Pierson, 1993: 602). Although insightful, this approach tells us too little about the 'non-cases' – the situations where policies were popular enough to be adopted but thereafter failed to endure, perhaps because positive feedbacks from supportive coalitions did not emerge, or because new forms of opposition appeared (i.e. negative policy feedbacks) that actively undermined them. In climate policy, the number of 'non-cases' is already too high to be ignored, even before policy designers attempt to design more durable and stringent policies to enable much deeper and faster decarbonisation.

Finally, existing accounts do not explicitly investigate whether policy durability is intentionally designed. This matters in a policy area such as climate change, where some policy makers are attempting to achieve highly ambitious long-term goals ('net zero' emissions) by nurturing virtuous cycles of mutually reinforcing feedback between durable climate policies and new countervailing coalitions that have a self-interest in promoting ever deeper forms of decarbonisation (Brunner *et al.*, 2012: 267; Huberty and Zysman, 2013: xiii).[4] One thing that renders climate change a particularly wicked policy problem is its inter-temporal nature – implying that policy designers should design solutions that are not only politically popular enough to be adopted and remain in place, but also stringent enough to bind their target groups to objectives that endure over time (Levin *et al.*, 2012: 124; Howlett and Rayner, 2013). The normative argument that politicians should intentionally design such policies is well known and has been repeatedly made (Levin *et al.*, 2012; Meckling *et al.*, 2015: 1171; Meckling, Sterner and Wagner, 2017: 918). However, whether and how often they successfully do so has not been definitively determined.[5] In fact, this important question is often left completely open (Edmondson *et al.*, 2018: 5; Pahle *et al.*, 2018: 861; Roberts *et al.*, 2018: 305; Meckling, 2019: 330). By referring to 'intentional design' we are not implying that there is a single, rational and omnipotent policy 'designer' (Goodin, 1996: 28). Rather, in thinking about durability from a policy design perspective we will illuminate how many different actors including, but not limited to, politicians interact with one another to shape, amend or hinder attempts to trigger deep and rapid decarbonisation (Levin *et al.*, 2012: 148). In his agenda-defining article, Pierson (1993: 624) argued that 'especially as government activity becomes widespread, politicians are likely to become aware that [their] policy choices have political consequences', leading them to consciously design with policy feedback in mind. Sadly, his point has been overlooked by a generation of policy feedback scholars (but see e.g. Schneider and Ingram, 1997: 101; Soss and Schram, 2007: 111; Jacobs, 2011; Pechmann, 2018). Indeed, the work that has been conducted on social policies has regularly made the rather gloomy prediction that the most positive policy feedbacks are likely to emerge slowly and in a largely *un*intentional manner (Soss and Schram, 2007: 111; see also Levin *et al.*, 2012: 148; Rosenbloom *et al.*, 2019: 172). Finally, intentional does not mean that all observed policy effects were necessarily intended (Goodin, 1996: 28); rather we seek to investigate the feedbacks that are generated when actors aim to shape their and others' long-term future.

1.2 Our Argument in Brief

Our broad aim in this book is to understand whether policy designers seek to intentionally create durable climate policies that are supported by positive policy feedbacks, and if so why, how and with what effects. We do so by exploring how policy designers combine or otherwise package together the various internal elements of policy (Schneider and Ingram, 1997: 2–3) – long-term goals, policy instruments, specific targets etc. – into an overall policy that facilitates deeper and more rapid decarbonisation. Many scholars have pinpointed the relationship between specific climate policy designs and their resulting effects and outcomes as a topic that deserves much greater analytical attention (Biber *et al*, 2017: 636; Schmidt and Sewerin, 2017: 2; Edmondson *et al.*, 2018: 11; Roberts *et al.*, 2018: 306; Skjærseth, 2018: 15). But with some exceptions (Hacker, 2004; Weaver, 2010; Jacobs, 2011; Schneider and Ingram, 2019), in the policy feedback literature issues of design and instrumentation have rarely been centre stage, in spite of Pierson's (1993: 603) suggestion that analysts should start with policy design processes and then move forwards to uncover their feedback effects and policy outcomes.

One of Pierson's (1993: 603) most thought-provoking research ideas was to carry out 'comparative analyses that examine the use of different policy instruments to achieve similar goals' in order to 'determine if the variation in instruments has political consequences'. We directly embrace this challenge by sampling across the main policy instrument types (regulatory, voluntary and market-based) and tracing out the policy feedbacks created by each instrument to determine how far they affected their durability. We adopt a 'within system' case design in order to hold relatively constant a range of 'non-policy' variables.[6] Our chosen political system (our 'locus') is the European Union (EU). The EU is a world leader in the adoption of new climate change policies (Jordan *et al.*, 2010) and hence has (unlike many comparable political systems such as the USA) adopted a sufficient number of policies to suggest it is at least broadly committed to intentional design (Huberty *et al.*, 2013: 254). We aim to break new ground by investigating the *post-adoption* policy feedbacks arising from these instruments to arrive at a fuller understanding of both their long-term political *durability* and their effectiveness at entrenching decarbonisation dynamics in wider society. We explore the design features that policy designers could in theory have drawn upon on to render their policies more durable, such as standards and technology requirements that force target groups to make significant, up-front investments in the policy's long-term existence. More specifically, we explore the thought-provoking – but largely untested – claim that genuinely effective policies are likely to incorporate a mix of design features that promote durability by locking certain aspects into place, but provide sufficient flexibility to prevent policy drift and redundancy (Jordan and Matt, 2014; Seto *et al.*, 2016: 437; Edmondson *et al.*, 2018: 1; Peters, 2018: 9).

Throughout, our approach is essentially empirical as opposed to normative, and is directly informed by relevant theories of politics and policy. We try not to fall into the trap of assuming that greater durability is necessarily more appealing than less durability. Our own sense of reflexivity is reinforced by the fact that many forms of policy durability are often regarded as something to avoid in environmental politics. In areas such as agriculture and transport, durable policies that lock in unsustainable forms of production and consumption have acted as formidable barriers to deep decarbonisation in the past (Unruh, 2000; Skovgaard and van Asselt, 2018). Hence for many environmentalists, the overriding design challenge in climate policy is how to break down 'carbon lock-in' (Unruh, 2000) and replace undesirable, yet politically durable, carbon-promoting policies with equally durable but environmentally more sustainable alternatives (e.g. Downie, 2017). In terms of the three dimensions of durability outlined earlier in this section (means, goals and outcomes), multiple changes in policy and governance are likely to be involved to achieve such a change. In the remainder of this book, we will therefore seek to understand policy durability as the outcome of a political process in which various actors are promoting particular forms and dimensions of durability, for different purposes and with different effects.

Having sketched out our broad argument, we now introduce the rest of this chapter. In the next section, we further elaborate the link between policy durability and policy feedback, our aim being to promote new work that links both (Campbell, 2012: 334; Mettler and SoRelle, 2014: 152). We then reconstruct the existing literatures on both concepts to address the policy design puzzles that loom large in relation to climate change mitigation.[7] Finally, we explore the claim that effective policies are likely to incorporate some design features that make them durable, but also others that provide designers with a degree of flexibility to cope with changing economic, technological and environmental circumstances (Peters, 2018: 136). The perceived need to craft policy designs that simultaneously incorporate durability and flexibility (Carlson and Fri, 2013: 119; Jordan and Matt, 2014) has been noted in the literature, but often only in broad terms and without a sufficient account of human agency in selecting one or the other type (Goodin, 1996: 39–43; Duit and Galaz, 2008: 311; Huberty, Kelsey, and Zysman, 2013: 252).[8] We address this research gap by developing and applying a new typology that distinguishes between *policy durability devices* and *policy flexibility devices*. In the final section, we conclude and signpost the remainder of the book.

1.3 Policy Feedback Effects, Mechanisms and Directions

In the last two decades, policy feedback has emerged as a significant organising concept in policy analysis, providing a framework for studying how policies affect subsequent politics and their own development over time (e.g. Béland, 2010; Mettler and SoRelle, 2014: 152). In this vein, Pierson (1993: 596) claimed that 'major public policies ... constitute important rules of the game, influencing the allocation of economic and political resources, modifying the costs and benefits associated with alternative political strategies, and consequently altering ensuing political development'. So rather than treat each policy battle as one in which all alternatives are equally plausible, he argued that scholars should understand how the political conflicts over new policies are structured by the actors and institutions established and/or remoulded by previous ones (Hacker, 1998; Weir, 2006: 171). Schattschneider (1935) was of course also concerned with understanding the various forms that the new politics took; policy feedback research arguably provides analytical tools and concepts to accomplish this task, going well beyond a policy's economic and social effects – the standard fare of *ex post* policy evaluation studies (Mettler and Soss, 2004: 55). Unlike many popular accounts of policy change (Howlett and Cashore, 2009), policy feedback scholars seek to identify and account for the *endogenous* sources of change, which over time can have important effects that often go under-reported (Greif and Laitin, 2004; Mahoney and Thelen, 2009). Finally, Pierson's definition makes it clear that the main focus should be on 'major' policies – or for us, the most durable ones – although this begs the question of how they became major in the first place.

Ever since Heclo (1974: 316) and Lowi (1972), policy scholars have been primed to expect policy to shape politics. In attempting to operationalise the general claim that 'past policies themselves influence political struggles' (Pierson, 1993: 596), we shall differentiate between a number of terms and concepts related to policy durability that are too often elided, specifically: policy feedback *effects*, the various *mechanisms* through which such effects are generated; the *directions* of feedback (positive, negative and/or combinations of the two); and the link back to specific policy *designs*.[9] In the remainder of this section, we review each of these in turn.

Policy Feedback Effects

Policy feedback effects, as we define them here, are the effects that a policy has on actors. The existing literature has identified a remarkably diverse array of policy feedback effects, ranging from direct effects on target groups and government ministries and agencies (Patashnik, 2008: 30), through to indirect effects on other interest groups (Mettler and Soss, 2004: 55; Kumlin and Stadelmann-Steffen, 2014: 6–8; Mettler and SoRelle, 2014: 151). Other work has uncovered much subtler, longer-term effects on wider society – on levels of civic participation (Mettler and Soss, 2004: 55), on public opinion (Soss and Schram, 2007) and even on fundamental conceptions of democracy and citizenship (Schneider and Ingram, 1997: 66; Schneider and Sidney, 2009: 110). Such potentially fundamental and far-reaching effects may surprise some climate policy analysts who are all too used to policies lasting for relatively short periods and contributing little or nothing to deep decarbonisation.

Orren and Skowronek (2002: 742) have tried to make sense of these rather varied effects by arguing that policies 'classify the groups, impart the identities, forge the divisions, and strike the alliances that channel future political action'. Pierson (2006: 118) later argued that policies 'can profoundly alter the political terrain over time'. What existing policies change 'are not just actors' perceptions of what is possible in political life, but also *the kinds of actors that are around, their capacities, and their policy preferences*' (emphasis added). These are undeniably big analytical claims. The key word is 'can' and it relates to the issue of contingency first noted by Schattschneider (1935) in the epigram at the beginning of this chapter. In an attempt to understand it, Skocpol (1992) distinguished between two main policy effects: those that transform *state capacities* (e.g. through the creation of new bureaucracies that support the development of 'their' policy programmes); and those that impact on the identities, goals and capabilities of *social groups*, but especially interest groups (for fuller reviews, see: Mettler and Soss, 2004: 55; Béland and Schlager, 2019: 186). Pierson (1993: 597) argued that feedback effects on publics could be the most wide-ranging and politically consequential of all, but at the time lacked the empirical evidence to confirm it. It is fair to say that much of the subsequent literature has utilised rather general categories of effect[10] that are difficult to relate back to particular policies. Moreover, as noted above, there has been a marked tendency to adopt backward tracing methods that document specific effects (e.g. on pensioners) in great detail,[11] rather than establishing causal links between specific policy designs and the full array of effect types and categories (Patashnik and Zelizer, 2013: 1075, fn. 44).

Policy Feedback Mechanisms

Causality is just as important in durability research as it is in other areas of policy analysis, but often the existing literatures have not fully explicated the underlying causal mechanisms of feedback (Kelsey and Zysman, 2013: 82). This criticism is particularly germane in the environmental policy literature, where feedback mechanisms are often conflated with feedback effects (Fahey and Pralle, 2016; Meckling, 2019: 319; see also Oberlander and Weaver, 2015: 41–42). This conflation is unfortunate because in his original stocktake, Pierson (1993: 597) clearly distinguished between two main types of causal mechanisms: 1. *resource/incentive mechanisms* that create or directly channel *resources* to actors and/or influence the alternative choices open to them; and 2. *interpretive mechanisms* that influence flows of information and, as a result, shape how actors interpret the world around them (see Table 1.1). For example, when policy feedback operates through *resource/incentive* mechanisms, policies channel new sources of revenue into government departments or to particular interest groups. They may also alter prevailing incentive structures, encouraging actors to make long-term, difficult-to-change commitments to certain patterns of living (e.g. government transport policies may directly affect where people

Table 1.1 *The dimensions of policy feedback*

		Actors affected		
		Government elites	Interest groups	Mass publics
Feedback mechanism	Resource/ Incentive	Administrative skills and capacities	Clienteles Direct funding Policy niches Access to decision makers	Lock ins: • Individual commitments
	Interpretive	Policy learning: • Cognitive shortcuts • Use of existing policy designs • Negative learning	Policy learning: • Negative learning • Focusing events • Effects – traceability and visibility • 'Quiet' policies	Effects: • Traceability and visibility

Source: based on Pierson (1993: 626).

choose to live and work). By contrast, *interpretive* mechanisms involve the channelling of information, e.g. by politicising previously uncontroversial policies by making their effects more visible whilst rendering others less visible, causing them to become more depoliticised. This second type of mechanism builds directly on Lowi's (1972) penetrating observation that some policies (such as regulatory ones) do not necessarily need to transfer significant financial resources to be politically influential.

Directions of Policy Feedback

The first generation of studies to emerge after the publication of Pierson's (1993) influential article mostly focused on only one direction of policy feedback – *positive* feedback. When positive policy feedback prevails, a cycle of self-reinforcing activity arises that follows a path-dependent pattern (Pierson, 2004: 18). In such a situation (originally hypothesised by Schattschneider (1935) and further discussed in Chapter 2), policies become steadily more durable as their feedbacks lock them into place. For example, some policies strengthen their own political support base by delivering highly visible, concentrated benefits to a particular group in society. Over time, external political pressures to dismantle them may grow, but the coalitions supporting them will leap to their defence (Biber, 2013; Patashnik and Zelizer, 2013: 1072; Oberlander and Weaver, 2015: 39).

Of course, Schattschneider (1935), Skocpol (1992: 531) and Pierson (1993: 600) had expected policies to generate feedback in not one, but two directions: positive and negative. By undermining a policy's own political support base, negative feedbacks are destabilising in their effects, opening up new opportunities to amend, weaken and possibly even dismantle the original policy. They are associated with the well-known patterns of incrementalism that characterise many areas of everyday policy making (Baekgaard, Larsen and Mortensen, 2019). But it is really only in the last decade or so that scholars have paid more attention to both types (Weaver, 2010; Jacobs and Weaver, 2015; Biber *et al.*, 2017: 612). A classic example is to be found in post-Civil War pensions policy in the USA, which prompted recipients to mobilise to protect it (positive feedback) but also generated opposition from those who claimed it was emblematic of corrupt or patronage politics (Skocpol, 1992; see also Mettler and SoRelle, 2014: 153). Scholars studying feedback from other perspectives (e.g. policy design) have also entertained this possibility (Schneider and Sidney, 2009: 108), as have those investigating longer-term processes of conversion and drift (Hacker *et al.*, 2015). However, policy feedback scholars have tended to adopt a rather binary view – either focusing on one direction or the other.[12] Consequently, the precise circumstances in which some policies generate different directions of feedback is still unclear, as is the scope for intentionally guiding them through conscious policy design.[13]

Policy Design and Feedback

For scholars of policy durability, a salient puzzle concerns the link between particular policy designs and various effects, mechanisms and directions of policy feedback. It is fair to say that scholars have not made as much progress in addressing this puzzle as Pierson (1993: 628) had originally hoped, largely because they have, as already mentioned, focused on the unintended (and very often choice-constraining) effects of durable policies (Campbell, 2012: 338). For example, in the welfare state literature, the rather blunt distinction between universal and means-tested welfare state programmes has long been held to be decisive, with the former assumed to produce more positive feedback than the latter, given that more people stand to benefit (Campbell, 2012: 338).[14] More recent studies, however, have tried to understand the effect of specific policy designs, showing how they affect the production of policy effects by altering the relative size, duration and visibility of benefit flows, as well as the proximity and nature of recipients (Campbell, 2012: 342). For example, welfare policies that are hidden (i.e. that distribute benefits indirectly via the private sector or through tax codes rather than cash payments) may generate weaker positive feedback because recipients believe that it is the market that is at work, not public policy (Mettler, 2011). Voters struggle to form a clear view of the extended or 'submerged state' that is delivering benefits to them. When they do form a view, it is that the benefits are mostly being provided by the private sector (Mettler and SoRelle, 2014: 171), not the government. Similarly, Patashnik (2008: 3, 155) and Jacobs (2011) have sought to explicate the conditions under which policy designers seek to manipulate both resource/incentive and interpretive mechanisms with the express intention of generating particular feedback effects. This type of more design-focused feedback research is noteworthy because it works across both of Pierson's mechanisms, but for reasons that will become clearer in Chapter 2, it remains all too rare (Jacobs and Mettler, 2018: 347, 349).

Empirical Foci

Finally, according to a recent state-of-the-art review (Mettler and SoRelle, 2014: 173–175), the existing policy feedback literature, while extensive, continues to offer a rather partial view of the relationship between durability and feedback because it mostly addresses the effects of a relatively small subset of cases (generally welfare state policies) in a limited number of jurisdictions (mostly the USA). Since the early 2000s, the effects on mass publics and voters have more or less become the default policy area to focus on (Mettler and Soss, 2004; Campbell, 2012; Mettler and SoRelle, 2014). By contrast, policies in areas such as the environment and climate change, where policy designers are more likely to be regulating than (re)distributing money, have attracted noticeably less attention. Comparatively little work has analysed policy durability and feedback in European and, in particular, EU settings (Meckling, 2019: 320; but see e.g. Daugbjerg, 2003; Jordan and Matt, 2014; Skogstad, 2017; Skjærseth, 2018; Kleine and Pollack, 2018: 1504). As we will show in Chapter 2, these analytical design choices have left many important features of the climate policy landscape in shadow, such as the role of interest groups in shaping (and being shaped by) the feedback effects of different policy instruments, including regulatory ones.

The importance of working across a fuller array of policy areas and jurisdictions has been noted (Pierson, 2006: 124), but not acted upon with sufficient vigour. New research that builds on Lowi's (1972) core argument (that policy determines politics) by analysing a broader range of cases could, we believe, be highly insightful.[15] Recall that in more regulatory policy areas, politics is normally dominated by powerful interest groups such as business, often vying for supremacy with policy entrepreneurs (Heidenheimer *et al.*, 1990: 309), particularly when they are representing diffuse interests (Wilson, 1980). In such conditions, significant political hurdles have to be surmounted even to get policies adopted, let alone ones that will endure and remain politically influential enough to make a difference. Hacker's (2004: 8–9) path-breaking work on the US welfare state – covering both its private and public components, and pensions as well as healthcare – suggests that policy feedbacks tend to play out differently in such settings.[16] Other things being equal, policies that seek to impose concentrated costs on small groups are less likely to be adopted. And if they are adopted, they are more likely to generate a very different – i.e. much more *negative* – direction of feedback, eventually rendering them less durable. Hacker (2002) usefully demonstrated how employers in the USA responded very differently to initial policies on social insurance (which they strongly opposed) and retirement (which they broadly supported). These responses had long-term and politically consequential effects. In fact, the tendency for small, contingent events in the policy formulation stage to subsequently generate profound effects is a recurring theme of the literatures on durability and path dependence (see e.g. Kay, 2012), again underlining the need for more forward-tracing approaches.

In Chapter 2 we explain why climate change offers a fascinating setting in which to look afresh at these post-adoption dynamics. But before we do so, in the next section we explain why key concepts in both literatures should first be re-thought and re-interpreted. This could, we believe, open up new opportunities for dialogue with communities studying other relevant topics including (intentional) policy design, policy instruments and the political power of incumbent interests, in a wider variety of policy areas than just the welfare state.

1.4 Restructuring Existing Research to Study Climate Change

Moving from Effects to Feedbacks

Policy feedback scholars have responded to Pierson's call (1993: 596) to specify when, where and how policy creates new forms of politics. Nevertheless, much of their work, especially recently, has centred on what we term 'policy feedback effects' (Schneider and Sidney, 2009: 108; Mettler and SoRelle, 2014: 156, 165).[17] These effects can be defined as a policy's immediate downstream consequences prior to any impact on subsequent policy making, i.e. before any complete feedback loop to the policy itself. Thus, if the policy in question (P) was adopted at time t, the most noteworthy first-order effects would be those appearing at t+1. However, in order to count as a *policy* feedback, those *effects* must have a politically significant impact not only on the original actors at t+1, but also on the original policy P, which may change to a greater or lesser extent (P2). A policy feedback can thus be defined as a politically consequential effect that operates via a set of intervening causal mechanisms to eventually affect the original policy.[18] To be sure, feedback does not have to produce significant policy changes in order to interest political scientists; positive feedbacks may have a politically consequential impact on the original policy by making policy change less likely. Our central point, however, is that a good deal of existing research has focused on first-order effects, *not* feedbacks (Pierson and Skocpol, 2002: 715). In making this distinction, we depart from some of the existing literatures, which generally treat policy feedbacks and policy feedback effects as the same concept (see e.g. Weaver, 2010: 138).

Moving from effects to feedbacks has some important implications. Firstly, it means looking at unfolding cycles of policy making, starting and ending with a particular element of policy such as a policy instrument (Sabatier and Jenkins-Smith, 1999: 119). Second, whereas first-order effects can in principle be studied over relatively short time periods, policy feedbacks require the study of at least one full cycle of policy making (to capture possible policy change) and hence potentially much longer periods of time. In a widely cited contribution, Sabatier and Jenkins-Smith (1999: 118) argued that the minimum time period for studying policy making should be at least ten years in order to capture multiple policy cycles (see also Campbell, 2012: 344). As explained below, our analysis passes this threshold.

Campbell's (2003) careful unpacking of how the US Social Security programme 'made' citizens indicates what can be revealed when effects and feedbacks are studied over long periods. She not only confirmed the presence of many different and interacting mechanisms and effects (Campbell, 2003: 6), but also how the citizen-level effects interacted with broader interest group-level effects. Thus, the Social Security programme empowered elderly beneficiaries with increased financial resources (through resource/incentive feedback mechanisms) while simultaneously encouraging them to lend their support to it (through interpretive mechanisms). Stronger and more mobilised beneficiaries in turn allied with and supported strong interest groups (including the American Association of Retired Persons), creating formidable new policy coalitions – notably the so-called grey lobby. However, in her analysis, Campbell also took the extra step and analysed how these clienteles not only resisted attempts to cut Social Security benefits but actually fought for new, more generous policies, i.e. she traced how first-order effects (e.g. increased resources through Social Security benefits) created policy feedbacks. She referred to these as 'spirals' (*Ibid*.: 2), showing that the policies were first a cause and then an effect of their beneficiaries' greater political participation (*Ibid*.: 66). We want to know whether her general approach can be adapted and applied to other policy issues and/or jurisdictions, namely climate change policy in the EU.

Explicating the Mechanisms of Feedback

Moving from effects to feedbacks also entails grappling with the vexed issue of causality. Policy analysts are becoming more conscious of the issue's importance (Falletti and Lynch, 2009; Grzymala-Busse, 2011; Capano *et al.*, 2019), and slowly the point is being taken on board as the various fields of research on policy durability evolve and intertwine (Béland, 2010: 582; Campbell, 2012: 345). After Pierson (1993), initial work usefully demonstrated the general utility of his two-fold typology of feedback mechanisms (Mettler and Soss, 2004: 60; Campbell, 2012: 338) and confirmed the value of studying both types together (Weaver, 2010; Skjærseth, 2018). Pierson (1993: 611, 625) was firmly of the view that the interaction between them was analytically puzzling and politically consequential, as the two types could simultaneously contradict and/or reinforce one another. We are also of the view that these are important and under-appreciated points, that are ripe for new empirical investigation (Pahle *et al.*, 2018: 862). Because we will sample across different instrument types in a regulatory policy area, the probability increases that we will encounter negative as well as positive feedbacks. And crucially, because we are examining a policy area in which the EU does not normally distribute significant financial benefits, we are primed to look for interpretive mechanisms and examine any interaction with resource/incentive mechanisms (Pierson, 1993: 611).

Incorporating Different Feedback Directions

Starting with a selection of policy instruments (as opposed to policies that are known to be durable) and tracing forwards also offers an opportunity to look afresh at the various directions of feedback. In Chapter 2, we will argue that only relatively recently have public policy scholars begun to build negative feedbacks[19] into their thinking (Howlett, 2009a: 253–254). If the overall direction of the feedback effects are positive, we would expect the initial policy P to become progressively more durable at t+1, t+2, t+3 etc. (Pierson, 2004: 174). As a consequence, what may originally have been a politically contested issue will gradually drop out of political debate as the policy becomes an accepted (and hence more durable) part of the broader policy landscape (Pierson, 2005: 46). As noted above, this possibility certainly aligns with the normative ambitions of many climate policy activists. But if the direction of feedback is negative, then we would expect P to be undermined at t+1, which could in turn trigger a set of policy responses ranging from fairly small adjustments through to its removal and possible replacement by a new and possibly weaker policy (P2) at t+1 etc. – an outcome that would surely alarm many environmentalists.

Very much building on Schattschneider's (1935) original insight, Weaver (2010: 159) has claimed that the concept of negative feedback is 'readily generalizable' to all policy sectors. However, this (broad) claim has not yet been put to the test (Baekgaard, *et al.*, 2019). It is rather puzzling that it has taken so long for analysts to do such a thing, given that Lowi's (1972) original 'policy determines politics' argument is such a key axiom of policy feedback thinking. In this book, we draw on Pierson's earlier work on how the interplay of institutional and policy-specific factors affected the opportunities to achieve cuts in welfare state policies (Pierson, 1994: 171–175), turn it on its head and process trace the political effects generated by three archetypal policy instrument types.

Working Across Different Levels and Areas of Policy

Concentrating on the most durable policies is entirely legitimate but for policy durability researchers it equates to sampling on the dependent variable (Campbell, 2012: 347). Having done just that, it was likely that scholars would discover that 'most [policies] ... [were] remarkably durable' and 'generally subject' to positive policy feedback (Pierson, 2004: 35). Indeed, Pierson (2006: 114) and others (Hacker, 2004: fn. 6) have argued that the 'major' policies are so durable that henceforth they should be re-conceptualised as institutions that essentially establish the rules of the game in politics. In this, they share the same tendency as other historical institutionalists who focus on other cases of deep institutionalisation such as the welfare state (Kay 2005) and some agricultural support policies (Daugbjerg, 2003).[20]

However, on closer inspection many of these studies are often pitched at the level not of single policy instruments, but much broader policy regimes and programmes (Pierson, 1994; Weaver, 2010).[21] Policy programmes comprise complex packages of multiple policy instruments that are directed at the achievement of a broader set of goals (Howlett, Mukherjee and Rayner, 2017: 130).[22] The broad focus of such work has encouraged analysts to categorise the resulting changes using similarly broad labels such as layering, drift and conversion (Hacker, 2004; Mahoney and Thelen, 2009; Jacobs and Weaver, 2015), which appear to conflate explanations of the underlying processes with descriptions of their outcomes. It is as if scholars are reluctant to move down a level of analysis and explore the feedback created by specific policy designs, perhaps believing that 'policy' is too ill-defined a concept to disaggregate into researchable categories (Pierson, 2006: 119). A significant analytical price has arguably been paid by opting to work mainly at a very broad level, in that it makes it hard to derive explanations for the precise feedback effects – i.e. both positive and negative – of specific policy instruments (Kay, 2012: 469). Furthermore, working at a broad level also delivers too little insight into the politics of designing the durable policies in the first place, 'black-boxing' the role of agency.[23] Yet it is precisely this topic which is at the forefront of contemporary policy debates on the governance of climate change.

Given that the central focus of policy feedback research is policy, one might have expected a more searching discussion of how to configure the policy variable in a way that facilitated more fine-grained empirical research. After all, one of the many contributions made by Pierson (1994: 175) was to unpack the welfare state into its constituent parts and show how the design of particular sub-elements generates different patterns of feedback, which in turn affects their vulnerability to dismantling. Yet the literature's reliance on a relatively 'blunt' (Kay, 2005: 556) conception of policy and the widespread practice of sampling on the dependent variable, has limited its ability to open up the 'black box' of policy design (Solmeyer and Constance, 2015: 1; see also Mettler and SoRelle, 2014: 165). In this book, we will explore what can be learned about policy durability when we unpack policy into its various sub-elements (Kumlin and Stadelmann-Steffen, 2014: 320), i.e. specific policy instrument types though to broader policy goals and paradigms. As we reveal in Chapter 2, this topic has long fascinated scholars working on single policy instruments (Ingram and Schneider, 1990: 67; Salamon, 2002: 11). If new bridges can be built between them and scholars of policy feedback and durability, what might the intellectual payoffs be? We return to this intriguing question in our final chapter.

The Intentionality of Design

Finally, we have already noted that the durability and feedback literatures have largely focused on effects that were at least partly or even wholly unintended by policy designers (Soss and Schram, 2007: 111). Examples in the social policy field include well-entrenched US policies that exacerbated racial and gender inequality. Campbell's (2015: 284) work on large policy 'juggernauts' such as the US Social Security programme could also be cited. These relatively durable policies have constructed elderly beneficiaries as worthy and deserving citizens, who now participate in politics at a higher level than other equivalent groups. It is worth noting that such policies first attracted scholarly attention not because they were difficult to adopt, but because they were either very effective or had become resilient to dismantling (Pierson, 1994). Some climate and energy policy scholars have adopted a similar approach (Levin *et al.*, 2012; Zysman and Huberty, 2013; Rabe, 2016: 139; Meckling and Nahm, 2018: 752; Pahle *et al.*, 2018: 861). For example, Rietig and Laing (2017: 576) selected a highly durable climate change law – the UK Climate Change Act – and subjected it to analytical scrutiny. Similarly, Stokes and Breetz (2018: 77) have examined the fastest growing alternative energy sources in the USA and tried to trace them back to the original policy drivers.

There is nothing intrinsically wrong with such research designs (Pierson, 1993: 602), but in focusing mainly on the 'victorious policy options' (Peters *et al.*, 2005: 1277), they risk being 'too contingent at the front end and too deterministic at the back end' (Pierson, 2004: 50; see also Kay, 2012: 471). Crucially they leave the effects of specific features of a given policy – such as its component instruments – in shadow.[24] By starting at the policy adoption process and tracing out the feedback effects of different types of instrument designs, we will examine how far it is possible to 'bring out ... the complexity and uncertainty that characterize formative moments in the creation of policies' (Peters *et al.*, 2005: 1277). Crucially, we will investigate what a forward-tracing approach reveals about the 'non-cases' of durability (Campbell, 2012: 347), i.e. where positive policy feedback fails to emerge or is quickly counteracted and overwhelmed by negative feedback (see also Patashnik, 2008). We are particularly interested to know whether studying the non-cases puts us in a stronger position to understand the conditions in which particular feedbacks do or do not occur. We return to these important matters in Chapters 2, 8 and 9.

1.5 Designing Durable Climate Policies

Combining Policy Durability with Flexibility

In many ways, policy durability has become *the* holy grail of those seeking deep decarbonisation (Rosenbloom *et al.*, 2019: 168). But how should policies be designed to bring it about with sufficient rapidity? Many literatures, covering credible commitments, political delegation and constitutional law, have identified a host of what we shall term policy *durability devices*, i.e. design components aimed at increasing a policy's durability (for a summary, see: Pierson, 2000b: 480–481; Glazer and Rothenberg, 2001: 84–87). Policy programme-level durability devices include long-term targets to create confidence that a certain policy direction will endure, and regular reporting obligations so that the policy's benefits are sufficiently visible to voters, interest groups and private investors, to trigger positive feedbacks. Politicians can also tie their own hands by handing over policy monitoring, evaluation and/or flexibility responsibilities to independent agencies. Finally, at the level of specific policy instruments, designers can employ regulations to force target groups to make 'sunk' investments in the long-term durability of a policy and/or discourage free-riding.

However, there is often an implicit assumption that the more *durability* devices that can be employed – and hence the more durable and constraining individual policies can be made – the better (e.g. Hovi, Sprinz and Underdal, 2009: fn. 1). In the opening section, we noted that environmental policies that become too heavily locked-in may be just as politically problematic as fragile ones. Locked-in policies – such as in the area of pensions or renewable energy subsidies – can become financially unsustainable (Béland, 2010: 574; Gürtler, Postpischil and Quitzow, 2019), piling pressure on politicians to introduce flexibilities.[25] From a democratic theoretical perspective, highly durable policies may also fail to adjust to the changing preferences of citizens and voters (Patashnik and Zelizer, 2013: 1083). And policies may become outdated if they are overtaken by new scientific information, such as in relation to the expected rates and impacts of climate change (Carlson and Fri, 2013: 119), or if new game-changing technologies enter the market (Auld *et al.*, 2014: 13). In short, removing the opportunity to revise policies risks locking in policy design errors (Weaver, 1988: 11) and/or increasing the risk of policy drift (Hacker, 2004). After all, it is entirely possible that some policies endure because they are so ineffectual that no one bothers to oppose them (Carlson and Fri, 2013: 123). Thus, in policy design a fundamental question regularly arises: how can predictable opportunities be created to regularly revisit and revise a policy's design without completely disrupting it?[26] In principle, there is a wide variety of what we shall refer to as *flexibility* devices that designers can employ. In Chapter 2, we will explain that they include monitoring systems to identify the need for revisions, together with time-specific targets and explicit flexibility clauses which create predictable opportunities for policy changes to be made.

Designing Durable Policies in Practice

If successful policy design is about crafting policies that are durable in some respects but flexible in others, precisely which elements of design can be altered to strike the right balance between the two? In Hall's (1993) highly influential formulation, a policy design has three main sub-elements:

- *Policy goals* which specify the objectives to be achieved; these change rarely, e.g. as a result of radical policy revisions;
- *Policy instruments* to implement the goals; these tend to change more regularly in the light of experience;
- The *calibration or setting of those instruments;* these change most frequently and are constitutive of what Hall termed 'normal' policy making.

Crucially, in this book we shall treat these elements or levels as potential entry points for inserting durability and/or flexibility devices into a given policy to generate particular policy feedback effects (Howlett, 2009b). And as these effects alter actor preferences and capacities, they may feed through to policy feedbacks at some, or indeed all, of these levels. Finally, these three sub-elements are embedded within a *policy paradigm* which Hall (1993: 279) defined as a 'framework of ideas and standards that specifies not only the goals of policy and the kind of instruments that can be used to attain them, but also the very nature of the problems they are meant to be addressing'. In climate policy, the beneficial nature of deep and rapid decarbonisation has become an integral part of the overarching climate policy paradigm in many EU countries.

As we noted in the first section, policy designers rarely design a whole policy programme from scratch (Levin *et al.*, 2012: 132–133). Rather, they tend to focus on trying to package together different elements in a manner which is broadly commensurate with their general aims and objectives, as codified in the broader policy paradigm (Howlett, 2014). A common entry point is the design of specific instruments because they constitute the bridge between broad policy objectives and day-to-day governing actions (Schneider and Ingram, 1997; Salamon, 2002; Kooiman, 2003: 29–30, 44–45). The design of instruments is often perceived to 'define' both policy making and feedback generation, because it affects the distribution of costs and benefits (Heidenheimer *et al.*, 1990: 344; Daugbjerg and Sonderskov, 2012: 402). It is for these reasons that policy instrument selection and change is afforded such a central place in the policy design literature (Meckling and Nahm, 2018: 744), and this particular book.

Accepting that there may be change at some or all three levels opens up many potential design choices, covering an almost infinite number of permutations of goals, instruments and settings (Howlett and Cashore, 2009).[27] Although it is true that policy instruments rarely appear pre-packaged in their archetypal or textbook forms, we argue that in practice they generally follow a set of basic categories (e.g. market-based, voluntary, regulatory; see Salamon, 2002), upon which the comparative research programme on policy durability foreseen by Pierson and others can be built. Crucially, these instruments types are most strongly differentiated in terms of their coerciveness (Salamon, 2002: 25) or stringency (Schmidt and Sewerin, 2018: 3, 11; see also Heidenheimer *et al.*, 1990: 310). In principle, regulation is the most coercive instrument. When selected, it is normally used by designers to generate effects with a relatively high degree of predictability, namely by imposing concentrated costs on target groups. At the other end of the spectrum of coerciveness we find voluntary instruments, which involve target groups volunteering to make short-term investments for longer-term societal benefits. Midway on the spectrum are market-based instruments which operate through the medium of market transactions. In Chapters 2 and 4 we discuss the most salient design features of these three instrument types, first of all in their textbook forms and then in the form in which the EU has actually used them to govern climate change over the course of the last thirty years.

In this book, we seek to investigate how far thinking about policy in terms of its instruments sheds new light on the links between policy durability and policy feedback. Salamon (2002: 24) famously argued that each instrument type has a specific set of internal 'dimensions', which give policy a distinctive 'spin' (Salamon, 2002: 11, 28), including, we might assume, the policy feedback it generates. In what follows, we sketch out the broad outlines of such a programme and explore its viability by testing it in a set of comparable empirical case studies within the EU. We focus on four instruments: the EU regulation on biofuel production, the market-based instrument of emissions trading (the EU Emissions Trading System), the voluntary agreement on carbon dioxide emissions from cars in force between 1999 and 2008, and the Cars Regulation that replaced it. These analyses explore how far each instrument type works through a set of feedback mechanisms to produce a distinctive set of endogenous policy dynamics, including – we expect – the opportunity to make subsequent changes that affect its durability.

1.6 The Broad Plan of the Book

Objective 1: Policy Design Intentions

Having summarised the research and policy gaps that motivated us to write this book, we are now in a position to outline our main objectives. Our first objective is to explore each instrument's formative moments in order to understand the intentions of its original designers with respect to policy feedback as well as the 'design space' in which they were operating (Howlett, 2011: 141–143). This space is bounded by a number of contextual constraints that make some options more politically feasible to accomplish than others. Within this space, we aim to understand the extent to which the nurturing of policy feedbacks was a conscious priority amongst designers. One standard assumption is that a potentially influential category of designers – politicians – are likely to be strongly motivated by an immediate desire to secure re-election, in which case manipulating feedbacks to deliver benefits over the long term may not rank as a particularly high priority (Patashnik and Zelizer, 2013: 1076; Oberlander and Weaver, 2015: 57). But what about other actors, possibly some with very different time horizons? In the EU, European Commission officials are unelected and hence may be more motivated to set and deliver against long-term policy goals. Meanwhile, some target groups such as businesses may be strongly motivated to minimise compliance costs, especially in the short run, but in the longer term may be alert to new business opportunities that have the potential to reap massive benefits by fundamentally reshaping the economic sector. By investigating these various actor types, their activities and their time horizons, we aim to understand whether there were discernible patterns in the policy designs they favoured (Mettler and SoRelle, 2014: 176) and, in particular, the entry points in Hall's three-level scheme that they gravitated towards. The standard advice from economists is that designers should first adopt broad, long-term objectives and independent agencies to instil policy making with credibility, and then (and only then) select the most appropriate instruments (Brunner *et al.*, 2012: 256). But others have advocated doing precisely the opposite – i.e. start with small, incremental re-calibrations of existing policy instruments and then, as positive feedbacks start to take hold, slowly 'ratchet up' to encompass ambitious policy programme-wide objectives that gradually lock in a new policy paradigm (Levin *et al.*, 2012: 125). By undertaking fresh empirical research, we hope to understand which of these two prescriptions approximates most closely to reality.

A key theme underpinning Objective 1 is that of *intentionality*. In the course of his work, Pierson (2000b) has repeatedly argued that designing effective and durable policies is next to impossible. If and when policy path dependence arises, it is more likely to have emerged in an unplanned rather than an intentional fashion. Moreover, if durable policies do take root, a fresh political problem almost inevitably arises: how to amend them (Pierson, 1994). But if this view of policy were true of all policy design situations, the scope for engaging in intentional policy design to deliver deeper and faster decarbonisation (Levin *et al.*, 2012: 138)[28] would be very limited indeed. Normatively, it also adds up to a rather alarming policy prognosis given the speed at which the world is hurtling towards dangerous levels of climate change.

Objective 2: Policy Feedback Mechanisms and Effects

Secondly, we follow Pierson's (1993: 602) suggestion and adopt a forward-tracing approach to map out the political feedback mechanisms and effects that have flowed from our instruments since their adoption in the early 2000s. We will examine important feedback mechanisms in each case and assess whether they were mainly resource/incentive or interpretive in nature. We have already noted that the existing literatures tend to subject the former to more detailed scrutiny. In the climate policy literature, the ability to impose costs on target groups in the short term is regarded as potentially decisive. But we are equally interested to know what happens when designers are forced (as they often are) to compromise and adopt less coercive instruments, or are distributing benefits (as in subsidies or emission allowances). Do interpretive mechanisms become more influential in such circumstances? Given the essential nature of climate policy, we expect negative policy feedbacks to be at least as influential as positive ones. Although myriad feedback effects could in principle be tested for (see Section 1.2 above), for the sake of convenience, we focus on the effects on some but not all actors, namely: target groups; government bodies; and other interest groups (Pierson, 1993: 624). Not all of these will have necessarily been part of the winning coalition that secured the adoption of the policy. Some, like the actors associated with Medicaid in the USA, may have been encouraged to support it (a positive feedback effect) having had no previous engagement (Campbell, 2015: 284). Others may have been unexpectedly drawn into policy design processes because the policy disadvantaged them in some way (i.e. they were newly created losers – hence manifestations of negative feedback effects). Following Pierson (2006: 118) and Skocpol (1992: 58), we will identify which of these three actor types were most heavily impacted by each instrument, document any significant effects on their capacity to act and any resulting changes to their policy preferences.

Objective 3: Policy Feedback and Durability

Our final objective is to bring the discussion back to the main theme of the whole book – policy durability – by examining how far the feedback mechanisms triggered feedback effects that altered the dynamics of subsequent policy making in a way that affected the initial policy. We will investigate whether feedback undermined the instrument (and with it, perhaps, the broader policy), or gradually made it more durable. We assess the degree of policy change according to the scope, the stringency and the durability of each instrument (i.e. how long it endured (in days) from the point of adoption to the point of revision) – three important degrees of change that we further explore in the next chapter. We will investigate whether this triad allows us to understand how policy feedback affected each instrument's subsequent development (Mettler, 2015: 271).

In order to address these three objectives, the rest of the book is structured as follows. Chapter 2 investigates positive and negative policy feedback in more detail and explores the role of different durability and flexibility devices. The next step in our argument involves showing how these devices vary across the main policy instrument types, which are summarised in their archetypal or textbook form. We conclude by reflecting on salient methodological challenges. The chapters in Part II relate these theoretical insights to the empirical experience of EU climate change policy. Because policy is rarely designed 'de novo' (Goodin, 1996: 30), we devote Chapter 3 to examining the prior development of EU climate policy, showing how policy programmes and instruments have co-evolved over time. We reveal that policy programme-level goals and objectives were originally established as long ago as the 1990s and were subsequently (and repeatedly) revised over time. Then we identify the general policy instrument preferences (Howlett and Cashore, 2009) that have slowly emerged in the EU since its founding in the 1950s. Together, these have heavily affected the design space in which climate policy designers worked. Chapter 4 examines the design features of our four instruments in much more detail. For each instrument, we introduce the relevant sector's greenhouse gas emission trends, give an overview of key policy actors and provide a brief preview of the instrument's early first-order feedback effects. Each instrument is subjected to more intensive, long-term analysis which traces out long, policy instrument change sequences in Chapters 5, 6 and 7, covering the period from the adoption of the initial instrument to June 2019. Given the known importance of stringency, the most obvious means to sample on the independent variable ('policy') is to move along the continuum of policy instrument types (Bemelmans-Videc *et al.*, 1998; Gunningham *et al.*, 1998: 344), i.e. starting with the most coercive (regulation – Chapter 5) and ending with the least coercive (voluntary action – Chapter 7) via the intermediate category of a market-based instrument – Chapter 6. In Chapter 8 we relate our empirical findings back to our theoretical framework, and in Chapter 9 reflect on our three objectives and identify new challenges for those who, like us, wish to understand how policy designers are rising to the politically demanding challenge of triggering deep and rapid decarbonisation.

Endnotes

1 Skocpol (1992: 58) usefully referred to this as a policy's political sustainability.
2 Hence, a policy can be politically successful but substantively ineffective (Skocpol, 1992: 58).
3 As noted above, they tend to have stable objectives and strong core coalitions, and over time garner support from a growing array of interest groups (Campbell, 2015).
4 Keohane (2015: 22) envisages these eventually coalescing into a larger and more powerful 'climate industrial complex'.
5 Some claim that intentionality is commonplace, whereas others disagree. Compare Meckling *et al.* (2015: 1171) with Huberty and Zysman (2013: 80) and Schneider and Ingram (2019: 194).
6 Political leadership, institutional structures etc. (see Campbell, 2012: 345).
7 Because of space constraints we set aside the related political challenge of adaptation – or of responding to climate impacts once they have manifested themselves (e.g. floods, heatwaves, forest fires).

8 This book is mainly concerned with public policy at EU level and not international climate diplomacy under the United Nations Framework Convention on Climate Change. In the latter context, flexibility refers to the ability of countries to purchase mitigation outcomes from other parties (Jackson et al., 2000).
9 Here understood as a noun, i.e. the architecture of a specific policy - see below and also Chapter 2.
10 Such as institutional drift, conversion and layering, etc. (Hacker et al., 2015).
11 What Pierson (2006: 124) termed 'demonstration projects'.
12 For analyses of both, see Weaver (2010: 142) and Skogstad (2017).
13 Here understood as a verb, i.e. the process of fitting together a set of policy means (instruments) to achieve specific policy ends (Howlett, 2014).
14 Hence the aphorism 'programs for poor people make poor programs... [because]... the coalitions that can form behind them are likely to be weak' (Amenta, 2003: 107).
15 It is telling that in his 1993 article, Pierson (1993: 599) generally refers to 'spoils', i.e. benefits. Later, he admitted that 'not all aspects of political life are subject to positive feedback' (Pierson 2004: 49) and later (Pierson 2006: 124) urged analysts to explore a wider variety of policy areas. It is also notable that Campbell's (2012: 338–341) more recent review was almost entirely concerned with policy benefits.
16 Patashnik (2008: 15) also concentrates on public interest reforms that do not generate concentrated benefits, a pattern not entirely dissimilar to climate mitigation.
17 In Campbell's (2012: 347) very useful turn of phrase they show 'the feed but not the back'.
18 But even Pierson has not been completely consistent on this point, having subsequently pleaded for new work on 'policy effects' (Pierson, 2006: 114).
19 Pierson barely mentioned negative feedbacks in his book (e.g. Pierson, 2004: 22 and 73). Ditto Campbell (2012) in her review.
20 The special attention afforded to pension policies is particularly noteworthy in this regard. It would be surprising if such schemes were *not* durable to some extent, given their age, scale and relative generosity, not to mention the significant personal commitments that individuals have made to their continuation (Béland, 2010: 569).
21 Note the affinities with the literature on policy regimes (May and Jochim, 2013: 427).
22 Interestingly, Pierson (2006: 121) has since backtracked on his initial claims, suggesting that it is 'not single policies operating in isolation that generate major effects, but clusters of policies with strong elective affinities'. Later he qualified that only '[...] *some* policies constitute enduring features of the political landscape that should be studied in similar fashion to traditional state institutions' (Hacker et al., 2015: 183, emphasis added).
23 Which in the case of climate change policy is heavily carbonised (Unruh, 2002; Levin et al., 2012).
24 Patashnik (2008: 12) adopted a slightly different approach to understanding the fate of large-scale public-interest reforms. Although he worked across a range of different policy types, he also (deliberately) sampled on the dependent variable, selecting cases of high and low durability.
25 This was of course Pierson's (1994) motivation for studying policy feedback in the first place.
26 Of course flexibility is not the only principle of 'good' policy design (for others, see Goodin, 1996: 39), but is the one that we will mainly focus on in this book.
27 This may partly explain why so many feedback scholars started with the most durable policy effects and/or types of mechanism and traced them back to their original instruments.
28 Levin et al. (2012: 138) claimed that there is no reason *a priori* why path dependence must emerge in an unpredictable and accidental fashion.

2

Designing Durable Policies

An Instruments Perspective

2.1 Introduction

Policy designers are actively searching for more durable climate policy designs to deliver deep decarbonisation. In Chapter 1, we noted that the existing distribution of resources and actor preferences in this area means that durable policies have proven immensely difficult to design in the past. Many difficult design choices and dilemmas will need to be confronted to ensure that future policies are more durable and more effective. These choices relate to the packaging together of various internal elements to produce an overall design that generates and is in turn sustained by positive policy feedback.

In this chapter, we explore the two main directions of feedback – positive and negative – and investigate how feedback thinking translates into the two interconnected worlds of politics and policy design. Section 2.2 outlines the factors that facilitate the creation of positive policy feedback effects, where appropriate referring back to Pierson's (1993) two causal mechanisms – namely resource/incentive and interpretive. Section 2.3 follows the same analytical steps, but this time for negative policy feedback effects. Section 2.4 compares and contrasts the two types, our aim being to move towards syncretic explanations that relate to both *policy* durability and feedback, work across both feedback directions and are applicable to a variety of policy sectors. Section 2.5 then considers how policy designers could intentionally design more durable policies, recalling that durability does not necessarily connote complete rigidity. It outlines what we mean by policy design before identifying the most important devices that designers can build into policies to promote different degrees of durability and/or flexibility. Section 2.6 explains how daily processes of policy design often centre on the selection and design of particular policy instruments. After outlining the essential features of voluntary agreements, regulation and emissions trading, it explores how each instrument type offers distinct opportunities to package together durability and/or flexibility devices. In general, we focus on how instruments appear in their idealised form; subsequent chapters analyse how climate policies have actually been designed and implemented in the EU. Finally, Section 2.7 outlines our methods, and Section 2.8 draws together our main conclusions, summarising the circumstances under which particular policy instruments are more (or less) likely to generate different types and directions of policy feedback.

2.2 Positive Policy Feedbacks

Positive Feedback

In systems analysis, positive feedbacks are self-amplifying (Richardson, 1991: 7). They occur 'when a change in one direction sets in motion reinforcing pressures that produce further change in the same direction' (Jervis, 1997: 125). Hence apparently small initial perturbations are amplified and, if there are no counter-reactions (i.e. negative feedbacks), they can eventually produce major changes (Baumgartner and Jones, 2009: 6). Everyday examples include the sudden emergence of consumer fads and fashions, or stampedes in large crowds (Richardson, 1991: 217; Jervis, 1997: 149). Systems analysts find positive feedbacks particularly interesting because they are inherently difficult to predict and explain (Bardach, 2006: 346). Indeed, very strong forms can produce entirely new features – or 'emergent properties' (Bardach, 2006: 340) – such as tailbacks in urban streets or collapses in banking systems.

Systems exhibiting positive feedback are said to have certain characteristics. Building on Arthur (1989, 1994), Pierson (2004: 18) argued that these include

- *Unpredictability:* because early events have large effects and are themselves partly random. Initially, many end states are possible and it may be very difficult to predict which will eventually occur.
- *Inflexibility:* the greater the positive feedback, the harder it becomes to shift from the selected path to an alternative one (i.e. path dependence).
- *Non-ergodicity:* small and accidental events early in a sequence do not cancel out. They are remembered and may have a decisive influence on the eventual end point.
- *Potential path inefficiency:* in the end, the path that is chosen may not necessarily be the best one; the process may be path-inefficient.

These characteristics have been used to account for the emergence of particular technologies, such as internal combustion engines powered with fossil fuel. In the past, many promising alternatives to these engines existed, including some using biofuel (see Chapter 5), but they were gradually abandoned (Arthur, 1989: 127).

Over time, fossil-fuelled cars have been gradually locked into society through their ubiquity and associated infrastructures of fuel supply and servicing (Rip and Kemp, 1998: 367; Kline, 2001: 101). Similar ideas have been employed to explain the triumph of technologies such as the QWERTY keyboard, the VHS video (over Beta versions), and the light-water nuclear reactor. As Arthur (1989: 128) explained, the interaction between seemingly random events and competitive forces can produce 'an outcome not necessarily superior to alternatives, not easily altered, and not entirely predictable in advance'.

As noted in Chapter 1, positive feedback is strongly implicated in the emergence of path dependence, when each step down a particular path produces consequences that increase the relative attractiveness of that path (Krasner, 1988: 83). As such effects begin to accumulate, they generate a powerful cycle of self-reinforcing activity which becomes biased in a particular direction (Pierson, 2004: 18). To put it slightly differently, 'once actors have ventured far down a particular path, they may find it very difficult to reverse course. Political alternatives that were once quite plausible become irretrievably lost' (Pierson, 2004: 10–11).

Positive Feedback in Politics

Positive feedback thinking has been embraced in the fields of political science and governance. At a very broad level, it has been used to explain long-term trends such as the growth in government activity over time (Baumgartner and Jones, 2009: 17) and the tendency for certain political issues periodically to 'catch fire' (True *et al.*, 2007: 160). In the policy sphere, positive feedbacks have been implicated in the long-term development of policy regimes (Weir, 2006: 172), in which problem framings, policy goals and instruments are arranged in a way that endures over a long period of time (Howlett *et al.*, 2009: 86). In relation to climate policy, regimes dependent on fossil fuels can be identified in a number of policy areas including transport, housing and agriculture (Seto *et al.*, 2016). Those advocating for durable decarbonisation policies are in effect seeking to replace those high-carbon policy regimes with low-carbon or carbon-free alternatives. A critically important question arises from this insight: in what circumstances are positive feedbacks more or less likely to appear and generate politically significant consequences? Systems analysts suspect that they are more likely to appear in systems which are deeply interconnected and densely populated with actors and institutions (Jervis, 1997: 253; Arthur, 1999: 107). As we shall see, it has proven more challenging to advance beyond this general claim and identify the precise conditions in which particular directions of feedback are more or less likely to occur.

Positive Policy Feedback

More recent work has, however, aided our understanding of the conditions in which particular policies generate positive *policy* feedback. Policies that do so are said to be self-reinforcing in the sense that they encourage actors – and specifically the 'target groups' which policies aim to influence – to define their preferences within their internal logic (Thelen, 2006: 155). The most durable policies strengthen their own political support base over time by enhancing the resources and power of existing supporters *and* by creating fresh supporters (Jacobs, 2009: 96). As such, durable policies not only 'promote [their] future development, [but] ... defend [their] future continuation and expansion' (Skocpol, 1992: 59). In Chapter 1 we noted Skocpol's (1992: 58) useful distinction between a policy's political success and its substantive success. Thus, politically successful policies are likely to be more durable, simultaneously triggering and being sustained by strong supportive coalitions. Less durable policies are more likely to target weak and divided actors, and as a consequence fail to encourage broad political support (Skocpol, 1992: 59–60).

As noted in Chapter 1, positive feedback thinking has been used to account for the long-term growth of broad policy regimes, and also explain their ability to resist reform (see e.g., Pierson, 1994). A durable, path-dependent policy (as opposed to politics – see above), is one in which previous policy decisions have 'act[ed] to circumscribe or foreclose parts of the policy space' for change (Kay, 2012: 462), by *limiting* future policy options. For policy designers intending to nurture different forms of policy feedback, a key challenge is how to secure agreement on which policy aspects to stick into place and which to leave open (i.e. render flexible). Before considering this important point, let us first consider the origins of positive policy feedback effects, i.e. the first-order effects prior to the full feedback loop.

Explaining Positive Policy Feedback Effects

Analysts have worked hard to go beyond sweeping accounts of the development of broad areas of policy and understand the precise circumstances in which policies (and specifically their policy instruments) produce particular positive feedback effects. Initially, it was not clear where they should begin, given North's (1990) argument that the ultimate causes of path dependence are highly contingent. If true, such cases would be very difficult to forecast *ex ante* (Mahoney, 2000: 511; Pierson, 2004: 44). For those who had adopted an historical institutionalist framing, the default answer has been to 'go back' and trace the most durable policies back to their origins. For example, in his backward-tracing work on welfare state dismantling, Pierson (1994: 142, 171–172) contrasted the weak and fragmented networks that emerged around housing policy in the United Kingdom with the far more unified and powerful pensioner lobby in the USA. Weaver's (2010) more recent work has more or less confirmed the same point, i.e. that specific policy designs have left a significant mark in pensions policy, both in terms of its initial development and its susceptibility to subsequent reform efforts (see also Jacobs, 2009: 99).[1]

Building on Arthur (1994), Pierson (2004) nonetheless claimed that certain conditions are especially conducive to the appearance of positive policy feedback effects. Of these, four in particular stand out: the presence of large set-up costs; significant learning effects; ongoing coordination effects; and the presence of adaptive expectations (for a summary, see Pierson, 2004: 24). The importance of *large set-up (or fixed) costs* falls squarely into Pierson's (1993: 609) category of resource/incentive mechanisms. Arthur's work had demonstrated that when set-up costs are high, individuals and organisations have an added incentive to identify and, most crucially of all, stick with a particular option (Pierson, 1993: 609). In environmental policy, a classic example is the 1977 US Clean Air Act, which forced polluting firms to bear the fixed cost of fitting expensive scrubbers to reduce air pollution, rather than burning cleaner coal supplies (for a summary, see Bardach, 2006: 340). This policy had significant policy feedback effects, reshaping the policy preferences of the firms that were required to fit scrubbers. Hence, when political circumstances changed and a new presidential administration sought to respond to rising energy prices by allowing all firms (including new entrants) to burn cleaner coal (Glazer and Rothenberg, 2005), the firms that had fitted scrubbers fought to protect their investments (and thus their competitive advantage). Through the feedback effect of the policy's initial design, opponents – namely firms that had originally opposed the fitting of scrubbers – thus became powerful interests advocating for the Act's durability.

Other analysts have since suggested that the same type of dynamic may now be playing out in relation to climate mitigation policy in the USA (Biber *et al.*, 2017: 614, 617) and other parts of the world (Levin *et al.*, 2012: 135; Meckling *et al.*, 2017: 920). And in an entirely different policy area – that of pensions – Weaver (2006) has shown how policy beneficiaries (namely working people) were asked to make significant upfront investments in exchange for a stream of future benefits. These upfront investments gradually nurtured powerful coalitions that have rendered contributory pension schemes more resistant to policy change (Campbell, 2003; Weaver, 2006: 223; but see Weaver, 2010).

However, policy coalitions only emerged in these cases because the government was able to force target groups to make upfront investments. If policy designers lack this power and/or target groups successfully resist them, then positive policy feedback effects could be neutered (see e.g., Meckling *et al.*, 2015: 1170). For this reason, designers may opt to nurture positive feedback effects not by imposing concentrated costs but by directing a concentrated stream of upfront benefits at target groups, via Pierson's (1993) resource/incentive mechanisms. Here, a classic example is Swedish unemployment policy which empowered trade unions by making them partly responsible for the disbursement of unemployment benefits (Rothstein, 1992; Pierson, 1993: 601). When the policies were challenged, the trade unions immediately leapt to their defence. Resource/incentive mechanisms have also been at work in the progressive empowerment of large farms and national agriculture ministries by the EU's Common Agricultural Policy (Daugbjerg, 2003), and in the rapid growth of renewable energy capacities through feed-in tariffs, which are a type of public subsidy scheme (Meckling, Sterner and Wagner, 2017: 919; Edmondson *et al.*, 2018: 5). Similarly, recipients of highly targeted long-term welfare support (for whom payments quickly become an integral part of their daily lives) provide another good example (Rose, 1990: 282). Therefore, other things being equal, we hypothesise that *policies which require large set-up costs and/or distribute significant and concentrated benefits, are more likely to produce positive policy feedback effects than those that do not.*

Learning has also been regularly implicated in the appearance of positive policy feedback effects. Arthur (1994) argued that with constant repetition, actors learn to reap increasing returns from a given technology, which in turn spurs further innovations in that technology. By taking that basic insight and transferring it to the policy world, both Skocpol (1992) and Hacker (2004) showed how government agencies that were established to implement new policies learned how to further their interests by interpreting their remits in a more expansive manner. For example, when the EU created the Common Agricultural Policy, national agricultural ministries hired new staff, who identified new ways to secure additional payments upon which their jobs partly depended (Daugbjerg, 2003: 433). These are classic resource/incentive feedback mechanisms. Two important implications follow from this observation. First of all, the absolute level of the benefits does not necessarily have to be that large to be politically consequential. Building on Wilson (1980: 371), Pierson (2015: 292) has argued that the recipients only have to perceive that the benefits are relatively important to support their continuation, which in part depends on their visibility and their predictability. Second, the more that recipients premise significant decisions on the continuation of the benefits, the more likely that positive feedback effects are to endure (Pierson, 1993: 608). Therefore, other things being equal, we hypothesise that *benefit-distributing policies which become large enough to constitute a significant premise of target groups' everyday existence, are more likely to generate positive policy feedback effects.*

Meanwhile, *coordination effects* occur in a situation where a policy's impact on target groups grows when other actors adopt the same behaviour. In the literature on technological innovation, coordination effects are assumed to be more likely when, as noted above, a particular technology is linked to a set of supportive infrastructures (e.g. cars and roads, fuel stations and tyre-repair facilities). Investments in the linked technology make the original technology more attractive to new adopters, rendering the associated policies more durable. Over time, the gradual, recursive development of technologies, durable public policies, consumer behaviours and supportive infrastructures produces vast interdependent webs of cause and effect which deliver 'massive increasing returns' to incumbent interests (North, 1990: 95). This line of reasoning is, as noted in Chapter 1, a mainstay of the sociotechnical innovation literature, but policy feedback scholars have also successfully applied it to understand the behaviour of big policy beneficiaries such as farmers, pensioners and the disabled, who premise their everyday behaviour on the expectation that the flow of policy benefits will be maintained into the future. Over time, durable policies beget durable politics, and vice versa. Therefore, other things being equal, we hypothesise that *policies which consolidate the status quo distribution of costs and benefits (and thus deliver further returns to powerful and well-organised incumbent actors) are more likely to generate positive policy feedback effects than those that work against them.*

Finally, *adaptive expectations* relate to the tendency for positive feedback processes to generate their own internal momentum as actors feel compelled to side with 'the winning coalition' (Baumgartner and Jones, 2002: 15). In Chapter 7 we will reveal how consumers have repeatedly shunned electric vehicles, fearing that the supportive infrastructure of charging points and repair facilities will not be installed at a sufficient rate. Although there are obvious links back to the dynamic associated with coordination effects (see above and, e.g., Pierson, 2004: 24), the dynamic of adaptive expectations has a somewhat separate origin – actors feeling under pressure to 'pick the right horse'. Thus, every motorist that purchases a fossil fuel-powered vehicle is in effect signalling to other buyers that theirs is the 'right' choice to make. In turn, they signal to others to behave in a similar way, thus increasing the likelihood that everyone's expectations become almost self-fulfilling (Bardach, 2006: 347). Pierson (1993: 608) was sufficiently intrigued to devote several pages to explicating what he referred to as 'policy lock-ins':

Policies may create incentives that encourage the emergence of elaborate social and economic networks [...] Major policy initiatives have major social consequences. Individuals make important commitments in response to certain types of government action. These commitments, in turn, may vastly increase the disruption caused by new policies, effectively "locking in" previous decisions.

Interestingly, he specifically mentioned transport and housing policies, both of which are relatively highly carbonised. Policy lock-ins are in effect extremely durable areas of government activity in which actor behaviour has, as noted above, unwittingly become self-replicating (Seto *et al.*, 2016: 434). Therefore, other things being equal, we propose that *policies which generate strong adaptive expectations are more likely to generate positive policy feedback effects than those that do not* (Béland, 2010: 574). Having explicated the triggers and facilitators of positive policy feedback effects, we now switch direction and consider negative policy feedback effects.

2.3 Negative Policy Feedbacks

Negative Feedback

In Chapter 1, we noted that negative feedbacks generally produce balancing or self-equilibrating effects (Richardson, 1991: 5; Bardach, 2006: 341). In systems thinking, they are strongly associated with the concept of homeostasis – the ability of a system to maintain stability in the face of external perturbations (Richardson, 1991: 48) – in a way which is analogous to how a thermostat maintains a room's temperature at a constant level. Negative feedback thus 'tends to diminish or counteract a change in any one of its elements' (Richardson, 1991: 5). In economics, negative feedbacks stabilise economies '...because any major changes [for example a sudden rise in the oil price] will be offset by the very actions they generate' (Arthur, 1994: 1) as actors seek to lessen their exposure (through fuel switching or by adopting energy conservation measures).[2]

Negative Feedback in Politics

Negative feedback thinking has become relatively well-absorbed in the fields of political science and governance. In politics, political systems are assumed to respond to some external perturbations by counterbalancing rather than reinforcing them (Baumgartner and Jones, 2002: 9). For example, as elite groups become more powerful, they tend to trigger counter-reactions from subordinate groups, who act to return the system to an even keel (Howlett, 2009a: 253). These arguments were central to Truman's 'disturbance theory' of American pluralism (Baumgartner and Jones, 2002: 12), to the notion of 'countervailing power' in the community power debate, and to the balance of power concept in international relations (Jervis, 1997: 121). More recently, they have been employed to construct theories of long-term policy change (Baumgartner and Jones, 2009: 288).

Negative Policy Feedback

Negative policy feedback undermines the original policy at t+1, which could in turn trigger a set of responses ranging from fairly small adjustments in the precise calibration of its constituent policy instrument, through to its complete removal and replacement with a new one (P2) at t+1, t+2, etc. Logically, it is reasonable to assume that negative policy feedbacks are just as likely to appear as positive ones. In Chapter 1, we noted that both types were mentioned by Skocpol (1992: 59) in her seminal contribution; Pierson also briefly referred to backlash dynamics in his review of the field (Pierson, 1993: 620). But soon after, negative policy feedback dropped out of the discussion. It is notable that in his book-length account of institutional change, Pierson only mentioned negative feedback on a handful of occasions (Pierson, 2004: 22, 73).[3] In fact, he claimed that '*most* policies are remarkably durable' and are 'generally subject' to positive feedback (Pierson, 2004: 15, 35; emphasis added). Self-reinforcing processes were, he added, especially prevalent in the political sphere; being 'arguably more pervasive and intense than they are in the economic sphere' (Pierson, 2004: 10). But if this were generally true, the overall policy landscape would quickly become 'frozen' (Skocpol, 1992: 59; Pierson, 2004: 77), leaving policy designers with nothing to do but tweak what is already there (Thelen, 1999: 396). Clearly, this is not happening in EU climate policy making, which – as we noted in Chapter 1 – is replete with many new policies.

In the 2010s, new scholarship rediscovered negative policy feedback. In a timely contribution, Weaver (2010) sought to understand why mounting fiscal pressures[4] arising from large pension programs had triggered policy reforms in some but not all countries. This finding was significant because positive feedback had been widely assumed to be the norm in that particular policy area (Marier, 2012: 403). Weaver (2010: 139) also noted that negative policy feedback may be equally influential in other non-distributive policy fields such as transport. He ended by noting that policy interventions to increase mobility in that sector had created many new problems, such as air pollution, congestion and accidents, that fuelled counter-mobilisations involving environmentalists and road safety campaigners. He concluded that negative policy feedback should become a new focus of attention, which he defined as the 'consequences of a policy that tend to *undermine rather than reinforce* the political, fiscal or social sustainability of a particular set of policies' (Weaver, 2010: 137; emphasis added).

Evidently, negative policy feedbacks arise from the tendency – noted by Schattschneider (1935) – for policies to create losers as well as winners (Jacobs and Weaver, 2015: 454). What might such losses entail? First and most obviously, they arise when there is continuing opposition from opponents who failed to get their way at the policy adoption stage. Such opponents do not simply disappear when the policy is adopted (Sheingate, 2003: 200); to quote Thelen (2003: 231–232) some may opt to stick 'around to contest the next round' of policy making. Very large and powerful incumbent interests such as oil and gas companies, may have an added incentive to do this, some having time horizons that may greatly exceed those of politicians, and the capacities to remain engaged with the policy process over long periods of time.

Second, negative policy feedback may be triggered by the emergence of opponents that did not mobilise at the policy formulation stage, but subsequently become more involved, either because they were simply biding their time and waiting for an opportunity to weaken the policy, or because it unexpectedly harmed them (e.g. through the imposition of costs – a resource/incentive feedback mechanism; see Weaver, 2010: 139; Jacobs and Weaver, 2015). Third, negative policy feedback may draw in completely new opponents (Mahoney and Thelen, 2009: 9–10), either from within the policy area or from cognate areas (Pierson, 1993: 600). Finally, negative feedback may create entirely new opposing groups that did not exist when the policy was created and whose entire *raison d'etre* is to weaken the policy in question (thus exemplifying the balance theory of interest group mobilisations noted above).

Regardless of whether the opponents pre-existed or are freshly mobilised, it is important to clarify which feedback mechanisms are at work. On this matter, there is still much analytical work to do, guided but not determined by Pierson's original distinction between two main types.[5] The policy could, for example, establish new sources of information (e.g. on polluting emissions) that, through interpretive mechanisms, alter who interest groups perceive to be at fault (Pierson, 1993: 632). Moreover, if emissions are found to have a detrimental impact on a particularly vulnerable social group or ecosystem, it may provoke what agenda-setting theories refer to as a 'focusing event' which generates broader disquiet about the policy amongst voters (Pierson, 1993: 619). Finally, if the original policy instrument is perceived to have unambiguously failed, it may trigger what Pierson (1993: 613) termed 'negative learning' about what does not work allied with an equally forceful desire to 'find something better'. Second and related to that, it is important to understand the interaction between the coalitions favouring the original policy and those advocating for change. If the opponents have weak capacities and are divided, policy designers may not be put under significant pressure to respond and may elect to stick with the policy *status quo*. But if the opponents are empowered by the policy (through, for example, the provision of new information – an interpretive mechanism), become more vocal and better organised, and/or external conditions suddenly change, designers may find themselves under pressure to step in and reform the policy. And if a policy is seen unambiguously as failing, even its original supporters may concede the need for change to protect it and the broader policy paradigm from further political damage.

Finally, negative policy feedback should not be confused with weak or even absent positive policy feedback (Howlett, 2009a: 247; Patashnik and Zelizer,

2013). At a minimum, negative policy feedbacks occur when a policy directly triggers political opposition to itself. In its most extreme form, it not only triggers opposition to the original policy, but to the adoption of new policies in the same and/or cognate areas (Skocpol, 1992: 59; Patashnik and Zelizer, 2010: fn. 3). In fact, a policy could conceivably trigger so much opposition to itself that designers are discouraged from adopting any further policy interventions in that issue area – a particularly extreme example of what Daugbjerg (2009: 399) referred to as 'the power of precedent'.

Explaining Negative Policy Feedback Effects

Although the policy feedback literature has only recently shown interest in negative policy feedback effects, the first-order effects that can eventually lead to a weakening of a policy's durability, there are clues as to when and where they are more likely to appear and be politically consequential. First of all, they are more likely to appear when a policy directly creates losers, chiefly through the operation of resource/incentive mechanisms. However hard designers sell their policies as *pareto* optimal (Bardach, 2007: 339), most will, as Schattschneider (1935) predicted, eventually produce some losers (Weaver and Rockman, 1993: 464). Whether by accident or by design, we therefore propose that *policies that impose immediate and relatively concentrated costs on particular groups are more likely to produce negative policy feedback effects than those that do not.*

Second, we hypothesise that negative feedback effects are *more likely when the losers – or those who perceive themselves to be at risk of losing – are powerful, well-organised and strongly mobilised* (Mahoney and Thelen, 2009: 17), as is often the case with many industries that support fossil fuels (Geels, 2010). Such actors tend to be especially assiduous and forceful defenders of the pre-adoption *status quo*. They are unlikely to stand idly by if policy designers try to 'lock in' radically different policy designs. On the contrary, they are very likely to aim at 'locking out' new policy interventions, either by diluting them during the policy formulation stage or undermining them during the implementation process.

Third, we hypothesise that *negative feedback effects are more likely to appear if the initial case for adopting the policy was weak, strongly contested and/or undermined by subsequent events*. In such cases, 'emergent losses' (Jacobs and Weaver, 2015) and/or gradual changes in the public's perception of problems are more likely.

Finally, we hypothesise that *negative feedback effects are more likely when opponents effectively have no alternative but to mobilise against the original policy*. In his seminal account of the US welfare state, Hacker (2004: 246) argued that target groups who suffer losses essentially have two options. They can opt to 'work within' the existing policy to achieve their ends, perhaps by engaging in selective non-compliance, adopting a new 'drop-in' technology to achieve compliance at a lower cost (Victor, 2011: 134), and/or by finding ways to pass on the additional costs to competing firms and/or their customers. Alternatively, opponents may opt (or have no alternative but) to 'work outside' the policy (Hacker, 2004: 246), by secretly engaging in incomplete implementation, pushing for some policy change or even openly advocating for complete dismantling. The choice between the two will in part be shaped by how directly and how heavily the target groups have been harmed by the policy in question.

2.4 Positive and Negative Policy Feedback Effects: Towards an Analytical Synthesis

Having now introduced both directions we are in a position to move towards an analytical synthesis. In Chapter 1 we identified an urgent need to connect policy designs with different first-order policy effects via the causal influence of specific feedback mechanisms. Table 2.1 is a first attempt to do just that, highlighting the implications for the most salient policy actors identified in Chapter 1 – namely target groups, government bodies and other interest groups. The existing literature has chiefly concentrated on the positive policy feedback effects on the left-hand

Table 2.1 *The main directions of policy feedback: typical effects*

	Positive policy feedback	Negative policy feedback
Target groups	Align their preferences and activities *with* the logic of the policy	Align their preferences and activities *against* the logic of the policy
Government bodies	New sources of authority and legitimacy to intervene	New sources of authority and legitimacy to intervene
	Greater bureaucratic capacity to support the policy	Greater bureaucratic capacity to block the policy
Other interest groups	Creation and expansion of pro-policy coalitions	Creation and expansion of anti-policy coalitions
Indicative examples	Major policies	Dismantled policies
	Super statutes	Retrenched policies
	Living legislation	Drifting policies
Impact on future design options	Contraction of the policy menu: path-departing reforms are less likely (policy durability)	Expansion of the policy menu: path-departing reforms are more likely (policy turbulence)

Source: own composition.

side of Table 2.1. Our expectation is that in a more regulatory setting such as climate policy, the effects on the right-hand side of the table are likely to be more prevalent leading to greater policy turbulence and change, although this is something we will subject to empirical study.

Second, putting positive and negative feedback effects alongside one another usefully reveals that they have rather similar analytical antecedents and hence should be studied together rather than separately. Counter-posing them also invites new questions to be asked about how well feedback thinking travels across different policy areas and modes of governing (Pierson, 2006: 130).

Third, by adopting a more syncretic approach we seek to understand better the interaction between Pierson's (1993) mechanisms. Table 2.2 draws on the existing literatures to illustrate the potential interaction between the two main types of mechanism and a range of observable effects. In general, Pierson's (1993) original argument that more is known about the operation of resource/incentive mechanisms than of interpretive mechanisms remains pertinent (see for example, Mettler and SoRelle, 2014). But in a more regulatory policy area such as climate change in which governmental actors are widely imposing costs, we should be especially

Table 2.2 *The potential interaction between policy feedback mechanisms and policy feedback effects*[1]

		Feedback effects		
		Government	*Target groups*	*Other interest groups*
Policy feedback mechanism	Resource and incentive	For *policy supporters* in government: New tasks, new mandates. New capacities e.g. revenue streams. New bureaucratic lobbies.	Stronger policy clienteles who reap policy benefits. More supportive coalitions. Stronger niches (for policy coalitions to exploit).	Bigger policy coalitions. New niches (for policy entrepreneurs to exploit).
	Interpretive	Policy learning on what works (the 'power of precedent'). New sources of data and information.	Policy learning on what works (the 'power of precedent'). New sources of data and information.	Creation of focusing events. New sources of data and information.

[1] The examples given are for positive feedback only.
Source: based on Pierson (1993); Campbell (2012); and Mettler and SoRelle (2014).

careful not to overlook the role of interpretive mechanisms as they may operate in subtler ways, for example through changing actors' cognition and understanding.

Finally, in Chapter 1 we declared that our ultimate goal is to move from mapping out first-order feedback effects, though to examining the resulting changes in inter-actor dynamics to eventually understanding the feedbacks on the original policy (i.e. completing the full policy feedback loop; Mettler, 2015: 271). The existing literatures suggest that four factors (some of them endogenous to the policy, some of them exogenous) will come into play as we move from the effects to the resulting policy feedbacks (Pierson, 2004: 154):

- The extent to which *the policy re-shaped the coalitions that existed at the point of adoption*. In general, positive policy feedback effects, perhaps intentionally nurtured by policy durability devices, expand the original winning coalition, lock the policy in place (greater durability) and limit the scope for future policy design. By contrast, negative policy feedback effects diminish the winning coalition, either by turning supporters into opponents or by drawing in new opponents. Consequently, they undermine policy durability by opening up new policy change opportunities and expanding the menu of new design options.
- The *mediating effect of the policy flexibility devices* that were (intentionally) incorporated into the instrument's design. For example, did active monitoring forewarn designers of impending shortfalls in performance so that policy changes could be enacted whilst safeguarding the broader policy paradigm? Or was a specific flexibility clause built into the design to force actors to consider new designs? In Hall's account of policy change, a growing perception that the policy is underperforming produces an endogenous push amongst actors to do things better within the existing policy paradigm (Baumgartner, 2013), although in the absence of exogenous pressures, this generally only results in incremental re-calibrations of existing instruments.
- The presence of *policy entrepreneurs* who are sufficiently well-motivated and/or resourced to maintain the policy status quo or, alternatively, suggest new changes. Such actors are widely known to play a key role in policy formulation (Wilson, 1980), but how far does their influence extend into the post-enactment phase, perhaps even intentionally enabled by policy flexibility devices? Without entrepreneurs, a policy may be so complicated and its effects so hidden (Mettler, 2011), that some actors – especially voters – may not even realise that they are being adversely affected (Béland, 2010: 579). But if negative feedback effects take hold, policy entrepreneurs may be able to exploit any available interpretive mechanisms to pressurise designers to alter the original instrument. By contrast, when positive feedback effects take hold, they may be able to use the power of precedent (another interpretive mechanism) to lobby for even stronger and more durable policies.

Table 2.3 *Positive and negative policy feedbacks: changes in scope, stringency and time horizon*

	Positive feedbacks	Negative feedbacks
Policy programme	More long term	More short term
	More stringent	Less stringent
	Broader in scope	Narrower in scope
Policy instrument	More deeply embedded	Challenged and possibly removed
Policy instrument settings (stringency, scope and time frame)	More stringent	Less stringent
	Broader in scope	Narrower in scope
	More long term	More short term

Source: based on Hall (1993); Howlett and Rayner (2013); and Pahle *et al.* (2018).

Either way, feedback mechanisms from the original policy instrument allow policy entrepreneurs to shape wider understandings of its fungibility.

- The presence of *exogenous pressures* for change which policy designers feel compelled to address (Thelen, 2003: 211). For example, to what extent do international negotiations put pressure on EU actors to secure faster greenhouse gas emission reductions? Or alternatively, does a worldwide recession persuade target groups to lobby for less stringent policy designs?

These dynamics will be explicated in the empirical chapters, and then more thoroughly discussed in Chapters 8 and 9. In the meantime, Table 2.3 builds on Hall's (1993) three-level model of policy change to formulate expectations about the policy changes that are more likely to appear at each level as a result of positive and/or negative policy feedback effects. Having now run through the entire causal sequence from the original policy through its first-order effects to policy feedback, the next section goes back to the start of that sequence and explores the scope for designing particular policies in ways that intentionally generate certain types and directions of feedback to increase a policy's durability.

2.5 Intentionality: The Conscious Design of More Durable Policies?

Policy Design: Key Meanings

In Chapter 1, we noted that the vexed issue of *intentionality* is connected to an even broader debate about the role of conscious, rational design in the policy design literature. Policy design first emerged as a research topic in the 1950s. It blossomed in the 1970s and 1980s particularly in relation to the development and application of particular policy instruments (Goodin, 1996). The literature on policy design ranges between two extreme positions. At one extreme are accounts which view design as not simply possible but normatively necessary. This literature, some of it directly addressing climate policy topics (see Chapter 1), has led to a good deal of 'policy analysis for policy' which seeks to identify and typologise all of the available policy instruments (e.g. Salamon, 2002). Not surprisingly, it has tended to reduce political contestation to a technical matter to be addressed by rational design (Howlett, 2011: 3). At the other extreme, we find studies that have robustly challenged the very idea of designing social life and/or raised doubts about whether design is even remotely possible in complex policy settings (Howlett and Lejano, 2013: 5).

More recently, a middle way has begun to open up between these two positions which underlines the importance of design in relation to grand societal challenges such as climate change, but emphasises the acute difficulty of designing more durable policies in practice (Peters, 2018: 3). Essentially, design is taken to refer to the process of creating policy responses to particular problems (Peters, 2018: 1). The emphasis is firmly on describing and explaining those policy processes as opposed to adopting a particular normative position (Howlett, 2019) – i.e. it is 'analysis of policy'. According to Bobrow (2005: 75), design processes tend to be 'ubiquitous, necessary and difficult': ubiquitous because they are expansive, recurrent and involve many different actors (i.e. there is no single rational designer); necessary – particularly if the aim is to address wicked policy problems (Pierre and Peters, 2005: 143); and difficult because of the multitudinous technical, political and legal challenges that inevitably arise along the way (Dryzek, 1983: 346).

Bobrow's useful insight relates back to a fundamental point made by Anderson (1971: 121) nearly five decades ago, when he argued that 'the skilful policy maker ... is [one] who can find appropriate possibilities in the institutional equipment of ... society to best obtain their goals.' If the aim is to design policies that are durable in some respects but flexible in others, which items of 'institutional equipment' can designers employ? Salamon's (2002: 24) systematic analysis of policy instruments offers the most detailed attempt to identify the key 'tool dimensions'[6] but none speak directly to the tension between flexibility and durability. In Chapter 1, we argued that Hall's (1993) typology of policy goals, instruments, and settings provides a new and potentially promising way to think about how that tension can be incorporated into design thinking. His typology identifies the most likely entry points for building durability and flexibility into policy designs. We also drew a distinction between durability and flexibility devices. In this section we will explain how these devices fit into Hall's scheme. In doing so, we will use the term policy design to mean two quite specific but in practice interrelated things (see also Schneider, 2013: 218): a *noun* (describing the 'architecture' of a policy – see Anderson, 1971) and a *verb* (describing the process through which designers produce policy in the real world).

Durability and Flexibility Devices

The general idea of designing for policy durability is a very old one (Bardach, 1977; Ingram and Schneider, 1990; Goodin, 1996). But what policy design features could be employed to increase the durability of a given policy? Building on the policy feedback literature, one obvious approach is to employ durability devices that induce actors to invest in a policy's long-term existence, over time transforming them from passive targets into active supporters (Glazer and Rothenberg, 2001: 76ff; Pierson, 2004: 24; Patashnik, 2008: 168; Jacobs, 2009). Durability devices can be built into overarching *policy programmes* (and thus operate at the level of policy objectives), into specific *policy instruments* and their *settings*, or into the broader *polity* (government departments, agencies and so on):

- *Programme-level durability devices:* these operate at the highest of Hall's three levels. They include long-term or intermediate programmatic targets to reduce emissions by a fixed amount by a certain date to nurture confidence that the broad policy direction will endure (Hovi *et al.*, 2009: 23). More specific enablers of action such as roadmaps and/or long-term strategies, perhaps co-produced with target groups, governments other and social actors, are another popular durability device (Greeuw *et al.*, 2000; Meckling, Sterner and Wagner, 2017: 919), again creating a shared vision of what the future will eventually look like (Skjærseth, 2018: 511–512).
- *Policy instrument-level durability devices:* these operate at the level of specific policy instruments (Hall, 1993). They can include standards, targets or goals that encourage and/or force target groups to make a 'sunk' investment in the policy. As noted above and by others (Kelsey and Zysman, 2013: 87), such investments have been a particularly popular and effective way to trigger positive feedback effects in environmental policy. However, designers can also trigger positive feedback effects by offering concentrated benefits, for example by providing subsidies for new forms of research and development (Pahle *et al.*, 2018: 864), or for producing a certain type of product (e.g. renewable electricity generation via feed-in tariffs). Other devices include forms of monitoring to highlight defectors and thus discourage free riding. Monitoring clauses are regularly built into the design of new EU environment laws to collect and disseminate information on how they are performing (European Court of Auditors, 2018: 4–5). In other circumstances, the durability devices can be designed to hinder and/or re-direct flows of information, particularly with respect to the imposition of immediate costs on target groups and/or to losers more generally (Jacobs, 2011: 246).
- *Polity-level durability devices:* politicians may be motivated to 'tie their hands' by handing over control to an independent regulatory agency (such as a central bank) (Glazer and Rothenberg, 2001: 84–87; Edmondson *et al.*, 2018: 6) to

oversee progress and/or protect their policies from being undone by their successors (Biber *et al.*, 2017: 632). For example, Meckling (2019: 326) argues that the International Renewable Energy Agency has performed this role in relation to the growth of renewable energy technologies. Finally, monitoring and evaluation bodies can be established to re-assure groups that the policy is performing well, and thus highlight what might be lost if it were to be changed.

In Chapter 1 we noted that excessively durable policies may also be problematic (Biber *et al.*, 2017: 610). Policy designers may therefore choose – or be forced by others – to build flexibility devices into policy designs that provide opportunities to revise policies (Parson and Karwat, 2011: 750).[7] Like the durability devices outlined above, flexibility devices can be programme-level, policy instrument-level or polity-level and function via both of Pierson's mechanisms:

- *Programme-level flexibility devices:* time-limited objectives offer an opportunity to revisit the policy's design at a pre-determined point in the future (Pierson, 2000b: 486; Heritier, 1999: 10). For example, in climate policy, emissions reduction targets are often tied to a particular deadline (e.g. 20 per cent by 2020), partly to drive progress (positive feedback) but also to take stock as circumstances change in the economy, in technology and in scientific understanding etc. In EU climate policy, we shall show that when high-level political agreements are set by EU Heads of State to achieve a particular emission reduction goal, a reference is sometimes inserted into the final *communiqué* to review the EU's commitment at a later date (this is known as a 'revert clause').
- *Policy instrument-level flexibility devices:* these include procedures incorporated into an instrument (such as a flexibility clause in related legislation) that provide an opportunity to revisit the policy's design in the light of changing conditions. They may be more or less prescriptive. Review clauses are regularly inserted into the design of new EU laws and are normally pre-programmed to be triggered at a fixed point in time (European Court of Auditors, 2018: 4–5). Other devices go further still and actually specify what should be done in the light of particular circumstances (Wilson, 1989: 37), such as a sudden change in the economy, an alteration in international policy or an extreme weather event such as a flood or a heatwave. Wilson (1989) termed them 'relational contracts'. By stabilising expectations, they seek to make policies more durable. By contrast, 'sunset clauses' have been inserted into the design of some US clean energy support instruments to scale them back at a given point in time, regardless of the situational environment (Stokes and Breetz, 2018: 84).
- *Polity-level flexibility devices:* these include monitoring and review systems to identify changes in performance and, where appropriate, flag the need for change.

Table 2.4 *Designing policy: different durability and flexibility devices*

	Means	Design aim	
		Durability	Flexibility
Polity-based	*Organisational*	Independent policy formulators and evaluation bodies	Independent policy formulators and evaluation bodies
Policy-based	*Policy programmes*	Specific objectives Specific targets Roadmaps	Time-limited targets and objectives (e.g. 20% by 2020) Conditional targets
	Policy instruments	Targets Objectives	Time-specific targets and objectives (e.g. 20% by 2020) Revert clauses
	Policy instrument settings	Targets Monitoring provisions *Ex post* evaluations	Flexibility clauses Relational contracts Sunset clauses *Ex post* evaluations

Note: these can operate manually or automatically.
Source: own composition.

Table 2.4 summarises examples of the main devices at each policy level.

To be clear, these are not devices to engineer agreement at the policy formulation stage (Weaver and Rockman, 1993: 458; Compston and Bailey, 2008). They seek to ensure that once adopted, policies *endure*. But what happens if the policy starts to head off track? To the extent that policy designers consider such possibilities in advance, they are confronted by a broad choice (Carlson and Fri, 2013: 124). On the one hand, they may adopt *manual* durability and/or flexibility devices that require an open and explicit agreement to adopt corrective measures (Patashnik, 2000: 16). Or they may adopt *automatic* devices that operate in the absence of an explicit decision to trigger them (Weaver, 1988; Hacker et al., 2013: 1). Manual devices have a number of attractive features. They may provide one particular group of designers – politicians for example – with opportunities to claim political credit for re-directing the policy. If they operate in an open and participatory manner, they may also allay fears that the design process is closed and unaccountable, and thus facilitate deeper trust and hence stronger political support. However, they also have well-known disadvantages. For example, in policy systems such as the USA and the EU, where power is widely distributed, they may function as veto points that target groups can exploit to block reform (Weaver, 1988: 260), perhaps leading to policy drift. Furthermore, the resulting political uncertainty – or worse still, complete paralysis – may reduce private investor confidence, chilling investment in new technologies – a risk that is often raised in relation to climate change policy (Stern, 2006: 368–370).

For all these reasons, designers have also invented devices that *automatically* align policies to changing external conditions. The best-known example in the social policy field is indexation, which adjusts benefit payments to reflect changes in the rate of inflation. Market-based instruments are perceived to be 'highly automatic' (Salamon, 2002: 32). Automaticity has, for example, been built into the design of emission caps in some national emission trading systems (Meckling, Sterner and Wagner, 2017: 921) and into the German and French system of feed-in tariffs (Cointe, 2015: 157; Pahle *et al.*, 2018: 863). Automatic devices have certain distinguishing features that may appeal to some politicians and certain times. For example, by locking-out opponents and/or avoiding the need to reassemble a sufficiently large political coalition, they are not as prone to institutional blockages as manual devices (Weaver, 1988: 243). By unburdening the policy agenda, they may also allow politicians to escape blame for unpopular decisions and/or when things go wrong.

However, automatic devices also have well-known drawbacks. For example, the loss of legislative discretion may deprive politicians of opportunities to claim political credit for avoiding drift; it may also undermine democratic accountability and hence system-wide trust and confidence. Second, in areas of regulatory policy such as climate change, disagreement in the formulation process may render it difficult to reach an upfront decision on which device to use in the first place, in which case manual devices in effect become the automatic option. This is precisely why Weaver (1988: 240) found that politicians tend to adopt polity-related devices, such as independent agencies, which can be tasked with achieving policy change in a more depoliticised setting.

Finally, the differences between manual and automatic devices may themselves have politically highly significant long-term effects on the visibility (or otherwise) of the costs and benefits generated by a policy, and thus the functioning of policy feedback mechanisms (Arnold, 1990; Hacker, Pierson and Thelen, 2013: 1). To put it slightly differently, one way in which designers can lock their policies into place is to prevent losers from realising that they are worse off and/or reduce their opportunities to mobilise against the policy (thus limiting negative policy feedback; Pierson, 2015: 292).

2.6 The Design of Policy Instruments

Policy Design Processes

In Chapter 1 we argued that in the real world policy designers rarely design policy programmes *de novo* (Levin *et al.*, 2012: 132–133). Instead, they expend their energies on adapting existing policy elements (policy goals, instruments and instrument settings; Howlett, 2009b) in a way that reflect new policy objectives. As we also noted in Chapter 1, a common entry point for these (re)design activities are specific policy instruments (Schneider and Ingram, 1997; Salamon, 2002). Instruments may appear towards the bottom of Hall's (1993) scheme, but the policy feedback literature reminds us that their design can be politically consequential (Mickwitz *et al.*, 2008: S169). If all policy instruments corresponded to a set of prepackaged archetypes, predicting those feedbacks would be relatively straightforward, but in practice they do not. No two policy instrument designs are ever exactly the same – in practice, there is an almost 'unlimited' variety of subtypes (Kooiman, 2003: 45).[8] However, the policy instruments literature helpfully suggests that each basic instrument type (e.g. regulation, voluntary agreements, market-based instruments etc.) has a distinctive design or set of 'internal dimensions' (Salamon, 2002: 24) that specify the roles and responsibilities of critically important actors . Crucially, it is this architectural design that allegedly imparts each instrument type with a distinctive 'spin' (Salamon, 2002: 11, 28) leading to a set of political (feedback) effects. In using that term, Salamon (2002) was not, we think, suggesting that the instrument's architecture would determine the resulting policy feedbacks. Instead, we think he was suggesting that by altering the flow of resources and information, instruments alter the capacities and preferences of actors, which in turn allows designers to (re)direct the timing and form of political conflict. Thus, while instruments will not fully determine outcomes, they may nonetheless influence what future politics is about – a set of interlinked causal steps which policy feedback scholars are uniquely positioned to elaborate. In the remainder of this section we briefly describe each instrument type and explore the conditions in which it is likely to generate distinctive feedback dynamics, including – crucially – the opportunity to make subsequent changes.

Policy Instruments: Opening the Toolbox

Policy instruments constitute the tools at the disposal of governments to implement their policy objectives (Wurzel *et al.*, 2013: 28). In Chapter 1 we distinguished between three types that are commonly used by the EU: (1) *regulatory instruments;* (2) *voluntary instruments,* principally voluntary agreements; and (3) *market-based instruments,* e.g. emissions trading. Of course, moving from this abstract threefold typology to real-world instruments requires careful empirical work which we will undertake in Chapters 3–7. For the time being, however, this typology allows us to explore their core design features in a little more detail. Thus *regulatory instruments* constitute a relatively coercive form of governing, through which targets are established (normally by public authorities) and then implemented by public and private actors. Failure to meet them usually triggers punitive action, although in practice they can be either mandatory or indicative. They can adopt different forms including bans and prohibitions, licenses and permits (Salamon, 2002; Taylor *et al.*, 2012). Command-and-control regulation is usually regarded as the 'hardest' policy instrument of all because it involves a relatively high degree of coerciveness. The 2003 Biofuels Directive (examined in Chapter 5) corresponds to this basic type of instrument.

By contrast, v*oluntary instruments* are agreed between public authorities and private actors who volunteer to adapt their behaviour. The Organisation for Economic Co-operation and Development (OECD, 1994: 4) has defined voluntary environmental policy agreements, as 'voluntary commitments of the industry undertaken in order to pursue actions leading to the improvement of the environment'. In general, they constitute the 'softest' and least coercive policy instrument type. Börkey and Lévêque (1998) further differentiated between negotiated agreements and unilateral agreements.[9] *Negotiated agreements* are slightly more coercive in the sense that they constitute formal contracts negotiated between industry and public authorities, often to address specific environmental problems. They may or may not be legally binding, but normally their contents are revealed to the public. The 1999 agreement on car emissions (covered in Chapter 7) corresponds to this type of instrument.

Finally, *market-based instruments* occupy a middle position in the spectrum of instrument types (OECD, 1994: 17). Eco-taxes and emissions trading schemes, long advocated by economists on cost-efficiency grounds, are the most widely used in the environmental field. The OECD (1980: 8) has of course continually emphasised their flexibility, but in practice much depends on how they are designed in practice. In principle, emissions trading is relatively simple and relatively flexible. In a cap-and-trade system, for example, a limit is set on overall emissions and target groups must surrender tradable emission allowances equal to their emissions. But in practice, allowances can be allocated for free (i.e. less coercive) or sold through auctions (i.e. more coercive). Where more flexibility is preferred, decisions about, e.g. allowance allocation can be discharged locally (e.g. by national governments) or centrally (e.g. by the European Commission). Cap-and-trade systems set a cap for the total amount of allowable emissions, leaving the market to determine the allowance price. Over time the cap can be lowered to bring about reductions in total emissions (i.e. more coercive). In theory, lowering the cap should increase the scarcity of emission allowances, pushing up their price and creating incentives for actors to reduce emissions. The 2003 Emissions Trading Directive (covered in Chapter 6) established such a system at EU level. Table 2.5 summarises these three instrument types.

How does this typology relate to the main themes of this book? First of all, instrument types may differ with respect to the feedback mechanisms that they

Table 2.5 *A typology of the main policy instruments*

Governance mode	Corresponding policy Instrument	Interaction between 'governors' and 'governed'
Hierarchy (Regulatory)	Regulation	Most coercive: 'Governance by government'
Market (Market-based)	Emissions trading Taxes	Intermediate: 'Governance with government'
Network (Voluntaristic)	Voluntary agreements	Least coercive: 'Governance without government'

Source: based on Wurzel *et al.* (2013).

harness to achieve greater policy durability and/or flexibility (Salamon, 2002: 25ff). At the coercive end of the spectrum, regulatory instruments could be expected to primarily harness resource/incentive mechanisms by imposing relatively concentrated costs on target groups. Voluntary instruments involve target groups volunteering to make the sunk investments needed to trigger positive policy feedbacks. Resource/incentive mechanisms are therefore not as likely to be heavily relied upon. Finally, emissions trading systems in general (and specifically cap-and-trade systems) rely upon target groups trading in allowances to emit pollutants; they thus sit in the middle of our typology. Thus, depending on how the scheme is designed (i.e. how the initial distribution of allowances is determined), there could be opportunities to distribute concentrated benefits to particular groups (via resource/incentive mechanisms). Alternatively, target groups could be forced to make sunk investments by auctioning the allowances to the highest bidder and/or rapidly forcing down the cap to reduce the supply of allowances.

Second, the three instrument types employ durability and flexibility devices in markedly different ways. Thus with command-and-control regulatory instruments, key powers to impose costs on target groups are vested with public authorities. Normally, the responsibility for initiating amendments also rests squarely with them. In the case of voluntary instruments, the design of the durability and flexibility devices is more heavily determined by what target groups are prepared to offer, although subsequently their pledges may be codified in a legal agreement with public authorities. Finally, in many market-based instruments, responsibility is shared among many actors operating in 'a market'.[10] Thus government actors will create the policy (governing the initial allocation of allowances in emissions trading etc.) and may set the overall cap, but thereafter the operation of the market is supposed to provide ongoing flexibility (Salamon, 2002: 32).

Thirdly, the three types differ significantly in terms of the means through which subsequent flexibility is achieved. Regulatory instruments tend to be the most reactive, typically requiring manual adjustments.[11] Market-based instruments are assumed to enjoy a much higher degree of automaticity (Salamon, 2002: 32). In fact, one of the theoretical advantages of textbook emission trading systems is that they offer highly dynamic incentives, as market prices adapt to changing external conditions. In practice (and as more fully explored in Chapter 3), the durability and/ or flexibility of any instrument depends on its specific 'real world' design (Carlson and Fri, 2013: 124).

Finally, in examining policy feedback over time, we remain cognisant of the possibility that in seeking a dynamic balance between durability and flexibility, designers may be operating in a changing context which has been shaped, amongst other things, by the initial instrument. If true, the choice between instruments (and, crucially, the selection of durability and flexibility devices) in the tool box at t+1 and t+2 may, if the feedback is sufficiently positive, be relatively *endogenous*.

2.7 Methods: Process Tracing and Counterfactual Analysis

In this book we employ process tracing to understand the relationship between policy feedback effects, policy feedback and policy durability. Process tracing is a method to collect 'evidence on processes, sequences, and conjunctures of events within a case for the purpose of either developing or testing hypotheses about causal mechanisms that might causally explain the case' (Bennett and Checkel, 2015: 7). It has been identified as a particularly effective within-case method to study path dependence and feedback (Bennett and Elman, 2006a, 2006b: 463–465; Falleti and Lynch, 2009: 1150). In each of the policy sub-areas discussed above, we use it to trace the development of a policy instrument before, during and after its adoption, including major instances of policy change (in stringency, scope and timeframe etc.), the formation of actor coalitions and the policy preferences of key actors such as target groups. We also collect temporal data on how long each instrument lasts in an essentially un-amended form (in days – i.e. how durable it was), and where relevant, how long it takes to agree a new policy design (the speed of amendment – again in days). In general, we hypothesise that as policy becomes more durable, the measures of scope and stringency will move in a similar direction, punctuated by relatively brief periods of policy amendment. If, on the other hand, the policy becomes less durable, the measures of scope and stringency will move in the other direction, and any amendments will take much longer period to agree upon (or result in no amendment at all – hence an increasing risk of policy drift).

The process tracing has two goals (Beach and Pedersen, 2013: 13–20): theory testing and theory building. As far as the former is concerned, we will seek to test the feedback-related causal mechanisms explored above, e.g. the expectation that concentrated resource flows to actors will make them more supportive of a particular policy instrument. As far as the latter is concerned, we will endeavour to create new theoretical expectations around the types and directions of feedback arising from the three instrument types.

In policy feedback research the use of process tracing is often connected to counterfactual analysis. A counterfactual describes an alternative world in which a particular object or process was not present, in our case corresponding to one in which there was no policy intervention. As Tetlock and Belkin (1996: 3) have argued, 'we can avoid counterfactuals only if we eschew all causal inference', in that a claim that 'X caused Y' rests implicitly on a counterfactual claim that 'if X did not exist, Y would not happen'. In other words, an approach which assumes necessary conditions – that certain factors were necessary for a certain process to occur or mechanism to operate – also implicitly assumes the 'counterfactual absence' of that factor (Fearon, 1991; Tetlock and Belkin, 1996; Mahoney, 2015: 213). Pierson noted the value of counterfactual analysis in analysing path dependence and positive feedback (2000a: 265), but did not discuss it at length or employ it in his own work. Yet as Kay (2005: 554) has correctly stated, in order to 'identify a path-dependent process, it is necessary to show that what did not happen could not have happened – that is, that certain options were not feasible because of earlier sequences of decisions'. In Chapter 9 we therefore discuss what we found by employing counterfactuals to understand policy durability and also critically reflect on some of the practical challenges that arise when employing this particular method.

2.8 Conclusions and Next Steps

We began this chapter by summarising the two main types of feedback – positive and negative. In spite of the bias in the existing literature towards positive policy feedbacks (see Chapter 1), many gaps remain in our understanding of when and how they arise. This omission is especially critical in an area such as climate change where policy makers are under political pressure to create self-reinforcing policy interventions. We then outlined some of the difficult choices that must be confronted by designers who are seeking to ensure that policies are both durable and flexible. In turn, we noted the importance of more syncretic explanations that work across *both* direction of feedback (Jervis, 1997: 168–169; Pierson, 2004: 50; Jacobs and Weaver, 2015).

In the second half of this chapter we considered how policy designers could intentionally design more durable policies. We outlined our interpretation of policy design and identified the durability and flexibility devices that policy designers can, in principle, utilise to achieve different degrees of durability and/or flexibility.

We then made new theoretical connections between the three main instruments, and different mechanisms and directions of feedback, showing how each instrument type offers distinctly different opportunities to package together durability and/or flexibility devices. We concluded by outlining our methods. In summary, this chapter has mostly focused on policy instruments in the idealised form that they are described in textbooks. In the next chapter we begin to analyse the forms that they have actually taken in EU climate policy.

Endnotes

1 In effect, endogenising issues such as programme maturation and slow growth that were exogenised by the 'New Politics' school of policy dismantling (Ross, 2000: 13).
2 It was this idea of self-equilibrium – a key axiom of standard economic approaches – that North and Arthur sought to challenge with their 'new' institutional economic approaches (Arthur, 1999: 108).
3 But see Pierson (2004: 135–7).
4 Note his reference to a resource/incentive mechanism.
5 Virtually all of the examples in Pierson (1993) relate to mechanisms of positive feedback.
6 He identified four: coerciveness; directness; automaticity; visibility (Salamon, 2002: 24–32).
7 Not just any changes, but particularly those which are deemed to be appropriate and relevant in the sense that they keep the policy as a whole on track (Goodin, 1996: 41).
8 This variety is probably why the policy instrument literature became rather obsessed with defining and topologising instrument types (Wurzel *et al.*, 2013: 23–8), rather than tracing out their feedback effects.
9 Unilateral commitments are less coercive and tend to consist of general promises made by individual companies and/or industry associations independently of public authorities. They do not appear in the EU's toolbox and hence are excluded from our sample.
10 Hence the economic argument that by taking matters out of the hands of bureaucrats and/or politicians, market instruments automatically instil policy with greater credibility.
11 But some regulations may be designed to be 'light handed' and/or 'smarter' to allow them to adapt more easily to changing exogenous conditions (e.g. inbuilt flexibility clauses and relational contracts etc.; see, for example, Gunningham *et al.*, 1998).

Part II

Designing Policy Durability

3
Designing Climate Policy in the European Union

3.1 Introduction

This chapter explores how policy designers in the European Union (EU) have addressed the challenge of climate change. In particular, it outlines the broad design space in which they have sought to create and sustain more durable policies. Starting with the broad aims of EU climate policy and then moving down to the establishment of particular aims, objectives and instruments, it reveals what design decisions were made, by whom and for what purpose. In particular, it focuses on how, when and why designers built durability and flexibility devices into their policy packages. Much of the previous work on policy durability and feedback has, as we noted in Chapter 1, concerned policies and design spaces that have a strongly distributive character. Therefore, Section 3.2 begins by exploring the nature of climate change as a distinct policy problem (Rosenbloom *et al.*, 2019: 169), pinpointing how the design challenges (and hence design spaces) differ from those in national social and welfare state policy. Section 3.3 builds on these insights by summarising the main instrument choices that were made in EU environmental policy in the past. In doing so, it reveals what Howlett and Cashore (2009: 39) would characterise as the EU's 'policy instrument logic'. Although there are well-known theoretical advantages of selecting from the full array of instruments (Jordan *et al.*, 2003: 12–16), we demonstrate that the EU has a strong preference for regulatory instruments. Our analysis then moves along the instrument continuum introduced in Chapter 1, i.e. starting with regulation and ending with voluntary action. Section 3.4 focuses on the historical evolution of EU climate policy since the late 1970s, noting how climate policies have incorporated different combinations of durability and flexibility devices. Finally, Section 3.5 summarises the main points about design choices and spaces in the EU.

3.2 Policy Durability, Policy Feedback and Climate Change

The concepts of policy durability and policy feedback emerged from studies of social, pension and welfare state policies, principally enacted in the USA. Such policies tend to have certain characteristics: they mostly deliver concentrated benefits to recipients (generally individual citizens); their public profile (or 'issue salience') amongst the general public is generally quite high; and their costs are dispersed across the wider population, chiefly those who pay tax. By contrast, the politics emerging in a policy area such as climate change are likely to be different (Lowi, 1972; Wilson, 1980): the issue salience amongst mass publics is often lower than amongst scientists and policy specialists; interest groups are likely to exert greater influence; and existing and as-yet-undeveloped technology is likely to play a more significant role. The remainder of this section unpacks these characteristics in more detail.[1]

First, *science* plays a relatively significant role in the politics of climate change, which increases the overall complexity of policy making and in turn creates a barrier to greater public understanding. The scientific complexity associated with understanding how greenhouse gas emissions impact the Earth's climate at various scales is relatively high. Natural cause-and-effect relationships are difficult to comprehend, let alone observe, and hence are much more difficult for non-experts (including voters) to appreciate. These difficulties are compounded when potential social responses to climate change are taken into account. According to one review of the literature, 'our ... brains and societal perspectives ... are not well suited to the timescales and time lags of climate change' (Pahl *et al.*, 2014: 377). Hence one of the pre-conditions for the appearance of positive policy feedbacks amongst mass publics – the presence of policies that have 'massive tangible impacts on citizens' lives on a daily basis (Patashnik, 2008: 29) – is less likely to be satisfied. In fact, the effects on mass publics of many climate change policies[2] are likely to rank fairly low in terms of their visibility and traceability (Pierson, 1993), leaving the door open for policy opponents to sow doubts in their minds and those of policy designers (Giddens, 2015: 157–158). But at the same time, their low visibility may create spaces in which environmental interest groups and policy entrepreneurs can raise the level of societal awareness to push particular policy instruments and devices.

Second, unlike many areas of social policy, climate policy makers are more likely to be (re)distributing *costs*, not benefits. As Hovi *et al.* (2009: 28) nicely put it: mitigation policies 'normally involve imposing costs on actors whose behaviour has to change'. In the aggregate terms employed by economists, it is completely rational for a society to completely decarbonise, especially if the net costs of doing so are lower than the costs of not mitigating (see Stern, 2006). However, politics complicates the analysis because the costs are often borne by some of the largest and most influential actors in the economy, such as electricity producers and the car industry (Unruh, 2002). Many of them have a strong interest in preserving the policy *status quo* (Bernauer, 2013). Moreover – and very much reinforcing the aforementioned point about public understanding – the costs and benefits of acting are associated with different levels of uncertainty. The immediate costs of decarbonisation tend to be more certain (i.e. traceable), whereas the benefits are more uncertain, less traceable and more likely to accrue far into the future (Victor, 2011: 41).[3]

Third, unlike many social policies, for whom mass publics are the standard unit of analysis (Mettler, 2015: 271), regulatory policies are generally targeted at organised interest groups, known as target groups in the policy design literature. Target groups are generally more powerful and find it easier to organise themselves into coalitions than the individual beneficiaries that dominate social policy (Béland, 2010: 577), and for whom collective action can be a significant obstacle to participation in policy design. In many cases, a policy's effects on the public, including voters, is easily drowned out by the continual 'din of politics' (Jacobs and Mettler, 2018: 359). By contrast, interest groups are more carefully attuned to how a policy affects them. They are more likely to have the motive, the extended time horizons and, crucially, the capacities to play a 'long game' and involve themselves in all the stages of policy design (Hacker and Pierson, 2014: 649). By comparison, the turnover of politicians, of policy issues and voter attention is often rapid. For Hacker and Pierson (2014: 651), 'organised groups are knowledgeable and care deeply about policies of which most voters are only dimly aware, and [...] policy makers [...] possess a range of techniques for exploiting this asymmetry'. Since Walker (1983: 403), political scientists have known that groups 'spring up' after the passage of new legislation. But when contemplating the feedback from climate change policies, it is important to remember that policy design processes were heavily populated with interest groups long before climate change became a salient political issue.

Finally, we know that climate policy is heavily affected by the interaction between policy and *technology* (Schmidt and Sewerin, 2017). Until now, the policy feedback literature (and indeed historical institutionalism more generally) has proceeded by analogising from the literature on technological innovation. But paradoxically, the politics surrounding policy feedbacks and/or the active steering of technological innovation has received relatively little attention amongst political scientists (Kay, 2005).[4] Yet when it comes to designing durable climate change policies, the past, present and future role of technology is likely to be crucial. In environmental policy, technology plays a deeply 'ambiguous' double role (Berkhout and Gouldson, 2003: 231), being both an important source of emissions and a means to reduce them. Moreover, we know that the most mature polluting technologies have co-evolved with policies and societies over time, generating significant policy lock-ins sustained by positive feedbacks. Pierson (2004: 27) has stressed the importance of the tightly interconnected 'institutional matrix' between policies, politics and technologies which generates 'massive increasing returns' to incumbents (North, 1990: 95). In Chapter 4, we will explore how the combustion engine forms a key component of car-based forms of travel, which in turn is deeply connected to everyday patterns of human interaction ('car dependency'; see Rip and Kemp 1998: 367). For policy feedback scholars, what is particularly distinctive about climate change is the depth and relative maturity of these entanglements. Unruh (2000: 818) has characterised them as not just a techno-institutional complex, but '... possibly the largest techno-institutional system in history and [one with] ... no real precedent' (Unruh, 2000: 828).

Together, these four characteristics – limited public awareness and understanding; an asymmetrical distribution of costs and benefits; powerful incumbent interest groups; and very sticky existing policy-technological interactions – are likely to bear upon the policy dynamics which shape how feedback effects are translated into policy feedbacks. In the past, they have arguably militated against the intentional generation of positive policy feedbacks that render policies more durable (Keohane, 2015: 22). Given their existence, negative policy feedbacks would seem to be more likely to appear in Chapters 5–7 than positive policy feedbacks. Powerful target groups, such as fossil fuel producers, enjoy massive advantages from incumbent technologies which may have originally developed in rather contingent circumstances, but have since become heavily locked in. They also have the means and motivation to mobilise to scale back policy stringency early in the design process. Politicians that manage to surmount these obstacles and adopt climate policies also risk being challenged by public protestors, as happened in relation to road fuels in the United Kingdom in 2001 and France in 2018.

In this context, in the remainder of this chapter (and the next) we will explore the policy design patterns and spaces that have emerged in the EU over the last four decades, noting how actors attempted to adopt durability and flexibility devices in the context of the four problematic characteristics noted above.

3.3 Established Policy (Instrument) Preferences

Polity and Policy Programmes

The EU is often described as a unique, multi-levelled system of governance (Hooghe and Marks, 2003; Schreurs and Tiberghien, 2007). The sheer number of actors (or 'veto players') that need to be satisfied before a new policy can be adopted or an existing one amended has led Hix (2007: 145) to describe it as 'hyperconsensual'. This situation has directly influenced the EU's ability to engage in durable environmental policy making. First, the EU's structure tends to limit its ability to coerce target groups into making the sunk investments that facilitate positive policy feedbacks (see Chapters 1 and 2). High-profile decisions on the EU's strategic direction, such as overall greenhouse gas reduction targets, are made in the European Council, an institution which brings together the Heads of State and Government of the Member States. It makes decisions by consensus, meaning that a single Member State can block agreement and no state can easily be coerced into doing anything. The European Commission, the EU's executive body, is tasked with acting in the long-term interest of the EU; it enjoys a sole right of initiative to formulate new policy designs that advance European integration. For most environmental legislation, the European Commission makes a proposal which must be adopted by a majority in the European Parliament and a 'qualified majority' in the Council of Ministers (which is made up of ministerial representatives from each national government). The European Parliament is seen as the 'greenest' EU institution, and often attempts to increase policy stringency (Burns et al., 2013). Finally, an independent agency – the European Environment Agency (EEA) – collects data on environmental quality and undertakes analyses of environmental policy performance. Particularly in areas where EU legal competence is weak and/or contested, policy designs have often been rendered less stringent in line with the preferences of the least ambitious actor (Jordan and Adelle, 2013).

Second, once the EU has adopted a policy, its hyperconsensuality means that it tends to remain in place, at least until a sufficiently large number of veto players are able to agree that it should be revised. This is one of the reasons why policy dismantling in EU-level environmental policy has generally been quite limited (Gravey and Jordan, 2016). However, policies that cannot be updated run the risk of succumbing to policy drift (Gravey and Jordan, 2019). Finding ways to ensure adequate flexibility is therefore a constant challenge in EU policy design. In some areas, EU law gives the European Commission delegated powers, through a process known as 'comitology', to amend existing policies to reflect changing circumstances (Blom-Hansen, 2011). These correspond to our category of manual flexibility devices. In Chapters 5–7, we will note other examples of devices that have been configured to operate in a more automatic fashion. Meanwhile, the Member States and the European Parliament have also tasked the Commission and the European Environment Agency to constantly evaluate the performance of EU policies and distribute information on what is working and what is not. As such, the EU is able to draw upon polity-based durability and flexibility devices (i.e. the top row in Table 2.4).

Third, the basic institutional structure of the EU affects the design space in which particular durability and flexibility devices are built into policy instruments (i.e. the bottom two rows in Table 2.4). It is widely known that the EU was consciously designed by its founders – the Member States – to operate with relatively limited financial resources. It does not, for example, tax in the way that conventional sovereign states do. Hence, it has relatively little money to spend – and virtually none in the environmental sector (Jordan *et al.*, 2012). As a result, the EU does not have the means (or the political support) to fund a (re)distributive welfare state policy, and it has a limited ability to fund subsidies or feed-in tariffs to directly cultivate positive policy feedback. As such, it cannot utilise resource/incentive feedback mechanisms in the same way that most of its Member States can. In fact, some believe that the EU has become so strongly associated with the use of a single instrument type – regulation – that it should be defined by it – hence, it is a 'regulatory state' (Majone, 1994). The next section explores the use of flexibility and durability devices at the policy instrument level (i.e. the bottom two rows in Table 2.4), moving from the most to the least coercive instrument types.

Policy Instruments

Regulatory Instruments

Regulatory instruments come in many different shapes and sizes (Keyes, 1996). Regulation certainly dominates the EU's environmental policy design activities (e.g. Holzinger *et al.*, 2006). Many EU regulations address products, the free trade in which is an integral part of the EU's trade liberalising ('single market') project. But they also govern processes such as waste disposal, land-use planning and environmental monitoring, which have little or no direct relationship to trade. By 2012, the total stock of environmental regulations had grown to roughly 1,000 items (Wurzel *et al.*, 2013). With reference to Table 2.4, individual regulatory instruments usually specify common objectives to be achieved and set specific targets and deadlines to achieve them (i.e. instrument-level durability devices). Some are implemented through EU Regulations, which means they are directly effective and immediately legally binding. EU Regulations are generally used to govern the trade in products – e.g. cars (see Chapter 7). However, the vast majority are implemented through a less-prescriptive sub-type of regulation known as Directives, which generally leave Member States with significantly greater leeway to determine how to apply durability and flexibility devices.

Why are the EU's policy instrument preferences so heavily tilted towards regulation? First of all, the EU's founding Treaties only explicitly mention regulatory instruments. The EU has tried to side-step this by using them to adopt non-regulatory instruments such as eco-labels, emissions trading (Chapter 6) and certain types of voluntary agreement (Chapter 7). However, these departures had to survive numerous challenges by veto players, especially those that sought to go beyond the limits of the EU's legally constituted design space. Second, using regulation to morally 'penalise' polluters may be regarded as a democratically more legitimate design priority than allowing them to pay to continue polluting (Dryzek, 2001). However, the relative importance of regulations has nonetheless declined in recent years as the EU has experimented – with varying degrees of success – with non-regulatory instruments (Jordan et al., 2005), to which we now turn.

Market-Based Instruments

In economic textbooks, a distinction is normally drawn between two main types of market-based instrument: environmental taxes and emissions trading. However, throughout the 1970s and 1980s, the use of taxes to supplement and/or replace regulation was completely absent from the EU's policy agenda. While Member States adopted a wide variety of environmental taxes at the national level (Andersen, 2019), regulation remained the main instrument of choice at EU level. Only in the early 1990s did the Commission, and in particular its environmental 'ministry', the Directorate-General for the Environment (DG Environment), push the idea of EU-wide environmental taxes and other economic instruments in the EU's 4th Environment Action Programme[5] (COM (86) 485: 16). However, the need for unanimity in the Council on tax affairs consistently allowed sceptical Member States to block individual proposals – including on greenhouse gas emissions. Frustrated by its inability to secure agreement, DG Environment switched direction and pushed for the adoption of another type of market-based instrument: emissions trading (see Chapters 4 and 6).

Voluntary Instruments

Similar factors have also constrained the adoption of voluntary instruments at EU level. They were able to flourish at the national level in Europe where the obstacles were less significant, although not in all Member States. By the 2000s, almost two-thirds were to be found in just two Member States – Germany and The Netherlands – although subsequently they have diffused to other countries (Wurzel et al., 2013). The EU only began to seriously consider a more voluntary approach in the late 1980s. After the publication of a White Paper on European Governance in 2001, many observers expected the Commission to adopt many at EU level (Wurzel et al., 2013: 127). However, once policy design discussions moved down to a more detailed level, the lack of a solid legal basis in the EU treaties again reared its head. It quickly became apparent that voluntary agreements could only be adopted outside the EU's formal decision-making procedures, thus side-lining two of its main policy bodies – the Council and the Parliament.[6] A number of actors, including the European Parliament, environmental NGOs, and Member States such as Denmark expressed various levels of scepticism about the efficacy of voluntary instruments when compared to regulation (see ENDS Europe 1998a, 1998b; European Parliament, 1998).

Despite this scepticism, several EU-level voluntary agreements were negotiated in the late 1990s, covering the energy efficiency of washing machines and televisions (Bertoldi and Rezessy, 2007: 56–67). The most high-profile of these agreements – which is discussed in Chapter 7 – was the 1998 voluntary agreement on CO_2 emissions from new cars. In this area, the EU-level automobile industry group, the European Automobile Manufacturers' Association (ACEA), preferred voluntary action to regulation. The Commission therefore set out to build new durability devices into an innovative, sector-wide agreement with the car industry that had the ambitious aims of reducing emissions and blazing a trail for many more voluntary agreements at EU level. However, that agreement's failure to drive sufficient emissions reductions led instead to its removal and replacement by an instrument that was more in line with the EU's pre-existing policy instrument preferences: the 2009 Cars Regulation and its successors.

Having now identified and explained the EU's pre-existing policy instrument preferences and the design spaces in which designers operated, the next section[7] explores how, why and in what form the EU began to design policies to address climate change. Throughout, we note the main durability and flexibility devices and explain the means through which they operated.

3.4 The Design of EU Climate Policy

The Origins of EU Policy

In 1986, the European Parliament was the first EU institution to publicly respond to scientific evidence of rising global temperatures by issuing a declaration (OJ C255 13.10.86). But given that previous attempts by the Commission to design an EU-wide response to the closely related problem of energy insecurity had amounted to little following the 1970s oil crisis, the likelihood that its declaration would culminate in significant policy innovation was not very high. As with matters of taxation, some Member States were quick to voice their opposition to the EU adopting new legal powers in this area. However, new opportunities began to open up at the international level. In 1987, the United States issued a proposal to create the Intergovernmental Panel on Climate Change (IPCC) and in 1988 an international conference was convened in Toronto to discuss possible policy responses. In June 1988, the European Council made an open-ended Declaration on the Environment, in which it stated that '...it is urgent to find solutions to such global issues as [...] the greenhouse effect' (Bull. EC 12-1988: 15). The

Declaration can be seen as an extremely weak programme-level durability device; it did not, for example, include any specific goals, targets or policies. However, it did create a policy-paradigmatic commitment to address the issue. And thus, shortly after, the Commission set out its own thinking in a Communication on climate change in the November of that year (COM (88) 656). Whilst acknowledging that policies to achieve emission reductions would not be immediately forthcoming, this Communication nonetheless marked the formal start of climate policy design at EU level. It was a good deal longer before the Commission mooted more specific policy programme-level durability devices: EU-wide targets for emission reductions (Wynne, 1993: 108–109). In December 1988, DG Environment began to engage other DGs in a discussion relating to the design of such devices.

In June 1989, the Council of Ministers issued a resolution on the broad, policy programme-level aim of EU climate policy, namely to mitigate greenhouse gas emissions in order to reduce the risk of disruptive climate change (89/C 183/03). One can detect in this early statement the slow emergence of a decarbonisation policy paradigm. Nevertheless, the most significant policy design initiatives were being enacted at the international level (i.e. principally through the United Nations (UN) and involving individual Member States acting independently of the EU). Following the Toronto meeting, a number of Member States attempted to force the pace by adopting broad, national emission reduction targets (a type of programme-level durability device). The Netherlands (1989), the United Kingdom (1990) and Germany (1990) were the first to do so.[8] By the Autumn of 1990, a number of Member States had adopted a national emission reduction target (Costa, 2008: 534). Yet there was still no common EU-wide target and, more importantly, no policy instruments to deliver the associated emission reductions.

The EU's First Bid for International Leadership

The Commission's Recommendation – published in March 1990 – to consider a time-specific (i.e. '1990 by 2000') EU-level emission stabilisation target (i.e. a policy programme-level durability device) was a calculated attempt to work with the grain of Member State preferences (Skjærseth, 1994: 26–27). In June 1990, the European Council subsequently called for the adoption of EU-wide targets and strategies to *limit* emissions. In terms of the menu of devices outlined in Table 2.4, this marked a conscious attempt to move from the broad level of policy programme targets, down to the design of specific policy instruments, both embedded in an emerging decarbonisation policy paradigm. During the second half of 1990, a policy entrepreneur, the Environment Commissioner Carlo Ripa di Meana, pushed Member States to adopt an even more ambitious policy stance, believing it would enhance the EU's identity as an international actor. In October 1990, a Joint

Energy/Environment Council agreed to stabilise the EU's collective emissions at 1990 levels by 2000. But again, this policy programme-level durability device only covered long-term aims, objectives and targets, *not* the policies and measures to achieve them (Oberthür and Roche-Kelly, 2008: 7). Wynne (1993: 110) dismissed this commitment as an 'ambiguous supranational concoction', which put off many potentially tricky discussions on their precise nature to some unspecified point in the future (Oberthür and Pallemaerts, 2010: 29). Nonetheless, it marked a further solidification in the EU's evolving and now increasingly interconnected multi-level climate policy design.

Meanwhile, discussions within the UN had progressed to the point that parties were able to adopt a broad agreement, the United Nations Framework Convention on Climate Change (UNFCCC) in June 1992. As a strong advocate of international cooperation, the EU eagerly signed and later ratified the UNFCCC even though it lacked the internal policy instruments to implement its commitments (Oberthür and Pallemaerts, 2010: 31). Just prior to the official signing ceremony in October 1991, the Commission published an integrated package of proposals for discussion (SEC (91) 1744). These covered four main areas (Haigh, 1996: 164). But as noted in the previous section, the fourth and, from a policy design perspective, the most innovative element – the common carbon/energy tax proposal – was eventually rejected by the Council (Skjærseth, 1994). In some respects, it hardly mattered because at that stage, the UNFCCC contained no significant programme-level durability devices, namely specific and binding targets (Oberthür and Pallemaerts, 2010: 32). But it left the EU in the awkward position of having signed up to a UN agreement that it did not have the policy instruments to implement. In fact, at the same time as the Commission's high-profile tax proposal was being discussed, a more technical decision on a monitoring mechanism to collect and communicate (via the Commission) information on national emissions and policy measures was being adopted (Decision 93/389/EEC, i.e. a polity-based durability device). After the tax proposal failed, the monitoring mechanism effectively became the EU's only major *de facto* climate policy instrument. Crucially, it required Member States (i.e. not the EU) to 'devise, publish and implement national programmes' (Pallemaerts and Williams, 2006: 43). However, these activities – to be led by the Commission but also involving the European Environment Agency (EEA), then only very recently founded (Hilden *et al.*, 2014) – allowed the EU to conduct 'distance to target' studies of whether EU emissions were on or off track: a potentially powerful interpretive feedback mechanism. The 1993 Decision on the monitoring mechanism thus created polity-based durability and flexibility devices which could, through processes of policy feedback, potentially support the design of future policy programmes and instruments. More importantly, it provided the Commission with information which it could use to make a more convincing case for new and/or revised policies if national-level policy instruments fell short of the EU's unilaterally adopted '1990 by 2000' stabilisation target.

A Widening Gap between Policy and Emissions

As it became clearer that the EU carbon/energy tax proposal was unlikely to be adopted, hopes for stronger EU and UN policies on other matters[9] were also receding as the world economy slipped into recession. So instead, the Commission opted to bide its time and build on the two least controversial elements of its 1991–1992 climate package. For example, a Decision (93/500/EEC) in another policy area – renewable energy generation – was adopted in 1993. Due to Member State opposition it only included indicative, non-binding targets, which Member States were only required to 'take note of' when framing their national energy policies. Although non-binding, the targets were relatively ambitious – such as increasing the share of the energy supply from renewables from 4 per cent to 8 per cent by 2005 and securing a 5 per cent share of the road fuel market for biofuels (up from virtually zero). In time, these indicative targets provided the foundation and stimulus for subsequent policy instruments after 2000 (e.g. the 2003 Biofuels Directive – see Chapter 5).

When the USA pulled back from the UNFCCC in 1993 (Oberthür and Ott, 1999: 44), the EU realised that if it was ever to be fleshed out with an emissions reduction protocol (containing binding targets and a specific timetable, i.e. programme-level durability devices), it would have to show the necessary leadership. So, in advance of the first Conference of the Parties (COP) to the UNFCCC, to be held in Berlin in 1995, the United Kingdom announced its readiness not only to stabilise, but cut its emissions in the period to 2010. In 1990, Germany had committed itself to achieving a 25 per cent emission reduction by 2005 (see Costa, 2008: 534). In both countries (the two largest emitters in the EU), greenhouse gas emissions were declining, albeit for 'non-climate' policy reasons.[10] Nevertheless, their pledges influenced an important political declaration of intent known as the Berlin Mandate (Oberthür and Ott, 1999: 46–47), which eventually paved the way to the adoption of the legally binding Kyoto Protocol in 1997. Oberthür and Ott (1999: 47) have identified the Berlin COP as a pivotal moment in the slow, step-wise development of the international climate regime.

In 1996, EU Environment Ministers agreed to seek 'significant overall reductions' in emissions after 2000 (Environment Council, 1996: para. 8). Even more importantly, following the publication of the IPCC's Second Assessment Report, they resolved that the increase in global temperatures should not exceed 2 °C above pre-industrial levels. Staying within the two-degree limit quickly became the overall objective of EU climate policy (Jordan et al., 2013). The adoption of this programme-wide durability device immediately generated a need for two further policy interventions. First of all, a complex formula was needed to allocate the necessary emission reductions amongst the Member States. This was finally accomplished in March 1997, after intense horse-trading. Little noticed at the time, the Environment Council's suggestion that industrialised countries should achieve a 15 per cent reduction by 2010 to remain within 2°C, marked another important landmark in the slow, stepwise development of EU and international climate policy. Second, the new reduction target underlined the need for new policy instruments. The Commission knew that it was starting from a very low base and so again focused on areas in which Member State support was likely to be forthcoming, i.e. relatively technical matters such as monitoring, reporting and energy labelling standards for traded products such as ovens, central heating boilers and refrigerators. It also launched a strategy to reduce CO_2 emissions from cars (COM (95) 689), another important traded product that was already a well-established focus of local air pollution policies at EU level. This strategy culminated in the voluntary agreement discussed in Chapter 7. At the time, transport was a highly anomalous sector from which emissions were increasing rapidly. Nevertheless, in spite of these new policy design activities, it was by no means certain that the EU would eventually deliver on the pledges it had made in the UN.

A Second Bid for International Leadership

The policy design debate inside the EU began to deepen after the adoption of the Kyoto Protocol in 1997. In order to secure agreement, the EU committed to achieving an 8 per cent reduction, whereas the USA and Japan accepted targets of 7 per cent and 6 per cent respectively. These numerical targets were in effect new policy programme-level durability devices but, in adopting them, the EU was forced to make some vital compromises including accepting a role for international emissions trading which, as noted above, was not in line with its existing policy instrument preference for regulation. Moreover, despite repeated predictions that emissions in the EU would rise (COM (1999) 230: 2), most Member States were still rather reluctant to adopt new EU-wide policy instruments, fearing that they would be economically too costly.

Then, in March 2001, there was an exogenous shock to the EU system: the newly elected Bush administration in the USA announced that it would not ratify the Kyoto Protocol, leaving the EU out on a limb. At the June 2001 Environment Council, Environment Ministers took the 'momentous decision' to go it alone and lead the climate regime (Bretherton and Vogler, 2006: 108). In March 2000, the Commission had initiated a large multi-stakeholder road-mapping exercise – a kind of policy programme-level durability device – known as the European Climate

Change Programme (ECCP). During its two stages (2000–2001 and 2001–2003), the ECCP identified numerous policy options, many of which were worked up into concrete proposals (Pallemaerts and Williams, 2006: 45) including, significantly, one on emissions trading (see Chapter 6).

After 2001, the pace of international policy design began to increase again. In 2001, the seventh COP (held in Marrakech) finalised most of the remaining operational aspects of the Kyoto Protocol, paving the way for its eventual ratification. Encouraging Russia to ratify the Protocol so that it could take effect arguably counts as one of the EU's greatest diplomatic achievements (Oberthür and Pallemaerts, 2010: 39). It followed up by designing and adopting a number of new internal policy instruments. These included the Directives on the Energy Efficiency of Buildings (2002), on Combined Heat and Power (2004) and, of particular relevance to us, on Emissions Trading (2003) and Biofuels in Transport (2003). In January 2005, the Commission issued a Communication which evinced a growing sense of confidence. In March 2005, Environment Ministers even overrode the Commission's advice and called for more ambitious policy programme-level goals and 'reduction pathways' equating to 15–30 per cent by 2020 and 60–80 per cent by 2050 (Pallemaerts and Williams, 2006: 47). It was almost as if the various EU institutions were competing with one another to set more stringent, more forward-looking and more durable policy designs.

In the mid-to-late 2000s, the EU's determination to play a leading role was reinforced by a number of focusing events. The first was Russia's decision (in January 2006) to temporarily halt gas supplies from the state-owned Gazprom company to Ukraine. This event – which was repeated almost exactly three years later in 2009 – helped to re-focus attention on the EU's ongoing attempts to coordinate its internal energy policy. According to two high-ranking Commission officials, this event gave them 'new impetus' to promote new policy designs (Delbeke and Vis, 2015: 86). A second focusing event in 2008 – the sudden surge in oil prices to an all-time high of nearly $150 per barrel – encouraged politicians to ask the Commission to explore lower-carbon energy options including biofuels and greater energy efficiency measures. The third event was the decisive public vote against an EU constitution in French and Dutch referenda, which had been originally drawn up to make EU governance more democratically accountable. In the ensuing political power vacuum, 'Brussels was looking desperately for something to give the Union a lift [and] Barroso [the Commission President] realised climate change was a good message to sell' to win over sceptical publics (Buchan, 2009: 14).

In January 2007, the Commission responded to these three events by launching a new strategy, which included a new policy programme goal of a 20 per cent reduction in emissions by 2020, rising to 30 per cent if other developed countries made comparable efforts after the Kyoto Protocol expired in 2012 (COM (2007) 2). In March 2007, the European Council offered its support for these new goals (7224/1/07; see also Bocquillon and Doebbels, 2014). Other new and potentially far-reaching programme-level policy objectives were adopted, including:

- *Renewable energy* – a target, binding at Member State level, that 20 per cent of total EU energy consumption should come from renewable sources by 2020, corresponding to about 34 per cent of electricity (COM (2006) 848);
- *Energy efficiency* – a non-binding commitment to reduce the EU's energy consumption by 20 per cent by 2020;
- *Biofuels* – a more binding target to ensure that biofuels accounted for 10 per cent of total transport fuel consumption in the EU by 2020, and move towards second-generation biofuels in the longer term (see Chapter 5);
- *Carbon capture and storage* – twelve large experimental installations to be in place by 2015 and all new coal plants to be carbon capture-ready by 2020 (COM (2006) 843).

In January 2008, the Commission launched an extensive package of proposals to achieve these goals. Entitled *20 20 by 2020: Europe's Climate Change Opportunity* (COM (2008) 30) it sought to explain the benefits of the EU's embryonic decarbonisation policy paradigm. It contained a number of inter-connected elements, including new amendments to the existing policy instruments addressing biofuels, CO_2 emissions from cars and emissions trading. Crucially (and for the very first time), it sought to address *all* emissions in one fell swoop (Oberthür and Pallemaerts, 2010: 47). The proposed EU-wide target would henceforth be translated into a 21 per cent reduction in sectors within the Emissions Trading System and a 10 per cent reduction in sectors outside it, both from 2005 levels (COM (2008) 30: 6–7). Recall that barely a decade earlier, EU-level policy instruments had only addressed a fraction of greenhouse gas emissions. And ten years before that, there were no policy instruments at all.

The Commission hoped to strike a rapid agreement on the entire package between the Council and the Parliament by the end of 2008 so that it could be adopted before the next COP meeting in Copenhagen in December 2009, at which it hoped to extend the EU's 'leadership by example' approach. Ever since the dawn of climate policy in the late 1970s, the EU had played a delicate, three-level game between international, EU and national policy and politics. But in 2008, the game became even more difficult to orchestrate as the world economy succumbed to a global financial crisis. Some of the newer Member States from Central and Eastern Europe viewed the EU's emerging decarbonisation policy paradigm as a direct threat to their economic prospects and ability to exploit domestic energy sources such as brown coal. Led by Poland, they fought to make the package less economically burdensome. For example, the revised Emissions Trading Directive (2009/29/EC) was amended to allow free allocation to Central and Eastern European electricity generators. In the new and much more stringent policy instrument governing car emissions, the compliance deadline was pushed back three years to 2015 (Regulation 443/2009). In the end, agreement on the whole package was only secured when the Parliament and the Council struck a broad package deal that traded concessions in one sub-area for more stringent targets in others (Skjærseth, 2015, 2016).

The Financial Crisis: A Period of Challenged International Leadership

The EU hoped that by offering a more stringent – but 'conditional' – greenhouse gas reduction target (30 per cent by 2020) ahead of the Copenhagen COP,[11] other major emitters could be lured into joining a political 'race to the top'. European Commission President Barroso's message to world leaders deliberately played on US President Obama's election slogan – 'Yes, you can. Yes, you can also do what we are doing' (Barroso, 2008). In October 2009, the European Council called upon other countries to embrace the EU's 2 °C objective. In turn, the EU pledged to adopt a new policy programme-level durability device: a goal of reducing emissions by at least 80–95 per cent by 2050. Reductions of this speed and magnitude effectively put deep and rapid decarbonisation on the EU's policy design agenda for the first time and marked a further evolution in the broader policy paradigm (from partial to deep and more rapid decarbonisation).

But other countries steadfastly refused to enter into a race to the top, rejecting a comprehensive treaty with binding targets and timetables and leaving the EU diplomatically isolated at Copenhagen. The result was a much looser agreement with voluntary pledges and reviews (Dimitrov, 2010). This outcome represented a significant defeat for the EU and forced it to come to terms with an even more discomforting reality: that other actors were not simply unwilling to follow but were willing to block its attempts to lead. For example, major airlines challenged the EU's plan to include the international aviation industry in the EU Emissions Trading System (see Chapter 4) and Canada reacted to new proposals governing the carbon content of fuels derived from tar sands. Moreover, the economic crisis in Europe, falling oil prices and the absence of a strong international treaty to replace Kyoto, made some EU Member States wary of adopting stronger internal policies and/or investing in unproven alternatives to fossil fuels. Despite the failure at Copenhagen, the Directorate-General for Climate Action (DG CLIMA) made another attempt to move the EU to the 30 per cent by 2020 target. However, it failed to secure sufficient internal support within the college of Commissioners and so, in May 2010, its proposal was not even formally published (ENDS Report, 2010; Skovgaard, 2013).

Nonetheless, in the run up to the 2011 COP in Durban, the EU managed to build new alliances with developing countries which enabled an agreement to 'develop a protocol, another legal instrument or an agreed outcome with legal force' by the end of 2015 (UNFCCC, 2012: 1). Against the odds, this amounted to another unexpected major diplomatic coup by the EU. In advance of that meeting, the Commission had published plans for a policy programme-level durability device (another 'road map') which sought to demonstrate that deep decarbonisation was both technologically and economically feasible to achieve by 2050 (COM (2011) 112; Delbeke and Vis, 2015: 22). As well as extend the time horizon out to 2050 (with intermediate milestones at 2030 and 2040), it also had the more immediate aim of extending the life of the Kyoto Protocol, which would otherwise have expired in 2012. After Copenhagen, these agreements suggested that the EU had reclaimed a degree of international leadership (Bäckstrand and Elgström, 2013). Furthermore, the deal struck at Durban helped the Commission to revive the internal debate within the EU over precisely what durability devices – chiefly policy programme-level targets – should be adopted in the period through to 2020 and on to 2030.

Preparing for the 2015 Paris Summit

In 2013, the European Council duly requested that the Commission re-examine the available design options. This time, many Member States forcefully demanded that the EU adopt a less prescriptive approach to deep decarbonisation. Circumstances were rather different than those that had prevailed in the brief period of intense policy innovation between 2007 and 2008 (Bürgin, 2015). Several Member States flatly opposed the introduction of new and binding renewable energy and efficiency goals (Flynn, 2013c). They were even joined by some parts of the Commission, including DG CLIMA (Fitch-Roy and Fairbrass, 2018: 66). These manoeuvrings had some influence on the Commission's proposals, which were hurriedly pushed through internal Commission consultations[12] and released on 22 January 2014 (COM (2014) 15).

After their publication, the conflicts did not take long to resurface. In broad terms, two coalitions had emerged in the Council. One coalition – known as the Green Growth Group of fourteen pro-climate Member States[13] – sought a more ambitious approach, although they differed on many specific policy design issues (Green Growth Group, 2014). Poland, on the other hand, emerged as a leader of a more fluid coalition of Central and Eastern European Member States, who were seeking to move ahead more slowly (Bocquillon and Maltby, 2017; Braun, 2019). The position adopted by these two coalitions varied across the different sub-areas in the package. For example, on greenhouse gas emissions, every Member State informed the Commission in 2013 that they preferred a common greenhouse gas reduction target for 2030, except one: Poland (European Commission, 2013: 2). On renewables, there was broader disagreement on the need for a new target and what form it should take. And on energy efficiency, Member States were divided on whether or not to adopt a new target (Skjærseth, 2015: 85). On specific policy instruments, even generally supportive Member States were willing to block agreement when it suited their national interests to do so (e.g. Germany in relation to cars, see Chapter 7). In many respects, the lack of agreement between Member States on internal and external policy matters harked back to the early days of climate policy, and suggested that the new, deeper decarbonisation policy paradigm was under political pressure.

In October 2014, the European Council finally secured internal agreement on the broad outlines of the 2030 Climate and Energy Framework. To have delayed any longer would have disrupted planning for the next COP scheduled for Paris in late 2015. The EU was anxious to strike a new globally binding deal at that meeting and for that to happen, new pledges needed to be tabled well in advance. With time running out (Keating, 2014e), the European Council managed to strike a deal on new policy programme-level targets for 2030: a new, binding 40 per cent reduction target for greenhouse gases, a 27 per cent renewable energy target (that was non-binding at national level) and an 'indicative' target of a 27 per cent increase in energy efficiency – all compared to 1990 levels. In stark contrast to what the EU had tabled prior to the Copenhagen COP,[14] these effectively amounted to two targets that were binding at EU level and one that was not.

According to Skjærseth (2015: 86), the EU's offer amounted to a complex, carefully negotiated package deal, hedged around with myriad compromises to bind everyone together. The Commission and the Member States that wanted a unilateral 40 per cent greenhouse gas reduction target in 2030 (including Denmark, the United Kingdom, Germany, Sweden, the Netherlands and France) were forced to compromise to secure the backing of Central and Eastern European Member States led by Poland, who were keen to assert their sovereign right to exploit their domestic reserves of coal and shale gas (Keating, 2014d). Poland in particular fought hard to delay agreement until after the Paris COP (Flynn, 2014). It also pushed for the insertion of a revert clause (a type of policy programme-level flexibility device, see Table 2.4) which would allow for a loosening of the target if a global treaty was not adopted in Paris. However, Herman van Rompuy, the then President of the European Council, claimed the opposite was in fact true, i.e. the revert clause would only activate if the Paris Agreement was more ambitious than the EU had expected (Keating, 2014f). Meanwhile, the United Kingdom failed in its attempt to include another flexibility device – a relational contract (see Chapter 2), i.e. an agreement to tighten the greenhouse gas reduction figure to

50 per cent by 2030 but only if a deal was struck at Paris (Marshall, 2014). But unlike under the Kyoto Protocol, the EU agreed that its pledge would be fulfilled by implementing emission reduction measures in Europe.[15] Van Rompuy pointedly described the whole deal as 'an ambitious yet cost-effective climate and energy path' (EUCO 230/14: 1). Examining the interweaving of various flexibility and durability devices at different policy levels allows us to understand better how the EU was able to strike such a deal, which involved securing agreement on the less contentious issues, but delaying agreement on the more contentious ones until after the COP.

Policy after Paris

In the run up to the Paris COP, the EU was able to reflect on some important achievements. It was still the most active global leader in international discussions and, as of 2018, was well on track to achieve its own 'by 2020' reduction targets.[16] At Paris, it managed to assemble a new 'High Ambition' international coalition, spanning richer and poorer countries; this was sufficiently strong to secure the agreement of virtually all UNFCCC parties on the world's first universally applicable agreement on climate change. This was undoubtedly another significant diplomatic achievement by the EU. The Paris Agreement sought to put the world on track to avoid dangerous climate change by committing *all* parties to keep long-term global warming 'to *well below* 2 °C above pre-industrial levels and *pursuing efforts* to limit the temperature increase to 1.5 °C' (UNFCCC, 2015: 2, emphasis added). It therefore reaffirmed the programme-level goal of 2 °C that the EU had originally (and unilaterally) committed to as long ago as 1996. Another new programme-level durability device – again, strongly advocated by the EU – committed all parties to a new goal of achieving net-zero greenhouse gas emissions by the second half of the century (i.e. balancing net global emissions with global carbon sinks). At first blush, it appeared as though the rest of the world had bought into the EU's deep decarbonisation policy paradigm.

However, the Paris deal hinges on the industrialised countries providing significant new financial and technological assistance to developing countries, a commitment which will be subject to delicate negotiation in the coming years. And the 187 pledges – or 'intended nationally determined contributions' – which were submitted ahead of the summit and together cover 95 per cent of global emissions – are not expected to keep warming below 3 degrees (UNEP, 2015), let alone 2 °C or even 1.5 °C of warming. A new set of international polity-based durability devices strongly advocated by the EU – the 'global stocktakes' – were adopted to assess the collective progress towards the new goals adopted in Paris. However, the first of these stocktakes will not take place until 2023. In the meantime, the developing countries will expect the industrialised countries to take early and purposeful steps to honour their pledges[17] on emissions and funding before 2025, when a new collective goal is expected to be adopted. In June 2017, Obama's successor, Donald Trump announced that the USA would withdraw from the agreement in 2020.

The Paris Agreement was widely interpreted as another diplomatic success for the EU. Chapters 4–7 will reveal that it also dovetailed with another round of internal policy review and reformulation activities in relation to emissions trading, biofuels and car emissions. The jury is still out on whether these policies and wider programmatic goals, politically challenging as they were to adopt, will be sufficient to allow the EU to decarbonise by 2050 (Oberthür and Dupont, 2015). In 2017, the European Environment Agency (EEA) (2017) concluded that the EU would need to significantly step up its efforts to achieve the interim cut of 40 per cent by 2030. In the spring of 2018, seven Member States – including France, Sweden and the Netherlands – called upon the EU to adopt more ambitious measures to achieve net-zero emissions by mid-century. In June 2018, Climate and Energy Commissioner Miguel Arias Cañete proposed raising the EU's national pledge from 40 per cent to 45 per cent by 2030 before the Katowice COP in 2018 and set out policy options to achieve zero emissions by 2050. However, at the beginning of 2019 there were few signs that Heads of State would agree to do so, with a number of Member States, including Poland and the Czech Republic, offering particularly stubborn resistance (Pickstone, 2019).

By contrast, post-Paris negotiations on the renewable energy and energy efficiency directives led to more stringent targets than were set out by the European Council in 2014. The recast Renewable Energy Directive increased the 2030 renewables target from the 27 per cent agreed in 2014 to 32 per cent (Directive 2018/2001).[18] The updated Energy Efficiency Directive similarly raised the headline reduction target from 27 per cent to 32.5 per cent. As noted above, neither of these new targets were made binding at national level.[19] In an attempt to improve long-term planning and coordination, a new Energy Union Governance Regulation (Regulation 2018/1999) established a new, collective road-mapping exercise. Crucially it obliges Member States to produce National Energy and Climate Plans covering the period 2021–2030, together with longer-term strategies to achieve net zero emissions 'as soon as possible'. These national roadmaps will be independently reviewed by the Commission, but if it finds them lacking, it only has the power to issue recommendations.

3.5 Conclusions

This chapter has described the complex and evolving policy design space in which the EU has formulated and adopted individual climate policy instruments. Today, climate change represents one of the most active areas of EU policy. But it had very modest and relatively recent beginnings – even referring to the various EU actions before c.2000 as 'a policy' probably imputes them with greater coherence and strategic direction than is warranted. With the exception of the Commission's monitoring function and its (relatively marginal) participation in international meetings, for the most part EU policy remained an empty shell – comprising some long-term programmatic targets and strategies, and an amalgam of national-level policies and instruments.

Given the EU's inner workings, it does seem remarkable that such a relatively complex and ambitious body of EU-wide policy even emerged. With hindsight it is possible to discern the influence of an ongoing 'game' (Putnam, 1988) of policy design that has simultaneously worked across and involved: (1) a wide variety of actors, including states, the EU institutions and non-state actors; (2) the use of flexibility and durability devices at all three levels of policy design (programmatic goals, instruments (including instrument goals) and instrument settings); and (3) the various levels of governance (i.e. international, EU and national). Starting with the first of these, policy designers have had to incorporate the preferences of many different actors, some of them veto players with the power to block legislation, within a hyperconsensual system of decision making. Several design strategies have been employed to engineer agreement (Eberlein and Radaelli, 2010). The first was to engage in policy packaging – linking policies in the legislative process (as happened in 2008 and 2014) to maximise the scope for striking deals that dissuaded veto players from exercising their vetoes. The other was to employ what Gibson and Goodin (1999: 363) have termed the veil of vagueness – that is, pushing for agreement on programme-wide durability and flexibility devices whilst using revert clauses and relational contracts to deliberately displace decisions on more contentious policy details into the future.

This takes us to the second aspect of the game: the various levels of governance over which policy designers operated. It is striking how developments in international and EU policy have not simply co-evolved, but have actively fed back on one another (Oberthür and Pallemaerts, 2010: 27). Until the early 2000s, the EU lagged behind UN policy, which the Commission used as a means to drive internal policy development forwards. DG Environment (and more recently its successor, DG CLIMA) was especially eager to lock the EU into the UNFCCC, hoping it would make policy at both levels more durable, whilst also generating a need for new supporting policies and measures (Pallemaerts and Williams, 2006: 43).

The third and final aspect of the game has related to the three main elements of policy design (Howlett, 2009b). In theory, policy designers can build durable interventions by starting at any level in Hall's (1993) scheme: policy goals, instruments or settings. Although incremental advances were made in relation to

Table 3.1 *EU climate policy: examples of policy durability and flexibility devices*

		Design aim	
	Means	Durability	Flexibility
Polity	*Organisational*	Progress reports by European Commission and the European Environment Agency	Progress reports by European Commission and the European Environment Agency
Policy	*Policy programmes*	Emission stabilisation by 2000 target (1990) Two degrees target (1996) 80–95% emission reduction target (2009) Roadmaps: the ECCP (I and II)	20-20-20 by 2020 climate and energy package (2007) 40-27-27 by 2030 package (2014) Revert clauses
	Policy instruments	Standards, targets and goals e.g. in: Biofuels Directive (2003) ETS Directive (2003) Voluntary Agreement on Car Emissions (1999) Cars Regulation (2009)	Review clauses, relational contracts and sunset clauses, e.g. in: Biofuels Directive (2003) ETS Directive (2003) Voluntary Agreement (1999) Cars Regulation (2009)
	Policy instrument settings	Stringency of the standard Monitoring provisions *Ex post* evaluation requirements	Deadline for the review *Ex post* evaluation requirements

Note: these can be designed to operate manually or automatically.
Source: own composition; see Chapters 4–7 for further detail.

monitoring and product standards, over time the EU has found that the most effective way to advance policy was to start at the level of broad, long-term goals and targets – with their associated programme-level durability (and flexibility) mechanisms – and then move down to the more detailed level of policy instruments and instrument settings (i.e. in effect moving down from the top to the bottom row of Table 2.4). Table 3.1 recasts Table 2.4 using examples drawn from this chapter. It suggests that the design space in which policy makers have worked to craft durability devices has not necessarily been equally open at all three levels. The constraints on the working space have been particularly noticeable when one moves down to the level of specific policy instruments. Table 3.2 summarises the main policy instruments found at EU level, grouped according to the main sub-types discussed in Chapter 2. In some cases, the EU has successfully 'imported' instruments first used outside Europe (emission trading for example) and built on pre-existing instrument choices at the Member State level (in the case of the voluntary agreement on car emissions as well as emissions trading). Nonetheless,

Table 3.2 *EU climate policy: selected major instruments, 1992–2019*[1]

Regulatory instruments	• 1992/2014 Monitoring CO_2 emissions
	• 2001 Electricity from renewable energy
	• 2003 Energy performance of buildings
	• ***2003/2009/2015/2018 Biofuels***
	• 2004 Promotion of combined heat and power
	• ***2009/2014/2019 CO_2 emissions from cars***
	• 2009/2018 Effort sharing of emission reductions
	• 2009/2018 Renewable energy promotion
	• 2012/2018 Energy efficiency
Market-based instruments	• 2004 Upper and lower limit for national fuel taxes
	• ***2003/2009/2015/2018 Emissions trading***
Voluntary instruments	• ***1999 CO_2 emissions from cars***

[1] The policy instruments covered in this book are shown in bold/italics.
Source: based on Jordan *et al.* (2012).

the most common instrument is still regulation (at least in terms of the number of measures adopted). Policy instrument innovation is only really discernible with respect to emissions trading and the voluntary agreement on CO_2 emissions from cars. The two tables also remind us that although the responsibility for determining the long-term aims and objectives of policy has steadily grown at EU level, shifts in the power to select and calibrate policy instruments has been rather more uneven.[20] Yet our analysis thus far also broadly confirms the veracity of a key point made in the existing literatures: that it is at the level of specific policy instruments that the political battles to generate positive policy feedback have been the fiercest of all. In view of this, the next chapter examines the instrument-level dynamics in more detail in the three policy sub-areas analysed in Part II of this book: biofuels (regulatory), car emissions (voluntary) and stationary emitters (market-based).

Endnotes

1. For a slightly different list of characteristics, see Rosenbloom *et al.* (2019: 169).
2. And arguably also climate change impacts in the absence of strong mitigation policies.
3. Policy designers can, however, manipulate climate policies to make benefits more concrete and push costs further into the future (e.g. Müller and Slominski, 2013; Wettestad and Jevnaker, 2019). See Chapters 5–7 for examples.
4. Possibly because technology is not normally such a critical factor in social and welfare state policy areas.
5. A regularly updated list of the main policy aims and objectives, and the policy proposals needed to address them.
6. Although in practice, the Council signed off on major agreements, and was engaged throughout the policy-making process that led to the voluntary agreement on cars studied in Chapters 4 and 7.
7. This section draws on Jordan *et al.* (2010), Chapter 3.

8. Sweden was the first European state to set a target in 1988, but it was not then a Member State of the EU.
9. Because the EU was by then the only consistent pace-setter in the world.
10. Economic restructuring in Eastern Germany, following the fall of the Berlin Wall, and fuel switching from coal to gas in the United Kingdom.
11. A type of revert clause.
12. In order, it was claimed, to secure Barosso's political legacy (Keating, 2014a). Russia's annexation of Crimea also reawakened fears of energy insecurity in Europe.
13. Belgium, Denmark, Estonia, Finland, France, Germany, Italy, the Netherlands, Portugal, Slovenia, Spain, Sweden and the United Kingdom.
14. Two binding pledges on emission reductions and renewable energy respectively, and an indicative pledge on energy efficiency.
15. Unlike the 2020 target, which could partially be attained by paying for 'flexibility' mitigation measures undertaken in developing countries.
16. In fact, the indications at the time were that it would collectively reduce its emissions by 20 per cent well before 2020 (Skjærseth, 2015: 87).
17. Including mobilising USD 100 billion per year to support climate actions in developing countries before 2025.
18. Chapter 5 discusses this important change in further detail.
19. Although the renewables target remained binding at EU level.
20. The power to set taxes, for example, still resides at the national level, while governance in other areas has shifted to EU level.

4

Climate Policy Designs

Contexts, Choices, Settings and Sequences

4.1 Introduction

Chapter 3 described the design space in which EU climate policies have emerged. It revealed an ongoing game of design that has simultaneously worked across and involved many different actors, governance levels and policy elements. One of the most significant policy design dynamics has been the one connecting programmatic goals and specific policy designs. In general, longer-term goals set at EU level to match international-level processes centred on the UNFCCC have been gradually back-filled with policy programmes and policy instruments.

This chapter examines the instrument-level dynamics and their initial feedback effects in more detail. Sections 4.2–4.4 provide more detail on the three policy areas that were originally introduced in Chapter 1. For each instrument, we briefly outline the relevant sector's emissions before the policy design process commenced, and introduce the main designers, target groups and interest groups. Then, the pre-existing policy design space is summarised and the most salient features of each instrument are described and an initial preview is given of the most significant post-adoption feedback effects. Over time, these effects have changed actor dynamics, leading to new policy changes and, eventually, long instrument sequences. These sequences, which are summarised in the concluding section, span many decades and will be discussed in much greater detail in subsequent chapters.

4.2 The Governance of Biofuels: An Extended Regulatory Sequence?

Emission Patterns

Biofuels are a type of bioenergy[1] resource that are derived from organic matter (International Energy Agency [IEA], 2011: 5; Bouthillier *et al.*, 2016). The 2003 Biofuels Directive – the EU's first main foray into biofuel-related policy design – defines them as 'liquid or gaseous fuel for transport produced from biomass' (OJ L123, 17.5.2003: 44). Unlike fossil fuels, biofuels are, at least in theory, a fully renewable resource because they derive from plant material (Environmental Audit Committee, 2008). They are also a central element of the EU's wider renewable energy ambitions. The economic potential of biofuels has been recognised for almost as long as cars have been produced: early versions of the diesel engine could run on a biofuel derived from peanuts (Knothe, 2001: 1104; International Energy Agency, 2011: 10). Since then, the economic fortunes of the industry have fluctuated, often in line with international energy prices. As an influential OECD review has noted, the high cost of biofuels relative to fossil fuels has repeatedly limited their uptake (Doornbosch and Steenblik, 2007: 11). Thus, biofuels were regarded as a technologically viable option until the 1940s, when falling oil prices rendered them uncompetitive (IEA, 2011: 10). They were actively re-promoted after the 1973 oil crisis when fossil fuel prices soared (COM (2001) 547: 5), and in the 2000s when they rose again.

However, in spite of these cycles, global biofuel production has nonetheless grown spectacularly by 525 per cent between 2000 and 2010, from 16 billion litres to 100 billion litres (IEA, 2011: 10). This growth was facilitated by a 'frenzy' of new policies, mostly adopted at a national level (Ackrill and Kay, 2014: 3). Nonetheless, the global uptake of biofuels slowed considerably after 2010 as fossil fuel prices dropped (IEA, 2019). In 2017 its share of the global transport fuel market still stood at only 4 per cent, up marginally from 3 per cent in 2010 (IEA, 2011: 1), leaving the biofuel industry as a relatively niche player in what is a huge, highly globalised market in transport and other fuels.

There are many different types of biofuel, but two in particular have repeatedly attracted the attention of policy designers: bioethanol and biodiesel, respectively accounting for 72 per cent and 27 per cent of global biofuel production in 2017 (IEA, 2019; see also Ackrill and Kay, 2014: 5). *Bioethanol* is a type of alcohol derived from corn, barley, wheat and sugarcane – i.e. food and fodder crops. It can be blended to produce a drop-in alternative to conventional petrol (Ackrill and Kay, 2014: 5). By contrast, *biodiesel* is an oil-based fuel derived from the fats and oils in rapeseed, palms, soya and even animal meat. It can be blended to provide a drop-in alternative to diesel fuel.

Over time, different generations of biofuel have been developed (IEA, 2011: 8). *First-generation biofuels* are produced using food crops. When combusted, they produce fewer pollutants than fossil fuels, but they also suffer from a number of well-known drawbacks. Production processes are relatively inefficient, typically requiring significant inputs of energy that is often, paradoxically, derived from fossil fuel (Charles *et al.*, 2007: 5738). In addition, first-generation biofuels are typically derived from feed stocks that require high-quality land for cultivation. As a result, there have been repeated claims that they undermine food security and encourage land-use intensification (through requiring chemical fertilisers and pest controls). *Second-generation biofuels* are derived from specially grown crops such as switch grass, the non-edible parts of food crops (husks, shells and cobs) and waste materials such as straw and cooking oil. Second-generation production processes tend to generate fewer greenhouse gases than those for first-generation biofuels (Charles *et al.*, 2007: 5738). However, they still require significant quantities of land for cultivation. Finally, *third-generation biofuels* are derived from algae (Ackrill and Kay, 2014: 9), do not compete with other potential land uses and have a lower greenhouse gas footprint, although they do require inputs (typically, sunlight, water and nutrients) that may not be available in all locations (IEA, 2011: 14).[2]

First-generation biofuels still account for the majority of current global production and consumption. By contrast, many second-generation and third-generation biofuels are still in the research and development stages. However, their market share has been growing significantly. In 2018, second-generation biofuels (both bioethanols and biodiesels) together accounted for 23 per cent of total biofuel usage in the EU (United States Department of Agriculture, 2018: 3–4). However, in order to fully appreciate the multifaceted challenge of developing durable policy designs, one needs to understand the distinction between different generations of the two main types of biofuel: bioethanol and biodiesel. Thus the most common first-generation *bioethanols* are derived from sugar and starch-based crops grown on high-quality agricultural land (Demirbas, 2009: s108; IEA, 2011: 8). The most common second-generation types derive from non-food crops such as perennial grasses (Sharman and Holmes, 2010: 310). However, only recently have these been produced at a sufficiently large scale to make them economically viable (IEA, 2011: 13). The most common first-generation *biodiesel* supplies derive from a variety of feedstocks including rapeseed in the EU and palm oil in tropical countries (Ackrill and Kay, 2014: 6). Second-generation biodiesels mostly derive from vegetable oils (Di Lucia and Nilsson, 2007: 534) including recycled cooking fats and oils (Ackrill and Kay, 2014: 8).

The main challenge facing policy designers is how best to incentivise the right type of biofuel use, which in practice entails matching production capacities with current and future levels of consumer demand. One influential OECD review identified a 'huge array' of policy design options for achieving these goals (Doornbosch and Steenblik, 2007: 24). However, according to the UN-affiliated High Level Panel of Experts on Food Security and Nutrition (HLPE), existing national-level interventions have tended to fall into two main categories: *demand-focused* and *production-focused* (HLPE, 2013: 11). Demand-focused policies have sought to create new markets for biofuels. They include tax exemptions for producers, so-called blending mandates that stipulate what percentage of fuel in a particular sector should be sourced from biofuel, and subsidies to nurture demand (e.g. encouraging private owners and fleet operators to convert to biofuels). By contrast, production-focused policies have targeted fuel producers and dealers by offering subsidies to compensate for the additional cost of producing biofuels (and especially the more advanced types) as compared to petroleum fuels, or alternatively establishing border taxes to give domestic producers a competitive advantage.

Why have so many policy designers sought to manipulate the demand for and supply of biofuel? The answer to this question is not straightforward – in fact, the perceived benefits of switching have changed quite significantly over time and within particular parts of the world (Demirbas, 2009: s109; Ackrill and Kay, 2014: 216). Three benefits in particular have been regularly cited by advocates: superior environmental performance (including lower greenhouse gas emissions); greater energy security through reduced reliance on imported fossil fuels; and economic benefits, particularly in rural areas that are reliant on agriculture (IEA, 2011: 7; Ackrill and Kay, 2014: 11). It is worth remembering that biofuel production first took off in Brazil and the USA in the 1970s, primarily to address energy security. In Europe, governments were much slower to promote production and use; when they did, decarbonisation, energy security and rural employment were the most regularly cited rationales (Palmer, 2014: 337–338), particularly after the early 2000s (Ackrill and Kay, 2014: 70).

The emergence of the Biofuels Directive in 2003 should be seen in the context of these broader technological, policy and scientific developments. In fact, many of them are explicitly cited in its opening recitals. The full story of the Directive's design is recounted in Chapter 5. It reveals that decarbonisation was one of the main rationales cited by advocates. As Palmer (2014: 337) explains, biofuels are, at least in theory, carbon-neutral: on combustion they release into the atmosphere the carbon which was originally sequestered during their growth. In a Communication published alongside the formal proposal for the Directive in 2001, the Commission boldly asserted that they 'offer an *ideal alternative* since, when based on EU grown crops, they are practically 100% indigenous and CO_2 neutral' (COM (2001) 547: 5, emphasis added). To be fair, it did qualify this headline statement with a discussion of the high cost of some production techniques. It also noted that 'up to half, or more than half, of the CO_2 benefit is offset in the production process for biodiesel and bio-ethanol respectively' (COM (2001) 547: 5). But it remains the case that, around this time, hopes in some parts of the Commission were high that biofuels would simultaneously solve many long-standing policy problems in the EU.

In practice, the emissions saved by switching to biofuels vary significantly (Ackrill and Kay, 2014: 24), depending on the precise type and generation of the biofuel used, and how it is produced, including how the land in which the feedstock was cultivated was previously used (Howes, 2010: 140). Biofuel production can lead to increased emissions from direct land use change, when the feedstocks displace food crops (Royal Academy of Engineering, 2017: 8; COM (2010) 811: 3). If, on the other hand, the feedstocks are grown on carbon-rich land which had not previously been farmed, such as forests, the resulting effects are categorised as indirect – hence the term 'indirect land use change' (ILUC) emissions. It has proven very challenging to quantify the scale of ILUC emissions from biofuel (Giljam, 2016: 102). As long ago as the late 2000s, scientists began to suggest that when the direct and indirect effects are fully accounted for, the total emissions arising from production may even exceed those associated with some fossil fuels (Environmental Audit Committee, 2008: 6; Ackrill and Kay, 2014: 24), although again the exact amount varies from one fuel type to another. Indeed, far from becoming more widely accepted as production has grown, the case for converting to biofuels to decarbonise society has become more contested as new information has emerged and circulated amongst actors.

As the biofuel industry has expanded in Europe, an increasingly complex set of feedstocks has been used, many imported from outside the EU. In 2015, the European Environment Agency (EEA) concluded that when the direct and the indirect effects arising from these extended supply chains are taken into account, the net environmental benefits of biofuels are subject to 'considerable uncertainty' (EEA, 2015a: 58). These uncertainties have stimulated – and in turn been greatly compounded by – a succession of political conflicts between actors promoting or opposing the use of different types (and indeed particular generations) of biofuel, many employing scientific information in a 'partial and tendentious fashion' (Ackrill and Kay, 2014: 217).

Target Groups and Other Interest Groups

The key policy actors related to EU biofuels policy have included the fuel producers, the vehicle producers, environmental groups, some (but not all) Member States and the EU institutions. Between 2000 and 2010, global biofuel production expanded massively from 16 billion litres per year to over 100 billion per year (IEA, 2011: 11). Growth then slowed, but by 2017 production had nevertheless increased to 143 billion litres annually (IEA, 2019). As noted above, production initially centred on the USA and Brazil; by 2016, these two countries still hosted 70 per cent of global production (IEA, 2017: 103). But gradually production has also taken off in some – but not all – Member States (Ackrill and Kay, 2014: 4). Our main point, however, is that production and consumption have rarely been uniformly distributed across time and space: certain countries and regions have actively promoted certain biofuel types for distinct reasons and using different mixes of policy instruments. These differences have led to countries trading in both fuels and feedstocks.

Globally, bioethanol is still produced at much higher volumes than biodiesel (IEA, 2017: 53). Global production grew much quicker between 1980 and 2007 – again, principally in the USA and Brazil. These two countries were anxious to secure new uses for existing agricultural production after the 1973 oil crisis (HLPE, 2013). By contrast, biodiesel production has grown more slowly, but has traditionally been the dominant biofuel in Europe (Demirbas, 2009: s110), strongly supported by biofuel producers associated with the agricultural sector, including farmers (Skogstad, 2017: 30, 34–35). The European car producers have generally been supportive of biofuels (see below), having staked their future profitability on 'dieselising' their car fleets to stay ahead of stricter greenhouse gas emission targets (HLPE, 2013: 12).

In the early 2000s, when the Biofuels Directive was being formulated within the Commission, biodiesel production in the EU stood at around 2.3 billion litres – i.e. around four times the total production of bioethanol (Demirbas, 2009: s109). However, only six Member States produced significant quantities (COM (2001) 547: 19), amongst which three were dominant (France, Italy and Germany), although there were also significant production facilities in Sweden, Spain and Austria. The remaining Member States produced very little or even no biofuel (COM (2001) 547, 19). In 2001, net consumption accounted for less than 0.5 per cent of overall fossil fuel consumption in the EU (COM (2001) 547: 6). In effect, policy designers were starting from a very low base.

When the European Commission began to seriously engage in policy design in the late 1990s, the biodiesel producers were better organised than the bioethanol producers. The key industry associations dated back to the late 1990s and included the European Biodiesel Board (EBB) (1997) and European Vegetable Oil and Proteinmeal Industry (FEDIOL) (1957). Bioethanol producers were initially represented by the European Union of Alcohol Producers. Formed in 1993 to represent producers of industrial alcohol as well as biofuels, it was renamed the European Union of Ethanol Producers in 2004. In 2005, the European Bioethanol Fuel Association (eBIO) was formed to specifically represent bioethanol producers. In 2010, the European Union of Alcohol Producers and eBIO merged to form the European Renewable Ethanol Association (ePure). As biofuel production expanded, other industry groups emerged claiming either to represent the interests of the whole industry (e.g. the European Biofuels Technology Platform (EBTP), established in 2006) or particular users and producers (e.g. the Leaders of Sustainable Biofuels, established in 2010 to promote the use of advanced biofuels in the aviation sector). Associations representing feedstock industries (e.g. COPA/COGECA – a very powerful interest group representing European farmers) and competing fuel types (e.g. EUROPIA for the oil and gas industries) also became more involved.

The involvement of environmental NGOs expanded from a small number (the European Environment Bureau [EEB], Transport and Environment [T&E] and the World Wildlife Federation [WWF]) to include most environmental NGOs campaigning on climate change-related themes (Skogstad, 2017: 30). As public awareness of the associated environmental and social impacts of driving up biofuel use grew, big international development charities such as Oxfam and Action Aid began to take a more active interest (Skogstad, 2017: 35).

The Design Space

The first policies to promote biofuels were adopted in Brazil and the USA and generally took the form of subsidies. By 2011, over 50 countries had become involved, adopting a much wider array of policy instruments, each having a distinctive national twist (HLPE, 2013: 11–12). Prior to the EU becoming more involved, those Member States that had biofuel-focused policies incorporated a mixture of production-focused and demand-focused instruments. Production subsidies (both direct and indirect, part or wholly paid through the EU's Common Agricultural Policy) were an important part of pre-existing national policy mixes. By 2006, the International Institute for Sustainable Development (2008) estimated that the EU and individual Member States were subsidising biofuels to the tune of around €3.7 billion per year[3] (see also COM (2001) 547: 17). But according to the Commission, these policy approaches were nonetheless still too weak and too diffuse to facilitate deep decarbonisation in the EU transport sector. Therefore, it began to explore ways to institute stronger and more harmonised policy support at EU level.

In theory, there were many ways in which policy designers at EU level could have approached the design challenge. Given the design space in which the Commission was working (see above and Chapter 3), it was entirely understandable that the Commission opted to employ regulation to set a blending mandate to drive new sources of production, although it also sought to shape demand. The objective of the 2003 Biofuels Directive was thus to promote the 'use of biofuels or other renewable fuels for transport' in each Member State 'with a view to contributing to objectives such as meeting climate change commitments, environmentally friendly security of supply and promoting renewable energy sources' (OJ L123, 17.5.2003: 44). Article 3 mentioned several renewable fuels, but the only ones then in existence were biofuels. Article 2 thus defined a number of different types of biofuel including bioethanol and biodiesel.

The Initial Policy Design

The Biofuels Directive was a form of command-and-control regulation. Thus Article 3 formally required Member States to ensure that a minimum proportion of biofuels were placed onto their national markets and 'to that effect ... set *national indicative* targets' (OJ L123, 17.5.2003: 44, emphasis added). But while the setting of these targets – which were essentially a type of blending mandate – was mandatory, their implementation was non-mandatory and they were established at national level by the Member States (i.e. the EU was simply facilitating national policy coordination). The targets were to be expressed in the form of two reference values, which were also non-mandatory: a reference value of 2 per cent (by energy content) to be achieved by the end of 2005; and a reference value of 5.75 per cent to be achieved by 31 December 2010. The policy instrument-level *durability devices* were therefore relatively weak. The Commission also proposed another, more novel *durability device*: an annual increase in blending levels by 0.75 per cent starting in 2005, to automatically raise the overall total from 2 per cent in 2003 to 5 per cent in 2009 (COM (2001) 547: 18). But this was quickly whittled away in the policy formulation process and did not appear in the final text of the Directive.

The Directive also did not say much about the precise actions that Member States should take to achieve their national biofuel targets, other than that governments should establish indicative targets to guide them (Haigh, 2009: 14–11) and regularly submit progress reports to the Commission. Significantly, the choice and calibration of specific, national-level policy instruments was left entirely to Member States (Di Lucia and Nilsson, 2007: 533). The only other *durability devices* included in the Directive related to monitoring and reporting. Thus under Article 4, Member States were required to submit annual reports to the Commission (a policy instrument-level *durability device*), in which they were supposed to explain their national indicative targets, set out the measures they had adopted to promote biofuels, and describe their impact in terms of national market shares. Each year, Member States were also required to explain and justify any difference between their national indicative target and the overall 'reference value' set at EU level. These reporting requirements were substantially stronger than those outlined in the Commission's original proposal and were the outcome of a complex trade-off between the European Parliament and the Council, in which the former insisted on stronger reporting in exchange for non-binding targets (see Chapter 5).

Crucially, Article 4 also included a flexibility clause, i.e. a policy instrument-level *flexibility device*. This obligated the Commission to publish, by 31 December 2006 'and every two years thereafter', an *ex post* evaluation report on the progress made by Member States (OJ L123, 17.5.2003: 45). Policy designers had evidently given some thought to this matter, because the text of the Directive included a detailed list of what the Commission should evaluate including *inter alia* the cost effectiveness of national policies, the economic and environmental costs of production, lifecycle analyses of particular biofuels, and the greenhouse gas emissions arising from each type. In hindsight, it is striking how many of these issues featured in the political controversies that gradually engulfed the sector. Finally, Article 4 concluded that 'if this report concludes that indicative targets are not likely to be achieved' the Commission should submit new proposals that 'address national targets, *including possible mandatory targets*' (Article 4 (2), OJ L123/, 17.5.2003: 46, emphasis added). In the terminology outlined in Chapter 2, this particular *flexibility clause* was a relational contract, not only designed to trigger at a precise point in time, but to be heavily biased in favour of more coercive controls at EU level.

Policy Implementation and Reform

The Commission eventually published its evaluation report in January 2007 (COM (2006) 845; see also Haigh, 2009: 14.11-11), by which point a wide variety of implementation problems had manifested themselves. In that report, the Commission confirmed what many policy designers had long suspected – the interim 2005 target had been missed and the other was 'not likely to be achieved' by 2010 (COM (2006) 845: 6). Consequently, the Commission duly recommended a new, mandatory 10 per cent biofuels target to be achieved by 2020 (COM (2006) 845: 8; see also COM (2006) 848). Moreover, it also sought to remedy a number of specific concerns that had emerged since the original Directive had entered into force. These included the direct and indirect impacts of growing crops for biofuels (e.g. the use of pesticides and fertilisers that could pollute local watercourses) as well as the mitigation potential of particular sub-types of biofuel. It claimed, however, that substituting up to 14 per cent of road fuels with biofuel would have a 'manageable' impact on agriculture (COM (2006) 845: 11; Haigh, 2009: 14.11-1), provided adequate policies were in place to encourage 'good' biofuels and discourage 'bad' ones (Haigh, 2009: 14.11-3). It did not specify what was meant by 'good' and 'bad', or how policy designs would produce them.

Far from resolving these ambiguities, what the Commission did next simply compounded them. Alongside the Biofuels Progress Report, it published a Renewable Energy Road Map (COM (2006) 848). Recall that the mid-2000s were a period in which the EU was setting increasingly ambitious policy programme-level targets (for details, see Chapter 3). The Road Map duly proposed a 20 per cent target for renewables by 2020 and, crucially, confirmed the need for a legally binding 10 per cent biofuels target, citing its own ex post-evaluation of the 2003

Directive. The new target proposed by the Commission was an explicit recognition that the national indicative targets mandated in the 2003 Directive had not provided a sufficient stimulus to biofuel production (particularly within the EU) and consumption to fulfil EU-wide goals (Johnson, 2011: 99). More detailed proposals to achieve the 10 per cent target, but for renewable fuels, were subsequently published by the Commission in January 2008 as part of a larger proposal for a Renewable Energy Directive (COM (2008) 19). These were adopted as part of the final new Directive (2009/28/EC) which promoted the use of energy from all renewable sources. Amongst other things, the 2009 Renewable Energy Directive repealed the Biofuels Directive as of the end of 2011, which by that point had only been on the statute book for around six years.

As well as introducing more stringent and binding EU-wide targets, the 2009 Directive included an obligatory template to improve the quality and timeliness of Member State reporting (Howes, 2010: 142). However, the cycle of policy change did not end there – a little over six years later (i.e. in 2015), the ILUC Directive (2015/1513/EU) was adopted which amended the biofuel provisions of the 2009 Directive to address the indirect land use change effects triggered by the 2003 and 2009 Directives. Finally, in 2016, the Commission issued a proposal for a recast Renewable Energy Directive (RED II), which brought biofuel policy into line with the EU's post-2020 targets (COM (2016) 767). When adopted, Directive 2018/2001 set a mandatory 14 per cent target for renewable sources in transport for each Member State. Unlike its predecessor, the recast Directive also capped the use of first-generation biofuels to meet this target at one percentage point above the share of those fuels in 2020. It also set a mandatory target for second- and third-generation biofuels of 3.5 per cent in 2030. The cycles of positive and negative policy feedback that facilitated this long instrument sequence are discussed in much greater detail in Chapter 5.

4.3 The Governance of Large Stationary Emitters: Locking In Emissions Trading?

Emission Patterns

Defining the scope of an emission trading system is not a given: it is a key policy design decision that can have important implications for the policy's effectiveness and durability. At a broad level, an emissions trading system can be designed to be either an *upstream* or a *downstream* policy. In an upstream system, fuel producers and importers of (for example) coal and oil must surrender allowances to cover the emissions embedded in the products they sell. In a downstream system, allowances must be surrendered for greenhouse gas emissions at source by (for example) the electricity generation industry (Foundation for International Environmental Law and Development, 2000: 23–26). In the case of the EU (and as explained more fully below), a decision was made relatively early on in the design process to create a downstream system due to fears that an upstream system would directly impact Member State energy systems and so require unanimity voting in the Council of Ministers (Foundation for International Environmental Law and Development, 2000: 23, fn. 21).

In a downstream system, design decisions about policy scope centre on both the types of greenhouse gases and the specific activities that will be covered (hence in the EU, stationary point-source installations such as power stations and/or diffuse sources such as transport). Emissions trading systems around the world have widely varying sectoral coverage, some relatively narrow (emissions from electricity generation and industry) others much broader (including road transport, waste and forestry, etc.; see International Carbon Action Partnership, 2019: 21).

The EU ETS covers emissions from electricity generation, energy-intensive industries such as steel production, and aviation. In 2018, ETS emissions (excluding aviation, which is not included in our study,[4] see Chapter 6) were estimated to be 27 per cent lower than in 2005, taking into account changes in the system's scope (EEA, 2018a, 2019). However, this overall pattern masked significant differences between the various sectors. Fuel combustion, largely for electricity generation, accounted for 63 per cent of emissions in 2018 and had witnessed a 25 per cent reduction since 2005. According to the EEA (2018a: 21), these reductions were the 'the main driver of the decline in emissions' across the entire system after 2013. Emissions from the energy-intensive industrial installations (e.g. steel and cement production) accounted for 33 per cent of emissions in 2018. In large part due to the 2008 financial crisis, industrial emissions fell by 12 per cent between 2005 and 2012, but by 2018 they were actually 4 per cent *higher* than when the system started. Similarly, aviation – while accounting for only 4 per cent of 2018 emissions – saw a 25 per cent increase in emissions between 2013 and 2018.

Target Groups and Other Interest Groups

The main industrial target groups can be placed in three broad categories: the electricity generation industry; the energy-intensive industries; and the aviation industry. The electricity generation industry was an obvious actor for the Commission to target, being a significant point-source emitter of CO_2. Around 40 per cent of total EU generation capacity was owned by seven companies in 2013, down from around 60 per cent in 1990 (Dahlmann *et al.*, 2017: 394). Between 2005 and 2012, seventeen of the twenty highest emitters in the Emissions Trading

System (ETS) were electricity companies, which were collectively responsible for nearly 40 per cent of emissions during that time (Bryant, 2016: 311). At EU level, electricity generators were represented by the Union of the Electricity Industry (Eurelectric), a well-resourced and well-staffed business association. The industry had been targeted by EU air quality policy for years, chiefly because of its contribution to acid rain. As a result, when emissions trading was proposed the industry was highly engaged from the outset, coordinating modelling exercises and working closely with the Commission (Braun, 2009: 481).

Companies in the electricity industry found that they shared a number of concerns when emissions trading was placed on the EU policy agenda. First of all, they generally did not sell electricity outside of the EU and hence had low vulnerability to global competition. They also calculated that they could 'work within' any EU-wide system; a significant percentage of any additional cost of purchasing emission allowances could be passed on to their customers (see Sijm *et al.*, 2006). Despite some shared interests, high industry concentration and unified EU-level representation by Eurelectric, emissions trading was still expected to generate different effects across the industry, largely depending on how carbon-intensive their operations were. High-carbon electricity companies such as Germany's RWE or Poland's Tauron Polska Energia – which relied on coal and had a relatively high CO_2 intensity of electricity production – preferred less-coercive policy instruments such as voluntary agreements. They were more reliant on allowances being allocated for free instead of being sold (see below) and would be disadvantaged by a high carbon price (Chen *et al.*, 2008). In contrast, low-carbon electricity companies such as France's EDF – which generated electricity from nuclear or renewables and therefore had a low CO_2 intensity of electricity production – perceived that they would be less vulnerable to auctioning and could actually benefit from high carbon prices by raising their electricity prices without significantly increasing their costs (Keppler and Crucini, 2010).

The second major target group was the energy-intensive industries, which included the steel, cement, refining, glass and paper manufacturers. Unlike the electricity industry, this was a much more disparate group of actors operating in many different markets that were relatively exposed to international competition. In some cases, they actively competed with one another: e.g. the steel and aluminium industries fought to supply car producers (Roth *et al.*, 2001). This fragmentation was reflected in the manner in which they were represented in Brussels. For example, a total of twelve EU-level associations representing energy-intensive industries responded to the European Commission's first consultation on emissions trading (see European Commission, 2001c). Initially, they did not place a high priority on participating in policy formulation activities and hence did not produce or actively communicate common policy positions (Wettestad, 2009b;

Skodvin *et al.*, 2010; Meckling, 2011: 38). However, in contrast to its effects on the electricity industry, the EU ETS created shared policy concerns for the energy-intensive industries (Wettestad, 2009b). A large number were intensive users of electricity, traded their products in global markets, benefited from freely allocated allowances and were disadvantaged when carbon prices rose. In Chapter 6 we shall show how the ETS forced them to coordinate more effectively (a policy feedback effect), eventually forming a new coalition in 2005 – the Alliance of Energy Intensive Industries (AEII). The initial preferences of the main EU institutions and NGOs are covered in more detail in Chapter 6.

The Design Space

The theoretical potential of emissions trading has been extensively debated by economists, but in the 1990s it remained a rather unappealing and 'peripheral' policy concept in the EU (Boasson and Wettestad, 2013: 56). It was, after all, a relatively novel instrument globally and ran counter to the EU's policy instrument preference for regulatory instruments.[5] However, these prior regulatory interventions furnished a good deal of usable knowledge about emissions from the sector (note the operation of an interpretive policy feedback mechanism) – detailed knowledge that proved to be directly salient to the Commission's emerging plans for emissions trading (Wettestad, 2005: 4).

Emissions trading had first been employed by US authorities in the 1980s (Voss, 2007; Hansjürgens, 2011: 639), and subsequently diffused to some EU Member States – principally Denmark (from 1999) and the United Kingdom (from 2002). Somewhat ironically, around fifteen years after it began operation, the EU ETS is still the world's only supranational emissions trading system. This is one of the main reasons why it has been described as a 'bold public policy experiment' (Ellerman *et al.*, 2010: 288) and 'a major feat of policy innovation' (Bailey, 2010: 145). According to one systematic analysis of the ETS's first trading period, it 'lifted the environment from the boiler room to the boardroom, from ministries of environment to ministries of finance, and from councils to Cabinet tables' (Ellerman *et al.*, 2010: 1; see also Ellerman *et al.*, 2016 and Wettestad, 2005: 19).

The Initial Policy Design

The ETS was adopted via a 2003 Directive (2003/87/EC) 'establishing a scheme for greenhouse gas emission allowance trading within the Community and amending Council Directive 96/61/EC'. The 2003 Directive laid the ground rules of the system and allocated governance tasks to the various participants. It established the ETS as a *cap-and-trade* system, capping the emissions from stationary emitters by allocating emission allowances, and then making trading of these allowances possible in order to achieve emission reductions at lower cost (Woerdman *et al.*, 2015: 43). Unlike the UK ETS (but like the Danish ETS), it was designed to be a *mandatory* scheme. Thus, installations covered by the system were required to hold a legal permit to emit greenhouse gases and to surrender allowances equal to their annual emissions. If they emitted more than that they would be fined. Article 10 of the Directive stipulated that at least 95 per cent of the emissions allowances would be allocated for free directly to target industries in Phase I (2005–2007), and at least 90 per cent in Phase II (2008–2012; see Woerdman *et al.* 2015: 56). Auctioning allowances to the highest bidder is the preferred allocation method advocated by many economists (Hepburn *et al.* 2006), but in the EU's scheme, free allocation was, as we shall explain in Chapter 6, eventually selected as 'the political price for ensuring' sufficient Member State support (Ellerman *et al.*, 2016: 4). In its first two trading phases, the EU's system was designed to be decentralised – many of the most significant decisions about the total quantity and allocation of the emission allowances were placed in the hands of Member States (Skjærseth and Wettestad, 2010b: 66). Crucially, no formal distinction was made between different types of emitters, e.g. the electricity generators versus the energy-intensive industries, although Member States de facto arrived at such a distinction when they began to allocate allowances (Wettestad, 2009a: 312).

The ETS mainly addresses CO_2 emissions from stationery sources, namely 11,000 power stations and industrial plants listed in Annex 1 (Delbeke and Vis, 2015: 41; DG CLIMA, 2016 : 4). It encompasses activities in 31 European countries – the 28 Member States of the EU plus 3 non-Member States (DG CLIMA, 2016: 96). The aims of the Directive were laid out in Article 1: 'to promote reductions of greenhouse gas emissions in a cost effective and economically efficient manner'. Other than one small reference to encouraging energy-efficient technologies (in the opening recitals of the Directive – number 20), no reference was made to other policy aims which emissions trading is often associated with, such as the nurturing of green technologies (Woerdman *et al.*, 2015: 61).

The system has been organised around a series of 'trading periods' (DG CLIMA, 2016). Thus, the main institutional structures of the policy were established before the initial period of trading in Phase I (2005–2007), later described as a pilot phase (Ellerman and Buchner, 2007; Ellerman *et al.*, 2010). During Phase I, the overall cap was set using emission estimates derived prior to the pilot phase (DG CLIMA, 2016: 4). Phase II ran from 2008 to 2012 and coincided with the first global trading period under the Kyoto Protocol. Phase III extended the lifetime of the system from 2013 to 2020, while Phase IV will cover the time period from 2021 to 2030.

The 2003 Directive allocated a number of important responsibilities amongst the various actors involved. As the system was – at least initially – decentralised, many of these responsibilities went to the Member States. Thus, Article 27 required them to bring into force all relevant legal and administrative provisions by 31 December 2003, draw up a publicly accessible registry of allowances and submit regular monitoring reports to the Commission (Haigh, 2009: 14.13-2). Importantly, Member States were empowered to decide how to allocate the allowances within their respective territories, through the drawing up of National Allocation Plans (NAPs) informed by 11 criteria listed in Annex 3 of the Directive. The EU cap comprised the sum total of the allowances allocated through the NAPs; other than the fines, the cap was in effect the main policy instrument-level *durability device*. In practice, we shall see that the vast majority of Member States opted to allocate their allowances to emitters based on their historical emissions (and indeed were constrained by the Directive from auctioning no more than a small percentage). Member States were also required to decide the fate of the relatively small percentage of allowances that could in theory be auctioned.

The act of continually trading in allowances is meant to guarantee that all trading systems achieve a basic level of dynamic flexibility. However, in the EU ETS two other obligations were placed on the Commission to introduce even more. First of all, the 2003 Directive required it to produce an *ex post* evaluation report on the application of the Directive by 30 June 2006. This report would consider no less than eleven specific issues which were outlined in Article 30 and, if relevant, make recommendations for a new Directive (hence it was a policy instrument-level *flexibility device*). The Commission eventually commenced its review in 2005 (Skjærseth and Wettestad, 2010: 70). Article 30 also gave the Commission the option to propose an amendment to Annex 1 by 31 December 2004 to extend the scope of the emissions trading system to other sectors, providing there was sufficient monitoring information on greenhouse gases – i.e. another policy instrument-level *flexibility clause*. During the policy formulation process, the chemicals, aluminium and transport sectors had been mentioned as possible candidates for later inclusion (Skjærseth and Wettestad, 2010b: 69). Second, Article 14 obliged the Commission to draw up more detailed monitoring and reporting guidelines (Haigh, 2009: 14.13-2), which were eventually formulated through the comitology process, and enacted via technical Regulation 2216/2004 (Haigh, 2009, 14.13-5). These could be thought of as another policy instrument-level *durability device*.

Over time, the 2003 Directive was gradually supplemented with more detailed policy guidance on a range of technical matters such as allowance allocation, monitoring and reporting. In general, these were formulated by the Commission via the comitology process, the aim being to speed up decision making to facilitate faster adjustments. However, in the formulation process, the Member States insisted that more far-reaching changes to the scope and functioning of the system[6] had to be adopted through primary legislation – i.e. via new directives – which of course brought in the other EU institutions. Eventually the 2003 Directive was amended, most conspicuously in 2009 and then again in 2018. With hindsight, the decision to distinguish between these two different routes to making subsequent adjustments was a fateful one, and led to a good deal of acrimony and, paradoxically for something that had sought to facilitate flexibility, significant delay.

The 2009 Directive, the design of which was informed by the 2005–2006 review mentioned above (Skjærseth and Wettestad, 2010a, was eventually adopted in just 457 days – an even more 'speedy' birth than the original 2003 Directive (Skjærseth and Wettestad, 2010b: 66). During Phase III, the overall cap was set centrally to reflect longer-term EU-wide emission reductions targets, 57 per cent of allowances were auctioned and there were more provisions addressing the concerns of the energy-intensive industries such as carbon leakage (Skodvin *et al.*, 2010). A fourth phase is scheduled to start after 2020. At the time of this writing, the system as a whole does not have an end date (DG CLIMA, 2016: 7), although this does not imply that its existence is fully accepted by all concerned.

Policy Implementation and Reform

The process of transposing the 2003 Directive into national law was supposed to have been completed by the end of December 2003, but only the United Kingdom complied on time and the Commission had to resort to extensive enforcement action against many Member States (Wettestad, 2005: 19). Then, the production of the National Allocation Plans (NAPs) proved to be a considerably more complex and time-consuming process than had been originally foreseen (Ellerman et al., 2015: 4), which triggered disagreements and delays; once again, the Commission resorted to legal enforcement measures (Haigh, 2009, 14.13-6). At first, allowance prices in the new system climbed steadily (Skjærseth and Wettestad, 2010b: 69), but then dramatically collapsed in mid-2006 when it became obvious that Member States had over-allocated allowances to the point-source emitters in their jurisdictions. When electricity generators in some countries passed on a substantial proportion of the higher market price of the allowances to their customers, they were accused of generating 'windfall' profits (Energy Intensive Industries, 2004; Woerdman *et al.*, 2015: 66).

The Commission began to tackle some of the fundamental causes of these problems in 2005, informed by the Article 30 implementation report noted above (Skjærseth and Wettestad, 2010b: 65). A formal proposal to amend the 2003 Directive was eventually published in 2008. The aims of the 2009 Directive

(2009/29/EC) were contained in its formal title, namely to 'improve and extend' the existing system. Amongst its most significant design features were:

- *A single, EU-wide cap*: between 2013 and 2020 this declined automatically over time (by 1.74 per cent per year – a downward slope known as the linear reduction factor) to ensure that the EU fulfilled its 2020 emission reduction target (Wettestad *et al.*, 2012: 73). In effect, this was a new, automatic policy instrument-level *durability device*. Accordingly, the decentralised (and manual) process of determining the overall cap (via the NAPs) was discontinued.
- *Much greater auctioning of allowances*: auctioning became the norm for electricity generators in 2013 (with partial derogations for installations in Central and Eastern European Member States), but energy-intensive industries continued to receive free allocation, albeit at a reduced level.
- *A wider scope*: more industries were included (e.g. aluminium production and petrochemicals) and some additional gases covered (DG CLIMA, 2016: 12, 18).

In some respects, the design of the system became significantly more complex (i.e. much greater differentiation between and within sectors), more centralised (i.e. a single, EU-wide cap and auctioning), and more automated (Wettestad *et al.*, 2012: 73–74; Müller and Slominski, 2013: 1437). The Commission was also given more administrative responsibilities. Chief amongst them was the production of carbon leakage lists (Article 10) to guide the allocation of free allowances; they were to be updated every year on the basis of state-of-the-art technology benchmarks. This proved to be a considerable new administrative task – the first list encompassed no fewer than 165 sectors (Müller and Slominski, 2013: 1437) – and quickly become a new focus of target group lobbying (an example of interpretive policy feedback). Member States were also required to make the collection and spending of auction revenues more transparent. In general, it maintained their right to determine how revenues were spent, but pledged that 'at least 50%' would be used to combat climate change (DG CLIMA, 2016: 35). The various other ways in which the 2003 Directive fed back on and in turn affected the design of the 2009 and 2018 Directives are discussed in Chapter 6.

Ex post evaluations of the EU ETS have focused on its first and second order effects on emissions, profits, investment and carbon leakage (Laing *et al.*, 2014: 510). They are technically quite complicated to produce as they require robust data and realistic counterfactuals (Laing *et al.*, 2014: 510; Branger *et al.*, 2015: 10). Confounding factors (the financial crisis, fuel switching, technological innovation, etc.) had to be identified and carefully disaggregated. Most have focused on emission reductions achieved, as that was (and remains) the declared aim of the system. Published evaluations have reported reductions of between 2 and 4 per cent of the total capped emissions, which may not seem substantial but is relatively significant given the massive allowance surpluses in Phases I and II (Laing *et al.*, 2014: 516). The effects of the system on private investment and technological innovation are thought to have been quite limited (Laing *et al.*, 2014: 516; Branger *et al.*, 2015: 12), reflecting the relatively low price of allowances.

The policy feedbacks created by the ETS have, by contrast, received relatively little attention in the existing literature (but see Skjærseth, 2018; Wettestad and Jevnaker, 2019: 6, 18). The electricity generators have proven particularly adept at passing through costs to their customers, although cost pass-through has occurred in all sectors (Laing *et al.*, 2014: 514), the precise extent being a function of sectoral- and firm-level characteristics (Convery, 2008: 128; Skodvin *et al.*, 2010: 860; Skjærseth, 2013: 46). Although modest at first, these feedbacks effects have, over time, became more pronounced and politically consequential, causing the 2003 Directive to affect the design of subsequent directives (see Wettestad, 2009b: 310), and encouraging actors such as the Commission to push for the scope to be expanded (see Graichen *et al.*, 2017). From 2005 to 2012, the system covered carbon dioxide emissions from electricity generation and industrial processes. Starting in 2012, it was expanded to cover aviation emissions from flights wholly within the EU. In 2013, the scope was again expanded to include several additional industries (chemicals and aluminium production) as well as emissions of non-CO_2 greenhouse gases from a specific, relatively limited set of industrial processes. Its scope has also expanded geographically as a result of the accession of new Member States – Bulgaria and Romania in 2007 and Croatia in 2013 – as well as its expansion to the EEA in 2008. If these extensions in scope had been in effect in 2005, the scope of the original 2003 Directive would have been approximately 15 per cent greater (Graichen *et al.*, 2017: 7). Further details of these changes in scope, stringency and timeframe are provided in Chapter 6.

4.4 The Governance of Car Emissions: From Voluntary Action to Regulation?

Emission Patterns

When, in the late 1990s, the EU came under international pressure to back up its emission reduction pledges with internal policies, political attention inevitably focused on the transport sector. A 1997 European Commission Communication noted that greenhouse gas emissions from the sector had risen by 10 per cent between 1990 and 1995 (Volpi and Singer, 2002: 143). More significantly, it predicted that without stronger internal policies, transport would account for nearly 40 per cent of total EU CO_2 emissions by 2010 (Haigh, 2009: 14.2-3). The Commission concluded that from both a political and an environmental perspective, the policy *status quo* was patently unsustainable. In the late 1990s, it warned that if the transport sector continued on the same trajectory, it would not only imperil the EU's international climate leadership ambitions, which significantly increased in the 2000s (see Chapter 3), but require other sectors to take up the difference (which it argued would be unfair to those sectors).

Fast-forward fifteen years to 2013 and the transport sector still accounted for around 25 per cent of the EU's total greenhouse gas emissions, of which passenger cars alone contributed 43 per cent (EEA, 2015a: 28). The Commission's earlier warning about rising emissions were thus well-founded. In fact, transport remained the only sector from which emissions increased year-on-year between 1990 and 2013 (EEA, 2015a: 6–7). The EEA has estimated that between 1990 and 2013, emissions rose by almost 20 per cent (against an EU-wide target of a 40 per cent *reduction* by 2030); from road transport, they had climbed by almost 17 per cent (EEA, 2015a: 8). In other sectors (principally electricity generation – which falls within the scope of the emissions trading system), emissions have fallen.

Cars, heavy goods vehicles, road fuels and spare parts are all traded across borders. As a result, the Commission has repeatedly argued that the EU should be involved in significant policy design decisions. However, there were and still are other large and powerful incumbent players, not least the fuel and car-production companies, many of which have existed for well over a century (Urry, 2008). One of the running themes of the ongoing politics in the transport sector has been the battle between the fuel and car industries to shape policy designers' perceptions of the prevailing design space (Weale *et al.*, 2000: 405). Politicians have certainly struggled to reach durable decisions on who should enjoy the benefits and shoulder the costs of transport-related climate policy: fuel producers, car producers and/or consumers?

The interaction between these aspects has done much to constrain the politically feasible design space. Thus the fuel economy of private cars improved significantly after the 1970 oil crisis, but declined throughout the 1980s and 1990s as the economy strengthened and consumers opted to purchase larger and heavier vehicles (HM Government, 2013: 13). This trend partly reflected consumer tastes (which the car companies arguably worked hard to influence), technological shifts and also, in part, related EU policies tackling urban air pollutants, noise and driver safety (Keay-Bright, 2000: 14). Against this backdrop, the EEA repeatedly argued that 'significant additional measures' (EEA, 2015a: 10) were needed to ensure the sector played its part in fulfilling the EU's decarbonisation ambitions. In principle, transport emissions occur along the whole supply chain, offering many potential points at which policies could be targeted. However, the direct emissions from car tailpipes were quickly identified as the key target for climate policy design activities: they were relatively easy to quantify and were already the subject of existing EU policies on localised pollutants.

Target Groups and Other Interest Groups

The car industry is large, interconnected and mature, employing millions of people either directly or in its expansive supply and servicing chains (Mikler, 2009). By the early 2010s, annual global car sales had climbed to some €2 trillion (Wells, 2010: 2). In the EU alone, around 13 million new cars were registered in 2010 (DG CLIMA, 2011). The industry is part of a much larger 'regime of automobility' encompassing the production and sale of new cars, through to their fuelling, maintenance and disposal (Smith *et al.*, 2010: 440). Twelve million people (around 6 per cent of total EU employment) currently manufacture and service them in the EU (European Automobile Manufacturers' Association (ACEA), 2017: 1; COM (2017) 676: 1). Moreover, the car is not just 'a technology': it is an entire 'way of life, an entire culture' for millions of people (Urry, 2008: 347), extensively underpinned by what Pierson (1993) would presumably recognise as policy lock-ins. These are not, one might think, conducive to the adoption of new policy instruments that trigger extensive positive feedback. On the contrary, history suggested that the sector would fight hard to 'lock out' disruptive policy change.

The car industry certainly offered few 'silver bullet' solutions to the challenge of rising emissions. More often than not, it presented the continuation of the dominant existing technology – the fossil fuel-powered internal combustion engine (Ntziachristos and Dilara, 2012) – as a given. The industry sought to preserve this core technology by supporting and often securing the adoption of policies that facilitated incremental or 'drop-in' technological responses. The most common examples included the fitting of catalytic converters (to address local air pollution challenges) and (in relation to climate change) making existing diesel engines more efficient, reducing air and rolling resistance, and introducing devices that automatically switch off engines at traffic lights. Additional incremental technologies suggested by the sector included biofuels (see above) and hybrid electric-diesel engines (Unruh, 2002: 318; de Wilde and Kroon, 2013: 2). However, while drop-in solutions might fulfil the EU's short to medium-term mitigation targets (i.e. until the late 2020s), environmental groups repeatedly maintained that more radical innovations, including hydrogen or electric vehicles, will eventually be required to fully decarbonise the sector (de Wilde and Kroon, 2013: 2; see also Chapter 3). At present, however, these innovations reside in technological niches: e.g. electric and plug-in hybrid vehicles accounted for only 1.5 per cent of total new car sales in the EU in 2017 (EEA, 2018b).

The Design Space

When climate change first rose up the EU's political agenda in the 1990s, the policy designers in the Commission had to decide which policy design levers to pull without becoming mired in a prolonged battle with powerful incumbent industries. The fact that the regulation of air pollution from vehicles represented one of the oldest sub-sectors in EU environmental policy created its own path-dependent effects. In fact, the most feasible design options that were available to the Commission in the 1990s were essentially the same as they had been in the late 1960s when the EU first became involved in governing the car industry (Weale *et al.*, 2000: 398). The first option was to focus on well-to-tank emissions by altering the quality of fossil fuels or switching to alternative sources such as electricity or hydrogen (hence primarily an issue for the fuel-supply industry). The second option was to focus on tank-to-wheel emissions and set car emission standards (hence primarily a concern for car manufacturers). The third was to modify driver behaviour (e.g. through education campaigns and altering the layout of roads). Given the balance of power between the various actors, it was almost inevitable that the process of selecting amongst these options would generate conflict, pitting EU institutions and Member States against one another, often backed by powerful interest groups (Wurzel, 2002: 134).

To complicate matters further, the main target groups, whilst united on broader issues, regularly disagreed on specific policy details. Intense disagreements between producers of large, premium vehicles (BMW, Porsche) and producers of smaller, more economical alternatives (Peugeot, FIAT, etc.) first surfaced in the 1970s and 1980s (Friedrich *et al.*, 2000: 608). Indeed, the European industry organisation, the European Automobile Manufacturers' Association (ACEA), was established in 1991 to give the industry a common (and, in particular, a more environmental) face (Wurzel, 2002: 141). By the late 1980s, the Commission had come around to accepting that a more collaborative approach would achieve environmental goals more quickly than resorting to *dirigiste* forms of regulation (Wurzel, 2002: 162). Dubbed the 'Auto-Oil' programme, it formally commenced in 1991 with the aim of building a more harmonious and forward-looking relationship between the main policy designers (Friedrich *et al.*, 2000: 609).

It was at this point that climate change started to rise up the EU's political agenda. Although the actors and the technologies (and hence the preferred solutions) were essentially the same, greenhouse gases nonetheless constituted a new category of pollutants, and hence a somewhat different policy design problem. Following a historic October 1990 joint meeting of the Energy and Environment Councils (at which the EU offered, for the first time, to adopt a collective emissions target – see Chapter 3), the Commission commenced detailed design work. Almost immediately, it ran into strong political opposition from ACEA, whose members lobbied their national governments to lock out radical new policy and technological innovations. Fearing a prolonged battle, the Commission opted instead to follow the grain of existing policy designs and focus on fuel quality and/or car emissions – the two main foci of the then ongoing Auto-Oil discussions.

But even so, the design process moved extremely slowly. The outcome – summarised in Chapter 7 – was one of the EU's first voluntary agreements in the environment sector, which sought to reduce CO_2 emissions from all new cars produced in the EU.

The Initial Policy Design

When it was eventually adopted in 1998, the voluntary agreement on CO_2 from cars was hailed as a policy innovation because it departed from the EU's established preferences for regulatory instruments (see Chapter 3). It committed European manufacturers to reduce average CO_2 emissions from all new passenger cars sold on the EU market from an average of 186g/km in 1995 to 140g/km by 2008, roughly equating to a 25 per cent cut over ten years (COM (1998) 495: 3; see also Bongaerts, 1999: 102). In turn, the agreement was expected to contribute around 70 per cent of the total reductions required to achieve a more ambitious longer-term target of 120g/km by 2012 (Recommendation 1999/125/EC). However, it took over three years to negotiate – the slowest adoption process of the fifteen policy instrument changes analysed in this book.

The agreement's objectives could be thought of as an instrument-level *durability device,* which aimed to encourage manufacturers to produce cleaner vehicles. To ensure that it remained relevant, it also incorporated several *flexibility devices.* For example, the emission target was time-specific (i.e. to be achieved by 2008–2012). It also incorporated a *flexibility clause* which committed ACEA (i.e. *not* the Commission), its main co-signatory, to review (by 2003) the potential for further improvements to be made (by 2012) to achieve a fleet average of 120g/km. This clause was, however, connected to a *durability device* (an intermediate target to achieve 165–170g/km by 2003), although the connection was ambiguously worded. Thus, if – and only if – ACEA failed to achieve the interim target (the degree of underachievement was not fully specified), would the Commission formally review the agreement (i.e. undertake an *ex post* evaluation – another type of *flexibility device*). Only then would it 'consider drawing up a proposal for binding legislation' (COM (1998) 495: 5). Furthermore, 'some European manufacturers' (no further details on their identify were given) were expected to produce cars that were capable of achieving the tougher 120g/km standard by 2000 (COM (1998) 495: 5). At first blush, the looseness of this commitment did not appear to put manufacturers under much pressure to make large, upfront investments in the durability of the policy. Finally, the Commission undertook to negotiate similar agreements with Japanese and Korean manufacturers to prevent them from securing an uncompetitive advantage – one amongst many pre-conditions that ACEA laid down before signing the agreement.

The agreement, incorporating ACEA's conditions (now re-termed 'assumptions'), was eventually published as an EU Recommendation in 1999, more than three years after the commencement of the policy design process (1999/125/EC). It was signed by the board of ACEA on behalf of its individual members, who, crucially, only 'endeavoured to contribute to' its implementation (Bongaerts, 1999: 102). It was presented as the centrepiece of a larger package of instruments addressing transport emissions, proposals for which were published by the Commission in December 1995 (COM (95) 689; see Bongaerts, 1999: 101; Haigh, 2009: 14.8-3). The other three elements in the package were designed to make up the missing 30 per cent reduction (i.e. to 120g/km) noted above. As Chapter 5 will show, this missing percentage turned out to be politically significant, because it equated to the difference between the reduction target sought by the Environment Council as far back as 1994 and the target (140g/km) which was included in the agreement after the prolonged, three-year design process.

An important additional part of the Commission's 1995 transport package sought to ensure that all new cars were better labelled so that consumers had access to more information on fuel usage and CO_2 emissions (these labelling requirements were adopted as Directive 1999/94/EC). The Commission hoped that this would inform purchasing decisions, which in turn would eventually incentivise manufacturers to produce cleaner and more efficient cars. After a great deal of discussion, an additional instrument was eventually adopted in 2000, which ensured that the right data was collected from the car manufacturers (Decision 1753/2000/EC). This Decision, which was in effect a polity-based *durability device*, also mandated the Commission to collect information about how the agreement was performing. However, the producers proved extremely reluctant to release it (largely, they claimed, to preserve their commercial confidentiality). For the first three years of the agreement (i.e. to 2003), ACEA was therefore only willing to supply data to the Commission; after 2003, it was independently verified by the Commission and released to the public in an anonymised form (Volpi and Singer, 2002: 150). The final part of the package was to have been another directive to stimulate green car purchases by adjusting national tax levels. However, this too foundered and was eventually shelved, blocked by Member States who were opposed to the EU becoming more involved in national tax affairs (Haigh, 2009: 14.8-7), leaving the whole proposal rather less package-like than the Commission had originally hoped.

Policy Implementation and Reform

At first, the implementation of the agreement proceeded smoothly and the car manufacturers met their targets with room to spare. But progress soon faltered and despite a late rally, the 2008 target was missed by some distance (Jordan and Matt, 2014). Having failed to achieve emissions reductions voluntarily, in 2009 the Commission claimed that it had no option but to change direction. It exploited the agreement's *flexibility clause* to formulate and then adopt a completely different policy instrument – a regulation – which was not only more coercive[7] and more finely tuned (i.e. through company-specific targets), but also had considerably stricter, binding standards set for 2015 and 2020. The instrument-level *durability devices* that were eventually inserted into the design of what came to be known as the 2009 Cars Regulation (443/2009) included fines for individual manufacturers that did not meet their company-specific targets. As the durability devices in the Regulation bore down on the producers, they were forced to make more significant investments in the long-term success of the EU's policy and more significant emission reductions eventually began to accrue (EEA, 2015a: 8). In fact, the time-specific *durability device* that required manufacturers to achieve a fleet average of 130g/km by 2015 delivered compliance a full two years ahead of schedule. Considerably more technological progress will need to be made to deliver on the 2020 target of 95g/km.[8] Designers were unable to agree on how to achieve such significant reductions when the Regulation was formulated in 2007–2008. Article 13 (5) of the 2009 Regulation thus committed the Commission to work with producers to review 'the modalities for reaching the 2020 target' by 1 January 2013 (i.e. a policy instrument-level *flexibility clause*) and issue a formal proposal to amend the 2009 Directive. A new policy proposal was duly published in July 2012 (COM (2012) 393), debated and discussed and eventually adopted as Regulation 333/2014.

After two decades of policy design, the core issues of responsibility and political feasibility are still as deeply contested amongst the major players as they were in the late 1980s. As will become clear in Chapter 7, even something as apparently self-evident as how to measure the tail-pipe emissions from particular vehicle types has proven difficult to agree upon. The 2009 Regulation reported emissions under something known as the standardised test cycle, which was applied by national authorities and certified by the Commission. Environmental groups claimed that it significantly under-reported emission levels – claims that were vindicated when (in 2015) the world's largest manufacturer of diesel engine vehicles – Volkswagen (VW) – was found to have deliberately cheated on them to achieve emission reductions at lower cost. This revelation triggered a worldwide scandal known as 'Dieselgate', after which the sale of new diesel cars in the EU plummeted and VW was forced to fight costly legal actions brought by car owners in the US. The whole affair shone an unflattering light on the lobbying activities of the car manufacturers in Brussels and eventually encouraged the EU to adopt tighter emission reduction targets and establish a new testing regime that better reflected 'real world' driving conditions (EEA, 2015a: 8).

When, as outlined in the previous chapter, the EU adopted its post-2020 emission reduction commitments in 2014, the Commission embarked on another reformulation of the EU's car emissions policy. It issued a new regulatory proposal in November 2017 that set an interim ('by 2025') target of a 15 per cent reduction from 2021 levels and a 30 per cent reduction by 2030 (COM (2017) 676). In December 2018, the Council and the Parliament agreed to an amended regulation which kept the Commission's proposed 15 per cent by 2025 target but set a more stringent target of 37.5 per cent below 2021 levels by 2030 (Regulation 2019/631). This equates to average emissions of 59g/km which, if achieved, would represent a 68 per cent reduction in the emissions from new cars since 1995 (COM (1998) 495: 3) – far more than had been envisaged when the voluntary agreement was adopted in 1998.

4.5 Conclusions

In this chapter we have introduced the three policy instruments – a regulation, an emissions trading system, and a voluntary agreement – that constitute the main foci of Chapters 5–7 respectively. For each instrument, we have outlined the pre-existing pattern of emissions, and the main designers and target groups. Then, we summarised the policy design space in each policy sub-area and noted the most salient design features of the instruments that were adopted. On closer inspection, these features include a complicated mix of durability and flexibility devices, operating at the level of policy instrument goals and policy instrument calibrations. If nothing else, we have confirmed that, to paraphrase Chapter 1, policy instrument design is more or less the essence of everyday governance. Policy instrument design processes in the real world often do take a long time to accomplish and, as we have shown, generate a good deal of political conflict. However, these three instruments were just the starting instruments in the respective sequences. Throughout this chapter, we have hinted at the existence of certain resource/incentive and interpretive feedback mechanisms and effects and noted them as priorities for more in-depth analysis in the next three chapters.

Endnotes

1 Biomass, biofuels and other non-fossil organic fuels are collectively known as bioenergy (Environmental Audit Committee, 2008: 5).
2 For a detailed list, see Annex IX of the 2015 Directive (OJ L239, 15.9.2015: 28-9).
3 Including all support mechanisms such as excise tax exemptions, capital grants and R&D funds.
4 Policy changes affecting the aviation industry are generally decided separately and the industry is still treated somewhat differently than other sectors (e.g. with a separate type of emission allowances). For further information, see Andlovic and Lehmann (2014).
5 The Large Combustion Plant Directive of 1988 and the Integrated Pollution Prevention and Control Directive of 1996 being especially relevant examples (for more examples, see COM (2000) 87: 8).

6 For example, the Linking Directive (2004/101/EC) linked the system to the other Kyoto Protocol flexibility mechanisms. In 2008, the EU adopted an Aviation Directive (2008/101/EC) which extended the system to the aviation sector. Because of space constraints, we mainly concentrate on the three core directives: the original 2003 Directive (2003/87/EC), and the two amending Directives adopted in 2009 (2009/29/EC) and 2018 (2018/410/EC) respectively.
7 And recall that, unlike directives, EU regulations are immediately effective (i.e. they do not have to be transposed in national legislation). See Chapter 2 for details.
8 In 2017, average emissions increased slightly for the first time since the 2009 Regulation came into effect (EEA, 2018b).

5

Regulation

The Governance of Biofuels

5.1 Introduction

The use of biofuel as a type of renewable energy dates back to the dawn of the global car industry in the nineteenth century. The attractiveness of biofuels derives from their ability to function as a drop-in alternative to fossils fuels such as petrol and diesel. According to the International Energy Agency, if the world is to stay within 2 °C of warming, annual production of transport biofuels must treble between 2017 and 2030 (Raval, 2018). The promotion of renewable energy has been actively discussed in the EU for many decades. But in the late 1990s, a period when EU climate and energy policies were evolving rapidly (see Chapter 3), the EU did not have a coherent, Europe-wide policy to promote the use of biofuels. So, the Commission began to prepare the ground, formulating fresh proposals for an EU-level policy to ramp up domestic production and use. The transport sector was an obvious target, the assumption being that from a technological perspective, greater biofuel use would not be overly disruptive.[1]

Adopted relatively quickly in 2003 (after just 557 days), the 2003 Biofuels Directive marked the EU's first significant attempt to actively govern the production of biofuels for use in the transport sector. Until that point, only a few Member States had the technological capacity to produce biofuels at a large scale within their territories; most had no policies at all to encourage production or consumption. This chapter documents the policy feedbacks created by the 2003 Directive and their unfolding impact on the 2009 Renewable Energy Directive as well as subsequent revisions made in 2015 and 2018 respectively. It reveals that the promotion of biofuels has not unfolded as the EU and, in particular the Commission, had originally expected. Confident expectations that they would address a triad of interlinked policy challenges – energy insecurity, rising greenhouse gas emissions from the transport sector and agricultural over-production in some EU Member States – have been repeatedly dashed. Eventually, policy designers were forced to accept that the €15 billion industry in biofuels that they had helped to nurture (van Noorden, 2013: 13) was generating many negative effects, both directly in the EU and indirectly in many other parts of the world. Many more actors began to take an interest in biofuels, many flatly opposed to any further expansion. By the late 2000s, the mood in the EU had shifted markedly against the first-generation of biofuels. While almost all actors could agree that the 2003 Directive was no longer fit-for-purpose, they struggled to agree on when and how to reform it. As wider public opinion began to swing decisively against not just first-generation biofuels but *all* biofuels, the Commission sought to tread a fine line between ensuring that producers were able to recoup their investments in first-generation biofuels, whilst giving a clear indication that the future lay in the second- and third-generation alternatives. The 2009 Renewable Energy Directive thus established a significantly higher and, for the first time, legally binding 10 per cent target for the minimum share of renewable fuels in the transport sector, but also introduced a new set of sustainability criteria to address the indirect effects of biofuel use. However, by the mid-2000s, biofuel had become 'a dirty word' in many quarters (Oliver, 2014) and despite the Commission's valiant efforts, the 2009 Directive conspicuously failed to improve its public image. In fact, the mounting controversy threatened to undermine not just the decarbonisation of the transport sector, but the Commission's long-term decarbonisation plans in other areas, such as switching to biomass-based forms of domestic heating and cooling.

In an attempt to recover the situation, the EU embarked on the design of yet another directive. However, it proved even harder to adopt than the 2003 and 2009 Directives. When it was eventually adopted after 1,058 days in 2015, the Indirect Land Use Change (ILUC) Directive sought to achieve three things simultaneously: cap the use of first-generation biofuel to fulfil Member States' renewable transportation targets; provide producers with a stronger incentive to invest in second- and third-generation alternatives; and minimise further indirect land-use changes. More significantly, the EU announced that no further policy support would be given to first-generation biofuel types after 2020. In 2018, the ILUC Directive was followed by a recast Renewable Energy Directive (RED II) – adopted in 742 days – that set a target of 14 per cent renewable energy in transport by 2030, capped the use of first-generation biofuels to meet EU targets at 1 per cent above 2020 levels and, for the first time, set a mandatory target for second- and third-generation biofuels at 3.5 per cent of the fuel mix in each Member State by 2030.

The remainder of this chapter recounts how the 2003 Directive was originally conceived within the Commission, how it was subsequently designed in close discussion with other actors and describes the policy feedback effects it generated after 2003. It then summarises the positive and negative feedback which shaped the design of the 2009 RED I Directive, and then traces how the feedback effects it set in train eventually impacted the design of the ILUC and RED II Directives.

5.2 The Policy Design Process: Creating the Biofuels Directive

The Promotion of Renewable Energy

The promotion of renewable energy has been actively discussed in the EU for decades (see e.g. the 1985 Directive (85/536) on the promotion of renewable energy; Scott, 2011: 828). Of the three main rationales for boosting biofuel use identified in Chapter 4, initially energy security was widely perceived to be the most important. For example, in the 1980s the EU explored ways to reduce excess food production by diverting Common Agricultural Policy funding to support first-generation biofuels (Ackrill and Kay, 2014: 53). In the 1990s, the production of biodiesel finally began to take off, encouraged by a patchwork of national fuel quality standards and blending mandates. As production in Germany and France grew, producers began to demand a more coordinated, i.e. EU-wide, set of policy supports (Ackrill and Kay, 2014: 53). Significantly, these calls were justified in terms of new policy goals, specifically addressing climate change (Ackrill and Kay, 2014: 54; Timilsina, 2014: 2). In November 1997, well over six years before the adoption of the 2003 Biofuels Directive, the Commission published a White Paper entitled *Energy for the Future – Renewable Sources of Energy*. It proposed a longer-term policy programme-level *durability device* – a target to raise the percentage of gross energy consumption derived from renewable energy from 5.4 per cent in 1995 to 12 per cent. But it also designed in some temporal flexibility by making the target time-specific, i.e. 'by 2010' (COM (97) 599). It also added in measures to increase the use of renewable energy in the transport sector (Del Guayo, 2008: 272). In doing so, the White Paper cited more rationales for boosting biofuel production and use, including employment generation in rural areas and, crucially for us, climate change mitigation. Throughout, the tone was confident and assertive, although it noted that some 'care will need to be taken to safeguard biodiversity in the EU' (COM (97) 599: 37).

In response to that White Paper, in June 1998 the Council and the European Parliament invited the Commission to develop more concrete policy proposals, specifically in relation to transport (COM (2001) 547: 28). The Parliament called for an integrated programme of measures to boost the market share of biofuels in transport to 2 per cent over a period of five years – a request that was explicitly referenced in the opening recitals of the Biofuels Directive (OJ L123, 17.5.2003: 43). At that point, any criticisms of expanding biofuel use were rather muted and the risk of triggering indirect land-use changes outside the EU was not widely acknowledged.

In November 2000, the Commission finally issued specific proposals in a Green Paper entitled *Towards a European Strategy for the Security of Energy Supply* (COM (2000) 769). It claimed that the EU was being 'held hostage by oil' (COM (2000) 769: 13) and recommended that renewable energy supplies be ramped up to account for at least 20 per cent of transport fuels by a new target year: 2020 (COM (2000) 769: 49). If achieved, it would have represented an enormous increase in deployment. For biofuels, the overall target translated into a specific target of 7 per cent by 2020, which may not appear much but would have represented an equally massive change to the status quo, given that at the time, biofuels had only a 0.3 per cent market share (see Skogstad, 2017: 29). Despite this, the 20 per cent figure quickly attracted political buy-in and was subsequently cited in the Commission's 2001 proposal for an EU directive (COM (2001) 547: 2). The Commission hoped that an eye-catching headline target would nurture new political support but admitted that it went 'well beyond what has been asked from the car and oil industry in the past' (COM (2001) 547: 2). In May 2001, the 7 per cent by 2020 target was re-stated in the Commission's proposal for an EU-wide policy programme addressing sustainable development (COM (2001) 264). It promised that a formal proposal on boosting biofuel use in the transport sector would be published in 2001 and expected it to be adopted by the end of 2002. The Commission also claimed that with the right mixture of policy supports, biofuel could account for up to 7 per cent of total transport fuel by 2010, and at least 20 per cent of fuel could derive from 'substitute fuels' by 2020 (Ackrill and Kay, 2014: 60). Later that year, the Commission re-endorsed the 20 per cent by 2020 target for 'substitute fuels' in a White Paper on transport policy (COM (2001) 370: 79). It suggested that 'the most promising forms [of alternative fuels] are biofuels in the short and medium term, natural gas in the medium and long term and hydrogen in the very long term' (COM (2001) 370: 86; see also Palmer, 2015: 275). The 20 per cent substitution target was eventually dropped during the policy design process (see Chapter 3), but the policy instrument-level *flexibility device* (the timeframe of 'by 2020') stuck and was eventually incorporated into the design of the 2009 Renewable Energy Directive.

An EU-wide Biofuels Policy

In its legislative proposal, published on 7 November 2001, the Commission argued that the overriding policy design challenge arose from the fact that 'the overall effort' in developing new production capacities was being 'provided by only a few Member States, whereas the benefits from promoting biofuels ... profit the Union as a whole' (COM (2001) 547: 29). Only at an 'EU-wide level', it continued, 'is it realistic to imagine the introduction of alternative fuels with significant market shares' (COM (2001) 547: 3). The Commission also maintained that 'biofuels are for the short and medium term the *only* option' (COM (2001) 547: 13, emphasis added). Interestingly, it appeared to frame this rationale in terms of nurturing policy feedback effects:

Without coordinated decisions [...] it is doubtful whether biofuels will ever reach a substantial share of the total fuel consumption in the EU. Actions at Community level [...] are therefore needed in order to create the basis for the investment required to promote sufficient quantities of biofuel.

(COM (2001) 547: 17)

The Commission must have known that the transport sector was the fastest growing source of greenhouse gas emissions in the EU (see Chapter 4) because it quickly identified it as being especially well-suited to using more biofuel. Use in this sector was, as noted in Chapter 4, perceived to be relatively straightforward, biofuel being a drop-in alternative to diesel and petrol. It believed that biofuels 'deserve to be exploited in the short to medium term because they can be used in the existing vehicles and distribution system and thus do not require expensive infrastructure investment' (COM (2001) 547: 6). A fuel-focused solution to rising emissions from the sector was certainly perceived to be more palatable to consumers than some of the alternatives (e.g. demand-side measures such as setting EU-wide speed limits, or policies requiring a technological step-change, e.g. switching to electric or hydrogen-powered cars; see Dunlop, 2010: 354). The Commission again cited many rationales for scaling up domestic production but emphasised three in particular: energy security, rural development and decarbonisation (COM (2001) 547: 2).

However, from the outset, the Commission knew that it was operating in a bounded policy design space. Although some Member States were keen to boost biofuel production and use in the transport sector, the rest were instinctively suspicious of attempts to adopt mandatory targets at EU level, to centralise reporting requirements or to establish stronger enforcement powers. The selection of policy instruments from the toolbox was also somewhat constrained. The Directorate-General for Energy and Transport (DG Energy), the lead DG on the proposal, lacked sufficient political support in the Commission, let alone in the Council, to expand the budget of the Common Agricultural Policy to subsidise domestic production or even divert existing payments to that goal (COM (2001) 547: 6). Consequently, the Commission was forced to conclude that the EU would not be self-sufficient in biofuel production in the short to medium term, which immediately implied some acceptance of imported biofuel supplies, possibly produced according to environmental standards that differed from those in the EU. Finally, the Commission was mindful that it would have to design its policies within World Trade Organisation rules. For instance, it risked provoking opposition from trading partners if it sought to use trade tariffs to privilege European producers (Ponte and Daugbjerg, 2015).

The Commission responded to these design constraints by proposing a phased approach. In the first phase there would be not one, but two interlinked directives: the first setting a reduced rate of excise tax on the sale of biofuels within the single market; and the second imposing an obligation on Member States to promote the use of biofuels in their own territories (COM (2001) 547: 8). The former would allow states to establish reduced rates of duty on biofuels without having to secure a formal derogation from the EU in advance. It would allow tax reductions of up to 50 per cent on pure biofuels, with a proportionate reduction for various biofuel blends (ENDS Report, 2001). The latter would require each Member State to establish formal targets at national level (Haigh, 2009: 14.11-1). It included an automatic *durability device* – a ratchet starting at a 2 per cent blending limit in 2005 and rising by 0.75 per cent per year to 5 per cent by 2009 (COM (2001) 547: 18). Subsequently – and assuming that things ran smoothly – the EU would, in a second phase, drive substitution rates above 5 per cent, by setting a mandatory, minimum blending mandate (COM (2001) 547: 8), the aim being to ensure that the overall share of total fuel consumption accounted for by renewable fuels rose to at least 20 per cent by 2020 (COM (2001) 547: 17).

The response to the Commission's proposals was somewhat mixed. The proposed directive on amending fuel duties was strongly opposed by several Member States; as a matter of principle, several did not want the EU becoming more involved in domestic tax affairs (Haigh, 2009: 14.11-1). However, the second proposal received a warmer reception. Nonetheless, the European Parliament and the Council disagreed on its design (Haigh, 2009: 14.11-2). The Parliament demanded mandatory targets to be included in the proposal but was fiercely opposed by the Council; in fact, Ministers voiced their firm opposition even before Parliament had commenced its first reading of the proposal. Crucially, all the policy designers seemed more concerned about selecting and calibrating the best policy instruments, than whether it was wise to seek such a significant increase in biofuel consumption.

However, some environmental NGOs were sceptical of the whole endeavour (cf. Rietig, 2018: 149). The European Environmental Bureau (EEB) flatly opposed all targets, stating that biofuels made 'no economic or environmental sense' and produced 'little or no climate or CO_2 benefits' (EEB, 2001; Euractiv, 2001). In a policy briefing entitled *Biofuels: Not as Green as They Sound*, it claimed that the projected emission reductions were 'by no means substantial'. From its perspective, what Europe needed was not another drop-in solution (and on that matter it pointedly referred to the superior performance of second-generation biofuels), but 'structural changes' that reduced the demand for car travel (EEB, 2002a: 4). It later claimed that the related proposal to allow tax reductions on biofuels was 'highly dubious' and that 'ministers were being asked to substantially reduce their national tax incomes on the strength of what was a very weak environmental case' (EEB, 2002b). Transport and Environment (T&E) – another NGO – was at least willing to support the general idea of incentivising production, but called for 'a comprehensive set of quality criteria' to ensure that they delivered verifiable climate benefits (ENDS Report, 2001). In 2002, it pushed for indicative, rather than binding, biofuels targets, arguing that the Commission's proposal was really 'motivated by agricultural support rather than environmental outcomes' (ENDS Europe, 2002).[2] The NGOs were joined in their criticism by the European Petroleum Industry Association (EUROPIA), a potential economic competitor to some biofuel producers, which warned against 'premature or prescriptive advancement of biofuels without sound environmental, logistical and economic consideration' (Euractiv, 2001). It is notable that prior to the adoption of the 2003 Directive, there was little recorded engagement in the policy design process by the biofuel industries, represented by organisations such as the European Biodiesel Board (EBB) and the European Union of Alcohol Producers (UEPA).

The Adoption of the 2003 Biofuels Directive

Having reflected on these criticisms, in September 2002 the Commission published an amended version of its proposal for a directive (COM (2002) 508). During the redrafting process, the Commission had removed the mandatory targets that the Council had opposed as well as all references to the calibration of national fuel duties. Mandatory targets were in effect shelved until indicative, i.e. non-binding, targets had had sufficient time to prove their worth (Di Lucia and Nilsson, 2007: 535; Del Guayo, 2008: 272). The Commission tried to derive environmental criteria to improve the environmental sustainability of transport biofuels – this was something that the Parliament and some environmental NGOs felt particularly strongly about – but these were, as noted in Chapter 4, rapidly chipped away during the policy adoption process (Ackrill and Kay, 2014: 57). The 2003 Biofuels Directive was finally adopted on 8 May 2003, a mere 548 days after the Commission had published the first version of its proposal in 2001. Of the three initial policy instruments studied in Chapters 5, 6 and 7, the Biofuels Directive was the most rapidly adopted. Lawyers have since remarked that its legal content was relatively low (its opening recitals being longer in length than the substantive legal text). This may be a reflection of the fact that its main purpose was not to achieve an immediate ramping-up of production, but rather to collect and share production information, and thereby learn more about the barriers to and opportunities of increasing indigenous production (Del Guayo, 2008: 274). Nevertheless, the 2003 Directive nonetheless marked 'the starting point of EU biofuels policy' (Ackrill and Kay, 2014: 56).

Having adopted the 2003 Directive, the EU began to explore new ways to encourage the wider uptake and use of energy from biomass. In December 2005, the Commission launched a wide-ranging Biomass Action Plan (COM/2005/628) followed by a broader biofuels strategy in February 2006. These aimed to explore approaches to more than double the use of bioenergy (defined in Chapter 4) 'over the next few years' across a much wider array of applications including electricity generation, and domestic heating and cooling. In the transport sector, the Action Plan admitted that second-generation biofuels were the more sustainable option in the medium-to long-term. But given short-term supply constraints (at the time, there were no second-generation production facilities in the EU), the Commission had to agree with producers that the EU should continue to support the production of first-generation biofuels. The Commission noted that while the other EU institutions generally endorsed its design aims, they disagreed on precisely how and over what timescale to achieve them (COM (2006) 845: 8).

5.3 The Implementation of the Biofuels Directive

Policy Instrument Implementation

Although most Member States transposed the 2003 Directive into their national policy systems on schedule, it was often on the basis of lower indicative national targets than had been originally foreseen by the Commission (Di Lucia and Nilsson, 2007: 541). When the consultants hired by the Commission added up these national targets in the period to 2005, they discovered that the average across the EU was only 1.4 per cent – around 30 per cent lower than the indicative value of 2 per cent contained in the Directive (COM (2006) 845: 16; Di Lucia and Nilsson, 2007: 535).[3] Because of the way that the Directive had been designed, the Commission was able to initiate enforcement proceedings against those Member States that had not established targets in national law (see Section 5.5 and also Chapter 4). However, it was powerless to act if they had adopted weak targets and/or the average of national targets fell below 2 per cent. Underlying the differences in national law and policy practice detected by the consultants were very different national policy instrument mixes. Crucially, Member States that had no – or only very immature – biofuel industries in 2003, tended to have weak and/or non-existent national support policies which the Directive, being essentially focused on information collection and dissemination tasks, was more or less powerless to overcome. The net effect could be likened to the relationship between a chicken and an egg: the gaps in some national instrument mixes could not be addressed overnight; but the resulting lack of policy certainty was delaying the construction of new biofuel production capacities and the stimulation of consumer demand (Di Lucia and Nilsson, 2007: 540).

The system of annual national reporting foreseen under Article 4 certainly offered no easy solution to this problem. In fact, the reports submitted by each Member State turned out to be very different in both their content and style (Howes, 2010: 142). This made it difficult for Commission officials to assess progress, let alone accurately forecast the development of new biofuel markets. In 2005, the Commission initiated infringement proceedings against around half of the Member States for not implementing certain parts of the Biofuels Directive (Di Lucia and Nilsson, 2007: 539–540). Some of the reasons cited by Member States for the lack of implementation were of a rather technical nature. Member States with weakly developed production capacities claimed that they needed more time to reconfigure their national policy mixes. Even if this could be achieved, many argued that they lacked the agricultural production capacities to upscale the production of feedstocks. It did not help that the EU's legal targets were essentially non-binding. Hence, the resource/incentive feedback mechanisms that could be wielded by the EU to force domestic producers to invest in new biofuel technologies (and hence increase the durability of the Directive) were weak (Di Lucia and Nilsson, 2007: 541).

More Fundamental Disagreements Over EU Policy

Underpinning these short-term implementation problems were, however, more fundamental disagreements (Di Lucia and Nilsson, 2007: 540). Even by the midway point in the implementation process (i.e. around 2005), more profound doubts were being aired about the EU's activities. Was the Directive about decarbonising road transport, achieving greater energy security or boosting agricultural development (Di Lucia and Nilsson, 2007: 542)? Even amongst the policy's strongest supporters, there were markedly different views. In Sweden, the overriding justification for EU-level action cited by supporters was to address energy security in as an environmentally sustainable way as possible. In Austria, by contrast, the focus was on promoting rural development (Di Lucia and Nilsson, 2007: 537). As more implementation reports were filed, it became abundantly clear that the Member States that had resisted the proposal at the policy formulation stage were the same as those reporting significant implementation problems (Di Lucia and Nilsson, 2007: 540). Academic analysts subsequently categorised Member States into those that were willing and able to develop new biofuel capacities and those that were not (and if so, what the constraints were) (Di Lucia and Kronsell, 2010). In short, what had originally appeared to be a policy panacea, was beginning to morph into something that EU actors wanted to interpret and implement in their own, rather different ways.

After 2001, EU production and consumption of biofuel continued to grow, rising from a combined market share of around 0.3 per cent in 2001 (COM (2006) 845: 3) to around 1 per cent in 2005, i.e. well below the indicative target of 2 per cent stipulated in Article 3 (Di Lucia and Nilsson, 2007: 537). In only three Member States (namely Austria, Sweden and Germany) did consumption exceed the relevant national target (Di Lucia and Nilsson, 2007: 537). That these three were positive about biofuels well before 2003 suggests that the Directive had not nurtured a dynamic, new pan-European market in biofuels (Di Lucia and Nilsson, 2007: 537).[4] The differences in national perspective and policy support were duly confirmed by the Commission's progress report. Published on 10 January 2007, it confirmed that the 2005 target had been undershot and that the 5.75 per cent target was also 'not likely to be achieved' by 2010 (COM (2006) 845: 6).

Globally, however, biofuel production was booming, growing at around 20 per cent per year between 2000 and 2010 (Timilsina, 2014: 15). This enabled the Commission to assert that biofuels were nonetheless worth backing as an alternative to fossil fuels. The EU should therefore run faster to seize the economic opportunities in what was clearly an expanding global market. By 2005, motorists in most Member States were buying diesel that had been blended with biodiesel (COM (2006) 845: 5), even if they had not consciously decided to support biofuel, be it indigenously derived or imported. Biofuels did, the Commission claimed, have a 'unique role to play'; in fact, in the medium term they were the only viable substitute for oil in the transport sector (COM (2006) 845: 2), offering 'large scale savings' in greenhouse gases (COM (2006) 845: 2). It argued that the reasonable response was not to dismantle the policy but to strengthen it 'to give confidence to companies, investors and scientists' (COM (2006) 845: 7). Consequently, the Commission announced its intention to plough on and publish a proposal for a new Directive, which incorporated the '10% by 2020' target that had been bargained out of the 2003 Biofuels Directive (Haigh, 2009: 14.11-1), but re-framed as a mandatory target.

Yet at this precise moment, a tide of political opposition to biofuels in general (and first-generation biofuels in particular) was rising across Europe. Importantly, biofuel's opponents began to exhibit more concern about issues that had been noted during the formulation of the 2003 Directive, but not acted on. These included the environmental sustainability of biofuels, the rather modest greenhouse gas reduction performance of many first-generation biofuels, and the slow arrival onto the market of second- and third-generation biofuel alternatives (Haigh, 2009: 14.11-2). What was particularly different about the policy design processes after 2005 was that more groups were articulating these doubts and were doing so in a much more vocal and organised fashion. Finding ways to respond to these criticisms, whilst simultaneously expanding biofuel production to fulfil the EU's greenhouse gas reduction targets, quickly emerged as *the* overriding policy design challenge in the European Commission.

5.4 Policy Feedback and Policy Instrument Redesign

A Step Change in Policy Programme Goals

Why was biofuel generating more opposition? Part of the explanation lies in the fact that by the mid-2000s the EU was intent on setting more ambitious targets at the policy-programme level covering the generation of renewable energy and, in addition, greenhouse gas mitigation. The publication in December 2005 of the Commission's action plan on bioenergy (COM (2005) 628) aimed, in effect, to replicate what was being pursued in the transport sector, but for a much wider array of sectors and uses including domestic heating and cooling. A few months later in February 2006, the Commission issued an *EU Strategy for Biofuels* (COM (2006) 34), which fed into several evaluations of the 2003 Biofuels Directive and several public consultations. Together, these informed a series of new EU-level road maps to boost domestic production. 'Almost all' of the respondents to one consultation agreed that EU policy should be made more mandatory, more consistent across countries and more environmentally friendly, informed by detailed sustainability criteria enshrined in legislation (Del Guayo, 2008: 280). But it is striking that, at this point, few were calling for a complete halt to biofuels expansion. The EEB was virtually alone in voicing its opposition, calling for the immediate and complete rejection of the Commission's strategy (ENDS Report, 2005). But by this point in the policy sequence, there appeared to be so much political momentum behind the EU's wider climate and energy policies that its criticisms went largely unheeded (Del Guayo, 2008: 275–276).

In January 2007, the Commission launched a comprehensive package of new proposals covering the period after 2012, which sought to forge a link between the EU's climate and energy policies – two policy areas that the Commission had hitherto struggled to connect (see Chapter 3 for details). In one Communication entitled *An Energy Policy for Europe* (COM (2006) 848), it re-committed itself to achieving the 20 per cent target for renewables by 2020. Whereas in the past this target had been largely exhortatory, this time it was more forcefully advocated, underpinned by feasibility studies and an impact assessment (see Chapter 3). In effect, the Commission began to argue that the long-discussed '20% by 2020' target was not simply necessary to achieve but was eminently feasible to implement with the right package of instruments. Crucially, the proposed policy programme would contain legally binding targets 'in order to ensure confidence and encourage investment' (Howes, 2010: 125). And instead of continuing with a sector-by-sector approach (i.e. addressing transport, domestic heating, etc.), there should be one policy programme-level *durability device* – an EU-wide target of 20 per cent by 2020 covering all forms of renewable energy (COM (2006) 848: 3). But yet again, a special exception was made for transport,[5] which would have its own binding sectoral target of 10 per cent of road fuel use to be supplied by biofuels by 2020 (COM (2007) 1).

In March 2007, Heads of State adopted these targets believing they would achieve the 'mutually supportive' integration of climate change and energy policies that they desired (European Council, 2007: 10). In doing so, they made a 'new starting point for a renewed and reinforced EU policy towards ... biofuels' (Del Guayo, 2008: 276). As regards biofuels, Heads of State underlined the need to find better ways to ensure that new biofuel production was environmentally sustainable and to accelerate the entry of second-generation alternatives onto the market (Haigh, 2009: 14.11-1).

Positive and Negative Policy Feedback Effects

Until this point, the political opposition to biofuels resided in a number of small pockets, generally at EU level. Evidence that a much wider political backlash against biofuels might be in the offing first began to emerge in late 2005 when the Commission announced a new Biomass Action Plan (COM (2005) 628; ENDS Report, 2006). At that point, three main concerns were raised by opponents, initially from within the environmental NGO community, but subsequently from well outside. First of all, concerns were voiced about the risk that rising consumption in Europe would trigger significant unintended effects outside its borders (for a summary, see Palmer, 2014: 341). In late 2007, the Organisation for Economic Co-operation and Development (OECD) published an evidence review which argued that the boom in biofuels would eventually put added pressure on the environment and particularly biodiversity (Doornbosch and Steenblik, 2007: 4). Throughout 2007 and 2008, a range of other respected international bodies including the UN Food and Agriculture Organization, the World Bank and Oxfam added their voices to what soon became a chorus of concern (Palmer, 2014: 337).

To understand this opposition, it is important to recall how different types of biofuel are produced (see Chapter 4). If biofuel feedstocks – essentially agricultural crops in the case of first-generation biofuels – displaced food crops, they could in theory exacerbate food insecurity. When global food prices rose suddenly in 2007–2008, it seemed to confirm that some of these hitherto theoretical fears were being realised, exacerbating concerns that biofuel policies in industrialised countries were putting poorer countries at greater risk of food shortages (Azar, 2011: 310). Since then, it has been accepted that the relationship between food security and biofuel production is far more complicated, varying by crop, biofuel type and the peculiarities of national biofuel markets (IEA, 2011: 16; HLPE, 2013: 13). But in 2007–2008, the sudden spike in global food prices acted to create what Pierson (1993) would recognise as a focusing event. After this event, biofuels began to attract even more critical media coverage, with international development NGOs arguing that cleaner transport fuel for the rich should not be secured by making the poor hungrier (Rietig, 2018: 149). This new framing jarred with the rosy picture that the Commission had been painting since the start of the decade.

Second, doubts about the emission reduction potential of first-generation biofuels began to grow (Sharman and Holmes, 2010: 315). As noted above, the EEB and T&E were the first European NGOs to cast doubt on some of the assumptions embedded in the Commission's original design work. These doubts hinged on some well-known facts: first-generation biofuel production normally consumes energy (cultivation requires fertilisers, etc.) and energy is then required to ship the finished fuels to market (more so when the supply chains are global in scale). Given the immature state of biofuel markets at the time, it was likely that this energy would be derived from fossil fuels. But the indirect emissions associated with biofuel production threatened to extend further still. If the crops grown for biofuels displace food crops, which are then grown on carbon-rich land such as forests, new emissions will be indirectly triggered. Amongst policy designers, these emissions are now known as ILUC emissions. The doubts about the emission reduction potential of first-generation biofuels subsequently attracted scholarly attention. A very well-cited paper published in 2008 in the prestigious journal *Science* gave added credence to claims that, at that time, were still largely hypothetical (Searchinger *et al.*, 2008). On the basis of modelling techniques, its authors suggested that when ILUC emissions were factored in, some of the first-generation biofuels produced in the USA generated *higher* emissions than fossil fuels.[6] Although some of their figures were eventually challenged (Timilsina, 2014: 12),[7] Searchinger *et al.*'s main claim – that some first-generation biofuels generate significant ILUC – was confirmed by a number of subsequent studies (Anderton and Palmer, 2015: 142). Much later (and without directly referring to anyone or any EU institution in particular), the EEA argued that those who were assuming that biomass energy was inherently carbon-neutral risked committing a 'serious accounting error' (EEA, 2011a: 1).

Just weeks before the publication of Searchinger *et al.*'s paper, the Commission published an impact assessment of a proposal for a new directive, in which it conceded that the risk of ILUC emissions was significant enough to merit more detailed research (Anderton and Palmer, 2015: 143). This assumption was subsequently confirmed by a number of Member States who were sufficiently concerned to commission their own studies (e.g. the Netherlands: Dehue *et al.*, 2008: 1). By this point, more forceful critics had concluded that all new policy development should be halted until cleaner biofuel production technologies were available, governed by strict sustainability standards (Environmental Audit Committee, 2008: 3). In effect, their critique implied that there should be no further increase in the consumption of first-generation biofuels, at the very point that EU production was finally beginning to take off, under the influence of policy feedback effects (Agra CEAS Consulting, 2013: 6). The growth in biodiesel production had been particularly pronounced, largely sourced from rapeseed oil and imported palm oil (Flach *et al.*, 2015: 21–23). By the mid-2010s, growth had expanded so much that the EU was widely regarded as a world leader (Flach *et al.*, 2015: 21–22). Many large fossil fuel producers had decided to convert their existing refineries into biodiesel production plants (Biofuels Barometer, 2015: 10). Between 2004 and 2008, the European Biodiesel Board (EBB) reported that EU biodiesel production had risen by 300 per cent, from 1.9 million to 7.7 million tonnes (EBB, 2019). In the same time period, the European Bioethanol Fuel Association (eBIO), formed in 2005, reported a 433 per cent increase in EU bioethanol production from 0.5 million to 2.8 million litres (eBIO, 2009). But the new research findings cast a pall of uncertainty across this fledgling industry.

Third, producers and non-producers were concerned that second- and third-generation biofuel production were not scaling up fast enough to make up the shortfall. In the mid-2000s, they accounted for just 1 per cent of the total fuel consumed in the EU transport sector (Peters *et al.*, 2015). A report commissioned by the European Climate Foundation claimed that the gap was mainly being filled by supplies imported from Brazil and the USA (Timilsina, 2014: 3; Peters *et al.*, 2015: 1). In Europe, some of the obstacles undoubtedly lay on the production side, including regulatory uncertainty and higher production costs relative to fossil fuels and first-generation biofuels (IEA, 2011: 39). However, the confidence of consumers (principally car owners), whose passive acceptance had initially been taken for granted by designers, could no longer be relied upon (Ackrill and Kay, 2014: 208). Throughout the mid-2000s, environment and development NGOs sought to reframe biofuels as a 'dirty' fuel that risked triggering myriad side effects (Ackrill and Kay, 2014: 180). Through their campaigning efforts, rather technical disagreements about how to stimulate and support biofuels began to escape into the wider public sphere.

5.5 A New Policy Design: The Renewable Energy Directive

The Formulation of a New Directive

These concerns were explicitly acknowledged by the Commission in its summary of a public consultation exercise (see above) on the direction of biofuels policy after

2010. The growing salience of the topic was confirmed by the number of organisations that responded (125 in total). The consultation confirmed that many respondents believed that the 2010 target would not be met, and revealed a strong assumption in the industry that the existing policy had to change. However, there were fundamental disagreements over what should be done, by whom and when (Londo *et al.*, 2006). The Commission eventually revealed its thinking in the 2007 progress report (COM (2006) 845). In very broad terms, it maintained that Europe needed biofuels as much as ever, but conceded that a more nuanced policy approach was needed which better incentivised the production of 'good' biofuels, whilst discouraging the production and use of 'bad' ones (Haigh, 2009: 14.11-3). However, this simple-sounding aim proved difficult to implement in practice because the world had changed, in part influenced by policy feedbacks generated by the 2003 Directive: the science of biofuels was better understood and more widely shared; fuel suppliers had adapted their operations and consumers were happily filling up their tanks with blended fuel; producers were finally reaping significant rewards from first-generation biofuels; and some investors had taken a risk and invested in the second- and third- generation alternatives. Moreover, because of domestic feedstock constraints, European producers and suppliers had factored the continuing availability of imported feedstocks into their business models, in doing so facilitating the rise of a global market in production and consumption, spanning a variety of sectors and users across many regions of the world. The EEA's Scientific Committee warned that the new 10 per cent target represented an 'overambitious [...] experiment whose unintended effects are difficult to predict and difficult to control' (EEA, 2008: 6). In reality, the policy experiment had been underway since before 2003.

The design work on the 2009 Directive was undertaken to fit in with the Commission's plans to overhaul the entire sweep of EU renewable energy policies. In turn, these were wrapped up into a larger package of climate and energy policy proposals to form what came to be known as the 2020 Climate and Energy Package (see Chapter 3 for more details). This policy programme demanded a much higher level of coordination between the various Commission DGs than had hitherto been achieved. The Heads of State were keen to adopt the whole package in one fell swoop to exert global leadership ahead of the December 2009 Copenhagen international summit. But they only managed to strike a deal on it in December 2008 after an unprecedented decision had been taken by the French Presidency to utilise a streamlined decision-making procedure (for further details, see Chapter 3). Two elements of the package addressed emissions trading (see Chapter 6) and renewable energy, although it also contained a new regulation governing car emissions (see Chapter 7). The 2009 Renewable Energy Directive was subsequently adopted on 23 April 2009, 457 days after the Commission tabled its proposal – even less time than it had taken to adopt the 2003 Directive.

The 2009 Renewable Energy Directive

Not surprisingly, the sub-element of the 2009 Renewable Energy Directive that related to biofuels proved to be one of the most difficult parts to agree (Howes, 2010: 124) given that it implied a 'massive scaling up in the demand for liquid biofuels' (Haigh, 2009: 14.11-4). It included a number of new features, the design of which had been strongly informed by lessons learned from the implementation of the 2003 Directive (Anderton and Palmer, 2015: 145). The stand-out design feature was of course the mandatory 10 per cent renewable energy target for transport, which was less prescriptive than the 10 per cent biofuels target that had originally been suggested (Egelund Olsen and Ronne, 2016: 165). The Commission's mid-term review had concluded that the *durability devices* in the 2003 Directive (i.e. the indicative targets) had not triggered significant positive policy feedback effects, despite some growth in EU production and consumption (Howes, 2010: 124). Other features included:

- A new provision (incorporated in Article 21.2) that allowed *second- and third-generation biofuels to count double towards the 10 per cent target*. This provision aimed to give producers added confidence to invest in the second- and third generation alternatives (Ackrill and Kay, 2014: 65), but it was the only specific policy support they received.
- A more rigorous and detailed *system of reporting* set out in Article 22. Member States were obliged to report every two years based on a template (a type of *durability device*), on many more issues including the production of advanced biofuels, biodiversity impacts and net greenhouse gas emission savings. The hope was that better reporting would convince critics and potential investors that EU policy was now heading in a more predictable direction – 'a core goal of the Directive and [...] a core element in policy stability to encourage investment' (Howes, 2010: 144). In addition, the Commission was required to produce a special report on ILUC by the end of 2010 (Article 23; see Anderton and Palmer, 2015: 145).
- A new set of *sustainability criteria* (Article 17) which all biofuels had to meet to be counted against the EU's renewable energy targets. Significantly, the criteria, which were a formal acknowledgment of the need to address direct and indirect land use changes (Afionis and Stringer, 2012: 116), applied both to indigenous *and* imported supplies (Woerdman *et al.*, 2015: 142). Biofuels that complied with the criteria, which were enunciated in Articles 17–19, could be counted against the 10 per cent target and become eligible for financial support (chiefly subsidies) at the national level (Scott, 2011: 829). The criteria addressed two main elements: greenhouse gas emissions (life cycle emissions should be at least 35 per cent less than fossil fuels)[8] and direct land use change[9] (cultivation of the

feedstocks should not cause direct changes to land with a high biodiversity value, i.e. primary forest, grasslands, wetlands etc.; see Woerdman *et al.*, 2015: 143). To further complicate matters, the application of the criteria varied by biofuel type.[10]

- A *system for certifying the sale and use of different types of biofuel*. This was the means by which economic producers and Member States would verify that the sustainability criteria were being complied with (Woerdman *et al.*, 2015: 143). The Directive provided for three main types of certification: bilateral agreements between Member States; national schemes within individual Member States; and voluntary schemes run by private actors but recognised by the European Commission. Of the three, voluntary schemes quickly proved to be the most popular. By the end of 2014, the Commission had recognised 19 such schemes (COM (2015) 293: 15).

It soon became clear that a significant price had been paid to secure agreement on the new Directive: its design was significantly more complex than that of the 2003 Directive.[11] Giljam (2016: 101), for example, notes how it sought to operate across many different dimensions simultaneously: various fuel types; along and between production chains (from the production of feedstocks to the labelling of biofuels on petrol station forecourts); across space (because the scope of the sustainability criteria were in part extra-territorial); and across time (stimulating a shift from first- to second-generation alternatives). These new dimensions of complexity were directly affected by the critiques of EU policy after 2003.

The Adoption of the 2009 Directive

That so much new policy was negotiated so quickly in the face of such strong criticism (particularly of the first-generation biofuels) has puzzled scholars of policy formulation. The adoption of a more stringent policy instrument-level *durability device* (the mandatory 10 per cent target) is particularly perplexing. Although the Commission was deeply split on the matter (Rietig, 2018),[12] the official drafting the proposal was sufficiently determined and well-connected to craft a proposal that convinced the other DGs to sign up to the headline 10 per cent target (Sharman and Holmes, 2010: 316). Another thing that facilitated agreement was the fact that Heads of State had already given their *de facto* blessing to the new target in March 2007, i.e. well before the publication of Searchinger's analysis, the spike in world food prices and the emergence of the cross-sectoral anti-biofuels coalition (Sharman and Holmes, 2010: 313; Rietig, 2018: 148). Crucially, they pledged to support the 10 per cent target 'before any discussion [...] about how it might be achieved' in practice (Ackrill and Kay, 2014: 62), and, crucially, before the publication (in 2008) of the detailed impact assessment that the Commission appends to all policy proposals. The European Council's determination to push ahead before the scientific evidence had been fully prepared and openly debated has been criticised as a striking example of 'policy-based evidence making' (Sharman and Holmes, 2010: 313). What it did was shift the focus of the policy design debate from ends to means; specifically, to the design of different combinations of *flexibility* and *durability devices* at the policy instrument level.

What appears to have pushed the proposal over the line was the sudden appearance of a supportive coalition within the Council. At the time, Member States were being heavily lobbied by biofuel producers (particularly of first-generation biodiesel) to provide greater policy support to the investments that they had made in the first-generation biofuels, and which they said were needed to fund investments in the second-generation alternatives (e.g. European Biodiesel Board, 2006; see Sharman and Holmes, 2010: 314). Member States with large agricultural production capacities were especially receptive to this line of argument, keen as they were to find new uses for land set aside as part of ongoing Common Agricultural Policy reforms[13] (Skogstad, 2017: fn. 3). More sceptical Member States (such as Denmark) and greener MEPs were gradually persuaded to align with what eventually became the winning coalition by the offer of sustainability criteria (Skogstad, 2017: 32), and a promise to draft more detailed proposals on the handling of indirect land use changes after the Directive had been formally adopted.

In some respects, the new Directive was a classic package deal. In other respects, it also owed its adoption to the unexpected opening of a window of opportunity in 2008–2009. Recall that this was a period during which the Commission President and the Heads of State were competing with one another to brand the EU as an international climate leader. The Council Presidency at the time was held by France. Its Prime Minister (Sarkozy) was in no mood to delay agreement and pushed hard for the entire package to be adopted in one fell swoop.

5.6 Policy Instrument Implementation and Redesign

Items of Unfinished Business

At the start of 2009, there were several items of business that still had to be addressed in order to strike a more politically sustainable balance between the policy's durability and its flexibility. The first and most urgent item was that of ILUC, which as noted above had been deliberately postponed during the negotiation process (Giljam, 2016: 102). However, public consultation exercises conducted by the Commission in 2009 and 2010 revealed very little agreement on what to do next (COM (2010) 811: 13). In a special report (COM (2010) 811), published in December 2010, the Commission conceded that without further policy intervention, ILUC emissions risked undermining investor confidence in *all* biofuels. In the same report, it noted that biofuels were projected to account for 9 per cent of transport fuels in 2020, making them by far the most important contributor to the mandatory 10 per cent target (COM (2010) 811: fn. 1). It promised to come forward with new legislative proposals by July 2011. A year later, the EEA (2011a) concluded that policies which generate ILUC 'may even result in increased carbon emissions' and called for all EU bioenergy policies to be comprehensively revised.

The second item was the functioning of the sustainability criteria. The immediate challenge was how to ensure that the various certification systems were fully up and running. Producers and environmental NGOs would only trust them if they were transparent, robust and, above all, fair. For the Commission, this meant creating a system that was both transparent and enforceable, and not only for EU-based biofuel supplies whose provenance could be verified relatively easily, but also stocks imported from other parts of the world (Scott, 2011: 831). Alternatively – and perhaps a little more straightforwardly – it could finesse these challenges by giving an even stronger push to the second- and third-generation alternatives than the 'double counting' rule implied. The problem was that producers said that they would only invest in such unproven alternatives if EU policy supported their investments in the first- and second-generation types. If this resembled a chicken and egg situation, then the producers argued that the Commission should move first.

Third, the 2009 Directive required a means to cope with changes in the (by then) rapidly developing science of biofuels whilst simultaneously offering support to investors. The discussions were heavily influenced by the failure of the 2003 Directive to respond to (i.e. have the internal flexibility to cope with) previous changes in scientific understanding. The Commission's first progress report on the new Directive was published in March 2013 (COM (2013) 175), and revealed that biofuels only accounted for 4.7 per cent of transport biofuels used in the EU (Flach *et al.*, 2015: 4). Its second progress report, published two years later in June 2015, predicted that use would climb to around 5.7 per cent in 2014 (COM (2015) 293: 14). The Commission blamed the limited growth rate on regulatory uncertainty and corresponding delays in the commercialisation of advanced fuels. But, in practice, a number of exogenous factors had also been at work. Falling world oil prices in the mid-2010s had made the second- and third-generation alternatives even less price-competitive than they would otherwise have been (Royal Academy of Engineering, 2017: 20). Meanwhile, declining sales of new vehicles in the wake of the global financial crisis had greatly reduced the demand for all types of road fuel (see also Chapter 7), including biofuel. Globally, production stagnated after 2010 (Timilsina, 2014: 15). After growing rapidly throughout the 2000s, biofuel consumption in the EU transport sector remained more or less static through the 2010s (Biofuels Barometer, 2017: 8). Therefore, in the early 2010s, all European biofuel producers found themselves confronting a perfect storm of declining revenues from the sale of first-generation biofuel and mounting policy pressure to invest in the alternatives, many of which were still stuck at the R&D stage.

5.7 Making Biofuels More Sustainable? A New Directive
Policy Formulation Begins

The Commission's hopes that it would achieve a swift revision of the biofuel-related elements of the RED by July 2011 were soon dashed. Yet again, its DGs struggled even to arrive at a common internal position, greatly delaying the publication of a new legislative proposal (Simkins, 2012). Almost two years after it had first consulted stakeholders, a draft was leaked to the press which created an uproar. It revealed that the Commission was actively considering tackling ILUC by capping the contribution of transport fuel from first-generation biofuel sources at no more than 5 per cent by 2020. In effect, this implied that only half of the existing (and widely discussed) 10 per cent target would be met from first-generation sources; the remaining 5 per cent would have to come from advanced sources or other types of renewable energy.[14] Given that consumption of first-generation biofuels was by that point fast approaching 5 per cent (see above), the leaked information implied that the new policy would not allow any additional growth in the first-generation types; all future growth would have to be met from other sources.

The details in the leaked proposal reflected the fact that the Commission was trapped in a 'policy lock-in' (Rietig, 2018: 156), partly of its own making: it did not want to close down first-generation production facilities in case the 5 per cent cap was not achieved, but it wanted to give a clear policy signal of support to producers who had invested in the second- and third-generation alternatives. Either way, the leak appeared to mark a significant U-turn in the Commission's thinking. Only five years before, it had steadfastly maintained that the 10 per cent target would be achieved with 'only limited reliance' on second- and third-generation alternatives (COM (2006) 845: 13). Its 2011 renewable energy progress report had subsequently stated that 'first-generation biofuels will be the predominant energy source over the period to 2020' (COM (2011) 31: 6).

The EBB's reaction to the leak was one of barely disguised fury, claiming that the proposals, if real, would 'definitely cause the immediate death of the whole EU biodiesel industrial sector' (ENDS Report, 2012b). Even independent academic commentators argued that it would 'shackle [...] the industry's growth possibilities' (Biofuels Barometer, 2015: 6). Jean Philippe Pui, the CEO of the French oil seed producer Sofiproteol, went further still, maintaining that it 'threaten[ed] an industry that arose as a response to [the EU's] policies and has invested massively in the next generation of biofuel technologies' (Keating, 2012e).

The Publication of a Formal Proposal

In October 2012, the Commission finally issued its proposal to amend the 2009 Directive[15] (COM (2012) 595), drawing to a close months of speculation, intense lobbying and very bitter argument. The Directorate-General for Climate Action (DG CLIMA) reportedly demanded rules that clearly differentiated between fuels based on their ILUC effects, but DG Energy felt there was insufficient scientific evidence to do this properly (Keating, 2012d). The Commission ruled out the idea of entirely excluding biofuels with very high ILUC effects from contributing to the biofuels target on the grounds that it could exclude biodiesel from vegetable oil, 'which [in 2012] represent[ed] the vast majority of the market' (Anderton and Palmer, 2015: 145). A joint statement by the biofuel producers and feedstock industries under the umbrella of a new cross-sectoral organisation, the 'EU Biofuels Supply Chain', argued that the ILUC proposal would have a 'devastating impact on the biofuels industries and diversification of farmers' revenues' and was 'based on unfounded and immature ILUC science' (COCERAL *et al.*, 2012: 1). Meanwhile, environmental groups claimed that the 5 per cent cap with a selection of fuel-specific ILUC controls was at best a very 'messy compromise' and at worse totally misguided (Keating, 2012d). In an editorial, *European Voice* accused the Commission of being 'intent on [...] creating a subsidy-dependent energy industry with the twin aim of propping up the farm vote and creating an illusion of energy security' (European Voice, 2012).

Eventually it became clear that the Commission was not the only EU institution riven by internal splits. In the Council, Member States such as the United Kingdom and Denmark demanded much tougher ILUC standards, whereas countries that depended more heavily on agriculture (including France, Poland and Hungary) felt the proposal was too stringent (Flynn, 2013b). Meanwhile, the European Parliament agreed to raise the cap on first-generation biofuel production from 5 per cent to 6 per cent to reflect the lobbying efforts of some producers, but was unable to agree on a clear negotiating mandate to guide its nominated rapporteur with the Council, Corinne LePage (Keating, 2013c). With time running out to complete the amendment before the Parliament ended its term in April 2014, the main environment and human development groups in Brussels launched a concerted 'Stop Bad

Biofuels' campaign to 'fix this broken policy once and for all' (Action Aid *et al.*, 2013: 3). When, in December 2013, a compromise brokered by the Lithuanian Presidency failed to secure agreement on an even higher cap (of 7 per cent, not 5 per cent), the Commission admitted defeat and shelved its proposal, which effectively brought the whole redesign process to a halt. The Lithuanian Energy Minister who chaired the key meetings claimed that a compromise deal had been scuppered by an 'exotic coalition' of Member States including Denmark and the Netherlands that wanted first-generation fuels to be much more heavily restricted and another (including Hungary and Poland) that essentially wanted to preserve the policy *status quo* (Keating, 2013g).

A few weeks later in January 2014, the Commission attempted to start afresh by issuing a Communication setting out a new vision for climate and energy policies (COM (2014) 15). Although biofuels policy was only briefly mentioned, what it included sent 'shockwaves' through the entire biofuels sector (Keating, 2014b). First of all, it confirmed that first-generation biofuels would no longer receive policy support after 2020, implying that the transport sector should either transition rapidly towards advanced biofuels or enact more fundamental changes, such as towards wholesale electrification (Flach *et al.*, 2015: 7; see also Chapter 7). Second, the transport sector would definitively lose the special status it had enjoyed in the early years of EU biofuels policy – henceforth, there would be no sector-specific biofuel targets after 2020 (see Chapter 3). Third, the EU intended to develop a broader and more strategic approach to the use of biomass across all sectors.

The Commission's intervention was a calculated attempt to reset the terms of the debate at EU level (Institute for European Environmental Policy, 2014: 5). Environmentalists were pleased that the Commission seemed at long last to be taking on board its warnings about ILUC. The various biofuel producers were, on the other hand, suddenly able to unite around a common condemnation of the policy's direction. In February 2014, a new coalition of biofuel producers wrote to energy ministers asking for the transport sector to retain its special status, with new sector-specific targets running until 2030. It claimed that the use of biofuels had grown to 4.8 per cent and that the EU's 'binding targets were key to providing the necessary guidance and predictability that encouraged investment in the sector' (Keating, 2014c). They argued that the abrupt shift in the Commission's position had 'badly shaken' confidence in the sector.

However, Ministers pressed on. In June 2014, the Council agreed to cap the contribution of first-generation biofuels at 7 per cent by 2020, thus providing some additional headroom through to 2020. But a significant number of Member States opted to align with the Commission's new position: they were either deeply worried about ILUC and/or did not produce significant quantities of biofuel.

On more detailed technical matters, however, disagreement quickly re-surfaced between the various producers. For example, Member States with large forestry sectors – principally Sweden and Finland – were keen to classify tall oil, a by-product of the wood pulping process, as a second-generation biofuel (Flynn, 2015b). ePure, the association representing bioethanol producers, wanted fuel-specific restrictions on first-generation biofuels to enable its members to continue to produce and market ethanol. Unsurprisingly, the EBB sought to ensure that biodiesel's dominant market position remained unaffected (Williams, 2014).

The Adoption of the Indirect Land Use Change Directive

In October 2014, the Council acknowledged that although better scientific understanding of the impacts of biofuels had cast doubt on their environmental effectiveness, it was not firm enough to inform the setting of fuel-specific ILUC factors. Instead, it opted to raise the generic cap on all first-generation fuels to 7 per cent whilst signalling that there would be no new targets after 2020 (Delbeke and Vis, 2015: 71). Meanwhile, the Parliament was even more deeply divided than the Council, both of whom were being heavily lobbied by the various competing industry associations. Given that talks had, by that point, reached the second reading stage, MEPs nonetheless opted to strike an agreement with the Council rather than risk the Council's position being automatically adopted. In turn, this allowed the ILUC Directive (EU/2015/1513) to be formally adopted by the Parliament and the Council on 9 September 2015, no less than 1,058 days after the Commission had published its initial proposal and over five years after it had published its initial report on ILUC. This was the slowest adoption process amongst all the instrument changes summarised in this book.

The ILUC Directive incorporated the 7 per cent cap (by 2020) which the Council had insisted upon but followed the Commission's recommendation that no new long-term targets should be set after 2020. As a further compromise, Member States were allowed to set lower caps in a number of clearly specified circumstances. The 'double counting' provision relating to advanced biofuels was also carried over from the 2009 Directive and a new policy instrument-level *durability device* adopted (an indicative target – akin to the ones contained in the 2003 Directive) which required Member States to 'endeavour to achieve' 0.5 per cent of consumption as advanced biofuel (OJ L239, 15.9.2015: 15). This meant that Member States could effectively set lower or no standards at the national level after April 2017 if they wished to,[16] subject of course to certain considerations (OJ L239, 15.9.2015: 15). During the negotiations, the Parliament's rapporteur, Nils Torvals, pushed for a binding and considerably stricter level of 2.5 per cent (Flynn, 2015a), but this failed to secure sufficient support. The ILUC Directive also built on the same pattern as the 2009 Directive and placed even more detailed reporting obligations on a growing cast of actors including suppliers, verifiers and Member States. This new information would be collated, reviewed and published by the European Commission.

5.8 Biofuels Policy After 2020: The RED II Directive
The Formulation of a New Directive

In late 2015 – around the time of the Paris climate summit – policy designers were still wrestling with precisely the same meta-issue that had vexed the Commission over twenty years before – how to trigger a durable, long-term deep decarbonisation transition in the transport sector. As far as biofuels were concerned, this was now thought to require a significant shift to the second and third generations of biofuels. In 2002–2003, there had been a widespread belief that first-generation biofuels would produce most of the required emission reductions. In its 2015 progress report, the Commission estimated that the share of the transport fuel market accounted for by biofuels had risen to 5.7 per cent in 2014 (COM (2015) 293: 3), of which 23 per cent were sourced from second-generation biofuel (up from just 1 per cent in 2009). As a result, the EU was finally on the way to becoming more self-sufficient – another one of the original rationales for EU-level action. Around 75 per cent of all the biofuels consumed in 2013 were produced within the EU (COM (2015) 293: 15).

In its 2015 Energy Union strategy, the Commission promised to come forward with a new bioenergy policy encompassing renewables and biofuels (COM (2015) 80). One of its primary motivations was to align all existing policy programme and policy instrument-level *durability devices* with the new 'by 2030' timeframe that the EU had adopted in advance of the Paris Agreement. Thus, in October 2014, the European Council announced a new combination of policy programme-level *durability* and *flexibility devices*, including an objective to achieve a 40 per cent reduction in greenhouse gas emissions by a new time-specific deadline: 2030 (European Council, 2014). The existing energy and renewable energy targets would also be amended to fit the new 'by 2030' timespan.[17] In February 2016, the Commission initiated a stakeholder survey on the main policy design options. The environmental NGOs firmly argued that the sustainability criteria in the ILUC Directive should be extended to *all* forms of bioenergy, a popular form of renewable energy (particularly in Eastern Europe). According to Sini Eräjää of the EEB, the EU 'must avoid repeating the mistakes made with first-generation biofuels' (Ala-Kurikka, 2015c, 2015d). In November 2016, the Commission published proposals to revise the Renewable Energy Directive to achieve the new

27 per cent target by 2030 under the heading of *Clean Energy For All Europeans* (COM (2016) 767). In the transport sector, a new proposal for what eventually came to be known as the RED II Directive included measures to cap the share of first-generation of biofuels at just 3.8 per cent in 2030, automatically decreasing via a series of steps from 7 per cent in 2021 (the target that had been originally introduced in the ILUC Directive). Furthermore, there would be a new mandatory target for the advanced biofuels: a minimum share of at least 3.6 per cent by 2030. The sustainability criteria from the ILUC Directive would also be extended – in a refined form – to all forms of biomass and biogas used for heat and power.

The Adoption of the RED II Directive

The immediate reactions were sufficiently critical to suggest that it would take time to hammer out a compromise. Significantly, they generally followed the same pattern as those to the Commission's proposal to amend the 2009 Directive. Thus ePURE welcomed the offer of further support after 2020 (which was rather at odds with what the European Council had indicated in 2014), but warned that the Commission was 'totally detached from reality if it expects that its proposal will result in significant investments in advanced biofuels, given that most of the potential investors have already been burned by the Commission's previous biofuels u-turns' (Ala-Kurikka, 2016a). Meanwhile, the environment and development groups, who by that point had organised themselves into an even more formal cross-sectoral coalition, tried to persuade the EU to abandon all biofuel targets after 2020 and end all national subsides of first-generation biofuel production (Birdlife International *et al.*, 2016). The industry committee of the European Parliament agreed that first-generation biofuels should be phased out by 2030 and recommended raising the overarching policy programme-level target for renewable energy from 27 per cent to 35 per cent by 2030 (Hodgson, 2017a).

The Member States eventually adopted a common position on the proposals in December 2017. Although they sided with the Commission's proposal to increase the renewable energy target to 27 per cent, they opted to maintain the existing 7 per cent cap on the use of first-generation biofuels 'to provide certainty to investors' (Hodgson, 2017d) and increase the target for all transport fuels from 10 per cent to 14 per cent. A deal on RED II (Directive 2018/2001) was finally concluded between the Parliament and Council in June 2018. It contained an overarching 32 per cent renewable energy target – significantly more stringent than the 27 per cent originally proposed by the Commission – with a *flexibility clause* that was primed to operate in 2023. The transport sub-sector target was increased from 10 per cent to 14 per cent, but the contribution of first-generation biofuels was capped at 1 per cent above 2020 levels in each Member State and set to gradually

Table 5.1 *Biofuels: significant policy instrument changes, 2003–2019*

Legislation (and speed of adoption)	Lifespan (days)[1]	Description
2003 Biofuels Directive (2003/30) (548 days)	3,151	• *Stringency*: indicative target. Biofuels to account for 2% (by the end of 2005) and 5.75% (by the end of 2010, set at a national level). • *Scope*: the 'use of biofuels or other renewable fuels for transport' in Europe. • *Timeframe*: to (2005 and) 2010.
2009 Renewable Energy Directive (2009/28) (457 days)	4,389	• *Stringency*: increased. Mandatory target that 10% of transport fuels to come from renewable sources in each member state; new inducements to produce advanced biofuels. • *Scope*: increased. Expanded to include sustainability of imported supplies as well as the use of indigenous biofuels, primary focus still on the use of fuels in transport. • *Timeframe:* increased. Extended to 2020.
2015 ILUC Directive (2015/1513) (1,058 days)	2,096	• *Stringency*: increased. Mandatory 10% of transport fuels to come from renewable sources in each member state, of which no more than 7% to be conventional biofuel; new indicative target to produce advanced biofuels. • *Scope*: stable. Still to include the sustainability of imported supplies as well as the use of indigenous biofuels. Primary focus still on the use of fuels in transport • *Timeframe:* stable. Remains at 2020.
2018 Renewable Energy Directive II (2018/2001) (742 days)	4,572	• *Stringency*: increased. 14% target for renewable energy in transport in each Member State by 2030. No more than 2020 level + 1% of transport fuels from conventional sources; new mandatory target that at least 3.5% of fuels should be advanced biofuels by 2030. • *Scope*: stable. • Still to include the sustainability of imported supplies as well as the use of indigenous biofuels. Primary focus still on the use of fuels in transport • *Timeframe:* increased. Extended to 2030.

[1] Expected at the time of writing (1 June 2019).
Source: own composition.

decline to zero by 2030. Finally, a new policy instrument-level *durability device* (namely a mandatory target) for advanced types of biofuel was adopted, equating to a minimum share of at least 3.5 per cent in each Member State by 2030. The text of the new directive was adopted on 11 December 2018, 742 days after the release of the Commission's proposal.

Chapter 4 briefly outlined the long sequence of policy instrument changes starting with the Biofuels Directive in 2003 and ending with the 2018 RED II Directive which, as noted above, will extend the timeframe of EU biofuel policy design out to 2030. Table 5.1 summarises each step in the sequence in considerably more detail, noting the most significant changes in policy stringency, scope and timeframe, and indicating the speed at which each change was agreed and its lifespan.

Endnotes

1 Initially by quite literally blending first-generation biofuels with conventional, fossil fuel-based transport fuel.
2 But aside from these two, most environmental NGOs were relatively silent. Some, including Friends of the Earth in the United Kingdom, briefly supported increasing biofuel production (Thompson *et al.*, 2004; Low Carbon Vehicle Partnership, 2005).
3 By contrast, the 2010 targets set by Member States were generally in line with the EU's reference value of 5.75 per cent.
4 In 2005, the share of transport fuels accounted for by biofuel was still effectively zero in nine Member States: Belgium, Cyprus, Estonia, the Czech Republic, Hungary, Ireland, Luxembourg, the Netherlands and Portugal (COM (2006) 845: 15).
5 According to two senior policy designers in the Commission, the 10 per cent target is the same for all countries because fuels are easily traded between states (Delbeke and Vis, 2015: 70).
6 In fact, the additional emissions could take up to 167 years to be reclaimed through the substitution of fossil fuels in the road transport sector (Anderton and Palmer, 2015: 141).
7 The science around ILUC emissions continues to be bedevilled by uncertainty (Giljam, 2016: 102).
8 From 2018, this value rose to 50 per cent. Installations commencing operation after 5 October 2015 must achieve emission savings of at least 60 per cent.
9 The decision was taken to defer the governance of ILUC to the Commission's comitology procedure (Haigh, 2009: 14.11-6).
10 All the criteria applied to first-generation biofuels; only the emissions-reduction criterion applied to the second-generation alternatives.
11 Recall that the opening recitals of the 2003 Directive were longer than the substantive provisions.
12 DG Energy was determined to adopt a more stringent policy than DG Environment (Skogstad, 2017: 32–33).
13 For example, land that could be used to grow subsidised biofuel feedstocks such as sugar beet.
14 There are essentially two main strategies for addressing ILUC: alter the feedstock (e.g. use waste products as feedstocks, thus producing second-generation biofuel); increase the intensity of production (Cowie *et al.*, 2016: 13–16).
15 And also the 1998 Fuel Quality Directive.
16 In effect, only 2.5 years before the compliance deadline of 31 December 2020.
17 Notably, to account for 27 per cent of total energy consumption by 2030 (see Chapter 3 for details).

6

Emissions Trading

The Governance of Large Stationary Emitters

6.1 Introduction

The concept of emissions trading has been actively debated by economists since the 1960s (Dales, 1968; Voss, 2007). In the 1990s, it began to attract the attention of large businesses in the EU, who were eager to investigate whether it offered a politically more palatable alternative to the Commission's default policy instrument – regulation. By the late 1990s – and buoyed by growing industry support – a small number of Member States began to adopt their own greenhouse gas trading schemes at the national level to bolster their existing policy instrument mixes which, at the time, were also heavily reliant on regulation and, in some cases, voluntary agreements (Wurzel *et al.*, 2013). The early 2000s were a period of intense activity for EU climate and energy policy, much of it directed at implementing the EU's increasingly ambitious long-term emission reduction goals (see Chapter 3). Internationally, emissions trading had been included in the recently ratified Kyoto Protocol. With other policy instrument options such as an EU carbon/energy tax seemingly unavailable, the Commission seized the opportunity to create an EU-wide trading system.

Adopted in 2003, the Emissions Trading Directive set up the EU Emissions Trading System (ETS). It was one of the EU's rare forays into market-based instruments and at first blush appeared to mark a significant break with its regulatory past (Wurzel *et al.*, 2013). After the ETS had been adopted, there was a lot riding on its success. It targeted some of Europe's largest point sources of emissions, which together accounted for approximately 45 per cent of the EU's greenhouse gas emissions (EEA, 2015b: 6). From a political and a bureaucratic perspective, the Commission's environment department (DG Environment) had invested significant resources in ensuring the system's adoption and was anxious to see it succeed. From the outset, it described trading as 'an important cornerstone' of the EU's entire climate policy (European Commission, 2001d; Wettestad, 2005: 1).

If emission trading failed, the Commission feared it would undermine EU climate policy and put a large dent in the EU's wider diplomatic ambitions.

The remainder of this chapter recounts how the 2003 Directive was originally conceived within the Commission, how it was subsequently designed in close discussion with other actors and describes the policy feedback effects it generated after 2003. It then summarises the positive and negative feedback which shaped the design of the 2009 Directive, and then traces how the changes that it subsequently introduced affected the design of the Market Stability Reserve in 2015 and another new Directive in 2018.

6.2 The Policy Instrument Design Process

The Formulation of the 2003 Directive

The 2003 Directive emerged rather suddenly from an unexpected confluence of exogenous and endogenous factors. The first exogenous factor was related to developments in the international climate regime. At the insistence of the US government, which had used emissions trading to address acid rain in the 1990s, the Kyoto Protocol opened the door to the use of trading between countries as a 'flexibility mechanism' (Skjærseth and Wettestad, 2008: 35; Braun, 2009: 470). At the time, many in the EU were suspicious of the US government's motives (see e.g. Ellerman *et al.*, 2010), but were willing to accede because the Protocol did not explicitly require every party to adopt trading (Skjærseth and Wettestad, 2009: 107).

The second exogenous factor was the growing interest in emissions trading within the oil and gas industry, which saw it as a way of forestalling the adoption of more intrusive instruments, particularly regulation. Major oil producers such as Shell and BP emerged as a 'key driver' of technical debates about how to trade across borders (Christiansen and Wettestad, 2003: 9; Wettestad, 2005: 10; Meckling, 2011a; Meckling, 2011b: 103–131). Over time, a transnational business coalition emerged, aiming to advance emissions trading globally (Meckling, 2011b: 44–45). Out of this, a dedicated international lobbying organisation – the International Emissions Trading Association (IETA) – was established in 1999 (Meckling, 2011a: 35).

Meanwhile, in the 1990s and early 2000s a number of developments within the EU made some actors more receptive to the idea of emissions trading. The EU had adopted legally binding emissions reduction commitments for the first time when it collectively signed the Kyoto Protocol in 1997. However, by the late 1990s, the Commission was warning that greenhouse gas emissions in the EU were rising (COM (1999) 230: 1), endangering compliance. In the early 1990s, the Council had blocked the Commission's efforts to adopt an EU carbon/energy tax (Jordan *et al.*, 2010: 61). As a matter dealing with taxation, that proposal had required the Council to act on the basis of unanimity and limited the Parliament to a marginal role (Skjærseth, 1994: 30). In political terms, this constituted an important barrier to new policy design. Therefore, the Commission realised that it 'desperately needed to develop another policy instrument' (Braun, 2009: 473). Crucially, because it was not a fiscal measure, emissions trading could be adopted by a qualified majority in the Council (Wettestad, 2005: 8), opening the door for adoption to take place. The Commission's research arm, the Directorate-General for Research (DG Research), began to prepare the ground with a series of studies on market-based instruments (Ellerman *et al.*, 2010: 14). Meanwhile, a small group of staff within DG Environment led by an environmental economist, Jos Delbeke, began to investigate the technical and legal feasibility of trading at EU level (see Delbeke *et al.*, 2006; Ellerman *et al.*, 2010: fn. 9; Dreger, 2014). A number of Member States, including Denmark, Sweden, the Netherlands and the United Kingdom, had already announced that they would develop their own national schemes. As these began to take shape, the EU institutions were pushed to act against what they saw as a threat to climate policy harmonisation (Christiansen and Wettestad, 2003: 7).

In June 1998, the Commission issued a Communication on the Kyoto Protocol (COM (1998) 353) in which it expressed its eagerness to establish an EU-level trading system to start by 2005. It also undertook to publish a Green Paper – a key stage in the policy formulation process – to inform an initial round of public consultations (Wettestad, 2005: 3; van Asselt, 2010: 127). As explained in Chapter 4, an important and early design decision was taken at this point to only target 'large emitters or a single economic sector' rather than emissions from myriad non-point sources such as cars or flights (COM (1999) 230: 16; see Wettestad, 2005: 3). In January 1999, DG Environment commissioned reports from two think tanks, the Center for Clean Air Policy (1999) and the Foundation for International Environmental Law and Development (2000), to prepare the ground for a formal legislative proposal (Skjærseth and Wettestad, 2008: 79).

In March 2001, another exogenous event – the US Government's withdrawal from the Protocol – created a further window of opportunity for the Commission to convince the other EU institutions of the need for this particular approach to emissions trading (Skjærseth and Wettestad, 2008: 155). This window of opportunity allowed policy formulators within the EU to connect a number of factors together in a way that facilitated rapid internal policy development (Skjærseth and Wettestad, 2009: 112). It also handed the EU a golden opportunity to seize climate leadership from the US, particularly regarding emissions trading (Meckling, 2011b: 37). Thus, it is slightly erroneous to suggest that trading was transferred from the USA to the EU (cf. Damro and Méndez, 2003: 74). The general concept of emissions trading was undoubtedly transferred, but the Commission still had to invest significant effort to win around those who doubted that a trading system would be sufficiently stringent to drive down emissions or could be made to work at a supranational level (Wurzel *et al.*, 2013). Chief amongst these were the environmental NGOs. The main alliance of NGOs working on climate issues in Brussels responded to the Green Paper by arguing that while emissions trading was 'a useful potential part' of EU climate policy, it was 'not the most important' (Climate Network Europe, 2000: 1). However, it accepted that trading could in principle reduce emissions, but only if it had clear targets, strict rules and was framed by suitably ambitious goals. In other words, it needed to be embedded in a much broader policy programme – which of course at the time the EU manifestly did not have.

After 1998, policy formulation activities accelerated rapidly. The Commission seized the initiative, building up its own technical expertise and using it to cultivate support amongst various potential veto players (Skjærseth and Wettestad, 2009: 110). Throughout, DG Environment was a key policy entrepreneur (Skjærseth and Wettestad, 2008: 189) – it was 'always [...] a step ahead' of other actors 'as regards knowledge' (Braun, 2009: 484). Its expertise – coupled with the need to implement the Kyoto Protocol – allowed DG Environment to sell the idea to more sceptical DGs in the Commission and to the other EU institutions. Second, the Council was in principle supportive of designing stronger EU policies, having agreed (prior to Kyoto) to adopt a new, EU-wide emissions reduction target (see Chapter 3). But on more detailed matters, several Member States harboured serious misgivings about emissions trading. In the end, however, there was a sufficient number of advocates within the Council to support the Commission's work (Skjærseth and Wettestad, 2009: 109).

Some potentially powerful target groups in industry were either supportive or able quickly to exempt themselves. Eurelectric (the European association representing electricity generators) was broadly supportive of cap-and-trade (Eurelectric, 2000). This was despite initial opposition from some of its members, including Germany's electricity association (VDEW, 2000). Eurelectric worked with the Commission to conduct economic modelling exercises that suggested that its members would largely be able to pass most additional compliance costs through to customers by raising electricity prices (Braun, 2009: 482; Skjærseth and Wettestad, 2010a: 111). Meanwhile, behind the scenes the European chemical and aluminium industries successfully manoeuvred themselves out of participation in the initial start-up phase (Christiansen and Wettestad, 2003: 9; Meckling, 2011b: 38).

By contrast, the energy-intensive industries such as steel, cement and oil refineries, which stood to be hit hard by any costs imposed by the ETS, initially held diverging positions across their numerous sector-specific interest associations (see Skjærseth and Wettestad, 2008: 84). For example, differences were especially pronounced in relation to the choice between free allocation and auctioning. This choice mattered because these industries were less able to pass through the additional cost of purchasing allowances to their customers because they were more exposed to global competitiveness pressures (see e.g. Demailly and Quirion, 2006). Be that as it may, in their responses to the Green Paper (see later in this section), the lime industry did not mention the allocation method at all, the steel industry could not achieve a common position on the matter, the paper industry called for free allocation, and the ceramics industry supported full auctioning (European Ceramic Industry Association, 2000: 1; Confederation of European Paper Industries, 2000; European Lime Association, 2000; European Confederation of Iron and Steel Industries, 2000: 1). In short, they were deeply divided on what eventually proved to be a highly consequential design matter because, unlike the electricity generators, they generally assumed that the proposal would suffer the same fate as the long-abandoned carbon/energy tax. This proved to be a 'strategic miscalculation' (Meckling, 2011b: 38) given that electricity generators were, by then, largely voicing their support for the proposal (Skjærseth and Wettestad, 2010a: 111) and it could not be blocked by a single Member State in the Council.

In March 2000, the Commission published a Green Paper to 'launch a discussion' on emissions trading, where it outlined the most significant design options, encompassing the scope of the proposed directive, the allocation of allowances and the degree of coercion (COM (2000) 87: 4). Although it was not made fully explicit in the Green Paper, DG Environment preferred a mandatory system, a narrow scope and the auctioning of allowances at EU level (European Commission, 2000: 2; Skjærseth and Wettestad, 2010b: 113; Boasson and Wettestad, 2013: 64; Dreger, 2014: 36–37, 53; COM (2000) 87: 18). The consultation eventually generated 700 pages of comments from 88 non-governmental respondents and 17 governmental actors, including 9 Member States (see European Commission, 2001b, 2001c). Although the Member States that submitted views 'disagreed on most aspects related to the design and harmonisation of' the system (Skjærseth and Wettestad, 2009: 111), the broad idea of emissions trading was nonetheless 'met with general approval' (Wettestad, 2005: 13). This did not in and of itself represent a new policy, but it was enough to enable the Commission to move to the next stage of policy design: policy formulation.

In 2001, it initiated much more focused discussions as part of a larger roadmapping exercise known as the European Climate Change Programme (ECCP) which encompassed various affected parties (see Chapter 3 for details). The ECCP's working group on flexible mechanisms was a more exclusive arrangement than the Green Paper consultation, comprising representatives from just seventeen organisations (European Commission, 2001a; see also Skjærseth, 2010: 299). This group eventually published its findings in June 2001 (COM (2001) 580), around three months after the US government's withdrawal from the Kyoto Protocol. Following that exogenous event, the working group participants were 'unanimous on the need to introduce emissions trading as soon as possible' (Skjærseth and Wettestad, 2009: 109), although important differences on its design remained (including on whether trading should be mandatory or be subject to an absolute cap).

The Commission's Formal Proposal

After one further round of brief consultations with some key organisations, the Commission published its legislative proposal in October 2001 (COM (2001) 581). In many respects, it was fully in line with DG Environment's long-standing aims. The proposed system would be mandatory, would start with a pilot phase, and would initially focus on a relatively narrow group of greenhouse gases and polluting activities. Formally linking the system to the Kyoto Protocol flexibility mechanisms was viewed as desirable but politically uncertain, and so was put to one side to be resolved at a later date.[1] However, the Commission did introduce two important changes in response to political opposition from Member States and industry:

- *Decentralisation* – each Member State would develop its own National Allocation Plan (NAP) to distribute allowances to industry within its territory. The Commission would, however, serve as an external watchdog (i.e. a polity-based *durability device*) to ensure that a number of common allocation criteria were adhered to.
- *Free allocation* – of all allowances in Phase I (2005–2007), with an as-yet-unspecified 'harmonised method' of allocation for Phase II (2008–2012) to be decided through the comitology system (i.e. a manual flexibility device).

As explained in Chapter 4, decentralisation compromised the effectiveness of the system, significantly weakening its ability to generate deep cuts in emissions in Phase I. Indeed, free allocation quickly became one of the main axes of conflict in a whole sequence of subsequent policy redesigns (Haigh, 2009: 14.13-4). The reason that the two changes were made was quite simple: the Commission was anxious 'to reduce complexity' where possible to 'ensure expediency in the policy making process' (Christiansen and Wettestad, 2003: 16) so that the 2003 Directive could be adopted. It generally succeeded in that endeavour because thereafter, 'the main shape and content' of its proposal 'remained intact through the complicated EU decision-making process' (Skjærseth and Wettestad, 2008: 45). However, some small, but important changes were nonetheless made to the text of the directive during the decision-making stage. Some of the most important of these related to the allocation process. The European Parliament and a few Member States – led by Sweden and Denmark – had originally pushed for various levels of mandatory auctioning (Council of the European Union, 2002: fn. 32; European Parliament, 2002). In the end, the Parliament and its allies in the Council were not able to force this through, in part because of the German coalition government's refusal to support it (Vis, 2006: 190). The final Directive did, however, provide for optional auctioning up to a maximum of 5 per cent in each Member State in Phase I and 10 per cent in Phase II. While this provision made auctioning possible, it also prevented Member States who were pro-auctioning (such as Sweden) from selling more than the maximum level.

The Adoption of the 2003 Directive

On 25 October 2003 – 733 days after the publication of the Commission's proposal – the 2003 Directive entered into force. Some have remarked on how rapid the adoption process was (Wettestad, 2005), but amongst our sample of instrument changes the speed was decidedly average (see Figure 8.1). Be that as it may, the Commission then set about establishing the system and Phase I formally commenced on 1 January 2005, a little over three years after the Commission launched its original proposal. Regarding endogenous factors, the existing literature puts the successful adoption of the proposal, in the context of the failed carbon/energy tax, down to four factors (Wettestad, 2005: 1). First of all, the Commission undertook a great deal of preparatory work before formulating its proposal. By shaping the views of other actors, it ensured that the main elements of its preferred design survived the adoption process (Skjærseth and Wettestad, 2010b: 68). Second, it was able to accommodate Member State preferences by making early and significant concessions – principally on auctioning and decentralisation (Müller and Slominski, 2013: 1433). Hence, when the Environment Council eventually debated the proposal it only suggested a few relatively minor changes (Wettestad, 2005: 5). Third, the European Parliament sought few far-reaching amendments (e.g. European Parliament, 2002). Some have suggested that it was slow to grasp the technical detail of emissions trading and struggled to focus its interventions (Wettestad, 2005: 14). The other EU institutions also deliberately put it under time pressure to adopt the proposal so that the system could be fully up and running by the time the Kyoto Protocol entered into force in 2005 (Skjærseth and Wettestad, 2008: 142; Skjærseth, 2010: 300). Finally, a number of potentially important non-state actors failed to effectively oppose the Directive. As noted earlier in the section, the energy-intensive industries (who stood to lose the most) did not actively mobilise until after the Commission had published its proposal.

This proved to be a serious mistake. Business was, however, generally united in opposing centralised auctioning (Boasson and Wettestad, 2013: 68), a key priority which was eventually incorporated into the text of the Directive. Meanwhile, environmental NGOs acquiesced to the Commission's efforts to fast track design, by working through the high-level road mapping exercise – the ECCP (Wettestad, 2005: 10).

6.3 The Implementation of the 2003 Directive

The publication of the NAPs provided for under the 2003 Directive proved to be a much more complex and drawn-out process than many had envisaged (Ellerman *et al.*, 2016: 92). Indeed, the Commission's earlier warning about the flaws inherent in decentralising allocation proved to be well-founded: the process facilitated a race to the bottom amongst Member States, some of whom were keen to shield their industries from global competitiveness pressures (Skjærseth and Wettestad, 2009: 115). Having accepted the general principle of mandatory emissions trading in the policy formulation process, some national governments were keen to exploit the flexibility that a decentralised allocation approach afforded them (Bailey, 2010: 148). Nevertheless – and very much against expectations – allowance prices in the system started to climb, reaching a high of €31 in April 2006 (Skjærseth and Wettestad, 2010b: 69; EEA, 2011b). However, in the same month prices began a dramatic collapse when it became clear that Member States had over-allocated allowances by a total of 4 per cent; the price of allowances in Phase I eventually fell close to zero by mid-2007. This fall in prices was due in part to incomplete information about actual emissions and overly optimistic economic growth forecasts (Woerdman *et al.*, 2015: 65), but fierce lobbying (of Member States) by some industries was also an important factor (see e.g. Anger *et al.*, 2016). In response, the Commission engaged in forms of limited 'unilateral' strengthening by scaling back the allocation proposals of some Member States (Müller and Slominski, 2013: 1427). In Phase II (2008–2012), it reduced them by an average of 10.5 per cent. Particularly significant cuts were made to those submitted by big emitters such as Poland and Germany (Skjærseth and Wettestad, 2010b: 70). Following the price crash in 2006, the Commission's interventions helped to restore prices to around €20 in early 2008 (Skjærseth and Wettestad, 2010b: 70).

As well as over-allocation (and hence low allowance prices), the system experienced a number of other problems arising from the design of the 2003 Directive. In Phases I and II (2005–2012), the electricity generators received most of their allowances for free. When they passed a substantial proportion of the higher market price through to energy users (including the energy-intensive industries), they were accused of generating excess revenues – or what came to be known as 'windfall profits' (Energy Intensive Industries, 2004; see Sijm *et al.*, 2006). As noted above and in Chapter 4, cost pass-through is entirely consistent with the axioms of economic theory (Laing *et al.*, 2014: 516). Despite this, when it was put into practice it provoked significant political opposition, especially from the energy-intensive industries (Wettestad, 2009b), i.e. there were negative policy feedback effects.

In January 2005, the Commission commenced work on its first evaluation report (an instrument-level *flexibility device*), as stipulated by Article 30 of the 2003 Directive (Skjærseth and Wettestad, 2010b: 65). It was informed by the work of consultants and included a web-based survey of stakeholders (DG Environment, McKinsey & Company and Ecofys, 2006). From the outset, it became apparent that several of them had markedly changed their views since the formulation process; there was a greater appetite for more auctioning and hence less flexibility (Skjærseth and Wettestad, 2010a: 108). When it was eventually published in November 2006, the evaluation report did not contain any specific recommendations, but its title, *Building a Global Carbon Market* (COM (676) 2006), signalled the Commission's eagerness to raise the EU's policy ambitions. Together, this information gave the Commission a 'strong impetus' (Skjærseth and Wettestad, 2010b: 70) and much ammunition to change the 2003 Directive. Moreover, the problems experienced during Phase I 'made it easier for the Commission to campaign for the development of a more market streamlined and more centrally steered system' (Boasson and Wettestad, 2013: 63). From a policy feedback perspective, this was broadly analogous to an interpretive mechanism.

6.4 Policy Feedback and Policy Instrument Redesign

The ensuing reform process should be viewed against the backdrop of three other important developments. First of all, there was a growing realisation that the EU's internal policies were insufficiently stringent to fulfil the bloc's Kyoto commitments (Boasson and Wettestad, 2013: 43). In March 2004, Heads of State demanded a new suite of policy programme-level goals and instruments to be considered at the Spring 2005 European Council. In February 2005, the Commission published a Communication to inform their thinking, entitled *Winning the Battle against Global Climate Change* (SEC (2005) 180). It was written in such a way as to not formally commit the EU to any new policy targets or *durability devices*, but it noted the need for new and/or stronger policy instruments, including in relation to emission trading. It also announced the launch of a second phase of the ECCP road-mapping programme to work through the details. The experience of the 2003 Directive suggested that a good deal of potential opposition could be identified and resolved in its various working groups.

Second, Heads of State began to view climate change as an area in which the EU could exert international leadership. By the mid-2000s, the United Nations Framework Convention on Climate Change (UNFCCC) process had become mired in a deep stalemate, following the US government's decision not to ratify the Kyoto Protocol (Boasson and Wettestad, 2013: 47). In January 2007, the Commission tried to burnish the EU's leadership credentials by publishing an integrated package of new proposals to support a 20 per cent reduction in greenhouse gas emissions by 2020 and support renewable energies and energy efficiency (see Chapter 3). The 20-20-20 targets (a policy-programme-level *durability device*) were subsequently endorsed by Heads of State in March 2007, who also requested the Commission to table new plans for a revised Directive 'which create[s] the right incentives for forward-looking, low carbon investment decisions' (cited in COM (2008) 16, Explanatory Memorandum: 3). In effect, the Heads of State backed a new policy instrument goal for the system midway through the road-mapping exercise and almost a year before the Commission had published a formal proposal.

Third, in the technical discussions between Commission officials and the energy-intensive industries who were by then actively engaged in emissions trading, the mood had turned altogether darker because of feedback effects generated by the system. Two issues drew their attention. The first was the steep (but eventually temporary) rise in allowance prices in 2005 and early 2006, which they framed as a 'double burden' on them as it increased the direct costs of their emissions and led to the indirect electricity cost increases that the electricity generators were passing on to them (e.g. Energy Intensive Industries, 2003: 2). The second issue arose from the EU's aforementioned desire to lead the world on climate change. The energy-intensives were alarmed at this, warning that any further strengthening of the system risked generating what they termed 'carbon leakage', i.e. the relocation of their operations to parts of the world with lower climate standards (Wettestad, 2009b: 317). This negative framing played into the ongoing debate about windfall profits (see Chapter 4), making their demands 'much more politically visible and salient, and functioned as an alarm bell for a wide range of industrial and governmental actors' (Wettestad, 2009b: 318). In the policy feedback literature, the sudden price increase (itself a direct product of allowance trading within the system), could be equated to an endogenously derived focusing event.

Some energy-intensive industries had begun coordinating on these issues in 2002 (Energy Intensive Industries, 2002). But in 2005, they formed a dedicated lobbying group to articulate their views – the Alliance of Energy Intensive Industries (Alliance of Energy Intensive Industries, 2005). More broadly, the number of groups who took an active interest in the detailed design of the system surged, drawing in new supporters but also some new opponents. It is telling that about six times more non-governmental actors participated in ECCP2 as had participated in ECCP1 (European Commission, 2001a; European Commission, 2007a). Having dominated ECCP1, the electricity generators suddenly found themselves confronted by many more opponents in ECCP2, led by the energy-intensives (Skodvin *et al.*, 2010: 861). Rising concern over windfall profits was an important driver of the decision to establish a dedicated High Level Group on Competitiveness, Energy and Environment within the Commission itself (Wettestad, 2009b: 314–315), and reporting directly to the Enterprise Commissioner. This group was in turn used as a platform by others seeking to block the Commission's attempts to increase the stringency and broaden the scope of the system (European Commission, 2005; High Level Group on Competitiveness, Energy and the Environment, 2006; Wettestad, 2009b; Dreger, 2014: 95). Although its origins lay in the reforms of the trading system, it was tasked with keeping an oversight on competitiveness issues across all areas of Commission policy making including, but not limited to, climate and energy. As the Commission prepared to launch a proposal for a revised Directive, the energy-intensives were described as being engaged in an 'aggressive lobbying effort' to protect their free allocation of allowances (cited in Wettestad, 2009b: 316).

The Commission's Proposal for a New Directive

In January 2008, the Commission finally launched its legislative proposal to revise the ETS (COM (2008) 16) as part of the broader 2020 Climate and Energy Package. In it, the Commission maintained that the proposed reforms were deliberately modest: to 'improve and extend' the system (COM (2008) 16). But the proposal included a number of significant changes, some with potentially far-reaching consequences, namely:

- *An EU-level cap:* decentralised NAPs would be replaced by a collective cap set at EU level.
- *Greater automaticity*: a 'linear reduction factor' would reduce the cap by a fixed amount (1.74 per cent) every year to reach a system-wide reduction target of 21 per cent below 2005 emission levels by 2020 (COM (2008) 16: 7).
- *Expanded auctioning:* with a distinction between electricity generators (auctioning from 2013) and energy-intensive industries (auctioning gradually introduced in Phase III – i.e. 2013–2020). The expectation was that 'at least' two thirds of all the allowances would be auctioned by 2013 (COM (2008) 16: 8). Companies deemed to be especially vulnerable to carbon leakage would, however, continue to receive free allowances.
- *Less flexibility*: more restrictions on importing emission reductions from abroad. No new credits would enter the system unless a satisfactory global climate

agreement was signed (updating the Kyoto Protocol) and the EU moved to a new policy programme-wide goal of a 30 per cent reduction.
- *Broader scope*: trading to be expanded to include more industries – chemicals, ammonia and aluminium production (COM (2008) 16: 4).

In an accompanying memorandum, the Commission used the disappointing environmental outcomes of Phase I to make a case for more stringent interventions (COM (2008) 16: 2). And crucially, as well as drive future greenhouse gas reductions (essentially reprising the main aim of the 2003 Directive), the Commission appeared more eager to nurture policy feedback effects, through creating 'incentives for forward-looking low-carbon investment decisions' (COM (2008) 16: 3). Finally, it indicated that it wanted the changes to be adopted quickly, that is by mid-2009, so the EU could shape the next big UNFCCC meeting in Copenhagen, then only eighteen months away. The imminent prospect of reform and the increased stringency of NAPII allocations increased expectations for higher prices: by July 2008, the price of allowances had climbed to nearly €30, the highest level since the Phase I price crash began in mid-2006 (EEA, 2011b, 2012).

Policy Instrument Redesign

The Commission's new proposal was, in many respects, aligned with the preferences it had held since the start of policy design, but had failed to satisfy during the negotiation of the 2003 Directive. During the implementation of the 2003 Directive it had successfully engaged in modest unilateral strengthening by tightening Member State allocation plans (see above), but with the new proposal it sought to achieve a more fundamental reform of the system. And crucially, an important interpretive feedback mechanism had been at work since 2003, i.e. the Commission could more confidently claim that 'on the basis of experience of [its] application' of the 2003 Directive (Article 30), reform was needed (see Skjærseth and Wettestad, 2010b: 81; Boasson and Wettestad, 2013: 63). Meanwhile, the European Parliament continued to support greater harmonisation and auctioning as it had done during the adoption of the 2003 Directive (Skjærseth, 2010: 303; Wettestad, Eikeland and Nilsson, 2012: 73).

Member States continued to broadly accept the main thrust of the Commission's thinking (e.g. European Commission, 2007b: 3). After the patchy performance of the system in Phase I, it was no longer credible for their officials to claim that all was well and no change was needed (Skjærseth and Wettestad, 2010b: 79). Increased support for EU cap-setting was influenced by Member State frustrations with the NAP process, which inflamed relations with the European Commission (Moore, 2018: 147–150). As the ECCP2 road-mapping exercise moved forward, increasingly positive signals emerged from the Council about increasing the share of auctioning in the ETS (ENDS Europe, 2007b). The biggest change was in Germany's position, given its key role in blocking an EU cap and mandatory auctioning previously (ENDS Europe, 2007a). It is also worth remembering that EU Heads of State had effectively already conceded the need for some strengthening when they approved the 20 per cent reduction target. Hence the question was not *if* the system should be reformed, but *how* it should be reformed to deliver greater emission reductions. In March 2008, when the Environment Council first debated the Commission's proposal, Member States offered it their broad support (Skjærseth, 2010: 301). This marked an important shift from their reaction to the 2003 Directive, when the Council was generally at odds with DG Environment and the European Parliament on the most critical policy design issues.

Industry had also changed its views. The preferences of particular industries had been heavily influenced by policy feedbacks from the 2003 Directive, which had affected the pre-existing distribution of costs and benefits amongst the main target groups (namely electricity generators and the energy-intensives). Free allocation in Phase I had largely been tied to historical emissions, meaning that businesses with higher emissions by and large received more allowances. The highest-carbon electricity generators (i.e. those that were more reliant on the burning of coal and oil) and the energy-intensives emerged from the national allocation process as the most significant beneficiaries of free allocation (Lise, Sijm and Hobbs, 2010; de Bruyn, Schep and Cherif, 2016). This distribution of policy costs and benefits both increased their support for emissions trading as the main policy instrument and encouraged them to push for continued free allocation. Although the energy-intensives began the policy redesign process by flatly opposing any shift in auctioning, by early 2008 they had realised that the game was effectively up and that 'all they could hope for was exemptions' and concessions chiefly in the form of free allowances (Boasson and Wettestad, 2013: 72). By contrast, low-carbon electricity generators who were more reliant on nuclear power and renewables, were less dependent on free allocation; many had directly benefited when higher allowance prices drove up electricity prices (Chen *et al.*, 2008: 271). A number of them therefore pushed to expand auctioning (e.g. Électricité de France, 2007). As a result of these inter-generator differences, the main EU-wide association – Eurelectric – decided not to adopt a common public position on auctioning during the development of the 2009 Directive (Eurelectric, 2007: 16). However, 61 CEOs of the largest energy generators agreed to go well *beyond* the EU's 20 per cent emission reduction target and completely decarbonise their operations by 2050, believing it would create new business opportunities (Eikeland, 2016: 51).

6.5 A New Policy Design

As soon as formal negotiations commenced between the main EU institutions, it became apparent that these policy feedback effects from the 2003 Directive were also interacting with a number of exogenous factors. First of all, in 2004 ten new Member States had joined the EU, many from Central and Eastern Europe. They were especially sensitive to the additional financial cost of more stringent policy measures (Boasson and Wettestad, 2013: 69). Polish representatives in the discussions made it abundantly clear that they were not prepared to accept greater auctioning if it imperilled the viability of their country's coal-fired power stations, which together met around 90 per cent of Poland's electricity needs (ENDS Europe, 2008a; Skjærseth and Wettestad, 2010b: 74, 81). Second, September 2008 witnessed the onset of the global financial crisis following the collapse of Lehman Brothers. By that point, negotiations over what eventually became the 2009 Directive were already at a comparatively advanced stage, but the worsening financial situation made many groups – and especially those in the Central and Eastern European Member States (Müller and Slominski, 2013: 1436) – even more reluctant to accept additional economic burdens (Skjærseth, 2010: 302).

The interaction between these endogenous and exogenous factors produced a number of unexpected shifts in actor preferences, which policy designers somehow had to bridge. For example, although Germany supported the shift to auctioning for electricity generation, it pushed for the continuation of free allocation to energy-intensive industries (ENDS Europe, 2008a; Skjærseth and Wettestad, 2010a: 110). In October 2008, MEPs in the Parliament's legislative committees found themselves bombarded by no less than 160 groups lobbying for free allowances (Skjærseth and Wettestad, 2010b: 81). It quickly became obvious to the Commission that a new directive would only be adopted if it treated industries in a more 'differentiated' manner. But the problem was that greater differentiation could only be achieved by making the design of the system, itself already quite complex, considerably more complicated (Wettestad, 2009a: 318).

And yet two months later in December 2008, i.e. a mere 457 days after the Commission tabled its proposal, the 2009 Directive (2009/29/EC) was adopted. This was considerably faster than the adoption of the 2003 Directive, which as noted in Section 6.3, took 721 days. Four factors facilitated its rapid adoption. First, positive policy feedback mechanisms had, as noted above, helped to nurture a new coalition of actors who preferred emissions trading to the alternative option of striking out in a new (e.g. more regulatory) direction. As a group, the Member States had also shifted to being more supportive of the Commission's plans for greater harmonisation, more auctioning and an extended scope. And if a fundamental reform of the system was not possible, many EU policy makers, including but not limited to the Commission's staff, feared the alternatives: a damaging loss of credibility in international negotiations and/or awkward demands for reductions to be made in sectors that sat outside the system, such as agriculture and transport, many of which were politically sensitive in some Member States. In effect, reform of the system quickly became the least-worst option for many concerned.

Second, the advocates of greater stringency were able to present their ideas as a 'sheer necessity' if the EU wished to be the main international climate policy leader (Boasson and Wettestad, 2013: 76). In fact, at the upcoming UNFCCC meeting in Copenhagen, EU Heads of State were fully expecting to enter a race with other parties to adopt more, not less, stringent targets. Third, the Central and Eastern European Member States had urged the French Presidency to switch to voting by unanimity in the Council on the broad 2020 Climate and Energy Package (Bocquillon and Maltby, 2017: 93). This successfully countered one source of pressure for greater stringency in the negotiations by marginalising the Parliament (Skjærseth and Wettestad, 2010b: 83), but it also strengthened the French Presidency of the Council by allowing it to engage in creative package deals across all the policy dossiers in the final rounds of negotiation (Skjærseth, 2010: 302).

Finally, the 2009 Directive proposal was significantly amended during the design process to bring losers on board whilst maintaining the support of potential beneficiaries. For example, costs were delayed into the future and potentially difficult decisions about the modes and timing of any compensatory measures (such as the allocation of free allowances) were referred to the comitology process (Müller and Slominski, 2013: 1429). The main design features of the 2009 Directive were described above. Chief amongst these was a new policy instrument goal – to achieve a 21 per cent reduction in emissions by 2020 from 2005 levels. Together, these changes simultaneously achieved greater harmonisation and greater policy differentiation (Wettestad et al., 2012: 73–74). The reformed system was thus both more stringent, broader in scope and more future-oriented, but also considerably more complicated than the original instrument, having a complex 'mix of provisions running in opposite directions' (Müller and Slominski, 2013: 1437). Yet again, complexity was the political price paid by the EU for adopting speedy internal policy changes before an important international conference.

6.6 Policy Feedback and Policy Instrument Redesign

Changing Exogenous Conditions

The Commission had originally banked on the Copenhagen conference being a diplomatic success for the EU, in which case the conditional 30 per cent EU reduction target would automatically have kicked in, and Article 28, a *flexibility clause* inserted by the Commission into the text of the 2009 Directive, would have triggered a new cycle of revision to the Linear Reduction Factor. The Commission and many market analysts had initially expected the post-2008 cap to be more difficult for the EU to achieve (e.g. ENDS Report, 2007). This increased stringency of the new Directive was also projected to lead to higher prices for emission allowances and thus drive greater emission reductions than had been achieved in Phase I.

Unfortunately, that is not how things worked out. Copenhagen was a diplomatic failure for the EU and, soon after, EU climate policy entered a period of much greater uncertainty characterised by what, in Chapter 3, we termed 'challenged leadership' (see Chapter 3). Moreover, the EU's diplomatic travails coincided with a period of financial austerity, which together made some parts of industry even more sensitive to changes to their economic competitiveness. The post-2008 financial crisis together with the post-2011 Eurozone crisis greatly undermined allowance prices in the ETS. First, they led to a sharp reduction in greenhouse gas emissions, driven in large part by reductions in the energy-intensive sectors (EEA, 2015b: 17–18). This meant that once again emissions across the system fell below allowance allocations, leading to a large allowance surplus and hence depressed prices. Second, allowance prices were pushed even lower by companies selling allowances to raise cash to keep themselves afloat in a crisis-hit financial environment (Capoor and Ambrosi, 2009: 6). As a result, allowance prices dropped rapidly from above €32 per tonne of CO_2 in September 2008 to below €10 per tonne by February 2009, where they hovered until 2011 (EEA, 2012). The price dropped again during the Eurozone economic crisis in 2011, to around €7 per tonne.

As a result, the Commission found itself facing a complex, multi-pronged dilemma. In 2010, Commission President Jose Manuel Barroso had created a DG for Climate Action (DG CLIMA), building it around the emissions trading unit that had originally been established in DG Environment. This change had occurred during the periodic restructuring of the Commission after the 2009 European Parliament elections (European Commission, 2010). Although the new DG had been mandated to advance EU climate policy, in the area of emissions trading it was anxious not to give the impression that it would continually intervene in the market to boost prices (ENDS Report, 2009; see also Wettestad and Jevnaker, 2016: 38). After all, emissions trading had been originally portrayed by its advocates as a flexible, automatically self-correcting policy instrument. After years of near-constant design interventions, designers in DG CLIMA wanted to stand back and give the market an opportunity to self-correct (Wettestad and Jevnaker, 2016: 38). To add to the Commission's dilemma, some of the system's most passionate supporters were too impatient to wait. In 2011, the UK government announced the creation of a national floor price (a kind of tax) to underpin allowance prices within the United Kingdom. It eventually took effect in April 2013. If other Member States followed suit, the Commission feared that it would trigger a renationalisation of EU climate policy (Wettestad and Jevnaker, 2016: 38), threatening the policy gains that it had achieved since 2003. The European Parliament also tried – and failed – to make changes to the system by amending related policy proposals that were going through the legislative process (e.g. on energy efficiency), but these attempts were firmly blocked by the Council (Wettestad and Jevnaker, 2016: 41).

6.7 Raising Allowance Prices: Backloading and the Market Stability Reserve

A New Policy Crisis

In a 2008 survey, market analysts predicted that allowance prices would be around €24 in 2010 and €35 in 2020 (Point Carbon, 2008: 31). When Phase III started in 2013, the actual price hovered at around €5 and the allowance surplus totalled over 2 billion (DG CLIMA, 2016: 92), putting the efficacy of the system in doubt. The Commission tried to intervene indirectly by redesigning the overarching policy goal to make it more stringent. In 2010, DG CLIMA sought to adopt a fresh proposal for a 30 per cent emission reduction target, but this failed to win sufficient support within the Commission and never saw the light of day (Skovgaard, 2014). When, three years later in 2013, the Commission finally secured internal agreement, Poland deployed its veto to block further progress in the European Council (see Chapter 3). So, after 2012, the Commission was left with no other option but to formulate a fresh set of amendments to alter the inner workings of the system.

If the Commission's default preference was for modest reforms that worked with the grain of existing patterns of emissions trading, what about other actors? In the Council, the United Kingdom, Denmark and the Netherlands were at the forefront of Member States advocating substantial reform to boost allowance prices. By contrast, Poland was still the prime mover amongst a group of Central and Eastern European Member States that wanted to block reform. The leak of an internal Commission document in March 2012 revealed that the Member States were far apart: some, such as the United Kingdom, wanted an entirely new Directive with a much tighter cap; others, such as Poland, argued for no change at all to the status quo on the grounds that low prices were a natural, market-based reaction to economic uncertainty (Bulleid, 2012a). Somewhere in the middle was a much larger group of Member States who were willing to entertain the idea of removing surplus allowances but divided on how best to do so.

For the Member States, a balance had to be struck. Withdrawing (or 'backloading') allowances from the auction share until the end of Phase III, would reduce the number that could be sold immediately by national governments. But any withdrawals could theoretically also increase the allowance price, meaning that each remaining allowance would be worth more. There was a good deal of uncertainty about the precise effects that backloading would have on revenues and prices – in effect, demonstrating one of the downsides of having adopted a market-based instrument rather than a regulatory one. Skovgaard (2017: 360) has written that the German finance ministry 'took a keen interest in [intervention], which they saw as crucial for avoiding a collapse in the allowance price', which was important because Germany's Energy and Climate Fund received funding from auction revenues. This gave it and other national finance ministries an endogenously derived incentive to support higher allowance prices in the system, which directly conflicted with their industry ministries who were concerned about the impact of higher prices on their domestic industries. As Skovgaard noted in the case of Denmark, 'a large increase in the allowance price would increase revenue but also raise production costs for Danish industry' (2017: 359).

Amongst businesses, the Alliance of Energy Intensive Industries was strongly against any intervention. In January 2012, it stated that it was 'opposed to any modification of the [...] rules which would damage further industry's competitiveness' (AEII, 2012: 1). The economic crisis had made its members even more determined to oppose policy change (Wettestad, 2014: 75). Most of the electricity generation industry – including Eurelectric – supported some reform, but a split between low-carbon and high-carbon generators was again apparent. Low-carbon companies such as EDF, GDF Suez, Fortum, and Statkraft were determined to push for changes that would increase allowance prices (see e.g. DG CLIMA, 2013). By contrast, high-carbon generators and actors that represented them opposed changes. Many that did so were based in Poland (e.g., the Polish Electricity Association, PKEE and Tauron Polska Energia). Meanwhile, market intermediaries such as allowance traders had been negatively impacted by the reduction in the volume of traded allowances and began to lose members (Moore, 2018: 164–165). As a result, they mobilised to support a strengthening of the policy (e.g. IETA, 2012). Environmental NGOs also supported reform (Climate Action Network Europe, 2012), although growing disillusionment with emissions trading led some of them to establish a 'Scrap the ETS' campaign (Corporate Europe Observatory *et al.*, 2013).

The Adoption of the Backloading Decision

Much as it may have preferred not to intervene, the Commission was eventually forced to act. In April 2012, the then Commissioner of DG CLIMA, Connie Hedegaard, announced that she intended to launch proposals to remove some surpluses from the system (van Renssen, 2012). In order to move quickly, DG CLIMA opted to implement backloading by delaying the sale of 900 million allowances rather than permanently retire them (ENDS Report, 2012c). It proposed to do this by amending the existing (2010) auctioning regulation (as noted in Article 29a of the 2009 Directive) via the supposedly more rapid route of comitology. Unlike the permanent cancellation of allowances or the adoption of a common floor price, it believed that this combination would provide a rapid, confidence-boosting approach to amend the existing Directive (Wettestad, 2014: 73). DG CLIMA's Director-General Jos Delbeke also thought that it would buy time to make more fundamental changes further down the line (Bulleid, 2012b).

However, this quick-fix rapidly descended into a long 'bitter, symbol laden and complicated battle' with the European Parliament (Wettestad and Jevnaker, 2016: 87), which again felt that it was being unfairly side-lined (Wettestad and Jevnaker, 2016: 89).[2] Hedegaard was eventually forced to plead with MEPs to 'act responsibly and support [...] back-loading' (Flynn, 2013a). In addition, old splits between Member States resurfaced in the Council. A group of Member States explicitly supported backloading, including Denmark, France and the United Kingdom (Wettestad and Jevnaker, 2016: 45; Skovgaard, 2017: 355). The German government remained undecided until late 2013 (Jevnaker and Wettestad, 2017; Skovgaard, 2017). Meanwhile, Poland, Greece and Cyprus openly opposed backloading (Skovgaard, 2017: 355). A 'nadir' was eventually reached when the Parliament voted down the proposal in plenary in April 2013, seemingly leaving the system on its 'deathbed' (Wettestad and Jevnaker, 2016: 3). However, eventually the amended Backloading Decision (1359/2013/EU) was adopted after it was agreed that it would only be used once. It entered into force on 17 December 2013, having taken 511 days to be agreed. Consequently, the auctioning of 900 million allowances scheduled for 2014–2016 was postponed until 2019–2020.

The Market Stability Reserve

The immense political effort required to secure what many had hoped would be a quick fix did not bode well for the success of more fundamental reforms to the ETS. In November 2012, the Commission had released a Carbon Market Report that sought to build a case for 'structural reform' to raise allowance prices, which at the time stood at around €8 per tonne (COM (2012) 652). It set out six possible policy response options: an increase in the EU's 2020 target to 30 per cent; limited allowance cancellations; an earlier increase in the linear reduction factor; direct forms of price management similar to the United Kingdom's carbon price floor; a new limit on the use of international credits; and an increase in the system's scope. The first four of these options had already been blocked or had failed to receive sufficient support, hence were unlikely to be adopted. Notably, the report did not include an option to pursue volume management.

Following several rounds of consultation (COM (2012) 652), DG CLIMA produced a new proposal for non-discretionary price interventions (COM/2014/020), which it termed the Market Stability Reserve (MSR). The general idea was to create a new 'objective and rule based' *flexibility device* that allowed the supply of allowances to respond automatically to changes in demand, thus dampening large fluctuations in the supply of allowances in the market (Delbeke and Vis, 2015: 51; DG CLIMA, 2016: 95). The political genius of the MSR was that it would be facilitated by market forces and hence could be presented as an automatic and permanent solution to the perceived need for greater flexibility (Wettestad and Jevnaker, 2016: 88). Nevertheless, the reaction of the various interest groups followed the same pattern as previous reforms, including backloading. Thus the market intermediaries and environmental NGOs were generally in favour (Flynn, 2013d). The energy-intensive industries opposed it, believing it would reduce the cost-effectiveness of trading (Flynn, 2013d). But having emerged battered and bruised from the long battle over backloading and with reserves of political goodwill towards their cause fast ebbing away, they struggled to mount an effective campaign (Wettestad and Jevnaker, 2016: 94, 106). Meanwhile, the split in the electricity industry continued, with Eurelectric and the low-carbon companies (e.g. Dong, EDF and the Danish Energy Association) supporting reform, and higher-carbon companies (including RWE and Tauron Polska Energia) opposing it.

The negotiations eventually focused on two main issues. The first was the reserve's start date. The Commission's proposal had suggested 2021, namely the start of Phase IV, which implied that the rules in Phase III would not be changed (COM/2014/020: 3). In the Council, the United Kingdom, France and Germany led a coalition that pushed for an earlier start date (2017), which fell squarely within Phase III (Kość, 2014). Poland, having accepted the need for the reserve at the October 2014 European Council meeting, successfully formed a blocking minority with the Czech Republic and Latvia that threatened to vote against an early start date (Ala-Kurikka, 2015b). Member States continued to circulate predictions of the impact of the MSR on auctioning revenues amongst themselves (e.g. a publicly available example being the United Kingdom's – see UK Government, 2014). In the Parliament, the centre-left, centre-right and liberals supported a 2019 start date (Ala-Kurikka, 2015a). The Greens and the left supported a 2017 start date and a cancellation of some backloaded allowances (more or less similar to the UK position supporting cancellation).

The second issue concerned the handling of backloaded and other unallocated allowances. These could either be returned to the market starting in 2019, as the Commission had proposed, or placed directly into the reserve. By December 2014, most Member States who supported a 2021 start date did not support putting these additional allowances into the MSR; while those that supported an early start date also supported the approach (Council of the European Union, 2014: 4). These policy design decisions would affect auctioning revenues by increasing the size of the reserve and preventing any additional allowances from being returned too quickly (i.e. by the end of Phase III). In the Parliament, a proposal to put these allowances in the Reserve was introduced by the centre-right's rapporteur, Ivo Belet, who enjoyed broad support across the party groups (Ala-Kurikka, 2015a; Williams, 2015).

The final agreement between the Council and the Parliament in May 2015 compromised on a 2019 start date and placed the backloaded/unallocated allowances directly into the MSR. When the Council voted on the agreement in September 2015, Poland, Bulgaria, Romania, Croatia and Hungary voted against. They argued that the October 2014 decision by the Heads of State had effectively ruled out an early start date, that the reserve (as well as backloading) amounted to an increase in the EU's 2020 reduction target, and that the decision should be subject to unanimity voting in the Council.[3] Poland even launched a legal challenge in the ECJ, arguing that it was not in line with the European Council's instructions (Court of Justice of the European Union, 2016), but eventually it failed.

A new Decision (2015/1814) establishing the Market Stability Reserve (by amending the 2003 Directive) was eventually agreed and formally entered into force in October 2015, 623 days after the Commission had first proposed it. The MSR was to take effect in January 2019, two years prior to the 2021 date the Commission had initially proposed. If the allowance surplus grew to more than 833 million allowances, a portion of the auction share equivalent to 12 per cent of the surplus would be automatically transferred to the MSR each year. If the surplus fell below 400 million allowances, the Reserve would automatically release 100 million allowances annually. These percentages and volumes were scheduled to be reviewed in 2021, three years after the MSR begins operating (Article 3). In a concession designed to bring on board the energy-intensive industries, the Commission agreed to monitor the impact of the Reserve on an annual basis to protect industries at the greatest risk of carbon leakage. This review will also consider EU measures to protect firms from the indirect costs of emissions trading through higher energy prices.

6.7 Emissions Trading towards 2030: The 2018 Directive

The Formulation of a New Directive

Many involved in emissions trading hoped that the adoption of the Market Stability Reserve would usher in a period of much-needed policy stability. But bubbling underneath were multiple long-running tensions that eventually combined to generate forces pushing for yet another round of policy changes (Wettestad and Jevnaker, 2019). As explained in Chapter 3, in January 2014 the Commission had released proposals for new 2030 emission reduction targets (COM/2014/020), but these had simply re-ignited long-running conflicts between the Green Growth and Visegrad coalitions. In October 2014, the Heads of State struck agreement on a new, long-term policy programme aim: a 40 per cent reduction in greenhouse gas emissions by 2030 (European Council, 2014). Again, the Commission argued that the ETS would have to be redesigned to incorporate this new aim and that to delay it any longer would disrupt the EU's planning for the next big UN summit scheduled for Paris in December 2015. In July 2015, the Commission duly produced a proposal for a new emission trading Directive (COM (2015) 337), as the 'first step in delivering' (European Commission, 2015: 1) on the new 40 per cent reduction target and, in doing so, establish a new, that is fourth, phase of trading. The main elements of the proposal included:

- *Increasing the linear reduction factor* from 1.74 per cent to 2.2 per cent every year starting from 2021 (European Commission, 2015: 1). This equated to a new policy instrument goal: a 43 per cent reduction in 2005 emissions by 2030 (up from 21 per cent by 2020), equivalent to an extra 556 million tonnes of CO_2 equivalent by 2030 (European Commission, 2015: 1).
- *Locking in auctioning:* the share of auctioned allowances would remain the same after 2020 (i.e. 57 per cent) (European Commission, 2015: 2).
- *Amending the free-allocation rules*: when the proposals were published, 97 per cent of energy-intensive sectors were in principle eligible for free allowances; henceforth, the focus would be on the sectors that were at the greatest risk of carbon leakage – using more fine-tuned criteria known as benchmarked values. Outside those sectors, free allocation would be gradually reduced and eliminated entirely after 2027.
- *Creating new support schemes to help industries decarbonise:* these included a new Innovation Fund for investments in renewables and carbon capture and storage, and a Modernisation Fund to help the ten poorest Member States decarbonise, funded by selling a portion of the auctioned allowances (COM (2015) 337: 3).

The Adoption of the 2018 Directive

The Commission's proposal explicitly stated that it merely created 'the necessary legal framework implementing the [...] principles' agreed by Heads of State in October 2014 (COM (2015) 337: 2). But Commission officials subsequently stated that the proposal was in fact still 'fairly open' and 'likely to be significantly altered during negotiations between lawmakers' (Keating, 2015). When policy design discussions commenced, it became clear that the proposal would in fact depart from the European Council's conclusions, partly because of the enhanced commitment that the EU had made in the Paris Agreement (i.e. to pursue 'efforts to limit the temperature increase to 1.5°C' rather than just 2°C; see UNFCCC). Starting in the second half of 2016, policy designers therefore began to tread a fine line between increasing the ambitiousness of the reforms to fulfil the EU's Paris commitments and not disturbing the political agreement that Heads of State had struck in October 2014.

A key question was whether to increase volume management through a proposed increase in the intake rate of the MSR or, more controversially, by cancelling more allowances. A group of Member States began meeting informally in the second half of 2016 to push for further volume management. By October 2016, that group consisted of Denmark, France, Luxembourg, the Netherlands, Sweden and the United Kingdom, with Slovenia joining a few months later (Moore, 2018: 208). Further changes were opposed by many Central and Eastern European Member States, including Romania, Bulgaria, Croatia, Lithuania, Latvia and Poland (Ala-Kurikka, 2016d), who argued that the reserve had only recently been adopted and should be allowed to operate before further changes were contemplated. Other Member States were initially rather sceptical; they included Greece, Ireland, and Spain (Ala-Kurikka, 2016d). The goal of building support for the volume management proposals outside of their core supporters in the Council – but especially the more controversial cancellation proposal – was facilitated by the fact that the proposals were meant to raise the allowance price and increase auction revenues. The proposals were supported in the Parliament by the centre-left parties, the Greens and the liberals, but initially opposed by the centre-right parties. When these groups finally reached a compromise in the Parliament's ENVI committee in December 2016, it included a pledge to cancel 800 million allowances in 2021 and establish a temporary increase in the Reserve's intake rate from 12 per cent to 24 per cent (Ala-Kurikka, 2016b, 2016c; Committee on the Environment, Public Health and Food Safety, 2017). The Environment Council eventually arrived at a common position by qualified majority in February 2017, with nine Member States voting against.

The 2018 Directive (2018/410) eventually emerged from trilogues between Member States and the Parliament in November 2017 and was published in the Official Journal in March 2018, 974 days after the Commission published its proposal. In a direct reference to the EU's multi-tiered climate policy design, the Climate and Energy Commissioner Miguel Arias Cañete proclaimed that the 'deal shows that the EU is serious about the Paris agreement implementation' (Ward and

Table 6.1 *Emissions trading: significant policy instrument changes, 2003–2019*

Legislation (and speed of adoption)[3]	Lifespan (days)[1]	Description
2003 Emissions Trading Directive (2003/87) (721 days)	3,356	• *Stringency*: Member states given option to auction an average of 8% of allowances (actual: 3%). Overall emission reductions based on member state allocation decisions. • *Scope*: Relatively narrow; 45% of EU greenhouse gas emissions from the electricity generation industry and energy-intensive industries. • *Timeframe*: 2005 to 2012.
2009 Emissions Trading Directive (2009/29) (457 days)	4,208	• *Stringency*: increased. Auctioning expanded to 100% for most electricity generators; 57% auctioning, 43% free allocation. Cap reduced 1.74% per year. • *Scope*: increased. Expanded to more sectors/gases (e.g. PFCs from aluminium production); Also expanded to within-EU aviation via a separate directive (2008/101/EC). • *Timeframe*: increased. 2013 to 2020.
2013 Backloading Decision (1359/2013) (511 days)	2,576	• Delays auctioning of 900 million allowances from 2014 to 2016 until the end of Phase III (2013–2020).
2015 Market Stability Reserve Decision (2015/1814) (623 days)	1,312[2]	• Creates the MSR, which automatically withdraws allowances from the auction share if the amount in circulation exceeds 833 million allowances. • *Timeframe:* 2019 onwards.
2018 Emissions Trading Directive (2018/410) (973 days)	4,651	• *Stringency: increased.* Free allocation expanded for energy-intensive industries and Central and Eastern European electricity generators. Cap reduced 2.2% per year starting in 2021; allowance cancellation from MSR beginning in 2024. • *Scope: stable.* No new additional sectors/gases. • *Timeframe*: increased. 2021 to 2030.

Notes
[1] Expected at the time of writing (1 June 2019).
[2] Does not have an end date. Lifespan calculated from legislation's entry into force until 1 June 2019.
[3] Significant policy instrument changes in bold.
Source: own composition.

Toplensky, 2017). But it was also, by some margin, the most time-consuming amendment in the entire policy instrument sequence, requiring deft policy design decisions to bridge the political differences between a number of key actors. For example, the Modernisation Fund was prevented from funding all new coal plants, with the exception of district heating facilities in the poorest regions of Romania and Bulgaria (Hodgson, 2017c). The reserve's intake rate was scheduled to increase automatically from 12 per cent to 24 per cent between 2019 and 2023. Starting in 2024, if the number of allowances in the MSR is higher than the number auctioned in the previous year, the excess allowances will be automatically cancelled. Free allocation would continue to energy-intensive industries, and governments in the Central and Eastern European Member States could allocate a larger share of their free allowances to their electricity generators. In the wake of these reforms, allowance prices rose steadily and, as of July 2019, consistently averaged above €20 per tonne for the first time since the 2008 financial crisis (Sandbag, 2019). As a result, in 2018 allowance prices were high enough to drive fuel switching in electricity generation from coal to gas for the entire year (Marcu et al., 2019).

Chapter 4 outlined the main policy changes starting with the 2003 Directive and ending with the 2018 Directive. Table 6.1 summarises each step in the sequence in considerably more detail, noting the most significant changes in policy stringency, scope and timeframe, and indicating the speed at which each change was agreed and its lifespan.

Endnotes

1 Via the 2004 Linking Directive – see Chapter 3.
2 See the voluntary agreement on cars for another example (Chapter 7).
3 Because it threatened, to paraphrase the Lisbon Treaty, to 'significantly affect the Member States' choice between different energy sources and the general structure of its energy supply' (Council of the European Union, 2015: 2–3).

7

Voluntary Action

The Governance of Car Emissions

7.1 Introduction

For as long as the EU has had a policy on climate change, transport has stood out as an anomalous sector. Between 1995 and 2004, greenhouse gas emissions across the EU declined by 5 per cent but grew by 26 per cent in the transport sector (COM (2007) 856: 2). As noted in Chapter 4, the sector's position is still anomalous today. Indeed, as the EU's climate policies have expanded, so too has the perception that the EU's ability to decarbonise – which by the 2000s had been elevated to one of its most significant strategic ambitions – may well stand or fall on the basis of what is achieved in the transport sector, and especially the road transport sector (ten Brink, 2010: 180–181), which today still accounts for around 70 per cent of overall transport emissions (COM (2016) 501: 2).

Even so, it took the EU a long time and a great deal of political effort to adopt any policies addressing CO_2 emissions from cars. A Directive on local car pollutants was adopted as long ago as 1991, which committed Environment Ministers to adopt binding regulatory standards on CO_2 by the end of 1992 (Haigh, 2009: 6.8-16). However, inter-state agreement proved impossible to achieve and it was not until 1998 – fully six years later – that the Commission completed the negotiation of a novel non-regulatory instrument: a voluntary agreement with the European Automobile Manufacturers' Association (ACEA). That agreement committed manufacturers to reduce average CO_2 emissions from all new passenger cars sold on the EU market from an average of 186–140g/km by 2008 (COM (1998) 495: 3), roughly equating to a 25 per cent cut over ten years (Bongaerts, 1999: 102; Gulbrandsen and Christensen, 2014: 509). ACEA's agreement was undoubtedly pioneering; it marked the first time that the EU had used a voluntary agreement to achieve a significant environmental policy programme-level objective. It has been widely recognised as constituting an important innovation in EU policy instrumentation, at least as significant as the adoption of emissions trading

(Wurzel *et al.*, 2013). However, within a few years the agreement was widely perceived to be failing and in 2009 was replaced by a new instrument – a binding regulation – thus drawing to a close a high-profile but short-lived experiment in EU-level voluntary action.

This chapter recounts the story of how that agreement was originally conceived within the Commission, how and why it was subsequently designed in the way it was, and how it was redesigned in the context of the policy feedback effects generated after 1998. It reveals how, over time, these effects gradually fed back through to undermine the agreement's durability, leading to a sequence of changes in policy instrumentation, starting with the regulation in 2009, itself subsequently amended first in 2014 and again in 2018. In broad terms, the first half of this chapter explains the genesis of the agreement. The second half summarises the various policy feedback effects that the agreement triggered and explores how, through time, these fed through to the revisions. We conclude by summarising the main sequence of policy instrument decisions which have unfolded over the – more or less – three decades since 1990.

7.2 The Policy Design Process: Creating the Voluntary Agreement on Cars

Rival Policy Design Options

The Commission began to investigate the scope for limiting transport emissions after a joint meeting of the Energy and Environment Ministers in October 1990. This meeting was pivotal because it established, for the first time, an EU-level target of stabilising EU-wide emissions at 1990 levels by 2000. In turn, this policy programme-level *durability device* triggered a search for implementing policy instruments. The Commission duly scoped out a range of options, including some relating to road transport. They covered plans for common speed limits and public transport schemes, but most proved too politically unpalatable for Member States and were quickly shelved (Wettestad, 2000). In September 1991, the Commission launched a brand new policy programme to limit CO_2 emissions, its centrepiece being an EU-wide carbon/energy tax (see Chapter 3). This tax – which the Commission thought would be more consistent with the EU's overarching plans for a common internal market – also foundered due to Member State opposition. It too was eventually shelved, setting back the development of an EU-wide climate policy by a number of years.

But in the transport sector, policy design activities continued to advance, pushed by more pro-environmental Member States such as the Netherlands and Denmark. A 1991 Directive on conventional car pollutants (91/441) was, as noted above, the first EU policy instrument specifically to mention the mitigation of CO_2. It committed Ministers to adopt standards by the end of 1992 (Haigh, 2009: 6.8-16). This gave the Commission a toe-hold and, in late 1991, it tasked its Motor Vehicle Emissions Group (MVEG) – a corporatist body comprising representatives of the Commission and the car industry – to scope out specific policy designs. These were sensitive matters, having been deliberately excluded from the Commission's ongoing Auto-Oil I Programme, a structured process of agreeing new standards for more localised pollutants (Friedrich, Tappe and Wurzel, 2000; Taminiau et al., 2006; see Chapter 4 for more details).

Sensing that the political wind was beginning to blow in the direction of more stringent policy interventions, in 1991 ACEA volunteered to reduce the emissions from all new cars by 10 per cent between 1993 and 2005. This opening gambit proved to be well below the Commission's expectations, but it was at least an explicit recognition that something had to be done. Within ACEA, however, a fierce battle was brewing between its various member companies over who should shoulder the burden of achieving the reductions (ENDS Report, 1992a). In February 1992, ACEA agreed that if the reductions were to be mandatory, the only realistic way to achieve them was via a mandatory EU-wide CO_2 tax.

Within the Environment Council, Ministers were also struggling to reach agreement. These differences cut across the main car-producing Member States, backed by their respective car industries, i.e. the main target groups, and various other interest groups (for a summary, see Chapter 4). In simple terms, the United Kingdom wanted a system of tradable permits to provide a progressively increasing incentive to improve fuel efficiency. Germany preferred a fixed legislative standard which differentiated between particular engine sizes and/or vehicle weights. However, other Member States perceived this to be a veiled attempt to allow its manufacturers to continue selling large, premium vehicles. Meanwhile, France advocated for a mixed system of regulation backed by fines and emissions trading, while the Netherlands pushed for a voluntary agreement incorporating different targets for specific engine sizes and vehicle weights. And finally, Italy preferred a graduated tax, with exceptions for the smallest vehicles which its manufacturers excelled at producing (ENDS Report, 1992a). Meanwhile, the European Commission remained internally split, with DG Environment pushing for stricter targets and shorter deadlines and DG Industry arguing for the exact opposite. As discussions dragged on into 1992, the feeling grew within DG Environment that CO_2 from cars was too difficult a matter to design a response to at that particular point in time (Keay-Bright, 2000: 16).

In November 1992, the MVEG produced a compromise proposal for a harmonised sales tax, differentiated into different weight categories. The baseline would start at zero in 1995 for all cars emitting more than 160g/km, and then decline via a series of planned increments to reach 110g/km in 2005. As a potential *durability device*, the proposal sought to offer manufacturers a dynamic incentive to produce more efficient cars in and across every weight category, as well as give consumers a financial incentive to buy smaller, more fuel-efficient cars. The planned increments would add a degree of policy automaticity that was relatively novel. Nevertheless, the proposal was a compromise. Had it established a technology-specific goal, it would almost certainly have been fiercely opposed by the politically powerful German car manufacturers, who were determined to preserve their ability to sell large cars in the most profitable premium segment of the market. It also offered to negate the need for additional policies to promote product labelling (which most manufacturers were averse to); the MVEG maintained that the price effect of the tax would be sufficient to indicate the environmental friendliness of different vehicles without the need for mandatory showroom labelling.

However, as we noted in the previous chapter, proposals for new EU-level taxes require unanimity: a high threshold. Given that a number of car-producing Member States (including the United Kingdom) were flatly opposed to the EU adopting any additional legal powers over tax matters, it was not entirely surprising that the proposal fell at the very first hurdle (Matt, 2012: 132–134). On 9 December 1992, Environment Ministers formally rejected the MVEG's proposal. Not a single Member State spoke in favour of it (ENDS Report, 1992b). The continuing deadlock ensured that the Commission missed its self-imposed deadline to submit policy proposals by the end of 1992. Having seen its proposal fall, the MVEG informed the Commission that it had done all it could do and politely suggested that the matter should be resolved at a higher level, beginning with the Commissioners. However, they remained split on the matter (ENDS Report, 1992b), so the deadlock persisted. Thereafter, three factors conspired to keep the issue well down the EU's political agenda. First of all, the pace of the international climate policy process dramatically slowed in the period after the 1992 Rio Summit. Although the EU ratified the United Nations Framework Convention on Climate Change (-UNFCCC), the US Government gradually pulled back from the process, leaving the EU with a difficult choice to make between either forging ahead on its own or hanging back (see Chapter 3). After some hesitation, it eventually opted for the latter. Yet an important source of internal friction remained because the European manufacturers were extremely wary of being undercut by manufacturers in countries with laxer standards. These tensions immediately manifested themselves when the EU began to search for new policy instruments to fulfil the policy programme-level target it had set to reduce its emissions.

Second, the European economy slipped into a deep recession after 1992 which severely affected the profitability of European car manufacturers, many of whom saw their sales plummet. Their collective appetite for any controls on emissions declined rapidly. In 1994, the Commission tried to revive support by suggesting that the production of 'clean, lean-produced, intelligent, quality, value' cars would boost economic growth and productivity (Matt, 2012: 134). The European Parliament also tried to restore political momentum by attempting to include CO_2 limits in the ongoing Auto-Oil programme, but it was firmly rebuffed by Environment Ministers (ENDS Report, 1994). Finally, following the Danish 'No' vote against the Maastricht Treaty in June 1992, the Commission became even more wary of intruding into sensitive areas of national policy where its legal competence to act was weak and/or contested. These included areas such as fiscal policy which the EU had sought to broach in the past and been rebuffed, as well as areas such as land use planning that were in principle highly relevant to reducing car emissions but were henceforth perceived to be similarly off limits.

Policy Instrument Selection

The political impasse was, however, eventually broken by Germany, revealing its somewhat 'paradoxical' ability to be both the EU's 'climate leader and green car laggard' (Hey, 2010). It was eager to make a success of the first UNFCCC COP in Berlin (Oberthur and Ott, 1999: 43; see Chapter 3 for details). To give that meeting a boost, in advance it made a unilateral pledge to reduce national CO_2 emissions by 25 per cent from 1990 levels by 2005 (Lenschow and Rottmann, 2005: 8). To support this goal, the German government brokered a voluntary agreement with the German car industry, under which manufacturers unilaterally committed to reduce average CO_2 emissions from their new cars by 25 per cent from 1995 levels by 2005. The core design principle that only average emissions should be encoded in the policy design was an absolutely critical one for the German manufacturers, who were, as noted above, very keen to maintain their ability to produce large premium-priced cars (Gulbrandsen and Christensen, 2014: 506). In exchange for their unilateral commitment, the German government agreed to postpone the introduction of binding regulation at the national level (ENDS Report, 1995).

Around the same time, other large emitters such as the United Kingdom agreed to reduce their greenhouse gas emissions, having perhaps noted that their emissions were declining because of the recession (Haigh, 2009: 14.1-2). In December 1994, Environment Ministers tried to raise the *ante* by asking the Commission to produce a proposal on car emissions corresponding to a limit of 120g/km by 2005, which the Commission felt was technically achievable in view of what the German manufacturers had pledged to achieve. The 1995 COP meeting in Berlin eventually culminated in a hugely important and far-reaching political agreement to negotiate a binding protocol to the UNFCCC (see Chapter 3). However, in spite of Germany's offer, the policy design process at EU level remained deadlocked.

Nevertheless, by mid-1995 one particular policy design – a voluntary agreement – began to emerge as the least-opposed option. The German manufacturers were comfortable with the idea – having already signed a similar agreement at the national level – as were other powerful industries in the German automotive sector (voluntarism being a well-developed practice in German environmental policy; see Wurzel *et al.*, 2013). Significantly, similar collaborative approaches were being trialled at EU level (Friedrich *et al.*, 2000), after many years of long and 'highly divisive' battles to agree car emission standards in the Auto-Oil process (Wurzel, 2002: 134). Voluntarism also fitted with a wider trend to experiment with new environmental policy instruments at EU level, chiefly to overcome the implementation problems that had long bedevilled regulatory approaches (Wurzel *et al.*, 2013). DG Environment's instinctive preference was still for some form of fiscal measure such as a tax, but political support for that option in the Council of Ministers and in other Commission DGs was not sufficient to overcome the unanimity rule. DG Industry maintained that a voluntary agreement would be more likely than a regulation to facilitate the sector's ongoing attempts to improve its global competitiveness.

So, in 1995, DG Environment seized the window of opportunity to act that Germany had opened up at EU level, launching a strategy on CO_2 emissions from new cars, which it described as a 'special concern' in the EU's fight against climate change (COM (95) 689: 2). In the strategy, the Commission sought to settle, once and for all, the matter of policy instrument selection. The proposal advanced a four-pronged approach:

1. *A voluntary agreement with car manufacturers*, which was eventually adopted as Recommendation 1999/125/EC. Although the Commission claimed that 120g/km by 2005 was technically achievable, it proposed extending the deadline to 2008 to give producers enough time to produce vehicles that were sufficiently affordable. It also suggested that 140g/km was a more feasible target than 120g/km, around 10 per cent of which could be achieved by the other three elements of the package.
2. A *directive on car labelling* to encourage greener purchasing (eventually adopted as Directive 1999/94/EC).
3. A *decision to monitor the voluntary agreement* (adopted as Decision 1753/2000/EC; see Gulbrandsen and Christensen, 2014: 510).
4. A *directive to stimulate green purchasing* through fiscal incentive schemes at the national level (which, as noted in Chapter 3, ran into fierce opposition and was never adopted).

Elements 1 and 3 were mostly targeted at the supply side, whereas elements 2 and 4 addressed the demand side.

To sum up, the coalition supporting the voluntary agreement (essentially Germany plus DG Environment) was small but strong enough to veto any alternative policy design option. As far as many environmental groups were concerned, a voluntary agreement was not their preferred approach, but it had the practical advantage that it could at least be adopted. However, they remained suspicious, believing that the experience of using voluntary agreements successfully at the national level was too limited to replicate them at EU level. Experience suggested that agreements were usually not stringent enough and tended to institutionalise incremental technological development (Rennings *et al.*, 1997). Meanwhile, the European Parliament – historically the EU's greenest institution – remained implacably opposed to using voluntary agreements. However, under the prevailing decision-making procedure, it was effectively excluded from the design process and so struggled to make its voice heard. These disagreements, many of them long running, quickly resurfaced once policy designers began to discuss the calibration of the agreement, including relevant policy durability and flexibility devices.

Policy Instrument Calibration

In its 1995 strategy, the Commission accepted that Environment Ministers were correct to assume that 120g/km was technically feasible to achieve by 2005 (Haigh, 2009: 14.8-3; COM (1998) 495: 2). It was supported by non-car producing countries such as Denmark and the Netherlands. But France and Germany insisted on more flexibility, pushing for the deadline to be put back to 2010. In 1996, the Commission established an internal working group to bridge these differences, which included DG Environment, DG Industry, and ACEA. None of the other parties – including the Parliament and the Member States – were invited (Keay-Bright, 2000: 21). However, ACEA continued to argue in the working group that a reduction of around 120g/km was 'unrealistic' (Haigh, 2009: 14.8-4), and instead offered to go to 167g/km by 2005 or, at the latest, 2010. This equated to a 9 per cent cut in average emissions rather than the 25 per cent reduction sought by the Commission and some national Environment Ministers. In their June 1996 meeting, Ministers broadly endorsed the Commission's proposed policy design, but given the number of dissenting voices in the room, had to settle for an 'uncomfortable compromise' on some of the fine detail (ENDS Report, 1996), namely a *durability device* (the 120g/km target) that had an important caveat: 'should it appear that it is not possible fully to achieve the [120g/km] objective by 2005, the phasing could be extended, but in no case beyond 2010' (in ten Brink, 2010: 182). At a stroke, Ministers effectively introduced a *flexibility device* (an extended timeframe) into the design process, which differed to the one they themselves had adopted just eighteen months before. But the Council also insisted on the insertion

7 *Voluntary Action* 165

of a relational contract (a type of *flexibility device*): if the agreement proved to be ineffective, the Commission should immediately examine new policy instruments including, crucially, binding regulations.

Ministers were keen to finalise the deal and urged the Commission to sign the amended text without further delay. However, other participants remained deeply concerned about what the EU was doing. Environmental groups were worried that the Commission was being put under political pressure to adopt something too quickly, and should dig in and use regulatory instruments to push the car manufacturers to go much further and faster (Keay-Bright, 2000: 20), in effect forcing technological transformations in the sector. They pointed to the fact that there would be no specific restrictions on the use of diesel engines (the drop-in technology favoured by many manufacturers, especially German ones). Fearing competitiveness pressures, ACEA argued that importers from Korea and Japan should adopt equivalent measures – committing the Commission to years of additional design work. As a condition for signing the agreement, it also insisted that oil producers should be required to deliver sufficient quantities of the relevant (low-sulphur) fuel (Keay-Bright, 2000: 44). The Parliament was equally concerned about the lack of more stringent, long-term targets and questioned the legitimacy of the process that the Commission appeared intent on following (there was, after all, no reference to voluntary agreements in the EU Treaties).[1]

Frustrated at the lack of progress, in late 1997 the then Environment Commissioner, Ritt Bjerregaard, threatened to table legislative proposals (Haigh, 2009 14.8-4). However, ACEA maintained that it was not feasible to achieve 120g/km by 2005 as it would 'would imply [a] radical downsizing of the whole fleet with cars that would neither be affordable nor meet the requirements of most car users' (quoted in Keay-Bright, 2000: 24). Bjerregaard was, however, fortuitously assisted by the earlier decision of the Heads of State (in December 1997) to sign the Kyoto Protocol, which committed the EU to making an 8 per cent reduction in its emissions from 1990 levels by 2008–2012. Until that point, the EU had only ever made a political commitment to stabilise its emissions.

This change in the broader, policy programme goals gave the design process the impetus that DG Environment had long been seeking. Discussions suddenly moved up to a higher political level in the Commission, to the Commissioners of DG Industry and DG Environment (Bangemann and Bjerregaard respectively) and Bernd Pischetsrieder, the CEO of BMW and the chair of ACEA (Keay-Bright, 2000: 25). Pischetsrieder had the experience of the German voluntary agreement to draw upon; he was eager to end the stalemate and strike a deal on behalf of ACEA that secured a greater degree of predictability for its members. In March 1998, ACEA slightly modified its position, announcing that it was prepared to commit to reaching 140g/km, but only over a somewhat longer timespan (by 2008, not 2005) and with all the pre-conditions outlined above, e.g. adequate provision of low-sulphur fuel, no specific targeting of diesel engines (ENDS Report, 1998; Bongaerts, 1999: 102, 41). All references to the original, more stringent *durability device* sought by the Commission – the policy instrument-level target of 120g/km – were removed from the draft agreement. Instead, ACEA merely restated the earlier offer made by some of its members to make available an unspecified number of cars that could, in theory, achieve the stricter target by 2000.

At first blush, the policy design that was eventually adopted at the high political level seemed to satisfy all of ACEA's key demands. At the March 1998 Environment Council, Ministers even praised ACEA's generosity, saying that the text provided a 'good basis for negotiation' (ENDS Report, 1998). But Denmark was amongst a number of Member States that disagreed and called upon the Commission to commence the drafting of a proposal for legislation in case the individual car producers failed to fulfil their obligations (Haigh, 2009: 14.8-4). This demand failed to generate sufficient political backing in the Council of Ministers, but Environment Ministers did agree that an interim target should be incorporated into the text of the agreement (see Chapter 3). The Ministers' final *communique* thus requested the Commission to explore the scope for inserting a *flexibility device* – an intermediate, time-specific target – to ensure that the emissions reductions remained on track (ENDS Report, 1998).

But even then, the saga continued. Another year passed before the agreement was finally signed and sealed by the main parties. There were two reasons for the additional delay. First, the Auto-Oil discussions with oil companies on fuel quality took more time to be concluded than expected (in June 1998). Second, ACEA presented its offer to the Commission in the form of a written letter, but the Commission had to formally reciprocate (COM (1998) 495), which took time to work its way through the EU's official policy design process. Eventually, in February 1999, the text of the agreement was published in the form of a Recommendation, a full decade after the historic Joint Council meeting in 1990, and no less than 1,144 days after the Commission had originally tabled its proposal. By some margin, this was the longest adoption period of any of the fifteen policy instrument changes covered in this book.

Reactions to the Policy Design

In public, the Commission professed to being pleased with the agreement, claiming it would be the first of many to be struck with large industrial sectors (Matt, 2012: 150). It maintained that the agreement 'correspond[ed] to the Council's expectations [in 1996, i.e. 120g/km by 2005] and the Commission's own original objectives [i.e. 140g/km by 2005]' (COM (1998) 495: 2). But many others emphatically disagreed (Taschner, 1998). The European Environmental Bureau condemned it as 'technically unambitious' and maintained that a 'far more ambitious target could have been set' (Keay-Bright, 2000: 27, 52). It claimed that the failure to insert durability devices into the final policy design left it lacking substantive content. Crucially, one of the most critical design issues of all remained open – namely, how the burden of compliance would be shared amongst the ACEA members (Volpi and Singer, 2002: 151). WWF maintained that the agreement conspicuously failed to comply with the Commission's own best practice guidelines on voluntary agreements and predicted that the reductions in fuel efficiency would slow down as the economy strengthened and consumers purchased larger, SUV-type vehicles (Volpi and Singer, 2002: 145). Ministers representing non-car producing Member States expressed similar doubts. The Danish Environment Minister, for example, repeated his call for the Commission to commence drafting a legislative proposal (Haigh, 2009: 14.8-4), but yet again this failed to generate sufficient political backing.

7.3 The Implementation of the Voluntary Agreement

In principle, the emissions reductions that ACEA had committed to could have been delivered via a number of different means, ranging from new engine technologies and fuels (e.g. electricity or hydrogen fuel cells), through to incremental adjustments in vehicle weight and engine size, vehicle shape (more aerodynamic) and tyre design (e.g. the use of low-friction variants). Environmentalists believed that regulation would provide the most stringent and durable means of determining what the manufacturers should do. But the manufacturers were adamant that the market was too dynamic and competitive for the exact mix amongst these measures to be known in advance and codified in legislation. From the outset, ACEA therefore repeatedly argued that the Commission should employ what it termed a more hands off or 'technologically neutral' approach that allowed 'markets [to] decide' (Bongaerts, 1999: 103) rather than legislators in Brussels.

In the late 1990s and early 2000s, exogenous conditions facilitated implementation. When world oil prices rose, car buyers responded by opting to purchase fewer and, in general, slightly smaller and/or diesel-fuelled cars, which generally produced fewer greenhouse gases (Matt, 2012: 174). Partly as a result, initially the European, Korean and Japanese producers made good progress in delivering emission reductions (ENDS Report, 2004). In fact, European manufacturers managed to reach the indicative target of 165–173g/km several years ahead of schedule (Matt, 2012: 180–181). Nonetheless, environmental groups remained unconvinced, believing that the delivery of the more demanding 140g/km by 2008 target should not be taken for granted. The way in which the agreement was designed certainly did not help them apply pressure, because it did not reveal why the reductions were being achieved. Were they due to 'the market', namely changing buying habits (e.g. for smaller cars), to the use of drop-in technologies such as diesel engines or to the existence of other policy instruments such as car labelling (ten Brink, 2010: 183)? Or was it because of national fuel taxes (which some Member States were increasing; see ten Brink, 2010: 186)? The monitoring information collected by ACEA members and handed over to the Commission made it difficult for the environmental groups and the Commission to evaluate what was going on.

In the early 2000s, exogenous conditions changed. Emission reductions began to plateau as economic growth returned in the Eurozone and, as environmental groups had warned, consumers promptly purchased larger and more polluting vehicles (Oosterhuis, 2006: 16). For most (but not all) car producers, such vehicles enjoyed bigger price premiums and represented a more profitable segment of the car market. Consequently, throughout much of the lifetime of the agreement, the average weight, engine power and size of the new cars sold in the EU steadily increased (COM (2010) 655). Had the economy not expanded and/or the agreement limited their production, ACEA would probably have reached its emission reduction target on, or even ahead, of schedule. As it was, the headline targets were missed (see Chapter 4). Environmental groups furiously accused the manufacturers of deliberately sabotaging the agreement by actively stimulating the demand for larger vehicles by devoting more of their advertising budgets to the more profitable SUV-style variants (Matt, 2012: 177–178). In turn, the producers (again) claimed that EU regulations governing local air quality and consumer safety had adversely affected their emission-reduction efforts,[2] and that the voluntary/technology-neutral approach should be retained (Gulbrandsen and Christensen, 2014: 512). In 2006, the blame-game took a slightly bizarre turn when ACEA claimed that the voluntary approach would only work if environmental groups persuaded their supporters to purchase smaller and more fuel-efficient cars (Matt, 2012).

Although average emissions did decline in the second half of the time period covered by the agreement (Matt, 2012: 183),[3] by 2008 the average still stood at 153g/km, a significant decline of 14 per cent but still well short of the 140g/km target. Once again, the design of the agreement came under critical scrutiny, as it only required the Commission to collect and publish industry-wide data on emissions. Although manufacturer-specific data was collected by ACEA and transmitted to the Commission as part of the monitoring Decision (see Section 7.2), the car companies claimed it was commercially sensitive and strongly opposed any attempt to release it to the public (Gulbrandsen and Christensen, 2014: 510). Environmental groups in turn countered that the absence of information made it very difficult to evaluate the overall performance of the agreement or hold individual manufacturers to account.

In response, groups such as Transport and Environment (T&E) adapted their tactics and began to exploit EU public access to information laws to obtain more detailed data, which they used to name and shame individual producers (ten Brink, 2010: 185). Starting in 2006, T&E published the first of what became an annual 'name and shame' report on emission trends across the industry. These confirmed what critics of the agreement had long suspected: hiding behind the average fleet emissions were significant inter-manufacturer and inter-country differences. Italian and French manufacturers specialising in smaller vehicles (FIAT and PSA, for example, which were the only two manufacturers to meet the 140g/km target) performed significantly better than German producers such as Daimler, Porsche and BMW specialising in much larger and/or faster vehicles.[4] In other words, the policy *durability devices* in the agreement were failing to prevent free-riding (Matt, 2012: 183–185). To give a flavour of the extent of the differences, in 2006 the average new car sold in Portugal emitted 144g/km, whereas in Sweden it emitted 187g/km (COM (2007) 856: 9). Evidently, the design of the agreement could not cope with such significant variations or, indeed, the fact that emissions were by then rising across the whole sector. A significant point was reached in 2004, when some ACEA members (including some of the German producers who specialised in mid-range cars) began to openly question the efficacy of voluntary agreements. They lobbied their governments for new policy designs, such as market-based instruments, that could respond more dynamically if emissions rose. However, ACEA remained more or less united on the unviability of regulatory approaches, such as those prevailing in the US, claiming that they threatened their international competitiveness (Wurzel *et al.*, 2013).

7.4 Policy Feedback and Policy Instrument Redesign

The Commission's annual monitoring report in 2006 revealed that average emissions were 163g/km and thus well in excess of the 140g/km target. It concluded that 'major additional efforts' were needed to get things back on track (SEC (2006) 1078; Haigh, 2009: 14.8-6). The data published in 2007 finally confirmed what many environmental groups had long expected:

> The voluntary approach has delivered a solid CO_2 reduction but has not been as successful as hoped. Given the slower than expected progress to date, the 120g CO_2/km target will not be met by 2012 without additional measures
>
> *(MEMO/07/597).*

These 'additional measures' included the long-awaited proposal for a binding EU regulation on car emissions, which the Commission eventually published on 19 December 2007 (COM (2007) 856), following more internal disagreements.

Its proposal suggested that producers should be compelled to cut CO_2 emissions from new passenger cars to 130g/km by 2012 (COM (2007) 19). Although this new target would be stipulated in the regulation, the producers could rely upon a range of so-called complementary measures – e.g. tyre pressure monitoring devices and gear shift indicators to promote eco-driving, better consumer information and traffic management, and, interestingly, biofuels (see Chapter 5) – to deliver the remaining 10g/km and thus reach 120g/km (Haigh, 2009: 14.8-8). And crucially, for the first time, the Commission proposed a more stringent policy *durability device* – a longer term 'aim' of achieving 95g/km – with a new deadline (2020). Such an aim had been repeatedly demanded by Members of the European Parliament (MEPs), equating to a 30 per cent reduction from 2011 levels of 135.7g/km (ten Brink, 2010: 195). They felt that it would reshape long-term expectations if the whole sector was much clearer about the intended, long-term direction of travel. The industry referred to the design of the new regulation as a more 'integrated approach' (Gulbrandsen and Christensen, 2014: 512), somewhat distinct from the voluntary approach enshrined in the agreement (COM (2007) 856: 2; Matt, 2012: 189–193).

The design of the 2007 proposal had been directly informed by four interconnecting policy debates. The first centred on what target manufacturers should eventually be asked to deliver. This debate had been informed by the findings of the *ex post* evaluation of the agreement that ACEA had offered to produce. Published in December 2003, it claimed that while it was technologically possible to fulfil the 120g/km target by 2012, the costs of doing so would be 'prohibitive' and would have a negative impact on the Eurozone economy (COM (2005) 269: Article 5). Instead of 120g/km, a reduction of up to 133g/km by 2012 would be more feasible (*ibid*). Environmental groups complained that 130g/km was patently unambitious and insisted that the manufacturers could easily achieve 120g/km by 2010 (EEB and T&E, 2004).

The second debate concerned the choice of policy instrument(s). Within the Commission, DG Environment had been preparing for the failure of the agreement since at least 2002, commissioning feasibility studies of a variety of alternative instruments including taxes, emissions trading and regulation (ten Brink, 2010: 189–191). On this matter, the various policy actors remained in broadly the same coalitions as they had when the agreement was first designed. Thus, DG Environment generally favoured regulation (Matt, 2012: 194), whereas the Directorate-General for Enterprise (DG Enterprise) preferred ACEA's integrated approach coupled to some form of emissions trading. The idea of adopting harmonising national taxes to reflect a given car's CO_2 emissions was opposed by several Member States including the United Kingdom (Haigh, 2009: 14.8-8). Meanwhile, manufacturers of the smaller vehicles were considerably keener on regulation than those that produced larger ones. Finally, environmental groups were even more determined that the EU should do what it had conspicuously failed to do in the 1990s and adopt strict regulations to force more radical technological innovations (Matt, 2012: 190).

The third debate related to the EU's broader, policy programme-level emission reduction goals. As noted above, a new policy driver emerged in 2005 when the Kyoto Protocol entered into force; for the first time, it committed the EU to deliver emission *reductions* (as opposed to stabilising emissions). In 2007, the Heads of State agreed that in order to meet the EU's new policy programme-level target of a 20 per cent reduction in emissions by 2020, sectors in which emissions were not falling fast enough or were, as in the case of transport, still rising, should do more (COM (2007) 757: 5, 8). In time, this debate directly informed the design of the component parts of the 2020 Climate and Energy Package (for details, see Chapter 3). The new proposal on car emissions was eventually incorporated into this larger package of policy measures, raising its profile within the EU institutions and increasing the time pressure on all designers to ensure that it was adopted alongside all the other component parts. Gradually, it appeared that transport was beginning to lose its hard-won status as a 'special' (or, in emissions terms, 'anomalous') sector.

The final debate concerned the economic competitiveness of the car sector in the context of rising political demands for more stringent environmental standards. The sector had historically been a cyclical part of the European economy, prone to suffer from significant periods of over-production. As climate change began to rise up the political agenda, uncomfortable questions began to be asked. Should it be treated as a malign threat to the viability of the sector? Or as an opportunity to address some of its underlying weaknesses, enabling it to compete more successfully in lucrative international markets such as the US, where many German producers had been planning to expand for some time? In January 2005, the Commissioner of DG Enterprise, Gunter Verheugen, launched the Competitive Automotive Regulatory System for the 21st Century (CARS 21) High Level Group to arrive at sector-wide answers and report back to him. Operating somewhat in parallel to DG Environment's efforts to draw the sector into the second phase of its own road-mapping process (the European Climate Change Programme (ECCP) – see Chapter 3), CARS 21 was dominated by industry and Commission representatives, with minimal input from environmental groups (Gulbrandsen and Christensen, 2014: 511). It incubated and became a strong advocate of ACEA's proposed 'integrated approach' (ten Brink, 2010: 194; Matt, 2012: 192). In general, CARS 21 mainly focused on how to meet the 2012 targets at lowest cost (to the manufacturers). In contrast, environmental groups continued to argue for more stringent *durability devices* (e.g. targets as low as 80g/km by 2020; see Matt, 2012: 192).

As these four debates coalesced, they generated a great deal of internal conflict within the Commission, forcing the then Commission President Barroso to step in and impose a policy solution (Gulbrandsen and Christensen, 2014: 512). The resulting Commission strategy was eventually published on 7 February 2007 (COM (2007) 19). Although its declared purpose was only to identify options and canvas opinions, it laid out a number of defining elements that eventually formed the basis of the 2009 Regulation. These were the overall target (120g/km), the additional 10g/km delivered by complementary measures (under ACEA's integrated approach – see above), and the longer-term target of 95g/km by 2020. Its publication gave environmentalists the high-level political commitment to regulation that they had long sought, and that even a few years before had been successfully opposed by ACEA. But the inclusion of the integrated approach in the strategy 'can be seen on the one hand as a necessary compromise to achieve [that] legislative outcome, and on the other hand as a major lobbying victory for the industry' (ten Brink, 2010: 194). After all, the 120g/km target had been demanded by some EU institutions as long ago as 1994 (see Section 7.2). Nonetheless, the balance of power within the policy design process did appear to be finally moving in the direction of the environmentalists.

During the next six months, the main target groups sought to shape the Commission's thinking as it drafted a formal legislative proposal. When this was eventually published on 19 December 2007, it triggered fairly predictable opposition from some Member States (notably France and Germany) that sought to lobby on behalf of their manufacturers for a raft of delays, exemptions and concessions which are described in the next section (Gulbrandsen and Christensen, 2014: 513). After it had been published, lobbying efforts shifted from the Commission to national governments and MEPs, who were expected to have a much greater say over the final outcome than the design of the voluntary agreement.[5] As the policy design process inched forwards, car producers were, however, still able to exploit the onset of the financial crisis (in 2008) to push for more concessions and additional policy supports (e.g. vehicle scrappage schemes at national level to promote the sale of new cars; European Investment Bank loans at preferential rates to fund industry restructuring). Without these, German manufacturers said they risked a near certain 'wipe out' (Gulbrandsen and Christensen, 2014: 513).

The design of the new Regulation (443/2009), which was informally agreed in December 2008, contained a number of important limitations to the durability devices originally suggested by the Commission, principally to secure the agreement of the German and French governments. The positions of these two countries were so important – but also so divergent – that the Regulation could not be adopted until their leaders, Angela Merkel and Nicolas Sarkozy respectively, had struck a high-level political bargain (Gulbrandsen and Christensen, 2014: 517).

Although it was much more involved in the final bargaining that it had been in the late 1990s, the European Parliament still found itself rather hamstrung. Not only did the other EU institutions put it under significant time pressure to endorse the proposal in time for the next big UNFCCC meeting in Poznan in late 2008 (at which the EU hoped to lead by example), there were also internal disagreements between its environment (Committee on the Environment, Public Health and Food Safety [ENVI]) and industry committees (Committee on Industry, Research and Energy [ITRE]) (Gulbrandsen and Christensen, 2014: 517). The ENVI committee held the lead role and its initial report was largely in line with the Commission's proposal (Burns, 2013: 996). However, it had to take into account the ITRE committee's position, which called for a phased approach to meeting the 120g/km target (Burns, 2013: 996–997; see also ten Brink, 2010: 198). The Parliament and Council eventually struck a deal on the proposal on 17 December 2008 along with the other parts of the 2020 Climate and Energy Package. It was formally adopted in early 2009, 492 days after the Commission issued its proposals – a considerably shorter period of time than the 1,144 days it had taken to adopt the voluntary agreement. The Regulation has been accurately described as a 'milestone' in the policy instrument sequence that was playing out in the sector (see Table 4.1), developing from no policy, to voluntary and then finally regulatory action (Gulbrandsen and Christensen, 2014: 504).

7.5 A New Policy Design

The best way to appreciate the main differences between the 1999 voluntary agreement and the 2009 Regulation, is to compare their respective designs. At first sight, the Regulation's headline target of 130g/km by 2012 was only slightly more stringent than the respective headline target (140g/km) in the voluntary agreement. Yet the design of the Regulation – at least compared to the form in which it was originally proposed by the Commission in December 2007 – was very different. In particular, the policy *durability devices* in the December 2007 proposal were greater in number and much stronger in their intended effect. For example, instead of one overall target, there would be average targets for each manufacturer, principally to overcome the free-rider problems that had afflicted the voluntary agreement.[6] The proposal also mentioned the European Parliament's insistence on a long-term aim (i.e. not a legally binding target) of achieving 95g/km by 2020. This was a goal that environmental groups and some MEPs had long advocated. And finally, the most significant indication that policy designers had adopted a more coercive approach was that the Regulation permitted the Commission to levy a fine on manufacturers that exceeded their targets.[7] These fines were designed to rise automatically to €95 per g/km exceeded *for every car sold* in the EU in 2015

(Haigh, 2009: 14.8-6). Given this formulation, if the Regulation was as poorly implemented as the voluntary agreement, manufacturers would be hit by fines running into many hundreds of millions of Euros.

Of course, during the subsequent policy design process, many of these design elements were whittled away and/or replaced with alternatives. For example, the 130g/km target was redesigned to phase in gradually rather than start abruptly in 2012 (ten Brink, 2010: 197); and it only covered 65 per cent of the total fleet by 2012, rising automatically via a series of intervening steps to 100 per cent by 2015 (Haigh, 2009: 14.8-9).[8] Second, the targets were further differentiated by vehicle weight using a design measure known as the limit value curve. Born of discussions in the CARS 21 process, this curve was drawn in such a way as to allow manufacturers of the heavier (and generally more polluting) cars to continue producing them, so long as they also produced smaller and less polluting cars (de Wilde and Kroon, 2013: 10). Not surprisingly, during the design process its precise slope became the focus of animated discussion between the various manufacturers (Hey, 2010: 214). Third, numerous other changes were made to allow particular manufacturers to continue producing the very largest vehicles (Bulleid, 2011). For example, they could claim 'super credits' for low emission cars[9] to lower their average fleet emissions (via the limit value curve).[10] Fourth, fines were reduced until 2019 for carmakers that narrowly missed their emission targets (ten Brink, 2010: 195). Only in 2019 would the maximum fine of €95 kick in (ten Brink, 2010: 200). In order to avoid perversely incentivising strict enforcement, ACEA convinced the Commission that any fines should go into the general EU budget, rather than its own coffers (ten Brink, 2010: 196).

Finally, and in the only example of legislative tightening during the entire design process, the target of 95g/km by 2020 was not merely retained but linked to a time-specific *flexibility clause*. This obliged the Commission to complete a review of the 'modalities for reaching' the 2020 target by 1 January 2013 (see Article 13 (5)). 'If appropriate' the Commission was mandated to propose an amendment to the Regulation. At the time, critics suspected that this particular *flexibility clause* would 'open [...] the door' to 'additional lobbying and negotiations', rather than legislative tightening (ten Brink, 2010: 200). Nonetheless, the policy sequence did appear to have shifted decisively towards regulation, because the relational contract in the Regulation only tasked the Commission to investigate regulatory policy alternatives.

ACEA claimed that the new regulation would allow its members to adjust their production cycles to cope with 'largely unpredictable factors including consumer preferences, market trends, economic developments and legal requirements in different fields' (ACEA, 2008). But environmental groups condemned the final text as a 'poor compromise' (ten Brink, 2010: 198). T&E claimed that, yet again, it was the same old 'story of special interests in industry and national governments preserving the *status quo*' (ENDS Europe, 2008b). In practice, it was a hard-won compromise. It was only by deferring agreement on future technological steps to the comitology process (Gulbrandsen and Christensen, 2014: 5201) that the French Presidency managed to broker a last- minute deal with the other EU institutions that allowed the EU to table more stringent policy programme-level targets at the UNFCCC meeting in Poznan. In truth, both sides had compromised to some extent. The car makers were forced to accept a more coercive approach grounded in regulation, linked to more transparent reporting (in Article 8) and underpinned by the threat of fines. But they also secured a number of significant concessions. By contrast, environmentalists finally secured the regulatory approach and longer-term target that they had long advocated, but had been forced to accept a less stringent interim target (130g/km instead of 120g/km) linked to a raft of offsetting measures such as pooling and super-credits of unknown efficacy. However, the *flexibility clause* in Article 13 gave DG Environment an opportunity to maintain pressure on the manufacturers.

7.6 The Implementation of the 2009 Regulation

In the years immediately after adoption in 2009, average emissions declined steeply to 132g/km in 2012. This was well below the 140g/km level that the voluntary agreement was supposed to have achieved by 2008, and just slightly above the 2015 target contained in the 2009 Regulation. The full data, when it was published by the EEA, indicated that the manufacturers were comfortably on course to comply with the 2015 target of 130g/km and were making good progress to achieve the 2020 target of 95g/km (Salvidge, 2012). In the event, Peugeot, Toyota and FIAT (companies that dominated the market in small cars) met the 2015 target four years ahead of schedule (T&E, 2012: 3) and the rest complied two years later in 2013 (EEA, 2016: 15). Manufacturers were quick to claim that their opposition to stricter standards during the design process had been vindicated: economic circumstances had unexpectedly changed, and this is what had facilitated faster compliance.[11] But, unsurprisingly, environmental groups arrived at precisely the opposite conclusion: regulation had finally been allowed to demonstrate its potential, emissions having declined three times faster after its adoption than before it (T&E, 2012: 14). They argued that this powerfully confirmed their long-held belief that the only sure route to deep decarbonisation was via a clear and firm regulatory approach. According to Jos Dings of T&E:

> The EU needs to learn lessons from this. When it comes to future targets [...] industry cost estimates should be taken with an SUV-sized pinch of salt
>
> *(quoted in ENDS Report, 2012a).*

7.7 Policy Feedback and Policy Instrument Redesign

As noted above, the 2009 Regulation contained two parts: (1) one concerning the definition of targets and modalities and (2) another determining the operation of those modalities (COM (2012) 393: 2).[12] But when the Commission commenced work on the second part in 2011 (via a review of the 2009 Regulation), several key performance indicators were beginning to head in the wrong direction. Thus, in spite of the reductions in emissions from smaller cars and a sharp decline in the total number of new cars sold (in 2012, sales dropped to their lowest level since 1995; see Keating, 2012c), emissions from the entire transport sector were still rising, as people opted to drive further each year (Le Goff, 2011). After 2008, emissions from freight transport (vans and lorries, etc.) declined, but car usage hardly dropped at all in spite of the financial crisis (EEA, 2011c). In fact, in the thirteen poorer Member States that joined the EU starting in 2004, transport demand outstripped the rate of economic growth (EEA, 2013: 8). By the late 2000s, it had become increasingly obvious that the manufacturers' long-term strategy, which pre-dated even the voluntary agreement, to 'dieselise' the European car fleet to attain CO_2 reduction targets, was also exacerbating local air pollution problems. By the early 2010s, concentrations of nitrogen oxides and particulate matter in many European cities were regularly breaching relevant World Health Organisation and EU standards (EEA, 2013: 8).

A White Paper published by the Commission in 2011 (COM (2011) 144) maintained that emissions from transport should *decrease* by at least 60 per cent from 1990 levels by 2050 to remain consistent with the sector's share of the EU's long-term target to achieve an 80–95 per cent reduction by 2050 (Le Goff, 2011; EEA, 2013: 6). However, once the Commission started to translate this line of thinking into amendments to the 2009 Regulation to extend its timeframe to 2030, old political battles resurfaced, often in an even more accentuated form than before. The German manufacturers, whose sales of luxury brands had held up relatively well during the recession, were determined to retain the existing limit value curve. They were especially wary of the 'by 2020' target of 95g/km, which was fast approaching. On the other hand, the French and Italian manufacturers had seen their sales plummet since 2008, but now regarded the re-writing of the 2009 Regulation as a political opportunity to produce and sell more of their smaller and less polluting vehicles. For a while, the divisions between the manufacturers prevented ACEA from arriving at a common position (Keating, 2012a, 2012b). As before, environmental groups such as T&E wanted the Commission to propose a tougher 2020 target of around 80g/km, insert an interim target of 60g/km for 2025, and introduce a new way of measuring car size to prevent further increases in vehicle weight that had done so much to undermine the voluntary agreement. They claimed that these policy designs (especially the extended timeframe through to 2030) were needed to spur greater industry competitiveness by keeping pace with new regulatory developments in Japan and California (Keating, 2012c).

An online consultation undertaken by the Commission confirmed that views were indeed 'highly divided' on whether the 2009 Regulation was performing satisfactorily (COM (2012) 393: 3). At a stakeholder meeting held in December 2011, environmental groups called for stricter targets (COM (2012) 393: 3) and claimed that compliance costs were far lower than ACEA had originally predicted in 2007–2008. From a policy feedback perspective, it was notable that new interest groups were beginning to make their presence felt. For example, the European aluminium trade body, European Aluminium, argued that weight-based targets gave manufacturers little incentive to use its members' products to make their cars lighter and less polluting (Salvidge, 2012).

7.8 Reaching the 2020 Target: The 2014 Cars Regulation

When, on 11 July 2012, the Commission finally published a proposal on new 'modalities for reaching' the 95g/km target (COM (2012) 393), some six months ahead of the January 2013 deadline specified in the 2009 Regulation, it became clearer how it intended to respond to these debates (Keating, 2012b). Thus, the German manufacturers were pleased to note that it preserved both the 95g/km by 2020 target and the existing limit value curve. During inter-institutional negotiations, the European Parliament had tried (but failed) to insert a considerably tougher *durability device*: an interim target of 68–75g/km by 2025 (Simkins, 2013). But as with the biofuels and emissions trading cases, it also became clear that the Commission had bridged some of the differences by inserting very detailed changes into the instrument's design, such as rules on how to calculate vehicle weights or how many 'super credits' to award manufacturers of particular types of electric vehicle (European Voice, 2012). In June 2013, the Council and the Parliament struck a deal which allowed car makers to 'double count' cars with low emissions (defined as below 50g/km) towards their targets in 2020. Much to the frustration of the environmental groups and some MEPs, a decision on the vexed issue of post-2020 targets was again deferred; the text of Article 13 (5) was simply amended to require the Commission to perform another review by 31 December 2015 with a view to proposing a new target and extending the timeframe 'to 2030'. Again, this came with the caveat that the proposals should be 'as neutral as possible from the point of view of competition and [...] socially equitable and sustainable'.

Normally, Heads of State rubber stamp technical deals hammered out in sectoral formations of the Council of Ministers. But on this occasion, the deal was unexpectedly blocked at a late stage by the German Chancellor Angela Merkel, who in the run up to federal elections had reportedly come under intense pressure from German manufacturers to expand the super credit scheme (Keating, 2013a). In what one respected EU newspaper described as a 'highly unusual move' (Keating, 2013b), she sought to build a blocking coalition with Central and Eastern European Member States, whose car industries were closely tied to her own. Later, it was revealed that Merkel's CDU party had received campaign donations from the family that owned BMW (Keating, 2013e).

At the Environment Council in October 2013, the blocking coalition was revealed to include Poland, Hungary, Slovakia, Estonia and Portugal, as well as the United Kingdom and Germany (Keating, 2013b). The French and Italian governments tried to push through the original deal, fearing that any extra modifications would give German manufacturers a competitive advantage. The pressure on the Parliament to acquiesce to Merkel's demands became intense. MEPs realised that if they did not back down, the entire dossier risked going back to a second reading which, given that the parliamentary term only had another six months to run, threatened to delay the adoption of new legislation by months and possibly even years (Keating, 2013d, 2013e). The Lithuanian Presidency eventually came to the rescue, brokering a deal that involved modifying the super credit scheme and the 2020 deadline (Keating, 2013f, 2013g). Under this fresh deal, the deadline for achieving 95g/km (which, recall, had been originally endorsed by the Heads of State as long ago as 2008) was pushed back a year to 2021. The super credit scheme was also significantly expanded to allow German manufacturers to continue selling large luxury cars. Greenpeace said the EU was:

... backtracking on earlier agreements to limit the climate damage caused by its cars. [It] has put a few companies' business interests before the interests of its citizens and the wider economy

(quoted in Flynn, 2013e).

According to T&E (2013), the deal implied that the CO_2 reduction target for 2020 would relax the overall target of 95g/km to somewhere around 100g/km. On 25 January 2014, the proposal was finally ratified by a plenary vote in the European Parliament and Regulation 333/2014 was added to the EU statute book on 5 April 2014, 609 days after being proposed by the Commission.

7.9 Policy Feedback and Policy Instrument Redesign

After the long and painful struggle to adopt the 2014 Regulation, a period of regulatory stability may have been expected. However, the 2014 Regulation included a *flexibility clause*, which committed the Commission to complete an *ex post* review of post-2020 targets by the end of 2015. In July 2016, the Commission duly published a *European Strategy for Low-Emission Mobility*, informed by that review (COM (2016) 501; Gibson *et al.*, 2015). The new strategy noted that a global shift to low emission mobility had finally begun 'but its pace should be accelerated' so that the sector was 'firmly on the path towards zero' emissions (COM (2016) 501: 2).

As before, a number of different factors had converged in a way that increased pressure on the car manufacturers and their supportive Member States to acquiesce to stricter targets and a new timeframe. First of all, the new strategy explained that the sector should make a greater contribution to fulfil the new policy programme-level emission reduction target of a 40 per cent cut by 2030, which the EU had adopted prior to the 2015 Paris Summit (see Chapter 3). Complex reforms of the EU Emissions Trading System were already under way (see Chapter 6) and the Commission explained that it was only fair that those outside it should do more. Again, transport's status as a special case was put under greater pressure.

Second, after meeting the 2015 deadline several years ahead of schedule, the progress in achieving emission reductions was stalling, leaving the manufacturers well off track to attain the more challenging target of 95g/km by 2021 (EEA, 2016). Exogenous factors were certainly at work: total car sales rose in the mid-2010s (Sharham, 2015) as growth returned to the Eurozone, reaching 15 million per year in 2017, the highest level since the financial crisis (EEA, 2018). The popularity of diesels also began to decline and, in 2017, they were overtaken by petrol cars for the first time since emissions data was collected under the voluntary agreement (EEA, 2018). The sale of electric and hybrids rose 42 per cent in 2017, but still accounted for only 1.5 per cent of total sales (EEA, 2018). It was rather ironic that while these trends alleviated local air pollution problems in some cities (average NOx emissions from petrol engines declined significantly after 2000, but hardly fell at all from diesel engines; EEA, 2016: 11, 27), they made it harder to fulfil climate change targets. This is because diesel cars generally burn fuel more efficiently than petrol engines and consequently produce less CO_2 per kilometre travelled than petrol cars.[13] In 2017, average CO_2 emissions from cars actually increased for the first time in over a decade, with petrol cars surpassing 50 per cent of total sales for the first time (EEA, 2018b). T&E blamed the increase partly on the shift back to petrol and partly on manufacturers selling more of the larger and heavier cars, whilst under-marketing low-emission electric vehicles (Delpero, 2018). If this sales pattern continues, it could prove to be highly significant, because according to the 2009 Regulation (and its relevant implementing instrument – Decision 2012/100), any manufacturer that exceeds its limits in 2021 will incur significant fines (Campbell, 2017).

Third, to make matters worse, the European car industry found itself under unprecedented public scrutiny following the revelation in 2015 that Volkswagen, the world's largest manufacturer of diesel engines, had deliberately cheated on air pollution tests in an attempt to secure a much greater market share for its diesels in the US market (EEA, 2016: 34; Ewing, 2017). The cheating was originally detected by a small environmental NGO in the United States, but once US authorities decided to act, the scandal rapidly escalated, drawing in more manufacturers (Roach, 2015; Simkins and Roach, 2015) and pushing what the previously relatively technical issue of vehicle emission testing up political agendas around the world. The scandal eventually resulted in the resignation of the company's CEO, the recall of millions of its vehicles, massive corporate losses and a raft of extremely costly legal actions in the USA (McGee, 2017). The Dieselgate scandal, as it eventually became known, led to a slew of regulatory inquiries into the behaviour of the car industry, including suspected cartel behaviour by the German manufacturers (Toplensky and McGee, 2018). If proven, cartel behaviour could lead to yet more fines (up to 10 per cent of global revenues on the product in question). Meanwhile, a special inquiry conducted by the European Parliament called for tighter controls on how new cars were tested and approved for use (European Parliament, 2017).

The reputational damage that the scandal exacted on the European car industry raised political awareness of the negative effects generated by its products (and especially diesel cars). For example, the EEA revealed that more than 30 per cent of NOx emissions in the EU derive from the road transport sector (EEA, 2016: 7), causing local air pollution standards to be exceeded in many large European cities. Armed with this information, activist law groups such as Client Earth used EU air quality standards to force cities such as Munich (the home of BMW) to institute city-wide bans on the use of diesel cars (Rojo, 2017a). Meanwhile, countries such as France, which specialise in producing smaller cars, sought to turn these regulatory developments to their commercial advantage. For example, in 2017 the French government announced that it intended to completely ban the sale of all new petrol and diesel cars by 2040 (Rojo, 2017b). This pledge, later repeated by the Swedish and UK governments, forced a significant shift in the car industry's climate change strategy, which until that point had been premised on negotiating incremental adjustments to petrol and, in particular, diesel car engine technologies. Finding itself wrong footed by these developments, the Commission at first sought to defend its incremental strategy when Elżbieta Bieńkowska, a European Commissioner, cautioned against kneejerk responses such as city-wide bans in case they undermined the integrity of the single market. She warned against demonising diesel cars 'which remain part of our lives and [hence] we must rebuild confidence in this technology [...] by having new and more reliable tests' (European Commission, 2017). The EU's testing regime was eventually overhauled in 2017.

Towards 2030: The 2019 Cars Regulation

But in DG CLIMA, attempts were being made to draft more policy proposals, nimbly exploiting the *flexibility clause* in the 2014 Regulation. Immediate reactions to its proposals ran along familiar lines. In general, manufacturers favoured less ambitious targets for 2030 differentiated according to vehicle mass, and no requirement to produce very low emissions vehicles. Environmental groups favoured more ambitious targets both for 2025 and 2030, based on a vehicle's footprint, with an explicit requirement to produce a certain number of very low emission cars (COM (2017) 676: 6). On 8 November 2017, the Commission published proposals for another regulation (COM (2017) 676). They sought to achieve a 30 per cent reduction in the CO_2 emissions from new cars, with a binding interim target of 15 per cent by 2025 to force the pace of change. These targets were based on a new Light Vehicle Test Procedure, introduced in September 2017. The rapidly collapsing sales of new diesel vehicles, which some manufacturers had banked on to comply with previous climate change targets, threatened to make these future targets much harder to meet, finally forcing all of them to embrace hybrid and electric technologies. Manufacturers that produced more of these so-called zero- and low-carbon vehicles would henceforth be rewarded with a less strict CO_2 target. However, the Commission stopped short of adopting environmentalists' demands to set a mandatory minimum production quota for them. A *flexibility clause* was included via Article 13, requiring the Commission to undertake yet another *ex post* policy evaluation in 2024 and 'where appropriate' develop a new proposal to amend the regulation. These proposed *flexibility devices* in effect committed policy designers to continue updating emissions controls for the foreseeable future.

Once again, the new proposal generated deep divisions in the Environment Council. Governments representing manufacturers of the small, petrol-powered vehicles (principally Italy, France and Sweden) demanded a stricter headline reduction goal (up to 40 per cent), whereas Slovakia and the Czech Republic claimed that a 20 per cent target would be 'sufficient' (Hodgson, 2018a). And yet again, positive policy feedback effects generated by the previous amendment, also began to manifest themselves, altering actor coalitions, capacities and preferences. New groups such as local authorities and city mayors entered the policy design process, pushing hard for tighter standards to reduce urban air quality problems (COM (2017) 676: 6). The electricity industry also joined in, campaigning for a growth in electric car sales to boost the demand for its electricity. The head of Eurelectric, Kristian Ruby, complained that 'the level of ambition [of the proposal] is too weak to trigger the necessary paradigm shift to electric mobility across Europe' (quoted in Hodgson, 2017b). Environmental groups concurred, pointing to the fact that some manufacturers had already set their own internal

Table 7.1 *Car emissions: significant policy instrument changes, 1998–2019*

Legislation (and speed of adoption)[3]	Lifespan (days)[1]	Description
1999 Voluntary Agreement (Recommendation 1999/125) (1,144 days)	3,615	• *Stringency:* reduce average CO_2 emissions to 140g/km by 2008–2009. • *Scope:* CO_2 emissions from all new passenger cars. • *Timeframe:* to 2008 (with a further review on changes by 2012).
1999 Directive (1999/94) (467 days)	7,074[2]	• Availability of consumer information on fuel economy and CO_2 emissions in respect of the marketing of new cars.
2000 Decision (1753/2000) (742 days)	3,411	• A scheme to monitor the average emissions of CO_2 from new cars.
2009 Regulation on CO_2 Emissions from New Cars (443/2009) (492 days)	2,398	• *Stringency:* increased. Reduce average CO_2 emissions to 130g/km by 2015 and 95g/km by 2020. • *Scope:* stable. CO_2 emissions from new passenger cars. • *Timeframe:* increased. Extended to 2015/2020.
2014 Regulation on CO_2 Emissions from New Cars (333/2014) (609 days)	2,825	• *Stringency:* increased. Reduce average CO_2 emissions to 95g/km by 2021. • *Scope:* stable. • *Timeframe:* increased. Extended to 2021.
2019 Regulation on CO_2 Emissions from New Cars (2019/631) (526 days)	4,249	• *Stringency:* increased. 37.5% reduction in CO_2 emissions per km from 2021 levels by 2030, and 15% by 2025. • *Scope:* stable. • *Timeframe:* increased. Extended to 2025 and 2030.

[1] Expected at the time of writing (1 June 2019).
[2] Does not have an end date. Lifespan calculated from legislation's entry into force until 1 June 2019.
[3] Significant policy instrument changes in bold.
Source: own composition.

corporate goals to phase in electric cars that were more ambitious than what the Commission was proposing, and should be formally incorporated into the proposal.

In September 2018, the Parliament's ENVI committee voted to support an increased 2025 target of 20 per cent and a 2030 target of 45 per cent (European

Parliament, 2018a; Gyekye, 2018b). Most of the party groups voted for the committee's report, but only one of twenty-three of the centre-right European People's Party members of ENVI joined them (European Parliament, 2018b: 4). In October 2018, the Parliament plenary voted for a compromise of 20 per cent in 2025 and 40 per cent in 2030 (Hodgson, 2018b). The Environment Ministers then agreed a general approach that kept the Commission's original proposal of 15 per cent by 2025 and increased the corresponding 2030 target to 35 per cent (Council of the European Union, 2018). In December 2018, after no less than five trilogue meetings, the Council of Ministers and the Parliament compromised on the final text of the regulation (see Council of the European Union, 2019). For cars, the compromise maintained the Commission's proposed binding 2025 target of 15 per cent and set a 2020 target of 37.5 per cent (Council of the European Union, 2019: 2). It also included the possibility of revising the 2030 target, and the setting of targets in 2035 and 2040, as part of a Commission-led review of the Regulation in 2023 (Council of the European Union, 2019: 73). The new 2019 Regulation (2019/631) was adopted on 17 April 2019, 526 days after being proposed.

Chapter 4 outlined the main policy changes commencing with the voluntary agreement with ACEA and ending with the 2019 Regulation. Table 7.1 summarises each step in the sequence in considerably more detail, noting the most significant changes in policy stringency, scope and timeframe, and indicating the speed at which each change was agreed and how long it lasted.

Endnotes

1 In November 1996, the Commission eventually produced guidelines governing the negotiation of voluntary agreements, which acknowledged that their legal ambiguity meant that they had to be non-binding (COM/96/561; see also Wurzel et al., 2013: 123–125).
2 Forcing them to fit heavy safety measures such as crumple zones, reinforced structures and air bags.
3 Possible reasons could have included the effects of the recession or a determined effort by the manufacturers to avoid legislation by meeting the reduction target (ten Brink, 2010: 185).
4 In fact, Porsche increased its fleet average emissions over the course of the agreement. Absent big increases in vehicle weight and engine power after the early 1990s, most German manufacturers would probably have met the 140g/km target (Hey, 2010: 219).
5 The proposal being for a regulation rather than a voluntary agreement or tax measure.
6 But under special provisions, manufacturers were able to form a pool in order to meet their targets (COM (2007) 856: 7).
7 Interestingly, the term used in the text of the Regulation is not fine but 'emission premium'.
8 In effect, the 2012 deadline was pushed back three years to 2015 (ten Brink, 2010: 198).
9 Namely, those emitting less than 50g/km in 2012.
10 These were eventually phased out in 2016, after which very low emission ('super') cars were counted the same as standard cars.
11 The emission reductions were thus an unexpected consequence of the financial crisis, which had encouraged consumers to purchase smaller and less polluting cars.
12 Namely the slope of the limit value curve, pooling, super-credits and the system of fines (see COM (2012) 393 for details).
13 Although the efficiency gap between the two has decreased in the last decade as diesel car have become larger, heavier and less fuel-efficient (EEA, 2016: 50).

Part III

Climate Policy

Durable by Design?

8

Climate Policy Feedbacks

Significant Mechanisms, Effects and Directions

8.1 Introduction

Policy designers are seeking to adopt more durable climate policies that not only endure but remain influential over the long term. Amongst target groups and other relevant actors, such policies seek to nurture a belief that deep decarbonisation will happen and that they should prepare for that possibility rather than working to prevent it. Schattschneider (1935), who we quoted at the start of Chapter 1, implied that some policies become durable because they foster and sustain their own political support base through processes of positive policy feedback but may remain vulnerable to negative policy feedbacks that render them fragile.

This chapter looks back across all five empirical chapters (Chapters 3–7) and forward-traces the policy feedback effects and mechanisms that flowed from the three original policy instruments on biofuels (Chapter 5), stationary emitters (Chapter 6) and car emissions (Chapter 7) respectively. In doing so, it seeks to address Objective 2 (on feedback mechanisms and effects) outlined at the end of Chapter 1. In the existing literatures, feedback mechanisms and feedback effects have often been conflated, resulting in a loss of precision about the causes of policy feedback and hence the underlying determinants of policy durability. In Chapter 1, we drew upon Pierson's (1993) influential distinction between two feedback mechanisms. *Resource/incentive mechanisms* have since become the stock in trade of policy feedback analysts and relate to the various ways in which policy instruments channel flows of benefits (in the form of resources) and costs (in the forms of burdens) to different actors and coalitions (Jacobs and Mettler, 2018: 346). By contrast, *interpretive mechanisms* have received less attention; they relate to the way in which policy instruments alter flows of knowledge and information in ways that reshape actor perceptions via processes of learning. In Chapter 3, we noted the possibility that policies may have important, long-term consequences even though they do not transfer significant financial resources.

As this chapter is primarily concerned with addressing Objective 2, it will chiefly examine the three original instruments (the 2003 Biofuels Directive, the 2003 Emissions Trading Directive and the 1999 Voluntary Agreement on CO_2 emissions from cars) and their first-order policy feedback *effects*, which we originally defined as downstream consequences with no complete feedback loop. In Chapter 1, we noted that scholars have studied a wide array of these policy feedback effects in the existing literature. Given that climate change is a wicked policy challenge (see Chapter 2), we will concentrate on the first-order effects on the identities, preferences and capacities of three main actor types: governmental bodies (in our case, the EU institutions and the Member States); target groups (i.e. the actors to whom the policy instrument was addressed); and other relevant interest groups. With some exceptions, the existing literature on policy durability has focused on the most durable policies and traced them back to their origins. As our approach relies on process tracing forwards from the original instrument, we seek to trace out the main feedback effects to understand how far they were either positive or negative in nature, thereby securing a better understanding of the 'non-cases' of policy durability. Once we have accomplished that task, we will be in a better position to analyse the complete feedback loops back to the original policy and subsequent feedbacks generated by later iterations of each instrument, as well as weigh the vexed issue of intentionality (i.e. which correspond to the third and the first objectives outlined at the end of Chapter 1). These two important topics are addressed in the next chapter.

Having outlined the aims and objectives of this chapter, the remainder unfolds as follows. Section 8.2 reviews the evidence of positive policy feedback effects generated by the three instruments, which appear in the order (more to less coercive) that we introduced in Chapters 1 and 2. Having done that, we critically reflect on the propositions that we developed (in Chapter 2) on when and where such feedback effects are more (and less) likely to emerge. In Section 8.3, we follow the same sequence of analytical steps but for negative policy feedback effects. In Section 8.4, we summarise and look forward to the concluding chapter.

8.2 Positive Policy Feedback Effects

In very general terms, positive feedbacks are self-reinforcing and self-amplifying. They occur 'when a change in one direction sets in motion reinforcing pressures that produce further change in the same direction' (Jervis, 1997: 125). Systems analysts and historical institutionalists such as Pierson (2004) have found them especially intriguing because they have a tendency to unfold in complex and unexpected ways (Bardach, 2006: 346). Policies generating positive feedback effects are held to be self-reinforcing in that they encourage actors – and specifically target groups – to align their preferences and activities with them (Thelen, 2006: 155). As a result, the original policy becomes more politically stable and hence more durable over time.

Regulation: Biofuels

The 2003 Biofuels Directive was adopted relatively quickly (in 548 days) and endured for 3,151 days – or over 8.5 years. It marked the EU's first foray into biofuel policy design, setting indicative regulatory targets to promote the production and consumption of biofuel in the transport sector across the EU. As noted in Chapter 5, the early 2000s was a period of rising political confidence in EU climate and energy policy, when Heads of State were eager to set more stringent and more long-term targets and biofuels appeared as a convenient policy solution to several long-standing and interconnected problems ranging from decarbonisation to rural economic renewal. Biofuels quickly gained a panacea status because they promised not only to meet the EU's escalating energy and climate policy ambitions, but also address many other long-standing problems, including excess agricultural production in Europe (Palmer, 2015: 281). Not only did they appear capable of displacing fossil fuels in the road transport sector (a sector in which emissions were rapidly rising), but they could also be reconfigured to facilitate decarbonisation in other sub-areas of the transport sector such as air and marine transport (IEA, 2011: 7).

Globally, biodiesel's share of global energy demand experienced an eight-fold increase in the period 2005–2015 and bioethanol a threefold increase (Royal Academy of Engineering, 2017: 17), albeit from relatively low levels. Starting in 2001–2002, there emerged the tantalising possibility that the main target groups in the EU – namely fuel and vehicle producers would buy into a positive vision of the future in which European biofuels production underwent a similar expansion. As noted in Chapters 4 and 5, biofuel production and consumption in the EU did grow substantially after 2003, underpinned by the 2003 Directive. Production of biodiesel in the EU grew by 250 per cent between 2005 and 2015, and bioethanol production grew by eightfold between 2004 and 2014. When it was eventually replaced by the 2009 Renewable Energy Directive, the policy instrument settings were made more stringent and more binding. The policy time horizon was also extended further into the future – from seven years (i.e. to 2010) in the 2003 Directive to eleven years (i.e. to 2020) – in order to give businesses greater confidence in policy support for biofuel production.

The *resource/incentive feedback mechanisms* in the period 2003–2009 were of varying importance, in part because the original directive was an example of a relatively weak regulatory instrument that set indicative targets that lacked strong coercive force. In fact, very few Member States had exceeded their interim targets under the Directive by the end of 2005. Crucially, while biofuel production in the EU increased significantly and related industries were strong supporters of the policy, the Directive did not compel target groups to make significant sunk investments in second- and third-generation biofuel production technologies and did not distribute concentrated benefits (in the form of targeted subsidies) to produce similar effects. Also, the policy feedback effects on government were not especially significant either – the 2003 Directive failed to direct new revenue streams into EU institutions that could be employed to create new bureaucratic coalitions that would in turn fight for the policy's expansion. The main target groups – namely biofuel producers – became more engaged with policy making after the 2003 Directive was adopted, with the European Biodiesel Board (EBB), the European Bioethanol Fuel Association (eBIO) and the European Union of Alcohol Producers (UEPA) becoming stronger supporters of EU policy support. In 2006, a pan-industry alliance (EBTP) emerged with the aim of encouraging all types of biofuel production, but it failed to bridge the differences between biodiesel and bioethanol producers on specific policy issues. It was only after the adoption of the 2009 Directive that new interest groups began to emerge, pushing specific types and niche uses of biofuel (e.g. advanced biofuels in aviation). Crucially, unlike some areas of social policy, the 2003 Biofuels Directive did not generate complex, society-wide commitments to biofuel among the public which could have increased broader support for the policy. In fact, because biofuels had originally been foreseen as a drop-in alternative to fossil fuels, the majority of the public were not aware of the Directive's existence or that the road fuel they were putting into their fuel tanks was blended with higher quantities of biofuel. The societal benefits of the Directive were therefore relatively diffuse at best and generally of very low visibility.

Positive feedback effects also emerged from the operation of *interpretive mechanisms*. For example, the Commission was able to cite the failure of the 2003 Directive's indicative targets in reaching the 2 per cent target in 2005 to argue for stronger targets to be included in the 2009 Directive (an example of the power of precedent). In effect, the failure to fulfil the targets allowed the Commission to argue that what had failed was not the long-term policy objective, but the (relatively) weak instruments chosen to achieve it. When the 2009 Directive was being formulated, the Commission again resorted to the power of precedent to argue for targets (in Article 21) that explicitly encouraged producers to produce more second- and third-generation biofuel. Until that point, its encouragement was rather unspecific, i.e. to produce 'more biofuel'. Second, Annex 4 of the 2003 Directive established a novel reporting and monitoring framework which helped to illuminate production trends in what was, by then, still an embryonic EU-wide market. As well as highlight and draw attention to the emerging boom in biofuels, it also indicated who the national leaders and laggards were. The major producers may have known what was happening, but at that point, smaller producers and those operating in the various supply chains (including feedstock producers, fuel suppliers and car manufacturers) were still operating in a state of uncertainty, with only partial access to information. This reporting framework was greatly strengthened by the more coercive provisions of the 2009 Directive which included a mandatory template to ensure more harmonised and more detailed reporting. Prior to 2009, countries had reported, but irregularly and rather inconsistently. The scope of the reported information expanded yet again with the adoption of the 2015 Indirect Land Use Change (ILUC) Directive, under which producers and Member States were required to report on the indirect emissions arising from all their production activities, sometimes spanning many different parts of the world.

Emissions Trading: Large Stationery Emitters

The original 2003 ETS Directive was adopted in 721 days and endured for more than nine years. When it was modified, the 2009 Directive made the instrument settings more stringent (comprising increased auctioning, EU-level allocation and cap-setting and a reduced cap) and increased the policy's scope (encompassing more sectors and gases). The policy time horizon was also extended out even further into the future (to 2020) so that target groups would have more confidence in the durability of emissions trading. These changes in stringency, scope and timeframe are typical of positive policy feedback. In many ways, the 2003 Directive actively facilitated these changes by generating significant new resource flows that, over time, had lasting effects on both target groups and government, especially at the Member State level and in the European Commission. The most significant *resource/incentive feedback mechanism* related to the emission allowances that were established when the system commenced in 2005. Unlike a tax (which extracts revenues from companies and channels them to governments), freely allocated allowances became a significant 'tradable asset' for industries that received them (Skjærseth and Wettestad, 2008: 75). Before the reforms of the 2009 Directive came into effect in 2013, allowance distribution was largely based on historical emissions. Thus the value of these new assets was disproportionately enjoyed by actors – such as high-carbon electricity generators and the energy-intensive industries – that during the formulation of the 2003 Directive preferred other policy instrument types such as an EU-wide voluntary agreement. This had two significant feedback effects. First of all, more actors became interested in trading. In particular, the allocation of free allowances created substantial 'incentives for lobbying' for all firms who were already in the system or were at risk of being included in its scope (Anger et al., 2016: 634). For example, during the formulation of the 2003 Directive, 93 non-governmental actors participated in the

European Commission's consultations. By 2007, the consultations related to the 2009 Directive attracted responses from 202 actors. In 2015, an online consultation on Phase IV of the trading system received more than 500 responses (as COM (2015) 337: 6).

Second, through time actors that benefited from trading became steadily more supportive of the ETS. The electricity generators had been largely supportive of it during the formulation process but became even more supportive when allowances were handed out for free, thus strengthening the 'instrument constituency' (Voss and Simons, 2014) that had advocated for the Directive in the first place. As we explained in Chapter 6, free allowances became a source of windfall profits for these actors during the first two trading phases (Müller and Slominski, 2013: 1434). And because many generators were not directly exposed to significant international competition pressures, they were able to pass through most of the additional costs to energy consumers in the form of higher electricity prices. As time passed, preferences changed: most generators became stronger advocates of the system as a whole, even when it began to attract more concerted political opposition from other actors (see below), fearing that policy dismantling would undermine their investments (Carlson and Fri, 2013: 122). Even the most opposed actors – namely the energy-intensive industries – stopped calling for alternative policy approaches, although they did advocate for major changes to the policy design to reduce their costs and increase free allocation (e.g. AEII *et al.*, 2007). Finally, all the firms included in the trading system had to make significant up-front investments in operational systems to monitor and report their emissions, and to administer the receipt and sale of allowances (Müller and Slominski, 2013: 1434). These investments helped to lock all target groups into the process of trading emissions, even those that remained opposed to it.

Resource/incentive mechanisms also had a significant effect on government actors. In the European Commission, what had initially been a small team of ETS-related officials in DG Environment rapidly expanded in number and was eventually shifted across into a new Directorate-General in 2010 (DG CLIMA). In effect, the ETS created a new bureaucratic lobby within the Commission for climate change mitigation in general and emissions trading in particular. Many of the core ETS team had worked hard to get the 2003 Directive adopted and had a 'strong "personal" interest in seeing [it] succeed' (Wettestad, 2009: 322). This expanding bureaucratic lobby certainly made its presence felt during Phase II, when the National Allocation Plans (NAPs) covering the period 2008–2012 were tightened significantly, very much against the wishes of some large Member States (Wettestad, 2009: 323). Later, DG Environment was a key advocate for replacing the NAPs with EU-wide cap-setting and allocation, as well as expanded auctioning (Wettestad, 2009: 324). In the late 2000s, staff in DG CLIMA became more heavily engaged in fulfilling a suite of new bureaucratic tasks, such as benchmarking free allowances and drawing up carbon leakage lists. By 2016, no less than 46 staff were working on emissions trading in DG CLIMA (European Union, 2016: 35–36).

One of the most consequential resource-related – and political – changes was the shift of resources to Member States through expanded auctioning, especially after 2013. For DG Environment, which played a central role in advocating increased auctioning, this shift was rationalised on the grounds that it would improve economic efficiency and welfare. The revenue flows to national treasuries – amounting to €11.8 billion between 2013 and 2015 (European Commission, 2017: 16) – were an important side effect, but were viewed as somewhat secondary in the Commission. The eventual selection of auctioning as the default method of allocation significantly impacted the preferences of the Member States, creating a material incentive to support reforms designed to raise allowance prices, including backloading, the MSR, and allowance cancellation in the 2018 Directive. Later on, in some Member States these dynamics pitted environment ministries and finance ministries (who fought to maintain high allowance prices to boost revenues) against industry ministries (who preferred lower prices to safeguard the competitiveness of some sections of business).

Finally, *resource/incentive mechanisms* actively encouraged other interest groups to align their activities with the trading system. Market intermediaries such as banks and consultancies were attracted by the prospect of new revenue streams in secondary markets related to banking and trading. It led to a sudden increase in the membership of organisations that represented major market intermediaries and lobbied on ETS topics, such as the International Emissions Trading Association. The importance of this mechanism weakened after late 2008 – due to the fall in the allowance price and tax fraud, among other issues – but still served as an important link keeping market intermediaries, and the policy actors that represented them, supportive and engaged with the ETS, even though they were not directly targeted by it.

By contrast, the public's direct participation in the functioning of the system remained limited. Indeed, some have argued that all trading systems have a 'special complexity' that actively hinders public access and understanding (Baldwin, 2008: 22), other than when particular focusing events propel it into the wider public discourse (e.g. in relation to windfall profits or allowance fraud). Indeed, the generally low visibility of resource flows generated by the ETS arguably facilitated the expansion in lobbying by target groups (Baldwin, 2008: 22).

The ETS also produced at least three significant positive feedback effects via the operation of *interpretive mechanisms*. First of all, there were significant, positive effects on the policy making capabilities of the European Commission. Many of its activities in Phases II and III addressed problems that originally emerged in Phase I (Mukherjee and Giest, 2017: 16). For example, the Commission had pushed for a more centralised system during the formulation of the 2003 Directive but had been firmly opposed by Member States. But when problems began to manifest themselves, thus becoming known 'facts on the ground' rather than hypothetical examples, DG Environment was able to cite them as evidence that a more centralised system was needed (negative learning; see Boasson and Wettestad, 2013: 63).

Second, once the ETS was up and running it too became a 'fact on the ground' that all actors had to calibrate their policy preferences and design activities against (Muller and Slominski, 2013: 1434). Some of the proposals for change involved relatively minor amendment to the existing policy (see Chapter 6). But several others, involved more significant structural changes, including the wholesale dismantling of the ETS (e.g. by the Scrap the ETS coalition of NGOs; see Corporate Europe Observatory *et al.*, 2013). But as EU policy – and thus the wider trading system – became steadily more durable, more and more actors opted to 'work within' the existing policy to achieve their preferences (see Hacker, 2004: 264), e.g. the energy-intensives shifted from advocating voluntary approaches to focusing on increasing free allocation from the existing policy. It is telling that within five years of the 2003 Directive being adopted 'the question of abolishing [it] was simply not on the table' (Boasson and Wettestad, 2013: 71). Given the intense battles over numerous, alternative instrument designs that had preceded the adoption of the trading system, the significance of this change should not be underestimated.

Finally, from the outset, transparent information on emissions was a vital but often taken-for-granted precondition for the successful functioning of the system (Delbeke and Vis, 2015: 128). Over time, this information provided a powerful 'cue' to new policy development in the manner suggested by Pierson (1993). It is worth remembering that very basic information on the distribution and quantification of emissions from installations later covered by the ETS simply did not exist when the system was being formulated, so a bespoke 'infrastructure had to be developed to generate and quality check' installation-level emissions data (Delbeke and Vis, 2015: 3). Indeed, the initial paucity of data and the associated complexity of collecting it was a major factor behind the decision to keep the system's scope relatively narrowly focused on a limited number of stationary ('point-source') emitters and only one greenhouse gas (Skjærseth and Wettestad, 2008: 62). At first, the emission estimates submitted by operators proved to be rather inaccurate, which partly explained why the national caps derived from them were so generous (Baldwin, 2008: 9). But as the quality of the information improved, so too did the trust of various actors in the robustness of the system. And as monitoring and reporting systems matured still further, the Commission was able to propose expansions in scope and stringency that would not have been possible before 2003. According to two senior Commission officials that oversaw these early design activities, the resulting information 'offered a transparent basis for the further refinement of measures or for concentration on areas that need[ed] to be brought to the attention of policy makers' (Delbeke and Vis, 2015: 128). Just as importantly, they helped to define carbon as a new commodity that could be traded in markets, which in turn fed through and affected allowance prices in the system, which in the view of many actors provided a real-time assessment of the overall performance of the system (Mukherjee and Giest, 2017: 7). In effect, the nature of the system changed over the course of a decade from one of partial information to one characterised by high levels of transparency – a shift that some of the new interest groups such as the NGO Sandbag both actively facilitated and benefited from. At several critical points after 2003 – e.g. when prices were perceived to be too high (as in 2005) or too low (as they were between 2008 and 2018) – greater data transparency provoked actors to adapt their behaviour and their preferences – very much as textbook accounts of market-based instruments assumed they would.

Voluntarism: Car Emissions

The instrument lying at the least coercive end of our continuum was the voluntary agreement on car emissions. It was adopted in 1998 after protracted negotiations lasting 1,144 days, during which a series of concessions were built in to pacify the car producers and their allies, especially in some Member States. Despite its drawn-out adoption, the agreement was relatively durable in a narrow sense, enduring for nearly ten years before being replaced by the 2009 Cars Regulation. In another sense, it was not durable, car emissions being the only case in which the main instrument was completely removed and replaced.[1] From the outset, environmentalists argued that the voluntary agreement was a weak and potentially ineffectual instrument, but were relieved that at least some controls on emissions had been adopted. After all, they considered the *status quo* – no policy at all – to be even worse.

Our expectations, formulated in Chapter 2, suggest that a voluntary agreement adopted in such circumstances was unlikely to generate significant positive feedback effects via *resource/incentive mechanisms*. These assumptions were largely confirmed by the main findings of Chapter 7. By their very nature, textbook examples of voluntary agreements involve target groups volunteering to make policy investments to achieve certain pre-defined environmental goals. However, the design of the 1998 agreement gave target groups little or no encouragement to invest in its long-term durability. In fact, it facilitated the adoption and continued use of simple, drop-in technological solutions such as low resistance tyres, turbocharged diesel engines and, of course, biofuels, the relatively minor cost of which could either be easily absorbed or be passed on to either customers, suppliers and/or fuel providers. By doing so, the agreement made it all too easy for car producers to withhold their investments and maintain the policy status quo extant. Moreover, because the agreement did not adequately address the delicate matter of inter-company burden sharing, free-riding remained a near constant possibility. Consequently, no single manufacturer (or group of manufacturers) felt sufficiently confident to invest in radical new technologies such as very low emission vehicles powered by electricity or hydrogen. To no one's great surprise, the agreement consequently failed to decisively restructure politics. It was only much later in the policy instrument sequence – when the controls were eventually tightened, first in the 2009 Regulation and then in 2014 and 2018 – that new interest groups (e.g. aluminium producers, electricity generating companies and municipalities demanding stringent, city-wide bans on diesel powered vehicles) began to enter the fray, lending their support to long-standing demands from environmental groups for more stringent and more durable targets. Finally, there were no new significant resource flows into government or, for that matter, the sudden emergence of a powerful new bureaucratic lobby within governments favouring deep decarbonisation. In marked contrast to some social policy fields, there were no elaborate unintended consequences for mass publics, for whom the policy conflicts in Brussels remained remote and irrelevant – at least, that is, until the Dieselgate scandal broke.

Yet despite the weakness of these *resource/incentive mechanisms*, the voluntary agreement managed to endure for over ten years. When it was eventually replaced, not only was the next instrument in the sequence (the 2009 Regulation) regulatory (and hence considerably more coercive), its settings were more stringent and its time horizon was set further into the future (out to 2020).[2] Therefore, although the policy instrument of the voluntary agreement was replaced, it also set in motion feedback processes that eventually strengthened the EU's overall policy towards CO_2 emissions from cars. These changes were, of course, consistent with processes of positive feedback, which suggests that *interpretive* mechanisms were probably also at work, much as they were in the case of emissions trading. What might these have been? First of all, although relatively low in coerciveness, the agreement and associated policies on monitoring nonetheless created substantial new sources of information on vehicle production and emissions that, over time, provided a powerful 'cue' to new policy development (Pierson, 1993). The manufacturers were originally very reluctant to share this type of information, even amongst themselves, arguing that it was commercially sensitive, but when it eventually entered the public domain it did lead to greater transparency.[3] This transparency, in turn, encouraged some manufacturers to take a calculated risk and invest in cleaner vehicles, more secure in the knowledge that they would not be undercut by free-riders. It was telling that the 2009 Regulation contained producer-specific targets, albeit arranged along a 'limit curve' that more or less entrenched existing inter-manufacturer differences to a relatively large extent.

Second, the information had a positive feedback effect on the policy making capabilities of DG Environment. As was noted in Chapter 7, DG Environment originally pushed for a more coercive approach during the policy formulation process but was repeatedly blocked by a small but powerful minority of Member States, backed by their respective car industries. Crucially, the provision of new information provided a forewarning to the Commission (from around 2002) that emissions reductions by the sector were well off track and gave it the confidence to push for new policy instruments. It was only when the widely expected failure of the agreement could be empirically verified (on which see Section 8.3), that the Commission was able to secure the breakthrough knowledge it needed to advocate successfully for a more coercive approach, which was eventually adopted in the form of the 2009 Regulation (an example of negative learning; see Boasson and Wettestad, 2013: 63).

Summary: When and Where Were Positive Feedback Effects Significant?

In Chapter 2 we noted that systems analysts expect positive feedbacks to be more likely in complex, deeply interconnected systems that are densely populated with actors, instructions and policy instruments. Arguably, modern policy systems in general (Pierson, 2004: 19) and the EU in particular exhibit such characteristics, and hence would appear to constitute fertile grounds in which positive feedback effects can emerge. Pierson (2004: 35) even went as far as to claim that they are 'widespread' in politics and that 'most policies ... are generally subject' to them. Positive feedback effects certainly featured heavily in his historical institutional interpretation of European integration (Pierson, 1996), which highlighted the ongoing inability of Member States to manage policy dynamics that they themselves had initiated. However, the existing literature on policy feedback and policy durability has not, as we also noted in Chapter 2, investigated the precise conditions in which feedback effects occur across the full range of policy areas. In Chapter 1 we argued that, in very general terms, they are probably less likely to appear in more regulatory policy settings such as climate change where governments are imposing concentrated costs on polluters to produce relatively diffuse social benefits.

How well do our empirical findings correspond to the four propositions that we originally formulated in Chapter 2? First of all, we proposed that *policies which require large set-up costs and/or distribute significant and concentrated benefits, are more likely to produce positive policy feedbacks effects than those that do not.* In their textbook form, regulations seek to impose significant up-front costs on polluters, unlike instruments further along the policy instrument coerciveness spectrum. But this is not how the 2003 Biofuels Directive was eventually formulated – opponents removed all but fairly weak, indicative targets. In general, feed-in tariffs and subsidies are regarded as the climate policy instruments that are most likely to generate positive feedback effects (Meckling et al., 2015). However, they lay outside the EU's policy design space and were not adopted. However, the ETS does seem to confirm the general validity of this proposition as do other prominent examples of emission trading (see Rabe, 2016: 10).

Second, we also proposed that *benefit-distributing policies which become large enough to constitute a significant premise of target groups' everyday existence are more likely to generate positive policy feedback effects*. The EU ETS case confirmed the general validity of this particular proposition. It also confirmed that the flow of benefits does not necessarily have to be particularly large in scale or long-lasting; just significant and immediate enough to encourage target groups to commit to the instrument's long-term durability.

Third, we noted the importance of coordination effects and proposed that *policies which consolidate the status quo distribution of costs and benefits (and thus deliver further returns to incumbent interests) are more likely to generate positive policy feedback effects than those that work against them*. Emissions trading confirmed the general validity of this proposition; the 2003 Directive survived its first few potentially perilous years of existence partly because it generated support amongst most of the actors to persevere with the existing instrument, albeit with marked differences of opinion on its precise calibration.

Finally, we proposed that *policies which generate strong adaptive expectations are more likely to generate positive feedback effects than those that do not* (Béland, 2010: 574). The 2003 Biofuels Directive could have shaped expectations had it provided a strong regulatory push in favour of first- and second-generation biofuels. But it was rendered too weak to do so because of concessions made at the formulation stage.

8.3 Negative Policy Feedback Effects

In systems analysis, negative feedbacks have balancing or self-equilibrating effects (Richardson, 1991: 5; Bardach, 2006: 341), which are analogous to the way in which a thermostat maintains a room's temperature at a constant level (Richardson, 1991: 48). In politics, negative feedback manifests itself in the appearance of countervailing coalitions which emerge to challenge new policy interventions and restore the system as a whole to its original position (Jervis, 1997: 125;

Howlett, 2009a: 253). In very general terms, policies that produce negative feedback effects actively trigger opposition to themselves that directly undermines their own durability (Weaver, 2010: 137), by opening up opportunities for opponents to weaken or dismantle them (Jacobs and Weaver, 2015). The effects of policy feedback on actors and on broad policy coalitions has been explored in a number of the existing literatures reviewed in Chapters 1 and 2. In Chapter 2 we noted, for example, some typical effects on prominent target groups as well as other interest groups. We hypothesised that the opposing groups may adopt a number of forms. Some groups may have unsuccessfully participated in the policy formulation stage, but then decide to stick around 'to contest the next round' of policy making (Thelen, 2003: 231–232). Others may have been supportive at the formulation stage but then switch their allegiance as the policy negatively affects them during the implementation phase. Still other groups may not have been involved in the design process, either because they did not expect to be targeted by the policy or because they operated in a different policy area (Pierson, 1993: 600), but then rise up in opposition as they are negatively affected by the policy (Weaver, 2010: 139). Finally, some policies may directly trigger the emergence of new groups or fresh alliances of existing groups whose entire *raison d'etre* is to push for reductions in policy stringency, policy repeal and/or a halt to similar policies in cognate areas (Patashnik and Zelizer, 2010: fn. 3). In Chapter 2, we suggested that one obvious *resource/incentive mechanism* is related to rapidly rising compliance costs that cannot be avoided. New sources of information on compliance costs that suddenly focus target group attention on the policy (via, e.g. a high-profile focusing event) constitutes a potentially important *interpretive feedback mechanism*. However, the mechanisms through which these effects are generated has so far received less systematic attention in the existing literature, which, as noted in Chapter 1, has generally been more concerned with only describing the most prominent positive policy feedback effects.

Regulation: Biofuels

In Chapter 5, we learned that the 2003 Biofuels Directive was designed relatively quickly inside the Commission's Directorates-General for energy and taxation, with relatively little consultation with other departments or wider interests. The primary target groups – the biofuel producers and the vehicle manufacturers – were generally supportive (or at least willing to acquiesce); the former because it promised to provide greater regulatory certainty, facilitate investment and generate a significant new revenue stream; the latter because biofuels were seen as a convenient drop-in technology that could be adopted with relatively little upheaval. Although environmental NGOs such as the European Environment Bureau (EEB) and Transport & Environment (T&E) were critical of the proposal, they were unable to build a blocking coalition of other actors. At the time, EU climate policy was still in its infancy and certainly did not attract the sustained interest of the EU Heads of State in the European Council. What had the potential to be strong environmental criteria in the Commission's original proposal were chipped away at during the policy formulation process, effectively removing any coercive push towards the second- and third-generation types of biofuel. The *resource/incentive mechanisms* most certainly did not impose significant additional compliance costs on producers and countries that were not already committed to producing first-generation biofuels. By the time the interim compliance milestone was passed in 2005 (when the indicative target was set at just 2 per cent), nine of the then fifteen Member States still had a market share of effectively zero per cent. And, as noted in Section 8.2, public awareness of the wider costs and benefits of expanding biofuel use remained relatively low, even though consumers in some Member States had been, often unknowingly, purchasing blended fuels for their vehicles for some time. Well before the passing of the formal compliance deadline in 2010, legal experts were bemoaning the 'predictable failure' of the Directive to sufficiently promote first-generation biofuels (Del Guayo, 2008: 275), let alone boost the production of the alternatives.

However, during the nearly nine years in which the Directive remained on the statute book, political opposition steadily began to grow. By 2008 – i.e. just four years after the date of adoption – aligned against the conventional biofuels was a phalanx of NGOs and charities representing a range of different concerns. Some, such as the EEB and T&E, had unsuccessfully voiced their doubts at the formulation stage, but had the resources and the self-interest to 'stick around' to establish whether these were well-founded. Others were new to the issue and/or had become more doubtful as implementation had proceeded and production had increased; these included several large international development NGOs. Their concerns were somewhat different – they claimed that using food crops to produce first-generation transport biofuels had inflated world food prices and exacerbated food insecurity in developing countries. By 2013, these opponents had united into a broader 'Stop Bad Biofuels' campaign, which was mostly directed at the first-generation biofuels, but also raised public doubts about *all* forms of biofuel production and use. Crucially, by the mid-2000s, negative policy feedback effects had begun to appear well beyond the borders of the EU, in the many locations across the world in which feedstocks were being grown, processed and transported. In 2008, even the scientific committee of the EU's own environment agency, the EEA, voiced its doubts, claiming that designers had initiated a huge policy 'experiment whose unintended effects are difficult to predict and difficult to control' (EEA, 2008: 6). No longer confined to the relatively narrow technical matter of how to source lower-carbon transport fuel, by the late 2000s *all* biofuel producers[4] found themselves at the intersection of some incredibly weighty global debates on issues such as global food production and supply, land use change, poverty and human development (HLPE, 2013: 11). What they and the Commission had originally assumed would be a handy drop-in solution to a set of carefully delineated policy problems – essentially greenhouse gas emissions from transportation – was being widely cited as a contributory cause of many others. And crucially, by the mid-2010s, preferences and coalitions had changed: the opposition by some actors to biofuels had expanded from the use of first-generation biofuels in transport to *all* types of biofuel use (and thus all biofuel-related policy making) in an array of possible new applications, such as biomass production, domestic heating and cooling.

These new endogenously derived sources of political opposition exerted enormous pressure on the once relatively united coalition of target groups, namely the biofuel producers and suppliers, and the car manufacturers.[5] New fault lines began to appear in that coalition between, for example, those that had invested in bioethanol and those that had invested in biodiesel, and between those that were keen to invest in new markets for second- and third-generation biofuels, and those that simply wanted to secure a rate of return on their existing investments in the first-generation types. Some producers claimed that they had to maximise production of the first-generation fuels, despite their flaws, in order to generate the revenue streams to support new investments in advanced biofuel (Levidow and Papaioannou, 2014: 294). Environmental NGOs felt that this line of argument was entirely circular and hence specious, but it was widely deployed by the pro-biofuel coalition during the formulation and adoption of the 2009 Directive. Quickly, the complexity of the issues under discussion began to escalate; even arbitrating over the various claims and counter-claims that swirled around one specific sub-issue – the potential indirect land use change effects of first-generation biofuels – mired the EU institutions in arcane debates that lasted for years after 2009. It is telling that the 2015 ILUC Directive took over 1,000 days to be adopted – twice as long as it took to adopt the 2003 Biofuels Directive or the 2009 Renewable Energy Directive. Amongst the fifteen policy instrument changes analysed in this book, the ILUC Directive was the second slowest to be adopted (after the voluntary agreement on cars).

Interpretive mechanisms also played a significant part in generating these feedback effects. First of all, the original Biofuels Directive did not, as noted above, directly generate significant new resource flows, but it established a new system of reporting on biofuel production, which was subsequently made more harmonised (and more binding) by the 2009 Renewable Energy Directive. The *interpretive mechanism* of reporting on a regular basis was designed to spur Member States to mobilise their national production facilities and thus render the whole policy more durable, but it also had the opposite effect of drawing unwelcome attention to the alarming speed at which the sector was developing inside and outside Europe. In addition, because EU supplies were still at that point insufficient to meet rising demands, the extent of Europe's reliance on complex and wide-ranging external supply chains became steadily more apparent. Second, both directives included new reporting provisions addressing matters such as *ex post* policy evaluation and ILUC emissions. Together, these two *interpretive mechanisms* helped to markedly increase the political profile of biofuel, which eventually fed through to more significant focusing events such as the food security crisis of 2007–2008, which in turn fed through to the ILUC debate that further sapped biofuels of political support after 2009. They also encouraged other influential actors – such as scientists, the OECD and the EEA's Scientific Committee – to subject the EU's emission-reduction claims to more robust and ultimately more critical analytical scrutiny. These challenges grew so much that after 2008, first-generation biofuels were no longer regarded as a panacea, but a problem: a 'dirty fuel' to be avoided wherever and whenever possible. The growing political opposition from both existing and new groups put the Commission in the especially awkward position of using durability devices to simultaneously promote the more advanced biofuel types (through, e.g., the 2018 Renewable Energy Directive) whilst limiting the production of first- and even second-generation types (through, e.g., the 2015 ILUC Directive). This delicate balancing act continues to this day, absorbing precious bureaucratic time that could have been devoted to more productive uses, as well as sapping biofuels of even more political support.

Emissions Trading: Large Stationery Emitters

Earlier in this chapter, we noted how the *resource/incentive mechanisms* based on free allocation increased support for the ETS. However, once trading commenced in 2005, allowance prices began to fluctuate in the manner that advocates of trading had long advocated. Importantly, this endogenous policy dynamic repeatedly altered the flow of resources to various target groups. Negative feedback effects appeared whenever allowance prices rose (as they did, albeit briefly, in 2005–2006), triggering new political opposition to the 2003 Directive. The energy-intensives, who by then had organised themselves into what would eventually become the Alliance of Energy Intensive Industries (AEII), reacted strongly against higher prices and the windfall profits they created for many electricity generators in the period 2005–2012 (AEII, 2005). In early 2006, this alliance successfully pushed to establish a new group within the Commission itself, known as the High Level Group on Competitiveness, Energy and the Environment (Wettestad, 2009b: 314). Although the AEII and its allies largely did not challenge the ETS as an overall policy approach after the adoption of the 2003 Directive, they were relatively effective at preserving free allocation against the wishes of DG Environment/CLIMA and the European Parliament, and strongly opposed efforts to raise allowance prices. They were joined by a substantial number of high-carbon electricity generators, especially from Central and Eastern Europe. These industries were eventually able to form strong alliances with existing policy-making actors – such as the European People's Party in the European Parliament, DG Enterprise, and the governments of Germany and Poland – that already enjoyed close ties to industry.

Other negative feedback effects related to emissions trading's policy settings were created by low prices. Between 2006 and 2007, and particularly in the period after 2012 and before 2018, allowance prices fell to low levels, sharply reducing the financial revenues from allowance auctioning that had originally increased Member State support for – and dependence on – higher allowance prices. In theory, the lost revenues could have been used to cultivate new policy coalitions.[6] Meanwhile, market intermediaries such as banks closed their allowance trading desks and membership of the pro-trading association (IETA) dropped by around 30 per cent between 2009 and 2017 (Moore, 2018: 164–165), robbing the system of supporters.

Finally, negative feedback effects also occurred through the operation of *interpretive mechanisms*, particularly the information relating to emissions, allowances and prices (Delbeke and Vis, 2015: 128). Information on the over-allocation of allowances in comparison to actual emissions between 2005 and 2007, along with sharply falling prices, played a key role in the shift away from the national-level allocation of allowances after 2013. This shift was arguably the most prominent example of policy change in the history of the ETS. It is puzzling, because the national allocation process gave Member States significant authority and gave industries an incentive (and opportunity) to push successfully for generous allocations. However, frustration with the process among Member State governments was the most important driver that facilitated a shift to a more centralised ETS. This was an endogenously driven shift arising from the original policy's decentralised design. During the 2005–2007 period, when allowance prices fell to near-zero and frustrations with the allocation plans mounted, there were few exogenous pressures that could be cited to explain such a shift (e.g. the economy was growing). These changes should, instead, be viewed as an unintended consequence of compromises that were made during the adoption of the 2003 Directive; compromises which, at the time, most Member States strongly supported. The allocation process did indeed give many ETS industries added influence over how allowances were henceforth allocated. But in the end, it was that very influence which led to Member State frustration and eventually to the shift to EU-level allocation and cap-setting.

Finally, information also produced a 'cue' to new policy development, through informing the demand from target groups for compensatory measures (such as continuing free allowances), which in turn required the collection of yet more information (to underpin sectoral benchmarks and criteria to determine which industries were at risk of carbon leakage and, as a result, eligible for continued free allocation). Information thus became a form of ammunition readily seized upon by opponents during what soon became a more or less constant policy design conflict. It shaped their preferences, i.e. their perceptions of how fairly they were or were not being treated relative to other groups. At the same time, the policy amendments that were adopted (such as backloading and the Market Stability Reserve) themselves became new institutional niches in which losers tried to press their case for further concessions.

Voluntarism: Car Emissions

We have already noted that the voluntary agreement on car emissions did not impose sufficiently significant or concentrated costs on target groups to force them to oppose it. Nor did it significantly weaken government capacities within the EU institutions by actively withdrawing resources from them. Consequently, *resource/ incentive mechanisms* did not produce significant negative feedback effects, at the least during the first five to ten years of the policy instrument sequence. In fact, the very lack of coerciveness made the agreement's continuation rather attractive to the main target group: the car producers. However, during the adoption of the 2009 Regulation – which introduced more coercive policy design features such as legally binding targets and even fines – the previously stable coalition of producers began to fracture. The existing literature on policy feedbacks has drawn attention to the way in which some social policies created new pro-policy coalitions within government. However, as in the case of emissions trading, negative policy feedback effects from the voluntary agreement led to the complete opposite – an anti-policy expansion unit within the Commission itself, in the form of a High Level Group on competitiveness (CARS 21). During the design of the 2009 regulation, it worked with the Commission to promote the so-called integrated approach to meeting the more stringent standards at lowest cost (to the producers). Meanwhile, the producers of the largest and most polluting vehicles also directly lobbied the German government to oppose the inclusion of more stringent standards. The manufacturers of smaller and less polluting vehicles pursued a different course, lobbying their governments to adopt stronger legal controls. Arguably, the latter were better able to stay ahead of events: the manufacturers that made the deepest commitment to a diesel-based solution – most dramatically VW – eventually discovered that they could only meet the reduction targets by cheating on them, a tactic which badly backfired when the Dieselgate crisis eventually struck.

We have already noted the significance of *interpretive mechanisms* in this particular case. The ability of the Commission to demonstrate empirically – through the collection and sharing of new information on emissions – that the voluntary agreement was ineffectual (negative learning) proved to be a decisive turning point in the policy instrument sequence, weakening the car manufacturers' long-standing argument that coercive forms of regulation were unreasonable, ineffectual and, above all, unnecessary. However, in the absence of strong policy programme-level decarbonisation goals (which highlighted the anomalous treatment of the transport sector relative to others), the sequence may well have followed a different path after 2005–2006, with the Commission struggling to make a compelling case for a regulation even though voluntarism had so manifestly failed. Be that as it may, once the policy instrument sequence unfolded after 2009, the provision of information arguably became more, not less, influential, being a significant underlying factor in the ensuing Dieselgate scandal and the resulting adoption of a more realistic 'real world' emission testing regime.

Summary: When and Where Were Negative Feedback Effects Significant?

It seems plausible to expect some negative policy feedback effects to appear in modern life. Otherwise, once adopted, most policies would stand a relatively good chance of enduring, leaving the wider policy landscape 'frozen' into place (Pierson, 2004: 77). However, the fundamental nature of climate change politics, which we summarised in Chapter 2, is likely to make this outcome somewhat unlikely in practice. That being the case, how well did the patterns of empirical change reported in Chapters 5, 6 and 7 relate to the four propositions that we originally formulated in Chapter 2? First of all, we proposed that negative feedback effects will be more common when policy designs directly create losers. More specifically, *policies that impose immediate and relatively concentrated costs on particular groups are more likely to produce negative feedback effects than those that do not.* The case of emission trading – and especially its impacts on the high-carbon electricity generators and the energy-intensives – provided the best and perhaps the only example of this. Second, we proposed that negative policy feedback effects are more likely to appear *when the losers – or those who perceive themselves to be at risk of losing – are powerful, well-organised and strongly mobilised* (Mahoney and Thelen, 2010: 17). Again, the emission trading case (and especially the behaviour of the energy-intensives) provided the most obvious and only illustration of this point, in the period after the creation of AEII. Third, we proposed that negative policy feedback effects are more likely to appear if *the original rationale for the policy was weak, strongly contested and/or undermined by subsequent events*. The events in the biofuels case provide the strongest confirmation of this point. Finally, we proposed that negative policy feedback effects are more likely *when opponents have no alternative but to mobilise against the original policy*. It is striking that across all three cases, target groups opted rather quickly to 'work within' the existing policy by reforming it rather than bring about its downfall by 'working outside' it (Hacker, 2004: 246). The most obvious examples to be found across the fifteen policy instrument changes are the energy-intensives (in the emissions trading case) and the opponents of first-generation biofuels (in the biofuels case). Having demonstrated through their own inaction the ineffectiveness of their preferred approach (voluntary controls), most car manufacturers[7] opted to work within EU regulatory controls to ensure that they support their long-term technological preferences.

8.4 Summary and Conclusions

Our main aim in this chapter has been to summarise the first-order policy feedback effects that flowed from the three policy instruments that were introduced in Chapter 4 and were subsequently subjected to more detailed analysis in Chapters 5, 6 and 7, with a particular focus on the effects created by the first policy in each sequence. We noted the role played by *resource/incentive* and *interpretive policy feedback mechanisms*. In Chapter 1, we defined policy feedback effects as the downstream consequences of an instrument without a complete feedback loop to subsequent changes to the instrument design itself. In this chapter we have uncovered and explored the first-order effects on the identities, preferences and capacities of three prominent actor types in climate policy: target groups, governments and other relevant interest groups. In the opening chapters, we noted that since the early 2000s, the post-Pierson literatures on policy feedback have had a strong focus on the effects on citizens and other mass publics; given their policy focus has generally been on distributive forms of welfare state policy, the effects on interest organisations and target groups have understandably received rather less attention.

In our analysis of policy feedback effects in a more regulatory policy setting (namely climate change), we have revealed two main findings. With regards to the policy feedback effects, we have demonstrated that the three original instruments generated feedback effects that affect all three group types, but that the depth and timing of those effects varied markedly across the cases and over time. Thus the only instrument to significantly affect government was emissions trading, which greatly empowered DG Environment/DG CLIMA with increased resources and expertise, while transferring significant revenues to national governments after

2013. The two instruments that had the most wide-ranging effects on other interest groups were those relating to biofuel and emissions trading, greatly expanding the number and diversity of those involved, as well as reshaping their policy preferences. The number of actors who have participated in designing car emissions policy has, by contrast, remained relatively stable over time.

With regards to the operation of *resource/incentive* and *interpretive feedback mechanisms*, our empirical chapters have usefully revealed that both mechanisms were at work, at least at some point, in all three instrument sequences. It is worthwhile recalling that in Chapters 1 and 2 we noted that the existing literatures on durability and feedback have mainly illustrated the functioning of particular types of mechanism, rather than test for the existence of the full array. However, only in the case of emissions trading did *resource/incentive mechanisms* play a pronounced role. This is at odds with the general assumption in the existing literatures that the most coercive instruments (essentially regulation)[8] produce the most significant feedback effects operating through *resource/incentive mechanisms*. By contrast, *interpretive mechanisms* – which have generally not received as much attention in the existing literatures – were at work in all three sequences but were especially important (at least relative to *resource/incentive mechanisms*) in two of the three cases: biofuels and car emissions.

Tracing out and explaining first-order effects is illuminating but time-consuming, especially across thirty years of policy making encompassing fifteen instrument changes. Nonetheless, it is not sufficient for an analysis of durability and policy feedback to only look at first-order effects. Rather, our analysis has revealed the existence of much longer-running sequences of change, rather than a series of one-off effects that were time-limited. Table 8.1 summarises the main sequences of instrument changes that have ensued in the three sub-areas over time, drawing together the detailed findings of Chapters 4–7.

If we begin with the most coercive instrument (regulation), Table 8.1 reveals that the governance of biofuels has evolved via a twenty-year sequence of changes that essentially remain regulatory in nature. At the other end of the spectrum (starting with low coerciveness), the governance of car emissions has moved – via another equally long and complicated policy design sequence – from a situation of effectively no controls on CO_2 emissions, to a fairly ineffectual voluntary agreement through to a considerably more coercive regulatory policy instrument which now appears to be rapidly locking into place. Finally, mid-way in our continuum of instrument types are the market-based instruments. With respect to the governance of large stationary emitters, Table 8.1 reveals that over the course of the last twenty years, emissions trading has gradually become locked in as the dominant policy instrument, although repeated policy amendments have greatly increased its complexity over time.

Table 8.1 *Policy instrument sequences in the three areas of governance, 2003–2019**

	The governance of biofuels	The governance of stationary emitters	The governance of car emissions
Starting point	**Regulation**	**Market-based**	**Voluntary action**
Original instrument	2003 Biofuels Directive (2003/30/EC)	2003 Emissions Trading Directive (2003/87/EC)	1999 Voluntary Agreement (Recommendation 1999/125/EC)
Policy change 1	2009 Renewable Energy Directive (2009/28/EC)	2009 Directive (2009/29/EC)	*1999 Directive (1999/94/EC)*
Policy change 2	2015 ILUC Directive (2015/1513)	*2013 Backloading Decision (1359/2013/EU)*	2000 Decision (1753/2000/EC)
Policy change 3	2018 RED II Directive (2018/2001)	*2015 Market Stability Reserve Decision (2015/1814)*	2009 Regulation (443/2009)
Policy change 4	–	2018 Directive (2018/410)	2014 Regulation (333/2014)
Policy change 5	–	—	2019 Regulation (2019/631)
Final instrument	**Regulation**	**Market-based**	**Regulation**

* Less significant instrument changes are shown in italics.

In Chapters 5–7, we also uncovered some notable temporal patterns in the way that the three sequences unfolded, principally relating to the time taken for each individual instrument change to be decided upon and adopted (i.e. equating to the ease of each successive amendment over time) and how long it existed (i.e. how long each amendment eventually endured), which we suspect offer insights into the overarching theme of the entire book: long-term policy durability. Figures 8.1–8.4 draw together data contained in Tables 5.1, 6.1 and 7.1. Figure 8.1 describes how long (in days) it took to make each instrument change in the respective instrument sequences. On closer inspection, the speed of adoption has varied quite significantly, ranging between 400 days (i.e. just over a year), for the 2019 Cars Regulation, to nearly 1,200 days (i.e. over three years) for the voluntary agreement on cars. There was no appreciable difference between the time taken to adopt instrument changes in one sub-area as compared to the other two. With the exception of the car emissions sub-sector, it was also not the case that the initial instrument took significantly longer to be adopted (the 2003 Biofuels and Emissions Trading Directives took 548 and 721 days to be adopted respectively) than its successors within each respective sequence.

8 Climate Policy Feedbacks 209

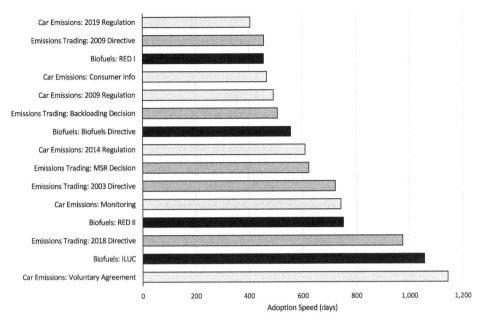

Figure 8.1 Significant policy instrument changes: speed of adoption (in days)

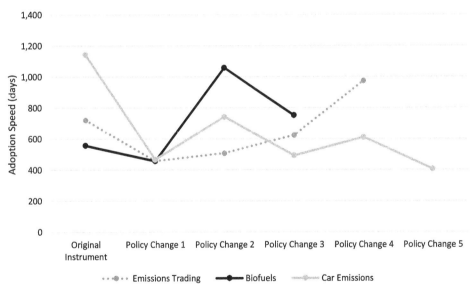

Figure 8.2 Significant policy instrument changes: variation in adoption speed over time

Figure 8.2 (which only focuses on the most significant instrument changes), displays the same data but reveals how the speed of adoption changed at each successive step in each sequence. It reveals that in the car emissions sub-area, the time taken to adopt each policy instrument change has declined significantly and

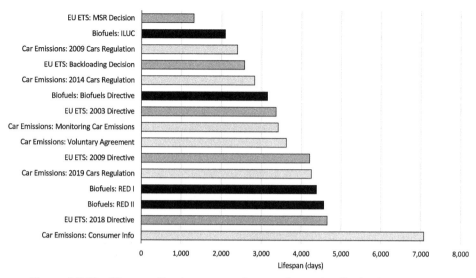

Figure 8.3 Significant policy instrument changes: longevity (in days)

consistently over time. In the emission trading area, the speed of adoption declined sharply at first, but after 2009 climbed steadily. In the biofuels area, no consistent temporal trend is apparent.

Turning to the related issue of instrument longevity, Figure 8.3 (which again encompasses all instrument changes) describes how long each instrument lasted for in an essentially unamended form. Leaving to one side the less significant instruments that do not have an end date (e.g. the 2000 Directive on consumer information related to car emissions), longevity has varied quite significantly, ranging from just over 2,000 days (i.e. just over five years – the 2015 ILUC Directive on biofuels) to over 4,500 days (i.e. nearly twelve years – projected for the 2018 Emissions Trading Directive). Given that the standard legislative term in the EU is five years (or circa 1,825 days), then every single instrument change in our sample managed to pass this basic durability threshold.[9] In fact, the vast majority of instrument changes lasted for well over eight years (circa 3,000 days), suggesting that in general, most of the instrument changes in our sample were relatively durable.

Finally, Figure 8.4 describes how each instrument's longevity (in days) varied across each successive step in their respective instrument sequence. It reveals that, in general, the second instrument in the sequence lasted considerably longer than the first, but as time elapsed, longevity (measured in days) declined but then eventually increased. To conclude, this chapter has mostly been concerned with describing and explicating the most significant first-order policy feedback effects created by the original policy instrument in each sub-area, although in passing we

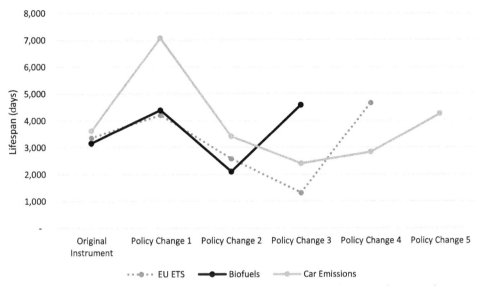

Figure 8.4 Significant policy instrument changes: variation in longevity over time

noted subsequent policy changes when and where they generally followed the same overall pattern of change as the initial amendment. The patterns in the data presented in this section have underscored the need to go beyond direct, first-order feedback effects and address the rather more vexed issue of policy *feedbacks*. In Chapter 1, we defined these as the politically consequential effects of a policy that operate via a set of intervening causal mechanisms to affect itself. This analytical shift – from policy feedback effects to policy feedbacks – is necessary to answer our first and third objectives, which we originally posed in Chapter 1. We address these challenges in our final chapter.

Endnotes

1. A situation that is also relatively rare across EU environmental policy (Gravey and Jordan, 2016, 2019).
2. Its scope, however, remained broadly the same. See Table 5.1.
3. ACEA's fall-back position was that it should be held by the Commission in an anonymised form.
4. In other words, not simply those producing the first-generation types.
5. Who by that time were under mounting pressure to achieve faster and deeper emission reductions (see Chapter 7).
6. For example, in relation to carbon capture and storage, new energy efficiency measures or new renewable energy technologies.
7. With the possible exception of companies such as VW that attempted to cheat the tests.
8. And of course subsidies, which are not included in our sample.
9. There are, of course, several other interpretations of policy durability (see Chapter 1), which we shall return to in Chapter 9.

9

Durable by Design?

Policy Making in a Changing Climate

> *You've got to think about big things while you're doing small things, so that all the small things go in the right direction*
>
> (*Alvin Toffler*)

9.1 Introduction

Policy durability is regularly identified as a critical ingredient in society's response to the wicked policy challenge of climate change. Over the course of the last three decades, many climate and energy policies have been adopted. In fact, in Chapter 1 we noted that climate change probably constitutes one of the most active sub-areas of environmental policy making. However, we also noted another, more 'inconvenient truth' about climate governance: that a surprisingly large number of climate policies are not sufficiently durable or effective enough (van Renssen, 2018). Indeed, climate policy is widely regarded as being especially susceptible to weakening and reversal (Rosenbloom *et al.*, 2019: 168), because it generally targets powerful vested interest groups and does not deliver immediate and visible policy benefits to voters.

The main aim of this book is to understand whether policy designers have sought to design more durable policies that are supported by positive policy feedbacks and, if so, why, how and with what effects. Across eight chapters we have explored how designers have packaged together different sub-elements of public policy – long-term goals, instruments and specific instrument-level settings – to achieve deeper and more rapid decarbonisation. We have done so in relation to the EU – an active adopter of new climate policies (Jordan *et al.*, 2010) and long-term decarbonisation targets stretching out to 2030 and beyond (for a summary, see Chapter 3). But have EU policy designers sought, to paraphrase the futurist Alvin Toffler who is quoted in the epigram of this chapter, to ensure that these sub-elements of policy move in the same direction and are mutually supportive?

We have attempted to break new analytical ground by going beyond their formative moments to study the post-adoption feedbacks arising from three important instruments in the EU's stock of policies – a regulation on biofuel production, a voluntary agreement on CO_2 emissions from cars and the EU Emissions Trading System – to arrive at a fuller understanding of both their durability over time and their ability to entrench deep decarbonisation dynamics in broader society.

In this chapter, we draw together the various threads of our argument and address the three overarching objectives identified in Chapter 1. In Section 9.2, we briefly restate the main findings of Chapter 8 on the main policy feedback mechanisms and effects that flowed from the three instruments in the period immediately after their adoption (i.e. Objective 2). In Section 9.3, we complete the feedback loop (or, more correctly, loops in extended policy sequences) by moving from first-order effects to explore how far they reshaped subsequent policy making in ways that affected the durability of policy in each sequence (i.e. Objective 3). In Section 9.4, we explore the motives of the original designers and the design space in which they were operating (i.e. Objective 1) to understand the extent to which they intentionally nurtured positive feedback to create greater policy durability. In Section 9.5, we return to the main theme of the book – policy durability *by design* – and derive some general conclusions about its determinants and unfolding effects. Finally, we reflect on the implications of our findings for debates on policy durability and policy design in other policy areas and political settings.

9.2 Policy Feedback Effects and Mechanisms

In our opening chapter, we noted that a durable policy generates positive policy feedbacks that foster and sustain its own political support base. Such policies trigger legacy effects that persist long 'after the waning of the political forces that generated their original enactment' (Jenkins and Patashnik, 2012: 15). In Chapter 1, we also noted that in order to understand how far and through which pathways policies feed back on themselves, analysts must first understand their first-order political effects on actors, their preferences and the coalitions that they build with other actors. We defined policy feedback *effects* as the downstream consequences of an instrument without a complete feedback loop to the original instrument. Strictly defined, policy feedback is both different and more difficult to study than effects: it relates to what happens when a given policy operates via a set of intervening causal mechanisms eventually to affect itself. Durable policies create positive policy feedbacks and reinforce themselves, whereas fragile policies create negative policy feedbacks and undermine themselves. Instrument sequences involve a series of interlinked policy changes, connected to one another via a series of policy feedbacks.

Our first aim was to employ process tracing methods to uncover the feedback effects and mechanisms that emerged after the initial moment of adoption (Objective 2). This type of analytical work sits squarely within the home domain of policy feedback research which has, as noted in Chapter 1, long sought to document the diverse array of feedback effects that can potentially arise in relation to government ministries and agencies (Patashnik, 2008: 30), through to voters and members of the public (Mettler and SoRelle, 2014: 151). The existing literatures suggest that some policies may have wide-ranging effects on such actors – altering their goals, their identities and their political strategies (Skocpol, 1992: 58). In Chapters 5, 6 and 7 we followed Skocpol (1992: 58) and Pierson (2006: 118) and concentrated on identifying which *actors* were most heavily impacted by each instrument, documenting relevant effects on their *capacity* to act and their *policy preferences*.

Changing Actor Identities, Capacities and Preferences

In terms of the *actors* that were impacted, in his influential agenda-setting article Pierson (1993) originally focused on government elites, interest groups and mass publics. Given that climate change is an essentially regulatory policy issue area, we opted to focus on the first-order effects on government, target groups and other interest groups. It is notable that all three of the original instruments we examined generated policy feedback effects on these actor types, including the least coercive one (the voluntary agreement on car emissions). However, the depth and timing of those effects varied significantly within and between the three sequences, as well as over time. The only instrument to have significantly affected government (particularly the European Commission and the Member States) was emissions trading, which greatly empowered DG Environment and DG CLIMA and reallocated resources to national governments via auctioning. This is a notable finding because bureaucratic effects were originally highlighted by Pierson (1993), but have since fallen out of academic fashion (Béland and Schlager, 2019: 201). The target groups that were most directly impacted were those in the emissions trading system, chiefly the low-carbon electricity generators (who benefited and/or could pass on any costs) and the energy-intensive industries and high-carbon generators (who bore many of the costs). By contrast, the two instruments that had the most wide-ranging effects on other interest groups were those related to biofuel and emissions trading; they significantly expanded the number and the diversity of the actors involved in the associated design processes.

Actor *capacities* were also directly impacted by policy feedback effects but to different extents and at different points in time. As noted in Chapter 6, the electricity generators (and especially those with low-carbon portfolios), were the chief beneficiaries of the ETS in the period 2003–2009. Their pre-existing capacity to engage in and influence design processes was already significant, but the ETS firmly entrenched their position as elite actors. By contrast, the car producers initially formed a powerful bloc that acted to foreclose the prevailing design space, but the failure of the voluntary agreement weakened their epistemic authority (through negative learning – the revelation that voluntary governance was not fit for purpose). In Chapter 8, we revealed that the environmental groups in all three cases were significantly empowered by interpretive feedback mechanisms, chiefly the information generated from monitoring emissions from ETS installations and biofuel production.

In principle, changes in actor *preferences* should provide an insight into the direction of any policy feedbacks. In very general terms, positive feedbacks are self-reinforcing and self-amplifying. Policies that trigger them directly incentivise actors – and specifically target groups – to align their preferences and activities with them (Thelen, 2006: 155). As a result, the policies become more politically stable and hence more durable over time. Emissions trading provided the best example of a positive feedback dynamic, that chiefly ran through to government and some target groups (namely the electricity generators), both of whom became increasingly convinced of the merits of trading. Had biofuel policies created a set of new interest groups favouring the expansion of second and third-generation biofuels (along the same lines as the powerful American Association of Retired Persons in the USA for example; Béland and Schlager, 2019: 188), the effects and the resulting feedbacks might have been more durable.

By contrast, policies that produce negative feedback effects actively trigger opposition to themselves, which can directly undermine their own durability (Weaver, 2010: 137) by opening up new opportunities for opponents to amend, weaken and possibly even dismantle them (Jacobs and Weaver, 2015). The most prominent example was the emergence of the new coalition against 'dirty' biofuels which expanded rapidly between 2003 and 2009, drawing in new members, many from 'non' environmental sectors such as international development organisations. Another example was the creation of the Alliance of Energy Intensive Industries in the early 2000s following the adoption of the 2003 Emissions Trading Directive. Initially weak and fragmented, the energy-intensives quickly coalesced into a new group which initially sought to replace emissions trading with another instrument, but gradually accepted that this could not be done and instead fought for a variety of opt-outs, delayed targets and special measures (e.g. free allowances). The emergence of new coalitions that are directly opposed to an instrument is a classic example of a negative policy feedback effect.

One of the most well-known challenges confronting policy feedback researchers is that of endogeneity (Campbell, 2012: 334; Mettler and SoRelle, 2014: 173), or of demonstrating that any observed effects were produced by the policy in question rather than other factors. In Chapter 2, we explained that we would address this challenge in three main ways: (1) by carefully uncovering the causal mechanisms (i.e. the feedback mechanisms) in the three sequences; (2) by employing counterfactuals; (3) and by explicating the interaction between endogenous and exogenous factors. With regards to the first of these, in Chapter 8 we sought to uncover the role of the two main feedback mechanisms across the three initial instruments, an important dimension that is routinely neglected by policy scientists (Capano and Howlett, 2019: 15). We revealed that both were at work, at least at some point in the opening parts of all three instrument sequences. It is worth recalling that the existing literatures on durability and feedback have tended to explicate the functioning of a specific mechanism (or mechanisms) rather than the full array.[1] Only in the case of emissions trading were *resource/incentive mechanisms* dominant. This is at odds with the general finding in the existing literatures that the most coercive instruments (essentially regulation)[2] produce the most significant positive feedbacks effects, largely via *resource/incentive mechanisms*.[3]

By contrast, *interpretive mechanisms* were at work across all three cases, but were relatively more influential in two of them – biofuels and car emissions – that at least initially, scored low in terms of coerciveness. There are several reasons why this is an important finding. First, *interpretive mechanisms* have generally received less attention in the existing literatures, despite Pierson's (1993: 611, 626) reminder that knowledge can be a very powerful political resource in design processes. Second, such mechanisms may generate significant feedback effects even in the absence of powerful new flows of finance or technology. Or to put it slightly differently, our cases revealed that the EU does not have to adopt stringent regulations or establish significant new resource/incentive flows (such as R&D subsidies) to decisively reshape the politics of decarbonisation (see also Béland and Schlager, 2019: 192). Third, the existing literatures have generally paid more attention to the effects of *interpretive mechanisms* on government than other actor types, but our three cases (and especially the ones relating to biofuels and the latter stages of the car emissions saga) reveal that they also have influential effects on other interest groups, including environmental groups for whom new knowledge became a vital new campaigning resource (see Pierson, 1993: 619 and Mol, 2006).

Turning to the second analytical response (counterfactuals – a structured exploration of what the world may have looked like 'without' the policy): these are sometimes employed by scholars of policy durability (Béland, 2010: 712), but they are not necessarily always employed in a consistent or analytically transparent manner (Pahle *et al.*, 2018: 865). In some respects, even during the initial stages of a long sequence, the potential number of 'no policy' scenarios can become unfeasibly large (Kay, 2005: 554). In order, therefore, to simplify as much as possible, we took the counterfactual situation to refer to what the world might have looked like in the first few stages of an instrument sequence (essentially

2003–2009) without any EU policy. What does this counterfactual look like? If we start at the coercive end of our instrument spectrum (regulation), the main reason that the 2003 Biofuels Directive was adopted relatively quickly was because it was relatively low in stringency, required no significant up-front investments and was restricted in scope to transport uses. Weak feedback effects in both directions were, therefore, *a priori* to be expected. However, by raising public awareness of the deleterious side-effects of rapid expansion, this directive aligned with and accentuated public concerns that were beginning to emerge in other parts of the world (such as the USA and Brazil) where biofuel production (and policies) was more advanced. These effects – principally generated via *interpretive mechanisms* – were the most significant of those generated by the Directive. As regards emissions trading, independent counterfactual analyses conducted by economists have already revealed that the emission reductions in the first two Phases (2005–2012) were relatively meagre (see Chapter 4). Our own approach reveals that the most significant differences between the 'with policy' situation and the counterfactual were, if anything, political not environmental, in the sense that the 2003 Directive altered actor coalitions and policy preferences amongst actors including the Member States, the electricity generators and the energy-intensives. Finally, the 'no policy' scenario in the area of car emissions is likely to have been very similar to the 'with policy' situation given how weak the voluntary agreement was (Jordan and Matt, 2014) and hence failed to generate significant feedback effects in either direction. We shall discuss the third analytical response (disentangling endogenous from exogenous drivers) in Section 9.3.

Different Policy Feedback Directions

In the opening chapter, we noted that the literatures on durability and feedback have been heavily preoccupied with documenting and explaining positive feedback effects. Pierson (2004: 35) even assumed that 'most policies [...] are generally subject' to them. More recent contributions have nuanced his claims by drawing more attention to the negative feedback effects generated by some policies (Weaver, 2010; Jacobs and Weaver, 2015). In a sense they recall the point originally made by Schattschneider (1935), whom we quoted at the start of Chapter 1, that most policies simultaneously create winners (and hence supporters) *and* losers (and hence opponents).

By employing a forward-tracing approach, we were able to confirm that both directions were present in all three sequences. There are three potentially significant implications of this particular finding. First of all, positive policy feedback effects were not, as Pierson originally claimed, the norm; both types were present. Just as importantly, negative feedbacks effects were not – as we suggested in

Chapter 2 – necessarily automatic either, which is significant given that climate policy is widely associated with activities that trigger political opposition from large, incumbent players such as stationery emitters, and in wider civil society (e.g., the 2018 Gilets Jaunes protests). Second, positive and negative feedback effects often flowed from the same policy instrument. Looking across the three sequences, it is striking that all three generated some positive feedback effects, although as noted above, their significance varied. The effects were most strongly positive in relation to emissions trading; they were much weaker and/or absent in the other two cases. By contrast, all three instruments generated at least some negative feedback effects, although their scale and significance also varied, as did the mechanisms at work. Only in two cases – emissions trading and biofuels – were we able to detect significant negative feedback effects during the immediate post-adoption period. Crucially, if the feedback effects run in both directions, what may ultimately matter more is not the absolute magnitude of either, but the net effect of both on actors, coalitions and, ultimately, the original policy.

Third, the positive and negative feedback effects were relatively long-running and long-lasting. This finding is probably less surprising for the positive feedback effects, being heavily tied to Pierson's (1993, 1994) evident fascination with the most durable and 'locked-in' policies. More puzzling, however, was the relative persistence of negative feedback effects, which were not only present in the first stage of the three sequences but persisted after subsequent policy amendments. Weaver (2010: 139) has helpfully argued that policies that generate negative feedbacks do not last long, yet some of the negative feedback effects in our policy sequences persisted for many decades, i.e. even when the policy in question was relatively durable. We shall return to this puzzling co-existence when we reflect on the nature of policy durability in Section 9.5.

Policy Feedback Effects: A Summary

Our analytical approach – of starting with policy designs and forward tracing the political feedback mechanisms and effects – has proven useful in revealing just how readily policy feeds back into politics – a long-standing and, in many ways, the most fundamental concern for all policy feedback scholars. Our analysis has confirmed that during the earlier phases of all three sequences, the initial design did not determine political effects in a crudely deterministic manner, but rather shaped the nature of the subsequent politics by affecting actor identifies, capacities, coalitions and preferences (Weaver, 1988: 261; Patashnik, 2000: 188). What was especially influential was not the absolute level of the resource flows generated by each instrument, but rather the size, duration and visibility of the benefits *and* the costs relative to the status quo (Jacobs and Mettler, 2018: 350; Béland and

Schlager, 2019: 192). In doing so, we have generated more conditional explanations of feedback effects that reveal 'how policies matter and under what conditions' (Pierson, 1993: 627). We have also demonstrated that in a more regulatory policy area, *interpretive mechanisms* seem to play a more significant role than is commonly thought. In recent years, the *interpretive mechanisms* operating through informational tools have been written off as 'cost efficient but often ineffective' (Howlett, 2019: 107). Our analysis has instead demonstrated that when adequately targeted at focal points in the design process (such as *ex post* evaluations and *flexibility clauses*), new information may trigger new political dynamics, culminating in focusing events such as the campaigns against 'dirty' biofuels and diesel engines (Dieselgate). Finally, starting with policy formulation processes and forward tracing out the subsequent political effects has furnished valuable new insights into which actors successfully anticipated the ensuing feedback effects, which often affected who enjoyed greater political power. The large electricity generators stand out in this regard; they have powerfully entrenched their dominant position in the energy sector. By contrast, the biofuel producers proved themselves incapable of anticipating let alone steering the political effects of the EU's policy designs. In the initial phase of the car emissions saga, the manufacturers successfully anticipated the policy's unfolding effects, but as time went on and exogenous conditions changed, some were better able to anticipate and prosper from the policy feedback effects than others, a dynamic which is now driving fundamental structural transformations in the entire sector (i.e. namely the decline of diesel, the electrification of powertrains and the advent of driverless vehicles).

9.3 Policy Feedback

From Feedback Effects to Feedback Loops

Our third objective was to understand why and to what extent the feedback effects outlined above affected the durability of the original policy and others. Did, in other words, the combined effect of the negative and positive feedback effects strengthen the original policy (thus rendering it more durable) or did they undermine it (thus rendering it more fragile)? At this point we have to move from somewhat linear (but still complicated) cause-effect relationships during the early phases of sequences (Meckling, 2019: 320), to more complicated instrument sequences of the type depicted in Table 8.1. In Table 2.3 we outlined two archetypal policy feedback sequences: one positive (leading to greater policy durability); the other negative (leading to greater fragility). When the *net* feedback effect is positive over time, we should expect the original policy P to be reinforced at t+1, t+2, t+3 etc. (Pierson, 2004: 174). As a consequence, what may originally have been a contested policy gradually drops out of political debate and becomes an accepted part of the wider policy landscape. Therefore, the original policy is reinforced at $t+1, t+2, t+3$, etc. (Pierson, 2004: 174), perhaps in the most extreme cases culminating in significant policy lock-ins (Béland and Schlager, 2019: 189). More specifically, in archetypal positive feedback sequences, policy instruments become more stringent, broader in scope and more future-focused (which in Table 2.3 we labelled 'stringency', 'scope' and 'timeframe' respectively). In Chapter 1, we also suggested that the lifespan of each amendment is likely to increase and the speed of adoption (of subsequent amendments) to decrease. In climate policy, this would equate to a sequence in which the policies, practices and technologies of deep decarbonisation become steadily more *locked in* over time.

If, on the other hand, the net direction of feedback is negative, then the initial policy P would be undermined at $t+1$, which could in turn trigger a set of responses ranging from fairly small adjustments in the precise calibration of its constituent policy instrument, through to its collapse and possible replacement with a new instrument (P2) at $t+1$ or $t+2$ etc. Therefore, in archetypal negative feedback sequences, instruments become less stringent over time, narrower in scope and less future-focused. In Chapter 1, we suggested that the lifespan of each successive amendment would likely decrease and the speed of adoption would decrease. In Chapter 2, we suggested that such sequences are more likely to appear when, as in climate governance, policy designers are under political pressure to impose upfront costs on target groups. This would correspond to a sequence in which the new policies, social practices and prevailing technologies of deep decarbonisation are gradually *locked out* over time.

Policy Feedback Sequences

From a purely policy feedback perspective, we suggested that the factor most likely to tip the balance in favour of one policy sequence as opposed to the other is the extent to which the first instrument reshapes the identities, preferences and capacities of the actors that sought to steer policy during the initial formulation and adoption processes. When the net effect is positive, the supportive coalition will prevail and/or grow stronger and the original instrument is more likely to be strengthened, and vice versa. However, in Chapter 1, we also suggested that three additional factors may be influential:

- The mediating effect of any *flexibility devices* that were incorporated into the instrument's design. For example, did monitoring reveal shortfalls in performance, or was a flexibility clause built in to provide a predictable opportunity to pursue policy change?

- The presence of *policy entrepreneurs* – for us, actors who have the means and the motivation to track sequences and seize new opportunities created by evolving feedback mechanisms. Target groups generally have a vested interest in remaining engaged. But in the absence of policy entrepreneurs, a policy may be too complicated and its effects too hidden for mass publics and other interest groups to appreciate that they are even being affected by it (Béland, 2010: 579) – a rather likely scenario in relation to many aspects of climate policy (see Chapter 2).
- The presence of *exogenous pressures* for change that policy designers may feel compelled to respond to. For example, to what extent did international climate negotiations put pressure on EU actors to secure faster and deeper emission cuts? Or did changes in the world economy motivate businesses to lobby for reductions in the policy's scope and stringency?

In Chapters 5–7, we described a number of significant alterations in the stringency, scope and timeframe of the instruments in each instrument sequence. Drawing on the material summarised in Tables 5.1, 6.1 and 7.1, Figures 9.1–9.3 depict the key characteristics of the three sequences. Again, we present these in order of the coerciveness of the initial instrument (i.e. regulatory, market-based and then voluntary). Figure 9.1 presents the main changes that have emerged in the area of biofuels, which in Chapter 5 we characterised as an extended regulatory sequence. The four boxes at the top represent the four main instrument changes in the sequence in which they were adopted (i.e. the 2003 Biofuels Directive through to the 2018 Renewable Energy Directive II), and the arrows represent the most significant feedbacks during the intervening periods. Lower down, we present key information on the speed of adoption (in days) and how long each amendment lasted for ('lifespan' – in days). Below that, we summarise the most significant changes in instrument stringency, scope and timeframe.

Figure 9.1 confirms that the governance of biofuels has indeed evolved via an extended sequence through which fairly weak regulatory targets relating to all biofuels have been replaced by mandatory targets, including a cap on the production of first-generation fuels and, more recently, binding targets that promote the consumption of the second- and third-generation types. None of the amendments triggered strong positive feedbacks; all have been somewhat undermined by medium to strong negative feedback effects. There has been no consistent trend in the adoption speed or lifespan of the instruments, which essentially remain regulatory in nature. Overall, deep decarbonisation in the sequence has neither been decisively locked in nor locked out; rather, policy has entered an inconclusive *cul-de-sac* (see also Biber, *et al.*, 2017: 640).

Figure 9.2 describes the key characteristics of the instrument sequence in relation to emissions trading. Although it covers roughly the same period of time as

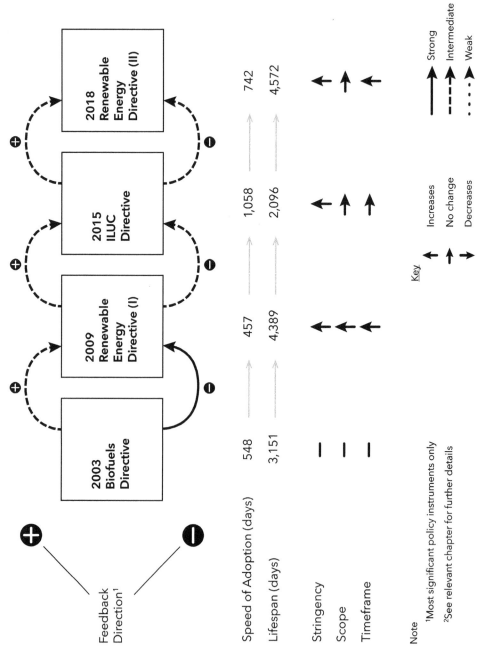

Figure 9.1 Biofuels: significant feedback directions

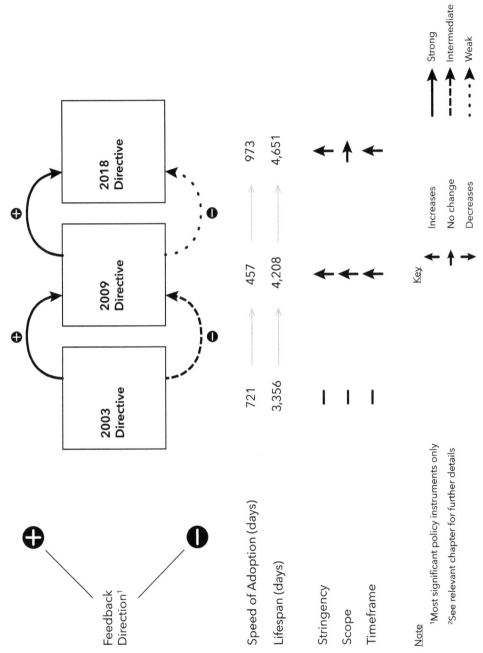

Figure 9.2 Emissions trading: significant feedback directions

biofuels (2003–2019), we have focused on fewer significant policy changes (three instead of four) and the combined feedbacks have been mostly positive. Although the speed of adoption has fluctuated, the lifespan of each instrument change in the sequence has generally increased (see also Figures 8.2 and 8.4). Over time, instrument scope, stringency and timeframe have increased. In Chapter 5, we described the overall sequence as one in which the instrument of emissions trading has been progressively locked in over time. In spite of the near constant travails experienced by the instrument, deep decarbonisation may finally be in the process of being locked in. At the time of this writing, allowance prices are around €30 per tonne and *resource/incentive* and *interpretive mechanisms* continue to strengthen the coalitions favouring even higher policy stringency. This case could therefore be described as one of *incipient* decarbonisation.

At the other end of the spectrum, the governance of car emissions has moved – via an equally long sequence – from a situation of virtually no controls on CO_2 emissions, through to a fairly ineffectual voluntary agreement and ending with a far tougher regulatory system. Figure 9.3 reveals that over time, the net policy feedback has shifted from roughly zero (i.e. positive and negative feedback effects more or less cancelling one another out) to broadly positive. In general, the speed of adoption has declined and the lifespan of each successive instrument change has generally increased. Over time, instrument stringency and timeframe have generally increased. Overall, deep decarbonisation in the sequence is finally – but gradually – being *locked in*, culminating in what appear to be long-lasting technological transformations across the entire sector (essentially from fossil-fuelled to electrically powered vehicles).

The Evolving Dynamics of Policy Feedback

Across all three cases, the unfolding sequences were heavily shaped by the manner in which each successive policy change reconfigured the coalitions favouring policy durability and/or change. In the area of biofuels, the negative effects of the original 2003 Directive fractured the coalition of existing producers that had originally favoured biofuel expansion. New fault lines began to open up between those that had invested in bioethanol and those that had invested in biodiesel, as well as those who were keen to exploit new markets for the second- and third-generation alternatives and those that simply wanted to secure a rate of return on their investments in the first-generation fuel types. No new pro-policy coalition has emerged within the Commission itself, supported and empowered by feedback effects from the original instrument in the sequence. On the contrary, conflicts between DGs and between the Commission and the Parliament have sharpened, as new opponents such as the international development charities have tried to force

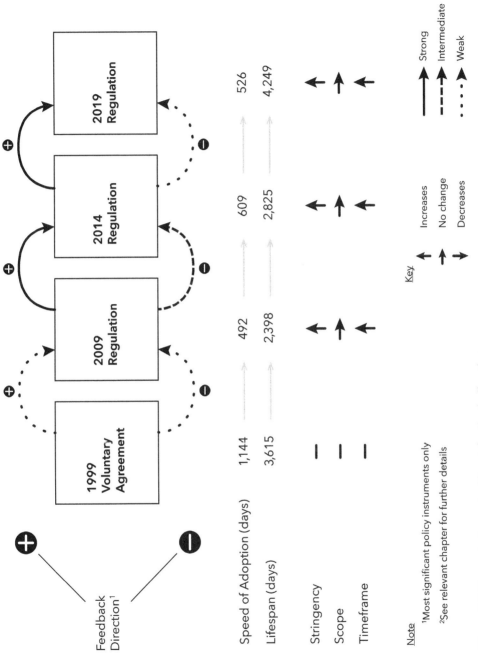

Figure 9.3 Car emissions: significant feedback directions

their way into policy design discussions. To quote Emmanuel Desplechin, Secretary General of ePure, the bioethanol industry association, the EU has, through an extended sequence of changes, gradually recognised that not all biofuels 'are created equal' (Gyekye, 2018a) – a fact that continues to feed into and energise politics across the sector, accentuating uncertainty, rendering policy fragile and repeatedly undermining new business investment (Oliver, 2014).

In the area of emission trading, the initially decentralised, free allocation-focused instrument disproportionately benefited those who were initially sceptical – the energy-intensives and the high-carbon electricity generators – who, buoyed by increasing support from government actors, environmental NGOs and market intermediaries, helped to enhance the instrument's durability. Low allowance prices and frustrations with decentralised allocation won the European Commission and the European Parliament new allies among the Member States for policy centralisation and increased auctioning. In turn, this dynamic gave Member States a new material incentive to seek policy reforms to push up allowance prices. Backloading and the Market Stability Reserve facilitated greater stringency, which was further enhanced after 2020 as a result of the 2018 Directive. The net effect of these changes was rather surprising: a policy instrument that for long periods had been derided as weak and ineffectual has been repeatedly tightened so that following the adoption of the 2018 Directive is now seemingly attaining the once elusive goal of consistently high allowance prices (Marcu *et al.*, 2019).

Finally, in the area of car emissions, existing scholarship has repeatedly demonstrated how politically and economically powerful incumbent players – namely the manufacturers of the largest cars – enjoy long-term influence over the direction and the temporality of policy design (Jordan and Matt, 2014). Initially, the long and painful process of adopting what was only ever a weak voluntary agreement followed a similar historical trajectory. The 1998 agreement fully reflected the producers' unwillingness to invest in the EU's plans for deep decarbonisation, thus permitting them to achieve incremental adjustments to their existing engine technologies. But endogenous pressures for change generated within the agreement itself gradually fed through to and destabilised that coalition of incumbent players, hastening the shift towards more coercive instruments. Even so, the coalition fought every single step of the way, such that almost every single policy design feature that could conceivably have been contested, was fiercely contested. Even seemingly inconsequential technical matters such as how to measure a vehicle's weight or its tail-pipe emissions were repeatedly and rigorously challenged.

Although the shifts in the coalitions within each sequence were influential, so too were the three other factors noted above. First of all, *exogenous* developments helped to shape the broad parameters in which new designs were bargained over amongst the pro- and anti-reform coalitions. For example, improvements in the global economic situation have generally increased economic activity within the EU, pushing up emissions, whereas worldwide recessions have generally had the opposite effect. To give an example of how this altered the interplay between the coalitions in the car sector, economic growth after 2000 increased the passenger kilometres travelled (together with the demand for larger and more polluting cars), fatally undermining the assumptions of the voluntary agreement. But by the time the Commission sought to secure political agreement on the 2009 Regulation, the worldwide recession had made it harder to design in more coercive measures. Suddenly, the car producers felt emboldened to fight for significant concessions and it was the pro-decarbonisation coalition that found itself on the back foot. Very similar cyclical dynamics were apparent in the other two sequences.

The other important exogenous dynamic lay in the international climate regime. In general, the international regime and its own development increased the political pressure to change the EU-level instruments studied in this book, a typical example being the effect of the Paris Agreement on policy stringency after the 2018 Emissions Trading Directive. However, at several critical points – noted in Chapter 3 – the European Commission found itself under pressure from EU-level actors (e.g. the Central and Eastern European Member States or the energy-intensive industry associations) to prevent EU policy from advancing too far ahead of other countries such as the USA and China. The most noteworthy examples of how these pressures affected policy design discussions can be found in the period immediately after the Copenhagen conference in December 2009. On some occasions, exogenous developments unexpectedly combined to exert pressure on pro-decarbonisation coalitions, e.g. after 2008–2009 when the global financial crisis (which dramatically reduced the price of emission allowances) coincided with the diplomatic failure at Copenhagen. They made all businesses wary of policy change, even those that were supportive of the general goal of deeper and faster decarbonisation over the long term.

Within these exogenous constraints, *policy entrepreneurs* were able to capitalise on endogenous dynamics to steer the three sequences towards deeper decarbonisation. Although many actors have performed important entrepreneurial functions (Sandbag in relation to emissions trading and T&E with respect to car emissions), chief amongst them was undoubtedly the European Commission. Freed from the need to continually seek re-election, it was able to play a long game, waiting for policy windows of opportunity and diving through them when they opened up (Di Lucia and Nilsson, 2007: 540; Palmer, 2015: 281). Amongst the main EU institutions and across all three sequences, it was the most persistent and forceful advocate of the instruments in the first place. Once they were in place and established (a not inconsiderable challenge in its own right – think back to the protracted battle to adopt the voluntary agreement on car emissions), it sought – albeit not always successfully – to increase their stringency, scope and timeframe. Although many unexpected design challenges had to be navigated along the way, positive feedback effects, as in the cases of the Emissions Trading System, gradually empowered it to seek continual reforms to entrench deep decarbonisation dynamics.

Finally, the EU may well be unusually open to policy entrepreneurs. But in a very basic sense, one of them – the European Commission – was itself a striking example of a polity-based durability device. The original designers of the EU created it to take a long-term view. But it was also instrumental in inserting flexibility clauses into new EU policies that required information to be collected and disseminated, ex post evaluations to be performed and new policy proposals to be produced. These flexibility devices, which often had the backing of the European Parliament, facilitated feedback mechanisms and created new opportunities to redesign existing policies well before their planned point of termination. Just as importantly, once triggered, the review clauses that the Commission had fought for functioned as important focusing events. They ensured that policy debates were never fully closed even when it was in the interest of powerful, incumbent actors to do so. Two cases in particular – biofuels and car emissions – were replete with examples of this phenomenon.

Policy Feedback: A Summary

There is a marked tendency in the existing literatures to only focus on some policy feedback effects and/or on certain actors, rather than the full array of effects and actors, rendering it difficult to understand the feedback loops back to the original policies. Consequently, many of the crucial determinants of policy lock-in remain in shadow and policy theories privilege exogenous over endogenous source of policy change. Admittedly, moving from effects to feedbacks is analytically challenging: it means studying long sequences of change over many decades (see Table 8.1), each interspersed by periods of feedback that may run in both directions at the same time. However, we have demonstrated that it has mostly been a fruitful strategy: across all three areas we have demonstrated that the original instruments did change, in at least one case (car emissions) by a significant amount, i.e. from one end of the coerciveness spectrum (voluntarism) to the other (regulation).

Second, we learned that the original instruments (P) were impacted in a host of different ways. The car emissions case offers the only example of wholesale instrument change, in stark contrast to biofuels in which the original regulatory sequence was only gradually amended. But at the level of instrument settings – the stuff of mundane, everyday governance – there was a near constant variation in stringency, scope and timeframe. In fact, the changes in instrument settings sometimes moved in different directions at the same time (see also Pahle *et al.*, 2018:

861). However, a close inspection of Figures 9.1–9.3 reveals that none resulted in a consistent reduction in stringency, scope and timeframe.[4] The Commission's strategy is very often to do just that: to make significant concessions during the initial adoption of an instrument in the sequence and then use that as a platform to build on. The resulting pattern – which has been described as 'ratcheting up stringency though policy sequencing' (Pahle *et al.*, 2018: 861) – has also been detected in areas such as renewable energy support (Seto *et al.,* 2016: 436).

Third, the instruments fed back not only on themselves, but on some of the other internal elements of policy elaborated in Chapter 3. For example, over time, positive policy feedback sustained the *instrument* of emissions trading, so that by 2008–2009 its complete removal was no longer regarded as a realistic design aim. Meanwhile, negative feedback related to the policy's *settings*, decreasing actor support for the status quo because of low allowance prices, allowed advocates of deep decarbonisation to increase the instrument's stringency and scope to address these issues.[5] Our findings therefore underline the importance of not treating policies as undifferentiated monoliths (Kay, 2005: 560). On the contrary, careful, multi-level analysis reveals how feedbacks operate simultaneously within the same instrument sequence as well as different levels of policy (goals, instruments and settings). In short, while undoubtedly challenging, such work is more likely to capture the multi-dimensionality of policy durability and feedback (Jacobs and Mettler, 2018: 350).

Finally, the one element of policy that was not significantly affected by negative feedbacks was the overarching paradigm[6] of deep decarbonisation. In relation to Hall's (1993) influential account of policy change, repeated negative feedbacks at the level of instruments gradually undermined the viability of the entire paradigm. But in our three sequences, the paradigm persisted. In fact, some negative feedback arguably contributed to the resilience of the broader paradigm. One explanation for this somewhat paradoxical outcome is that instruments do not simply generate negative feedbacks; they may also generate positive feedbacks (in this study, emissions trading and car emissions after 2009). What mattered in other words, was the *net* effect.[7]

9.4 The Policy Design Process: The Designers and Their Intentions

Having examined policy feedback, we now turn to Objective 1, which related to the formative moments of each instrument. In this section we shall identify the main designers, examine their intentions and priorities, and the constraints they were operating under. We shall conclude by examining the extent to which the conscious manipulation of policy feedback to achieve greater durability was an explicit priority – as originally suggested by Pierson (1993: fn. 59) – and expressed in the title of this book – Durability *by Design*. To be clear, in Chapter 1 we argued that to count as 'intentional' any observed effects do not have to perfectly correspond with what was originally intended (Goodin, 1996: 28); rather, we have attempted to investigate what effects were generated when actors consciously sought to shape the future.

The normative case for taking bold and decisive steps to accelerate decarbonisation transitions is well known (Eskridge and Ferejohn, 2001: 1271). In some respects, it has become the holy grail of climate activists (Parson and Karwat, 2011: 751; Rosenbloom *et al.*, 2019: 168). In Chapter 1, we noted that hopes have regularly been expressed that more durable policies will nurture a sense of expectation within broader society that deep decarbonisation is inevitable and will steadily become locked into societies (as in Hacker and Pierson, 2014: 652). Henceforth, all actors – including but not restricted to target groups – should adapt accordingly because henceforth society is on a path to net-zero emissions and there will be no going back. And yet for those of us who are prepared to study policy design 'as it is and not as we would like it to be' (Flanagan *et al.*, 2011: 711), we should remember that even when some actors are more future-focused, some will not be and hence intentional policy design for the very long term is likely to remain immensely difficult (Pierson, 2000). When path dependence takes root – as it arguably has in relation to the heavily carbonised ways of living that underpin everyday life in all policy sectors – it is often the unintended outcome of a multitude of individual steps (cf. Levin *et al.*, 2012: 138; Rosenbloom *et al.*, 2019: 172). And once policy lock-ins become entrenched, they can be exceedingly difficult to dislodge or, to use Pierson's (1994) terminology, 'dismantle'. If this is as true for deep decarbonisation as it has been for welfare state reform, the probability of limiting warming even to 2°C is likely to be very low indeed.

Who Were the Designers?

In Chapter 1, we explained that our aim was to empirically explore the middle ground between two somewhat polarised views of policy design (Peters, 2018). This middle ground regards design as a process though which policy makers respond to problems; those like us who are working in the middle ground seek to describe and explain that response process. They appreciate the importance – perhaps even necessity – of design in relation to some especially wicked problems such as climate change but seek to understand the political challenges that arise in practice. In climate policy, after securing agreement on the need for a new policy, the next most difficult challenge is probably how to strike a balance between simultaneous demands for greater durability *and* flexibility within its design (Goodin, 1996).

Chapters 3–7 amply confirmed that design within the EU was not dominated by a single rational policy designer. Rather than a single path or sequence to deep decarbonisation that all actors agree upon, they reveal an almost constant process of contestation involving many actors, centring on both the means and the ends of policy (Rosenbloom *et al.*, 2019: 169). For us, the key designers were governments, target groups and other interest groups. Their behaviour often confounded general expectations. Politicians – and chiefly Heads of State – are often assumed to be myopic and incrementalist, but at key junctures (such as the agreement of policy programme-level goals for 2020 and 2030) they aimed for – and in large measure were able to adopt – a longer-term view in collaboration with proposals from the Commission. By contrast, target groups – and specifically large businesses – are often assumed to be well-organised repeat players that have the means and the motivation to think well beyond the next election (Hacker, Pierson and Thelen, 2013: 32–33). But in all our cases business was not monolithic: at many critical junctures, industries clashed with each other (electricity generators vs. the energy-intensives; biodiesel producers vs. bioethanol producers; car manufacturers vs. fuel suppliers etc.). Even the European Commission, which as we have already noted is in principle the EU's policy formulator and thus the closest approximation to a decarbonisation transition 'manager', was forced to bargain and compromise to advance deep decarbonisation. Sometimes, even it struggled to act coherently, e.g. when its own Directorates-General repeatedly and openly disagreed on the 2030 reduction targets.

Policy Design Intentions

It is a truism that policy design is an inherently constrained activity (Bobrow, 2005; Peters, 2018). All actors were forced to operate within exogenous constraints arising from prevailing legal and political institutions. But our forward-tracing approach also detected significant constraints of a more endogenous nature. For example, the EU has a set of historically well-defined instrument preferences (see Chapter 3) which it continually struggles to escape. It is telling that with the sole exception of emissions trading, there are still virtually no environmental market-based instruments and voluntary agreements at EU level. And second, we revealed that once an instrument sequence has been initiated, the search for alternatives occurs on a terrain that has been altered by those policies. One of the most well-known design recommendations in the environmental policy instrument literature is that designers should start with the least intrusive instruments and only then move along the coerciveness spectrum (Howlett, 2019). By examining the feedbacks generated by individual instruments, we have revealed how the instrument toolbox on occasions becomes steadily more endogenous over time, i.e. once an instrument sequence takes hold[8] (amongst our cases, emissions trading and the regulation of car emissions after 1999), it significantly affects subsequent choices.

Amidst these complex and fluid alliances, a long-running battle has been waged at the level of policy paradigms between environmentalists wanting to accelerate and deepen decarbonisation, and a range of incumbent players demanding to slow and/or narrow its scope (Goldthau *et al.*, 2019: 31). Importantly, in policy design terms, the battle was not simply between environmentalists fighting for greater durability and incumbent players seeking flexibility; things were altogether more complicated. Sometimes, actors favouring deeper decarbonisation such as the European Commission aimed to retain some flexibility to prevent existing policies from becoming outdated or misaligned with changes in technology (e.g. the review requirements in the voluntary agreement). Meanwhile, at some points industry groups preferred more policy durability to squeeze more income from their existing investments – in diesel-powered cars, for example, or first-generation biofuels.

As the process of design unfolded, various actors sought to shape the adoption of durability and flexibility devices to alter the timing and direction of the policy sequence and thus the broader decarbonisation transition. In Chapter 2, we outlined the conceptual distinction between durability devices and flexibility devices at different levels of policy. Policy programme-level durability devices include long-term targets to breed confidence that a particular direction will endure. At the level of specific instruments, designers can also force polluters to make significant 'sunk' investments to make the overall direction more durable. By contrast, *instrument-level devices* such as flexibility clauses provide an opportunity, known by all in advance, to revisit the policy's design in the light of changing conditions.

In Chapters 5–7 we noted that in everyday governance many of these devices are designed to operate at the level of specific instruments. With regards to promoting durability, Figures 9.1–9.3 usefully reveal how the stringency, scope and timeframe of the goals embodied in the instruments changed as the respective sequences unfolded. Monitoring clauses were a near standard design feature of all the instruments. Their role in facilitating *interpretive feedback mechanisms* was noted above. The use of instrument-level flexibility devices was also apparent in all three sequences. For example, Article 30 of the 2003 Emissions Trading Directive required the Commission to draw up an *ex post* evaluation by a specific date (30 June 2006), 'accompanied by [new] proposals as appropriate'. This gave the Commission an opportunity to document the failings of the existing instrument and initiate a new round of policy making without having to wait for the Member States to offer their blessing. Finally, relational contracts bound the Commission to act in a particular way, e.g. maintain the regulatory approach to car emissions governance after 2009. Of course, in practice, the Commission was never able fully to control the instrument sequences because unintended consequences inevitably began to emerge and affect the prevailing design space. However, it repeatedly extolled the need for a coherent, long-term perspective. According to the two most senior officials in DG CLIMA who oversaw the design work:

Policymaking on the basis of facts and figures [...] [and] an active engagement with stakeholders [was] [...] more rewarding than overly concentrating on what is considered politically opportune in the short term

(Delbeke and Vis, 2015: 2).

It is also worth noting that the devices that were eventually adopted were generally of a manual rather an automatic nature. Although on many occasions the Commission tried to introduce greater automaticity (e.g. in the early stages of the biofuels and emissions trading sequences), it was almost always opposed by Member States. Other than comitology (which on occasions spectacularly failed to deliver rapid policy amendment),[9] the only automatic devices that were adopted (namely the linear reduction factor, the Market Stability Reserve and automatic allowance cancellation in relation to emissions trading, and the gradual phasing out of first-generation biofuels) arrived relatively late in the respective sequences when policy was effectively already quite durable.

We shall say more about precisely how the EU engaged in long-term design in the next section. But as part of that endeavour, did the EU – and specifically the Commission – consciously design policies to generate particular feedback effects, which was the more specific dimension of intentionality raised by Pierson (1993: 624)? More often than not, the Commission's proposals were framed in terms of the need to generate broad environmental outcomes – specifically greenhouse gas reductions[10] – or attain generic objectives such as preserving the single market. There were, however, some hints in design-related documents that acknowledge the importance of cultivating the political support of key players. For example, the Commission's (2001: 17) proposal on biofuels noted the importance of nurturing 'the investment required to promote sufficient quantities of biofuels' and likened the relationship between investment and policy durability to a chicken and an egg (p. 3). Later in the sequence, the opening recitals (paragraph 14) of the 2009 Renewable Energy Directive underlined the value of securing greater 'certainty for investors' in all types of renewable sources. And in preparing proposals to adapt the 2003 Emissions Trading Directive, the Commission emphasised the importance of 'creating the right incentives for forward looking low carbon investment decisions by reinforcing a clear, undistorted and long-term carbon price signal' (COM (2008) 16: 3). Therefore, the answer to Pierson's question is probably no: designers did not intentionally design policies to produce certain political feedback effects, although given the increasing political salience of deep decarbonisation, this topic merits further research.[11]

The Policy Design Process: A Summary

Policy feedback scholars have generally evinced more interest in the politics that emerge after the enactment of a policy; all too often, the 'pre-policy' period, encompassing the policy formulation and decision-making stages of design, are bracketed off (Peters *et al.*, 2005: 1277).[12] However, by adopting a forward-tracing approach that links formulation to feedbacks, we have been able to shed light on two important aspects of policy durability that until now have mostly lain in shadow. First of all, we have demonstrated that policy durability and flexibility are not simply fixed policy attributes to be used by policy scientists to describe policies – i.e. as more durable (or flexible) than others. In real-world design processes, actors readily adopt and agitate for the adoption of their own interpretations of durability; hence, its real-world meaning is the focus (and outcome) of political debate and conflict. Furthermore, because of policy feedback, these struggles have a tendency to shape the design of the next amendment in a policy instrument sequence.

Second, we have shed new light on just how uncertain and contingent the formative moments in some sequences are. Even instrument sequences that may now appear with hindsight to be relatively locked in (emissions trading, for example, or car emission regulation after 2009) may initially have had rather uncertain origins, particularly in hyperconsensual policy-making systems such as the EU which are riddled with veto points and inhabited by many powerful incumbent actors. There are many durable policies in the world today (Adam *et al.*, 2019). But durable and effective policies that do not succumb to drift are much rarer; they certainly do not appear to readily 'design themselves' (Howlett and Lejano, 2013: 367). Rather, the EU institutions have had to struggle long and hard to build more durable instrument sequences. In the initial, formative moments the overriding aim was to make the most of available policy widows and get something – and on occasions anything – adopted, and then build up from there.[13] During the early stages of all three sequences, adoption was the overriding priority, perhaps alongside avoiding strong initial negative feedbacks that could conceivably have imperilled the policy's very survival (Mukherjee and Giest, 2017: 275).[14] Even once the sequences had evolved, the level of stringency changed more regularly than the instruments' scope (see Figures 9.1–9.3), hinting at the existence of more systemic limitations to the prevailing design space. Technologically and politically challenging issues (such as how to reduce emissions from heavy lorries or international airlines, or reduce the underlying demand for car travel) were repeatedly kept outside the scope of policy design discussions to ensure the survival of the sequence, thus revealing how near-term compromises may, on occasions, buy much needed time and political space to build longer-term policy durability.

9.5 Policy Durability

The Dimensions of Durability

Durability is commonly equated with persistence and steadfastness. In Chapter 1 we noted how there is a common assumption amongst policy scientists that durability is relatively common, albeit with some ambiguity about its precise meaning. In Chapter 1, we therefore tried to introduce more clarity and precision to the debate by distinguishing between three dimensions of durability:

1. Its *means*, as measured by how long its implementing instruments last. An instrument is not durable if it is rapidly weakened or even completely dismantled.
2. Its *objectives*, as measured by their stability over time. A policy is unlikely to be durable if its overriding objectives are rapidly and significantly amended over time.
3. Its *outcomes*, as measured by how far they are delivered over time. Policies are unlikely to be durable if they fail to generate substantive outcomes and/or succumb to policy drift.

The first dimension arises from the recognition that the most common entry point for designers wishing to build more durable designs is often at the level of specific instruments, rather than long-term goals and policy programmes (Levin *et al.*, 2012: 132). Policy sequencing, it has been claimed, is (and indeed should be) the norm, not single 'big bang' policies (Levin *et al.*, 2012: 125) that seek to fix long-term targets. Our forward-tracing focus on instruments has generated new insights into how designers actually go about crafting policies that seek to lock certain aspects into place, whilst providing sufficient flexibility to prevent policy drift and redundancy (Jordan and Matt, 2014). In Chapter 8, we revealed that every single one of the fifteen instrument changes in the three sequences surpassed a very basic durability threshold (i.e. surviving the standard EU legislative term of five years). In fact, the vast majority lasted well over eight years, even the dismantled voluntary agreement on cars. In the previous sections, we also noted how each one has been designed in such a way as to balance demands for durability and flexibility. Two obvious cases in point are the Emissions Trading System (Woerdman *et al.*, 2015: 74) and the policy on biofuels (Egelund Olsen and Ronne, 2016: 181), each now constituting complex policy sub-areas in their own right, with distinct rules, terminologies and temporal rhythms.[15]

In theory, designers can accept Levin *et al.*'s (2012) advice and opt to build path-dependent policy interventions by continuing to work only at the level of instruments. In Chapter 3, we noted that in the formative moments of EU policy in the 1980s and 1990s, the Commission did rely on such a strategy, focusing on areas of 'low politics' such as monitoring, evaluation and the calibration of standards covering white goods such as fridges. Such a strategy corresponds to the 'Monnet method' of deepening European cooperation 'by stealth' (Jordan and Adelle, 2013: 382). However, our forward-tracing and multi-element approach to understanding design has also revealed how in seeking to balance durability and flexibility, the EU has sought to adjust other policy elements, specifically policy-programme-level goals and targets ('the durability of objectives' – the second dimension noted at the beginning of this section). There have been two notable features of the EU's behaviour. First of all, as well as crafting specific instruments, the European Commission has pushed the EU – and specifically Heads of State in the European Council – to adopt longer-term goals and targets – e.g. relating to 2000, 2020 and 2030. We repeatedly uncovered evidence that the EU Heads of State signed up to such targets (such as the 20% by 2020 renewables target) without fully appreciating their near-term implications (see also Buchan, 2009: 137). Only later, when the Commission started to back-fill the targets with new and/or reformed instruments, did the political implications of adopting them become fully apparent. At that point, the Commission sought to use its exclusive power of initiative to speed up the process, pushing designers to reach agreement by presenting an upcoming international conference as a non-negotiable decision point. In effect, it employed what Gibson and Goodin (1999, 363) have termed the veil of vagueness – pushing for agreement on programme-wide durability and flexibility devices (time-limited targets, strategies and revert clauses) whilst deliberately leaving the detail about their implementation for another day (Jordan *et al.*, 2010: 203). At other times, the Commission used its power of initiative to forestall conflict by withdrawing (or not publishing) a proposal to slow down the policy design process. By delaying the adoption of new long-term targets (e.g. for 2030) until it was politically propitious to do so, the Commission was able to prevent internal conflict from escalating to the point that design entirely broke down.

Second, designers in the EU have come to realise the importance of working across different levels of governance at the same time (Levin *et al.*, 2012: 133). With the benefit of a thirty-year perspective on climate policy design, we have been able to reveal how developments in international, EU and national policy did not simply co-evolve, but actively fed off one another (Oberthür and Pallemaerts, 2010: 27). For example, before the early 2000s the EU lagged behind UN policy; the Commission used this as a stick to drive Member States towards more stringent internal policy designs. After the US government's withdrawal from the Kyoto Protocol in 2001, the EU came under international pressure from other countries to step into the vacuum and adopt a lead-by-example approach. Each successive international meeting then became a focal point for engineering internal agreement on new design activities to ensure the EU's international credibility. After a particular international meeting (such as the one in Berlin in 1995), policy designers favouring stronger internal action used the agreements struck there as a 'force majeure' (Jordan et al., 2010: 205) to drive the rest towards stronger internal targets, policies and measures.

By constantly looking for and exploiting windows of opportunity at multiple levels of policy and governance, the Commission was able to foster and maintain a sense of 'irreversibility' amongst a sufficient number of key actors (Eberlein and Radaelli, 2010: 788), thus displacing potentially awkward political conflicts into the future or to other policy venues. In doing so, long-term targets were gradually moved in a more stringent direction (or stayed the same), instrument sequences were sustained and losers kept on board using a mixture of concessions such as the delayed entry of a new standard.

The third and final dimension relates to the durability of policy *outcomes*. At a broad level, the EU is now decarbonising. Its greenhouse gas emissions are in long-term decline (Delbeke and Vis, 2015: 3), it easily fulfilled its 2012 reduction target and is on track to fulfil its 2020 emission reduction target (EEA, 2018). However, the current portfolio of policies and near-term targets is insufficient to ensure that the EU fulfils its more demanding targets for 2030 and 2050, let alone achieve deep decarbonisation ('net-zero' emissions) by 2050 (a long-term goal which in 2019 began to be actively debated amongst the EU institutions – see Chapter 3).

The three sequences neatly illustrate many of the practical difficulties that the EU has experienced in delivering durable policy outcomes. If we start with biofuel, the much-vaunted internal market in biofuel remains highly fragmented and the 10% target (by 2020) will be very challenging to fulfil, in spite of the immense effort that has been invested in policy design processes since 2000. In 2017, the EU's statistics agency Eurostat (2017) declared that the EU had only achieved a 6.7% share of transport fuels in 2015 as against 1.4% in 2004. As regards actual emission reductions – the overriding justification for initiating the sequence in the first place – the complexities associated with tracking emissions along complex supply chains means that the EU may never know what the net outcomes of its design efforts were. It is telling that some of the large incumbent players such as the oil and gas producers are beginning to invest significant resources to develop third-generation alternatives (Raval, 2019), but the long promised 'breakthrough' (COM (2015) 293: 16) to achieve 'clean' biofuels still appears a long way off (Royal Academy of Engineering, 2017: 21).

The emissions trading sequence has undoubtedly reduced emissions but not to the extent that many, including the main designers in the Commission, originally hoped. Chapters 4 and 6 catalogued the long litany of problems that have been experienced, culminating in long periods when allowance prices hovered just above zero (Sandbag, 2019). However, it is inherently uncertain what the future holds for allowance prices and thus the policy's long-term effectiveness at driving decarbonisation. And yet, in spite of the modest outcomes generated, the ETS remains firmly in place – seemingly politically too big to dismantle, but for many years too ineffective to set the EU firmly on a trajectory to net zero emissions by 2050.

Finally, average fleet-wide CO_2 emissions from cars are falling in line with increasingly stringent targets and deadlines contained within EU policies, but several manufacturers may struggle to fulfil even their near-term obligations, which could result in some incurring significant fines after 2021 (Campbell, 2017). The greenhouse gas emissions from trucks and buses have only recently been addressed by designers (Delbeke and Vis, 2015: 83), a tricky challenge given that the main alternative to diesel (electrification) is not as easy to deploy as it is in the car segment of the sector. Furthermore, there remains a significant risk of policy drift across the sector. The Commission has conceded that a much faster and more 'holistic' approach to deep decarbonisation is urgently required, encompassing the way in which all vehicles are produced, fuelled and disposed of (COM (2016) 501). Certainly, the longer that diesel vehicles remain on the roads of Europe, the more challenging it will be to address local air pollution problems in towns and cities. In Chapter 7, we noted that systemic change is beginning to occur in some parts of the sector, as more manufacturers switch to selling electric and hybrid cars. It is telling that VW – the company at the epicentre of the Dieselgate scandal – has committed itself to becoming the world's largest producer of such cars. Even so, there is a seemingly ever-present risk of drift – that any environmental improvements made are eaten up by the relentless increase in car ownership and distances travelled (EEA, 2015: 24). The EEA has repeatedly underlined the need for a systemic shift towards public transport, sharp reductions in air travel and strenuous efforts to reduce the demand for road transport (EEA, 2016). As yet, the EU has barely begun to deliver it.

Policy Durability: A Summary

Policy durability is often equated with policy lock-ins and hence undesirable forms of rigidity. In economics, durability is chiefly viewed in terms of setting very long-term targets (known as pre-commitment strategies) and/or establishing independent institutions (akin to central banks). Amongst policy scientists, durable policies are those that 'tie the hands' of target groups (Patashnik, 2008: 167; see also Levin *et al.*, 2012). However, we have revealed that in everyday policy design processes, deep decarbonisation entails the adoption of policies that are durable in some respects, but also flexible in others.

Our forward-tracing approach has usefully revealed how the EU has sought to strike a dynamic balance between the two. The incorporation of flexibility and durability devices within individual instrument sequences has, however, proven to be a complex and iterative challenge, encompassing many elements of policy and levels of governance. We have demonstrated that policy durability in the EU is a multi-dimensional phenomenon, encompassing three key dimensions – policy means, policy objectives and policy outcomes. The first of these is widely understood in existing scholarship. Our findings demonstrate that it is probably also the easiest of the three to address in practice. In EU climate policy, programme-level objectives have also tended to be rather stable over time. The durable, ongoing delivery of satisfactory outcomes has long been the Achilles heel of EU climate policy. Yet arguably, the most difficult challenge of all has been to ensure that policy sequences simultaneously perform strongly against all three dimensions. Of the three sequences, the one addressing biofuels has performed the least satisfactorily in this regard, being trapped in the policy equivalent of a *cul-de-sac*. However, for various reasons, all three sequences have failed to deliver the environmental outcomes that were originally promised. Drift is normally thought of in terms of the ability of a given policy to adapt to the changing world around it. What was particularly striking about the three policy sequences was that the pressure to adapt emerged as much from endogenous dynamics as exogenous ones (namely, the economy, environmental quality etc.). Thus in the biofuels area a key pressure derived from rapid changes in the scientific understanding of its environmental consequences, for emissions trading it derived from the changing allowance price and in the car sector it arose from the public's preference for particular vehicles (diesel or petrol, large or small). Evidently, simply keeping pace with a policy's own unfolding feedbacks constitutes a significant policy design challenge in itself, even before any exogenous factors are considered.

And yet, in spite of all these setbacks, the decarbonisation policy paradigm in the EU has remained relatively immune to sustained political challenge. In fact, after over three decades of policy design activity the EU arguably remains the world's only consistent leader in international climate politics. There is a live debate amongst scholars on how best to design policies (Iacobuta *et al.*, 2018: 18; Pahle *et al.*, 2018; Schmidt *et al.*, 2018; Rosenbloom *et al.*, 2019: 170). Our analysis reveals that it involves crafting policy designs that are able to anticipate and weather changes, be they endogenously and/or exogenously derived. A significant – but greatly overlooked – aspect of the EU's overall approach has been the near continuous backwards and forwards movement between the main sub-elements of policy – long-term goals, policy programmes and instruments. This recursive strategy is how the EU thinks about 'the big things while doing the small things, so that all the small things move in the right direction'. It is a strategy to achieve *active durability*, through which different policy elements are combined in such a way as the overall package is 'sufficiently robust to sustain [a] degree of modification and still accomplish its desired goals' (Peters, 1999: 86). When durability is actively accomplished through myriad interconnecting elements, even strong negative feedbacks may serve a positive political function. They are akin to policy alarms, alerting designers to the fact that broader programmes and paradigms are under mounting political pressure. The alarms prompt key designers such as the Commission to re-orient instrument sequences to safeguard the broader programmes and, perhaps even more crucially, maintaining the overarching policy paradigm.

9.6 Final Reflections and New Directions

Policy feedback is a key piece of the broader puzzle of how to understand and ultimately deliver greater durability in instruments, objectives and outcomes. In this book we have sought to go beyond the very general argument that policy somehow reshapes and re-orientates politics to offer more conditional explanations on how it feeds back into political life, through what mechanisms, in what directions and with what effects including, crucially, on the original policy. In doing so, we have developed and tested new definitions of key terms and concepts drawing on fresh empirical work in an area (climate change) and institutional setting (the European Union) that have been largely overlooked by policy feedback researchers in the past (Béland and Schlager, 2019: 201). By investigating the relationships between specific policy designs and feedbacks, we have identified new and potentially fruitful ways to significantly advance Pierson's (1993) original research programme. In making new theoretical and conceptual linkages between policy durability and policy feedback – two sub-areas of the policy sciences that have largely developed along separate tracks – we have identified a rich new agenda for future research.

Which topics merit further analysis? Three, in particular, stand out. One is the relationship between policy and politics. It is worth recalling that while the title of his 1993 article referred to policy feedback, Pierson (1993: 596) was mainly motivated to better understand everyday politics, *not* policy. We have confirmed that a great deal of everyday politics is shaped by previous policy interventions (see also Jacobs and Mettler, 2018: 358). But we have also demonstrated that the resulting political effects on actor identities, preferences and capacities subsequently feed back into and shape the politics associated with the next round(s) of design. As such, policy feedback research also greatly enriches our collective understanding of *policy* as well. It is fair to say that most policy scientists have not grasped the importance of this point as fully as they could and should have done. First of all, our work informs research on the selection, adoption and redesign of instruments, a classic topic that is rightly enjoying a renaissance (Howlett and del Rio, 2015: 1234–1235). The instrument sequences described in this book confirm that there is an inescapably historical dimension to policy instrumentation that is all too often neglected in favour of static typologies and one-off snapshots. We have also shown that the tension between flexibility and durability is resolved through employing a whole series of devices that have largely been unreported in the policy instruments literature. Our typology of the main devices could be used to study a much wider array of instrument types and design situations.

Our findings also inform broader policy theories, the majority of which do not explicitly attend to the relationship between feedback and durability (Béland and Schlager, 2019: 185). Unlike mainstream accounts of policy change (which stress the importance of exogenous drivers in generating significant change), our forward-tracing approach has usefully drawn attention to the role played by *endogenous* sources of change, which over time may have slow moving but ultimately significant effects. The destabilising effects of the Dieselgate crisis, the persistently low price of allowances in the ETS and the cross-sectoral campaign against biofuel certainly cannot be fully appreciated without thinking about the interaction between exogenous and endogenous factors. An increasingly popular way to understand the role of such gradual policy changes is to employ the terminology of institutional layering, drift and conversion (see e.g. van der Heijden, 2011). Although we could have employed this terminology to describe the three sequences,[16] our forward-tracing approach has the potential to explicate and explain the recurrent processes of policy feedback and policy change in much finer detail.

Our study also identifies opportunities to make new linkages between the literatures on policy durability, feedback and design. Policy design is commonly thought of as being characterised by failure and disappointment – of doing little more than 'tilting the odds' in favour of important new societal objectives such as deep decarbonisation (Bobrow, 2005: 78). While it is undoubtedly true that incumbent interests do enjoy significant agency to block or deploy policy change, including via forms of negative feedback (Béland and Schlager, 2019: 190), so too do those advocating for faster and deeper decarbonisation. For example, we have demonstrated how the European Commission has developed a whole repertoire of design actions: offering concessions to bring on board losers and thus ensure that instrument sequences are maintained (Goldthau *et al.*, 2019: 30); slowing down or speeding up decision making; moving institutional venues or shifting the focus of design discussions from the instrument level up to the policy programme level and back again. Indeed, the manipulation of time itself (Nowotny, 1994: 145) may well be one of the most powerful – but least appreciated – tactics in its toolbox of policy design. By shifting the focus ten or twenty years into the future and then back again, this strategy not only avoids becoming too bogged down in bitter contemporary political battles, but shapes future expectations about what may eventually be possible and desirable in the fullness of time, be that much cleaner and quieter cars powered by electricity or biofuels sustainably produced from algae (Rosenbloom *et al.*, 2019: 174). Mettler and SoRelle (2014: 152) are surely correct in arguing that new research on these kinds of design activities could greatly inform our understanding of how current politics shapes future design possibilities, and vice versa.

The second topic which merits further research is the unfolding relationship between policy and technology. In Chapter 2 we noted how the literatures on technologies, socio-technical systems, policy feedback and path dependence have indirectly informed one another (Hess, 2014; Seto *et al.*, 2016: 435; Edmondson *et al.*, 2018; Roberts *et al.*, 2018; Schmidt and Sewerin, 2019). Our analysis has certainly shed new light on the deeply contingent roles played by governments and other state actors in initiating and accelerating decarbonisation transitions. That role goes significantly beyond the rather narrow one envisaged in the socio-technical transitions literature – essentially of creating protective niches in which new environmental technologies can emerge (Hess, 2014: 279) – to encompass the near constant interventions that designers make to steer ongoing policy sequences towards deeper and faster decarbonisation. In that regard, we have shown how small and seemingly inconsequential differences in policy design – an additional flexibility clause here or a requirement to perform an *ex post* evaluation there – may become politically consequential in the fullness of time (Kemp and Pontoglio, 2011).[17] Our work certainly resonates with (but adds considerably more nuance to) the claim that transitions are heavily shaped by the conflict between broad coalitions of actors (Hess, 2014: 282), by revealing the importance of policy feedback effects from previous policies.

At the same time, policy scientists could benefit from engaging more positively with transitions scholars in order to understand how technologies and associated market structures shape the politics of policy design. Usually policy scientists in general (and policy feedback scholars in particular) tend to bracket off these aspects (Béland and Schlager, 2019: 190).[18] But across all three sequences, basic technological differences (such as between electricity generators and energy-intensives, different electricity companies, or manufacturers of diesel and electric cars) were a significant contextual factor that not only shaped initial actor preferences during the formative moments of policy design, but greatly mediated the ensuing feedbacks (Kelsey, 2018: 616).[19]

The third and final topic concerns the role of the wider public. The effects of welfare state policies on mass publics has become a standard feature of the contemporary policy feedback literature, and one in which significant intellectual advances have recently been made (Béland and Schlager, 2019: 191). In Chapter 1, we explained our rationale for bracketing off such mass effects. To a very large extent it was justified, as the formulation, adoption and refinement of policy instruments did largely occur within non-majoritarian venues well away from the public's gaze. Other than the big international meetings at Copenhagen and Paris, other endogenously structured focusing events such as the Dieselgate crisis or the cross-national campaign against 'dirty' biofuels, policy durability was largely shaped by elite actors operating in elite venues. However, neither deep decarbonisation nor, for that matter, European integration can be assumed to be truly durable goals if they fail to win and secure the support of the wider public. The EU's declining support amongst voters and the associated rise in anti-EU politicians and parties is already widely known and understood (Jordan and Adelle, 2012: 382–383).[20] What is not so well appreciated – and hence would make a good topic for future research – is how these issues interconnect with and are shaped by the feedback from existing and new policies (Skocpol, 2013), particularly those that seek to decarbonise areas of private life such as diet, thermal comfort and mobility that lay so far outside the EU's current design space that they have barely been touched by policies in the past.

In view of what is known about the subtle, long-term effect of policies on mass publics (see Chapter 1), two potential scenarios are possible, which could form the focus of a new programme of research. The first is that new policies provide an opportunity for designers to build stronger public support for both European integration and deep decarbonisation by explaining the need for and collective benefits of EU-wide action (Patt and Weber, 2014: 226), i.e. positive policy feedback. The second is that the adoption of more stringent policies is used by opponents of European integration to blunt the EU's policy ambitions by sowing doubts in the minds of voters about the benefits of deep decarbonisation, i.e. negative policy feedback. In Chapters 5–7 we noted how the lack of agreement in and with the European Parliament in the 2010s significantly slowed down the adoption of amendments, significantly limiting the EU's ability to recalibrate its existing policies to ensure that EU climate policy as a whole remained durable. Given its importance in driving forwards international climate politics and policy making in pursuit of net zero emissions, the EU's ability to manage these internal tensions could well have a significant bearing on the extent to which the world avoids dangerous climate change in the years ahead.

Endnotes

1 Hence going beyond what Pierson (2006: 124) termed analytical 'demonstration projects'.
2 And of course subsidies, which are not in the EU's environmental policy toolbox (see Chapter 1).
3 For example, by forcing polluters to make upfront investments in certain pollution control technologies required by the policy. In doing so, they are actively supporting the durability of the policy (see Chapter 2 for details).

4 The closest example being the capping of the expansion of first-generation biofuels.
5 In fact, they were forced to provide special concessions to opponents such as continued free allocation.
6 A policy paradigm 'specifies not only the goals of policy, and the kind of instruments that can be used to attain them, but also the very nature of the problems they are meant to be addressing' (Hall, 1993: 279). It equates to a policy's 'overarching orientation' (Rosenbloom et al., 2019: 169).
7 See also Oberlander and Weaver (2015: 58).
8 And especially those that foster strong positive policy feedbacks.
9 The attempt to backload emission allowances being the best example (see Chapter 6).
10 To stray too far from these could, of course, run the risk of acting *ultra vires*.
11 For example, through interviewing policy designers about their motivations and understandings.
12 And similarly, the policy formulation literature brackets off policy feedbacks (Jordan and Turnpenny, 2015).
13 On the formidable obstacles to policy adoption, see Weaver (1988: 212).
14 Figure 8.4 revealed that, in general, the second instrument in each sequence lasted considerably longer than the first.
15 Thus echoing Salamon's (2002) earlier point that often in policy instrument design the political price paid for securing adoption is greater technical complexity.
16 Until recently, emission trading exhibited evidence of policy drift whereas biofuels involved repeated layering. By contrast, the car emissions example provides the only example of displacement – when the instrument sequence flipped from voluntary to regulatory.
17 A recent systematic review of literature concluded that inter-instrument differences are indeed less decisive in shaping effects than the internal design of single instruments (Kemp and Pontoglio, 2011: 34).
18 And, in fact, private actors more generally.
19 Such as the basic choice between 'working within' or 'working outside' the existing policy sequence (see Chapter 1).
20 This area is ripe for new research drawing together different strands of the policy feedback literature. It is an open question as to whether European voters regard the EU in much the same way as some US voters perceive their government to be a 'submerged state' (Mettler, 2011), that delivers policy benefits to them in a remote and hidden manner.

References

Ackrill, R. and Kay, A. (2014). *The Growth of Biofuels in the 21st Century: Policy Drivers and Market Challenges*. Basingstoke: Palgrave MacMillan.

Action Aid, Birdlife Europe, European Environmental Bureau et al. (2013). *Biofuels: EU energy ministers must choose right path for our world's climate and food security*. NGO Media Advisory, 9 December.

Adam, C., Hurka, S. and Knill, C. (2019). *Policy Accumulation and the Democratic Responsiveness Trap*. Cambridge: Cambridge University Press.

Afionis, S. and Stringer, L. C. (2012). European Union leadership in biofuels regulation: Europe as a normative power? *Journal of Cleaner Production*, **32**, 114–123.

Agra CEAS Consulting (2013). *EU Biofuels Investment Development*. Wye, UK: Agra CEAS Consulting.

Ala-Kurikka, S. (2015a). EU Parliament backs faster CO_2 market boost. *ENDS Europe*, 24 February.

Ala-Kurikka, S. (2015b). Latvia seeks compromise on early ETS reform. *ENDS Europe*, 6 March.

Ala-Kurikka, S. (2015c). MEPs accept weaker biofuel cap. *ENDS Europe*, 14 April.

Ala-Kurikka, S. (2015d). Campaign turns up heat on bioenergy. *ENDS Europe*, 28 April.

Ala-Kurikka, S. (2016a). Winter Package: renewables proposals cap food-based biofuels at 3.8%. *ENDS Europe*, 30 November.

Ala-Kurikka, S. (2016b). MEPs clinch ETS reform deal in time for Thursday vote. *ENDS Europe*, 14 December.

Ala-Kurikka, S. (2016c). MEPs vote for higher emissions cuts in ETS reform. *ENDS Europe*, 15 December.

Ala-Kurikka, S. (2016d). Council pushes for February deal on ETS position. *ENDS Europe*, 19 December.

Alliance of Energy Intensive Industries (AEII) (2005). *The Impact of EU Emission Trading Scheme (ETS) on Power Prices: Remedial Action Urgently Needed 10 Months After Start of ETS*. Brussels: AEII.

Alliance of Energy Intensive Industries (AEII) (2012). *Position of the Alliance of Energy Intensive Industries on the Commission Proposal to Back-load (set-aside) EU ETS Allowances*. Brussels: AEII.

Alliance of Energy Intensive Industries, Cefic, and the International Federation of Industrial Energy Consumers (2007). *Contribution Paper for the EU ETS Review: Alliance of Energy Intensive Industries + CEFIC / IFIEC*. Brussels: AEII.

Amenta, E. (2003). What we know about the development of social policy: comparative and historical research in comparative and historical perspective. In *Comparative Historical Analysis in the Social Sciences*, eds. J. Mahoney and D. Rueschemeyer. Princeton: Princeton University Press, pp. 91–130.

Anderson, C. W. (1971). Comparative policy analysis: the design of measures. *Comparative Politics*, **4**(1), 117–131.

Andersen, M. S. (2019). The politics of carbon taxation: how varieties of policy style matter. *Environmental Politics*, **28**(6), 1084–1104.

Anderton, K. and Palmer, J. R. (2015). Evidence-based policy as iterative learning: the case of EU biofuels targets. *Contemporary Social Science*, **10**(2), 138–147.

Andlovic, M. and Lehmann, W. (2014). Interest group influence and inter-institutional power allocation in early second-reading agreements: a re-examination of aviation emissions trading. *Journal of European Public Policy*, **21**(6), 802–821.

Anger, N., Asane-Otoo, E., Böhringer, C. and Oberndorfer, U. (2016). Public interest versus interest groups: a political economy analysis of allowance allocation under the EU emissions trading scheme. *International Environmental Agreements: Politics, Law and Economics*, **16**(5), 621–638.

Arnold, R. D. (1990). *The Logic of Congressional Action*. Yale: Yale University Press.

Arthur, W. B. (1989). Competing technologies, increasing returns and lock in by historical events. *The Economic Journal*, **99**(394), 116–131.

Arthur, W. B. (1994). *Increasing Returns and Path Dependence in the Economy*. Ann Arbor: University of Michigan Press.

Arthur, W. B. (1999). Complexity and the economy. *Science*, **284**, April, 107–109.

Auld, G., Mallett, A., Burlica, B., Nolan-Poupart, F. and Slater, R. (2014). Evaluating the effects of policy innovations: lessons from a systematic review of policies promoting low-carbon technology. *Global Environmental Change*, **29**, 444–458.

Averchenkova, A., Fankhauser, S. and Nachmany, M. (eds.). (2017). *Trends in Climate Change Legislation*. Cheltenham: Edward Elgar.

Azar, C. (2011). Biomass for energy: a dream come true … or a nightmare? *Wiley Interdisciplinary Reviews: Climate Change*, **2**(3), 309–323.

Bäckstrand, K. and Elgström, O. (2013). The EU's role in climate change negotiations: from leader to 'leadiator'. *Journal of European Public Policy*, **20**(10), 1369–1386.

Baekgaard, M., Larsen, S. K. and Mortensen, P. B. (2019). Negative feedback, political attention, and public policy. *European Journal of Political Research*, **97**(1), 210–225.

Bailey, I. (2010). The EU emissions trading scheme. *Wiley Interdisciplinary Reviews: Climate Change*, **1**(1), 144–153.

Baldwin, R. (2008). Regulation Lite: The Rise of Emissions Trading. LSE Law, Society and Economy Working Papers 3/2008. London: LSE.

Bardach, E. (1977). *The Implementation Game: What Happens After a Bill Becomes a Law*. Cambridge: MIT Press.

Bardach, E. (2006). Policy dynamics. In *The Oxford Handbook of Public Policy*, eds. M. Moran, M. Rein and R. E. Goodwin. Oxford: Oxford University Press, pp. 336–366.

Bardach, E. (2007). Why deregulation succeeds or fails. In *Creating Competitive Markets: The Politics of Regulatory Reform*, eds. M. Landy, M. Levin and M. Shapiro. Washington, DC: Brookings Institution Press, pp. 331–342.

Barroso, J. M. D. (2008). European Council Press conference. SPEECH/08/711, 12 December.

Baumgartner, F. (2013). Ideas and policy change. *Governance*, **26**(2), 238–258.

Baumgartner, F. R. and Jones, B. D. (2002). Positive and negative feedback in politics. In *Policy Dynamics*, eds. F. R. Baumgartner and B. D. Jones. Chicago: University of Chicago Press, pp. 3–28.

Baumgartner, F. R. and Jones, B. D. (2009). *Agendas and Instability in American Politics.* 2nd ed. Chicago: University of Chicago Press.

Beach, D. and Pedersen, R. B. (2013). *Process-Tracing Methods: Foundations and Guidelines.* Ann Arbor: University of Michigan Press.

Béland, D. (2007). Ideas and institutional change in Social Security: conversion, layering and policy drift. *Social Science Quarterly,* **88**(1), 20–38.

Béland, D. (2010). Reconsidering policy feedback: how policies affect politics. *Administration and Society,* **42**(5), 568–590.

Béland, D. and Schlager, E. (2019). Varieties of policy feedback research: looking backward, moving forward. *Policy Studies Journal,* **47**(2), 184–205.

Bemelmans-Videc, M.-L., Rist, R. C. and Vedung, E. (eds.). (1998). *Carrots, Sticks and Sermons: Policy Instruments and Their Evaluation.* London: Transaction Publishers.

Bennett, A. and Checkel, J. T. (eds.). (2015). *Process Tracing: From Metaphor to Analytic Tool.* Cambridge; New York: Cambridge University Press.

Bennett, A. and Elman, C. (2006a). Complex causal relations and case study methods: the example of path dependence. *Political Analysis,* **14**(3), 250–267.

Bennett, A. and Elman, C. (2006b). Qualitative research: recent developments in case study methods. *Annual Review of Political Science,* **9**(1), 455–476.

Berkhout, F. and Gouldson, A. (2003). Inducing, shaping, modulating: perspectives on technology and environmental policy. In *Negotiating Environmental Change: New Perspectives from Social Science,* eds. F. Berkhout, M. Leach and I. Scoones. Cheltenham: Edward Elgar, pp. 231–260.

Bernauer, T. (2013). Climate change politics. *Annual Review of Political Science,* **16**, 13.1–13.28.

Bertoldi, P. and Rezessy, S. (2007). Voluntary agreements for energy efficiency: review and results of European experiences. *Energy & Environment,* **18**(1), 37–73.

Biber, E. (2013). Cultivating a green political landscape: lessons for climate change policy from the defeat of California's Proposition 23. *Vanderbilt Law Review,* **66**(2), 399–462.

Biber, E., Kelsey, N. and Meckling, J. (2017). The political economy of decarbonisation: a research agenda. *Brooklyn Law Review,* **82**(2), 605–643.

Biofuels Barometer (2015). *Biofuels Barometer – 2015.* Available at: www.eurobserv-er.org/biofuels-barometer-2015/

Biofuels Barometer (2017). *Biofuels Barometer – 2017.* Available at: www.eurobserv-er.org/biofuels-barometer-2017/

Birdlife International *et al.* (2016). *Bioenergy Laid Bare: Fuelling Climate Change, Fuelling Hunger.* Brussels: Birdlife International.

Blom-Hansen, J. (2011). The EU comitology system: taking stock before the new Lisbon regime. *Journal of European Public Policy,* **18**(4), 607–617.

Boasson, E. L. and Wettestad, J. (2013). *EU Climate Policy: Industry, Policy Interaction and External Environment.* London: Routledge.

Bobrow, D. (2005). Policy design: ubiquitous, necessary and difficult. In *Handbook of Public Policy,* eds. B. G. Peters and J. Pierre. London: Sage, pp. 75–95.

Bocquillon, P. and Dobbels, M. (2014). An elephant on the 13th floor of the Berlaymont? European Council and Commission relations in legislative agenda setting. *Journal of European Public Policy,* **21**(1), 20–38.

Bocquillon, P. and Maltby, T. (2017). The more the merrier? Assessing the impact of enlargement on EU performance in energy and climate change policies. *East European Politics,* **33**(1), 88–105.

Bongaerts, J. (1999). Carbon dioxide emissions and cars: an environmental agreement at EU level. *European Energy and Environmental Law Review,* **8**(4), 101–104.

Bongaerts, J. (1999). Carbon dioxide emissions and the ACEA agreement. *European Energy and Environmental Law Review*, **8**(4), 101–104.

Börkey, P. and Lévêque, F. (1998). *Voluntary Approaches for Environmental Protection in the EU*. ENV/EPOC/GEEI (98) 29/final. Paris: Organisation for Economic Cooperation and Development.

Bouthillier, Y., Cowie, A., Martin, P. and McLeod-Kilmurray, H. (2016). Introduction. In *The Law and Policy of Biofuels*, eds. Y. Bouthillier, A. Cowie, P. Martin and H. McLeod-Kilmurray. Cheltenham: Edward Elgar, pp. xxi–xxvii

Branger, F., Lecuyer, O. and Quirion, P. (2015). The European Union Emissions Trading Scheme: should we throw the flagship out with the bathwater? *Wiley Interdisciplinary Reviews: Climate Change*, **6**(1), 9–16.

Braun, M. (2009). The evolution of emissions trading in the European Union – the role of policy networks, knowledge and policy entrepreneurs. *Accounting, Organizations and Society*, **34**, 469–487.

Braun, M. (2019). The Czech Republic's approach to the EU 2030 climate and energy framework. *Environmental Politics*, **28**(6), 1105–1123.

Bretherton, C. and Vogler, J. (2006). *The European Union as a Global Actor*. 2nd ed. London: Routledge.

Brunner, S., Flachsland, C. and Marschinski, R. (2012). Credible commitment in climate policy. *Climate Policy*, **12**(2), 255–271.

Bryant, G. (2016). Creating a level playing field? The concentration and centralisation of emissions in the European Union Emissions Trading System. *Energy Policy*, **99**, 308–318.

Buchan, D. (2009). *Energy and Climate Change: Europe at the Crossroads*. Oxford: Oxford University Press.

Bulleid, R. (2011). Accounting rules agreed for car eco-innovations. *ENDS Europe*, 25 July.

Bulleid, R. (2012a). Poland pushes for ETS changes at council meeting. *ENDS Europe*, 18 April.

Bulleid, R. (2012b). EU official urges caution on ETS floor price option. *ENDS Europe*, 31 May.

Bürgin, A. (2015). National binding renewable energy targets for 2020, but not for 2030: why the European Commission developed from a supporter to a brakeman. *Journal of European Public Policy*, **22**(5), 690–707.

Burns, C. (2013). Consensus and compromise becomes ordinary – but at what cost? A critical analysis of the impact of the changing norms of codecision upon European Parliament committees. *Journal of European Public Policy*, **20**(7), 988–1005.

Burns, C., Carter, N., Davies, G. A. M. and Worsfold, N. (2013). Still saving the earth? The European Parliament's environmental record. *Environmental Politics*, **22**(6), 935–954.

Campbell, A. (2003). *How Policies Make Citizens: Senior Political Activism and the American Welfare State*. Princeton: Princeton University Press.

Campbell, A. (2012). Policy makes mass politics. *Annual Review of Political Science*, **15**, 333–351.

Campbell, A. (2015). The durability of Pierson's theory about the durability of the welfare state. *PS: Political Science & Politics*, **48**(2), 284–288.

Campbell, P. (2017). Carmakers on course for CO_2 fines as diesel wanes. *Financial Times*, 23–24 September.

Capano, G. and Howlett, M. (2019). Causal logics and mechanisms in policy design: how and why adopting a mechanistic perspective can improve policy design. *Public Policy and Administration* (online version).

Capano, G., Howlett, M., Ramesh, M. and Virani, A. (2019). *Making Policies Work: First- and Second-Order Mechanisms in Policy Design*. Cheltenham: Edward Elgar.

Capoor, K. and Ambrosi, P. (2009). *State and Trends of the Carbon Market 2009*. Washington, DC: World Bank.

Carlson, A. E. and Fri, R. W. (2013). Designing a durable energy policy. *Daedalus*, **142**(1), 119–128.

Center for Clean Air Policy (CCAP) (1999). *Design of a Practical Approach to Greenhouse Gas Emissions Trading Combined with Policies and Measures in the EC*. Washington, DC: CCAP.

Charles, M. B., Ryan, R., Ryan, N. and Oloruntoba, R. (2007). Public policy and biofuels: the way forward? *Energy Policy*, **35**(11), 5737–5746.

Chattopadhyay, J. (2015). Are press depictions of Affordable Care Act beneficiaries favorable to policy durability? *Politics and the Life Sciences,* **34**(2), 7–43.

Chen, Y., Sijm, J., Hobbs, B. F. and Lise, W. (2008). Implications of CO_2 emissions trading for short-run electricity market outcomes in northwest Europe. *Journal of Regulatory Economics*, **34**(3), 251–281.

Christiansen, A. C. and Wettestad, J. (2003). The EU as a frontrunner on greenhouse gas emissions trading: how did it happen and will the EU succeed? *Climate Policy*, **3**(1), 3–18.

Clemens, E. S. and Cook, J. M. (1999). Politics and institutionalism: explaining durability and change. *Annual Review of Sociology*, **25**, 441–466.

Climate Action Network Europe (2012). *Contribution to the European Commission's Public Consultation on Review of the Auction Time Profile for the EU Emissions Trading System*. Brussels: CAN Europe.

Climate Network Europe (2000). *Emissions Trading in the EU*. Brussels: Climate Network Europe.

COCERAL, Copa-Cogeca, EBB *et al.* (2012). *About-turn by EU Commission on Biofuels Policy Set to Decimate Biofuels Industry in the Midst of the European Economic Crisis*. 17 October.

Cointe, B. (2015). From a promise to a problem: the political economy of solar photovoltaics in France. *Energy Research and Social Science*, **8**, 151–161.

Committee on the Environment, Public Health and Food Safety (2017). *Report on Interinstitutional File: 2014/0011 (COD). Document Number A8–0003/2017*. Strasbourg; Brussels: European Parliament.

Compston, H. and Bailey, I. (2008). Political strategy and climate change. In *Turning Down the Heat: The Politics of Climate Policy in Affluent Democracies*, eds. H. Compston and I. Bailey. Basingstoke: Palgrave.

Confederation of European Paper Industries (CEPI) (2000). *CEPI's Views on the Emission Trading – Responses to the Commission's Green Paper on Emission Trading*. Brussels: CEPI.

Convery, F. J. (2008). Reflections – the emerging literature on emissions trading in Europe. *Review of Environmental Economics and Policy*, **3**(1), 121–137.

Corporate Europe Observatory, AITEC, Northern Alliance for Sustainability *et al.* (2013). *It is Time to Scrap the ETS! Civil Society Organisations Demand That the EU Scrap Its Emissions Trading Scheme*. Brussels: Corporate Europe Observatory.

Costa, O. (2008). Is climate change changing the EU? The second image reversed in climate politics. *Cambridge Review of International Affairs*, **21**(4), 527–44.

Council of the European Union (2002). *Interinstitutional File: 2001/0245 (COD) – Progress report. Document Number 10002/02, 19 June 2002*. Brussels: Council of the European Union.

Council of the European Union (2014). *Interinstitutional File: 2014/0011 (COD). Information note from the Presidency on the state of play. Document Number 16360/14, 5 December 2014*. Brussels: Council of the European Union.
Council of the European Union (2018). *Interinstitutional File: 2017/0293(COD) – General Approach*. Document Number 12903/18. *10 October 2018*. Brussels: Council of the European Union.
Council of the European Union (2019). *Interinstitutional File: 2017/0293(COD) – Analysis of the Final Compromise Text with a View to Agreement*. Document Number 5091/19. 17 January 2019. Brussels: Council of the European Union.
Court of Justice of the European Union (CJEU) (2016). *Case C-5/16: Action Brought on 4 January 2016 – Republic of Poland v European Parliament and Council of the European Union*. Luxembourg: CJEU.
Cowie, A., Cowie, A. Soimakallio, S. and Brandão, M. (2016). Environmental risks and opportunities of biofuels. In *The Law and Policy of Biofuels*, eds. Y. Bouthillier, A. Cowie, P. Martin and H. McLeod-Kilmurray. Cheltenham: Edward Elgar, pp. 3–29.
Dahlmann, F., Kolk, A., & Lindeque, J. (2017). Emerging energy geographies: scaling and spatial divergence in European electricity generation capacity. *European Urban and Regional Studies*, **24**(4), 381–404.
Dales, J. H. (1968). *Pollution, Property, and Prices*. Toronto: Toronto University Press.
Damro, C. and Méndez, P. L. (2003). Emissions trading at Kyoto: from EU resistance to Union innovation. *Environmental Politics*, **12**(2), 71–94.
Daugbjerg, C. (2003). Policy feedback and paradigm shift in EU agricultural policy: the effects of the MacSharry reform on future reform. *Journal of European Public Policy*, **10**(3), 421–437.
Daugbjerg, C. (2009). Sequencing in public policy: the evolution of the CAP over a decade. *Journal of European Public Policy*, **16**(3), 395–411.
Daugbjerg, C. and Sondeskov, K. M. (2012). Environmental policy performance revisited: designing effective policies for green markets. *Political Studies*, **60**(2), 399–433.
de Bruyn, S., Schep, E. and Cherif, S. (2016). *Calculation of Additional Profits of Sectors and Firms from the EU ETS*. Delft: CE Delft.
de Wilde, H. P. J. and Kroon, P. (2013). *Policy Options to Reduce Passenger Cars CO_2 Emissions after 2020*. Amsterdam: Energy Research Centre of the Netherlands.
Dehue, B., Meyer, S. and Hettinga, W. (2008). *Review of EU's Impact Assessment of 10% Biofuels on Land Use Change*. Utrecht: Ecofys.
Del Guayo, I. (2008). Biofuels: EU law and policy. In *Beyond the Carbon Economy: Energy Law in Transition,* eds. D. N. Zilman, C. Redgwell and L. K. Barrera-Hernandez. Oxford: Oxford University Press, pp. 265–286.
Delbeke, J. and Vis, P. (eds.). (2015). *EU Climate Policy Explained*. London: Routledge.
Delbeke, J., Hartridge, O., Lefevere, J. G., *et al.* (eds.). (2006). *EU Energy Law: The EU Greenhouse Gas Emissions Trading Scheme*. Deventer, the Netherlands: Claeys & Casteels.
Delpero, C. (2018). New car CO_2 up for first time in a decade. *ENDS Europe*, 24 April.
Demailly, D. and Quirion, P. (2006). CO_2 abatement, competitiveness and leakage in the European cement industry under the EU ETS: grandfathering versus output-based allocation. *Climate Policy*, **6**(1), 93–113.
Demirbas, A. (2009). Political, economic and environmental impacts of biofuel: a review. *Applied Energy*, **86**, S108–S117.
Di Lucia, L. and Kronsell, A. (2010). The willing, the unwilling and the unable – explaining implementation of the EU Biofuels Directive. *Journal of European Public Policy*, **17**(4), 545–563.

Di Lucia, L. and Nilsson, L. (2007). Transport biofuels in the European Union: the state of play. *Transport Policy*, **14**, 533–543.

Dimitrov, R. S. (2010). Inside Copenhagen: the state of climate governance. *Global Environmental Politics*, **10**(2), 18–24.

Directorate-General for Climate Action (DG CLIMA) (2011). *CO_2 Emissions from New Cars Down by Almost 4% in 2010*. Brussels: European Commission.

Directorate-General for Climate Action (DG CLIMA) (2013). *Review of the Auction Time Profile for the EU Emissions Trading System. Summary of the Public Consultation, 25 July 2012–16 October 2012*. Brussels: European Commission.

Directorate-General for Climate Action (DG CLIMA) 2016). *EU ETS Handbook*. Brussels: European Commission.

Directorate-General for the Environment, McKinsey & Company and Ecofys (2006). *Review of EU Emissions Trading Scheme: Survey Results*. Brussels: European Commission.

Doornbosch, R. and Steenblik, R. (2007). *Biofuels: Is the Cure Worse Than the Disease?* Report SG/SD/RT (2007) 3/REV1. Paris: OECD.

Downie, C. (2017). Business actors, political resistance, and strategies for policymakers. *Energy Policy*, **108**, 583–592.

Dreger, J. (2014). *The European Commission's Energy and Climate Policy: A Climate for Expertise?* Basingstoke: Palgrave MacMillan.

Dryzek, J. (1983). Don't toss coins in garbage cans: a prologue to policy design. *Journal of Public Policy*, **3**(4), 345–367.

Dryzek, J. (2001). *The Politics of the Earth*. Oxford: Oxford University Press.

Duit, A. and Galaz, V. (2008). Governance and complexity: emerging issues for governance theory. *Governance*, **21**(3), 311–335

Dunlop, C. (2010). The temporal dimension of knowledge and the limits of policy appraisal. *Policy Sciences*, **43**(4), 343–363.

Eberlein, B. and Radaelli, C. (2010). Mechanisms of conflict management in EU regulatory policy. *Public Administration*, **88**(3), 782–799.

Edmondson, D. L., Kern, F. and Rogge, K. S. (2018). The co-evolution of policy mixes and socio-technical systems: towards a conceptual framework of policy mix feedback in sustainability transitions. *Research Policy* (online version).

Egelund Olsen., B and Ronne, A. (2016). The EU legal regime for biofuels. In *The Law and Policy of Biofuels*, eds. Y. Bouthillier, A. Cowie, P. Martin and H. McLeod-Kilmurray. Cheltenham: Edward Elgar, pp. 164–190.

Eikeland, P. O. (2016). Electric power industry. In *Corporate Responses to EU Emissions Trading: Resistance, Innovation or Responsibility?* Eds. J. B. Skjærseth and P. O. Eikeland. London: Routledge, pp. 45–98.

Électricité de France (EDF). (2007). *EDF Position on EU ETS Review*. Paris: EDF.

Ellerman, A. D. and Buchner, B. K. (2007). The European Union Emissions Trading Scheme: origins, allocation, and early results. *Review of Environmental Economics and Policy*, **1**(1), 66–87.

Ellerman, A. D., Convery, F. J. and de Perthuis, C. (2010). *Pricing Carbon: The European Union Emissions Trading Scheme*. Cambridge: Cambridge University Press.

Ellerman, A. D., Mercantonini, C. and Zaklan, A. (2016). The European Union Emissions Trading System: ten years and counting. *Review of Environmental Economics and Policy*, **10**(1), Winter 2016, 89–107.

ENDS Europe (1998a). Green light for EU car CO_2 reduction deal. 30 June.

ENDS Europe (1998b). EU ministers approve CO_2 from cars deal. 6 October.

ENDS Europe (2002). Ministers clip wings of biofuel package. 10 June.

ENDS Europe (2007a). Gabriel urges 100 per cent carbon permit auction. 31 May.
ENDS Europe (2007b). Ministers to urge more carbon permit sales. 22 June.
ENDS Europe (2008a). EU carbon leakage exposure criteria under attack. 31 October.
ENDS Europe (2008b). EU strikes deal to delay car CO_2 curbs. 2 December.
ENDS Report (1992a). Competing options for EC curbs on CO_2 emissions from cars. 31 March.
ENDS Report (1992b). Deadlock over CO_2 controls on cars. 1 December.
ENDS Report (1994). European Parliament backs down over vehicle emissions. 1 March.
ENDS Report (1995). German industries follow Dutch in volunteering CO_2 reductions. 30 April.
ENDS Report (1996). Car industry lashes out at Auto/Oil proposals. 31 May.
ENDS Report (1998). Car makers give ground on fuel efficiency agreement. 1 March.
ENDS Report (2001). Commission backs biofuels despite doubts over environmental benefits. 1 November.
ENDS Report (2004). Car industry drifting on CO_2 targets. 1 February.
ENDS Report (2005). Biofuel plan risks backlash from green groups. 1 December.
ENDS Report (2006). Green groups criticise biofuels strategy. 1 February.
ENDS Report (2007). What price the cost of carbon? 23 November.
ENDS Report (2008). Consensus still limited on EU climate package. 19 November.
ENDS Report (2009). Carbon market crash imperils green investment. 1 February.
ENDS Report (2010). Hedegaard retreats on EU 30% emissions target. 27 May.
ENDS Report (2012a). Carmakers zoom past European carbon targets. 23 January.
ENDS Report (2012b). Latest draft suggests major shift in EU biofuel policy. 25 September.
ENDS Report (2012c). Commission opts for middle ground on EU ETS set-aside. 13 November.
Energy Intensive Industries (2002). *Energy Intensive Industries' Concerns Regarding the Proposed Emissions Trading Directive*. Brussels: Energy Intensive Industries.
Energy Intensive Industries (2003). *Energy Intensive Industries' Position on the Amendments Voted by the EP's Environment Committee on 11 June*. 16 June. Brussels: Energy Intensive Industries.
Energy Intensive Industries (2004). *Energy Intensive Industries Call Upon EU Decision-Makers to Pay More Attention to the Impact of Emissions Trading Upon Their Competitiveness*. Brussels: Energy Intensive Industries.
Environment Council (1996). *Conclusions of the 1939th Environment Council, Meeting 25–6 June*. Brussels: Council of Ministers.
Environmental Audit Committee (2008). *Are Biofuels Sustainable? First Report of Session 2007–8*, Vol. 1. London: House of Commons.
Eskridge, W. N. and Ferejohn, J. (2001). Super-statutes. *Duke Law Journal*, **50**, 1215–1275.
Euractiv (2001). Industry and environmentalists oppose EU biofuel plans. 20 September.
Eurelectric (2000). *EURELECTRIC Position Paper on the Commission's Green Paper on Greenhouse Gas Emissions Trading within the EU (COM 87/2000)*. Brussels: Eurelectric.
Eurelectric (2007). *Position Paper: Review of the EU Emissions Trading Directive (2003/87/EC) and the Linking Directive (2004/101/EC)*. Brussels: Eurelectric.
European Automobile Manufacturers' Association (ACEA) (2008). Tough CO_2 legislation must be matched by support for the automotive industry. ACEA Press Release, 17 December.
European Automobile Manufacturers' Association (ACEA) (2017). *The Automobile Industry Pocket Book*. Brussels: ACEA.

European Biodiesel Board (EBB) (2006). *EBB Comments to the Commission Consultation on the Revision of the EU Biofuels Directive.*
European Biodiesel Board (EBB) (2019). *Previous Production Statistics: The EU Biodiesel Industry.*
European Bioethanol Fuel Association (eBIO) (2009). *2008 Fuel Ethanol Production in the EU*. Brussels: eBIO.
European Ceramic Industry Association (Cerame-Unie) (2000). *Comments on the Green Paper on Greenhouse Gas Emissions Trading within the European Union COM (2000)87*. Brussels: Cerame-Unie.
European Commission (2000). *European Climate Change Programme, Chairman's Background Document 2: Allocation Methodologies and Recognition of Early Action.* 7 December. Brussels: European Commission.
European Commission (2001a). *Final Report: ECCP Working Group 1 'Flexible Mechanisms'*. 2 May. Brussels: European Commission.
European Commission (2001b). *Green Paper on Greenhouse Gas Emissions Trading Within the European Union: Summary of Submissions*. 14 May. Brussels: European Commission.
European Commission (2001c). *List of Comments Sent for Green Paper on Greenhouse Gas Emissions Trading Within the European Union*. Brussels: European Commission. 14 May.
European Commission (2001d). *Commission Proposes Ratification of Kyoto Protocol and Emissions Trading System*. Press Release. 23 October. Brussels: European Commission.
European Commission (2005). *Energy, Environment, Competitiveness: Commission Launches High Level Group – IP/06/226*. Brussels: European Commission.
European Commission (2007a). *List of Participants, ECCP Working Group on EU ETS Review: The Scope of the Directive, 8–9 March 2007*. Brussels: European Commission.
European Commission (2007b). *Final Report of the 3rd Meeting of the ECCP Working Group on Emissions Trading: The Review of the EU ETS. Further Harmonisation and Increased Predictability, 21–22 May 2007*. Brussels: European Commission.
European Commission (2010). *Commission Creates Two New Directorates-General for Energy and Climate Action*. Press Release IP/10/164. 17 February. Brussels: European Commission.
European Commission (2013). *Green Paper 2030: Main Outcomes of the Public Consultation*. Commission Services Non Paper. Brussels: European Commission.
European Commission (2015). *European Commission Fact Sheet: Questions and Answers on the Proposal to Revise the EU ETS*. Brussels: European Commission.
European Commission (2017). *New and Improved Car Emissions Test Become Mandatory on 1 September*. Press Release, 31 August. Brussels: European Commission.
European Confederation of Iron and Steel Industries (Eurofer) (2000). *Eurofer View on Emissions Trading – Comments to the Green Paper COM (2000) 87*. Brussels: Eurofer.
European Council (2007). *Brussels European Council, 8–9 March 2007 – Presidency Conclusions*. Brussels: European Council.
European Council (2014). *Presidency Conclusions of the European Council – 23/24 October 2014*. Brussels: European Council.
European Court of Auditors (2018). *Ex-Post Review of EU Legislation: A Well-Established System, but Incomplete*. Special Report 16/2018. Luxembourg: European Court of Auditors.

European Environment Agency (EEA) (2006). *Greenhouse Gas Emissions Trends and Projections in Europe 2006*. EEA Report 9/2006. Copenhagen: EEA.
European Environment Agency (EEA) (2008). *Suspend 10 Percent Biofuels Target, Says EEA's Scientific Advisory Body*. Copenhagen: EEA.
European Environment Agency (EEA) (2011a). *SC Opinion on Greenhouse Gas Accounting in Relation to Bioenergy*. Copenhagen: EEA.
European Environment Agency (EEA) (2011b). *EUA Future Prices 2005–2011*. Copenhagen: EEA.
European Environment Agency (EEA) (2011c). *Laying the Foundations for Greener Transport: TERM 2011 Report*. EEA Report 7/2011. Copenhagen: EEA.
European Environment Agency (EEA) (2012). *EUA Future Prices 2008–2012*. Copenhagen: EEA.
European Environment Agency (EEA) (2013). *A Closer Look at Urban Transport: TERM 2013 Report*. EEA Report 11/2013. Copenhagen: EEA.
European Environment Agency (EEA) (2015a). *Evaluating 15 Years of Transport and Environmental Policy Integration*. EEA Report 7/2015. Copenhagen: EEA.
European Environment Agency (EEA) (2015b). *Trends and Projections in the EU ETS in 2015*. EEA Technical Report 14/2015. Copenhagen: EEA.
European Environment Agency (EEA) (2016). *Explaining Road Transport Emissions*. Copenhagen: EEA.
European Environment Agency (EEA) (2017). *Trends and Projections in Europe 2017: Tracking Progress towards Europe's Climate and Energy Targets*. Copenhagen: EEA.
European Environment Agency (EEA) (2018a). *Trends and Projections in the EU ETS in 2018: The EU Emissions Trading System in Numbers*. EEA Report No 14/2018. Copenhagen: EEA.
European Environment Agency (EEA) (2018b). *Progress of EU Transport Sector towards Its Environment and Climate Objectives*. EEA Briefing 15/2018. Copenhagen: EEA.
European Environment Agency (EEA) (2019). *EU Emissions Trading System (ETS) Data Viewer*. Accessed 13 June 2019.
European Environmental Bureau (EEB) (2001). *Press Release: EEB Asks Commission to Scrap Biofuels Proposal*. 18 September. Brussels: EEB.
European Environmental Bureau (EEB) (2002a). *Biofuels: Not as Green as They Sound*. May. Brussels: EEB.
European Environmental Bureau (EEB) (2002b). *Press Release: EEB Urges ECOFIN Meeting to Reject Current Biofuels Proposal*. 17 June. Brussels: EEB.
European Environmental Bureau (EEB) and Transport & Environment (T&E) (2004). *Input to Environment Council Debate on Sustainable Road Transport*. Position Paper, 11 October.
European Lime Association (EuLA) (2000). *The Green Paper on Greenhouse Gas Emissions Trading within the European Union: Updated EuLA Position Paper*. Brussels: EuLA.
European Parliament (1998). *Resolution on Climate Change in the Run-Up to Buenos Aires (November 1998)*. Document B4–0802/98. Brussels: European Parliament.
European Parliament (2002). *European Parliament Legislative Resolution on the Proposal for a European Parliament and Council Directive Establishing a Scheme for Greenhouse Gas Emission Allowance Trading Within the Community and Amending Council Directive 96/61/EC*. Strasbourg; Brussels: European Parliament.
European Parliament (2017). *Report on the Inquiry into Emission Measurements in the Automotive Sector (2016/2215(INI)*. Committee of Inquiry into Emission Measurements

in the Automotive Sector, A-0049/2017, 2 March. Strasbourg; Brussels: European Parliament.

European Parliament (2018a). *Draft Report on the Proposal for a Regulation of the European Parliament and of the Council Setting Emission Performance Standards for New Passenger Cars and for New Light Commercial Vehicles as Part of the Union's Integrated Approach to Reduce CO_2 Emissions from Light-Duty Vehicles and Amending Regulation (EC) No 715/2007 (recast)*. Committee for Environment Public Health and Food Safety, PE619.135v01–00. Strasbourg; Brussels: European Parliament.

European Parliament (2018b). Result of roll-call votes of 10.09.2018. Committee on Environment, Food Safety and Public Health. Strasbourg; Brussels: European Parliament.

European Union (2016). *Official Directory of the European Union: European Commission*. Brussels: European Union.

European Voice (2012). Barroso II closes its eyes to the evidence: The Commission reveals its true colours on climate change. 17 October.

Eurostat (2017). *Share of Transport Fuel from Renewable Energy Sources*. 14 March. Brussels: Eurostat.

Ewing, J. (2017). *Faster, Higher, Further: The Inside Story of the VW Scandal*. London: Bantam Press.

Fahey, B. K. and Pralle, S. B. (2016). Governing complexity: recent developments in environmental politics and policy. *Policy Studies Journal*, **44**(S1), S28–S49.

Falleti, T. G. and Lynch, J. F. (2009). Context and causal mechanisms in political analysis. *Comparative Political Studies*, **42**(9), 1143–1166.

Fankhauser, S., Gennaioli, C. and Collins, M. (2015). The political economy of passing climate change legislation: evidence from a survey. *Global Environmental Change*, **35**, 52–61.

Fearon, J. D. (1991). Counterfactuals and hypothesis testing in political science. *World Politics*, **43**(2), 169–195.

Fitch-Roy, O. and Fairbrass, J. (2018). *Negotiating the EU's 2030 Climate and Energy Framework: Agendas, Ideas and European Interest Groups*. London: Palgrave MacMillan.

Flach, B., Lieberz, S., Rondon, M., Williams, B. and Teiken, C. (2015). *EU-28 Biofuels Annual*. GAINS Report NL5028. Washington, DC: USDA Foreign Agricultural Service.

Flanagan, K., Uyarra, E. and Laranja, M. (2011). Reconceptualising the 'policy mix' for innovation. *Research Policy*, **40**(5), 702–713.

Flynn, V. (2013a). CO_2 price slumps as MEPs oppose backloading. *ENDS Europe*, 24 January.

Flynn, V. (2013b). ILUC proposal criticised by EU energy ministers. *ENDS Europe*, 22 February.

Flynn, V. (2013c). EU member states divided on post-2020 targets. *ENDS Europe*, 3 September.

Flynn, V. (2013d). Expert talks home in on ETS reform option. *ENDS Europe*, 25 September.

Flynn, V. (2013e). Lawmakers agree to water down car CO_2 deal. *ENDS Europe*, 27 November.

Flynn, V. (2014). Fault lines emerge in ministers' 2030 debate. *ENDS Europe*, 3 March.

Flynn, V. (2015a). Lead MEP calls for stronger biofuel reform. *ENDS Europe*, 5 January.

Flynn, V. (2015b). Lead MEP supports wood-based biofuels. *ENDS Europe*, 8 January.

Foundation for International Environmental Law and Development (FIELD) (2000). *Designing Options for Implementing an Emissions Trading Regime for Greenhouse Gases in the EC*. Final Report to the European Commission, DG Environment (Contract B4–3040/98/000795/MAR/B1). London: FIELD.

Friedrich, A., Tappe, M. and Wurzel, R. K. (2000). A new approach to EU environmental policy making? the Auto-Oil I Programme. *Journal of European Public Policy*, **7**(4), 593–612.

Geels, F. (2010). Ontologies, socio-technical transitions (to sustainability), and the multi-level perspective. *Research Policy*, **39**(4), 495–510.

Gibson, D. and Goodin, R. E. (1999). The veil of vagueness. In *Organizing Political Institutions: Essays for Johan P. Olsen*, eds. M. Egeberg and P. Lægreid. Oslo: Scandinavia University Press, pp. 357–385.

Gibson, G. Kollmthodi, S., Kirsch, F. et al. (2015). *Evaluation of Regulations 443/2009 and 510/2011 on CO_2 Emissions from Light-duty Vehicles*. Ricardo-AEA and TEPR. 8 April. Brussels: European Commission.

Giddens, A. (2015). The politics of climate change. *Policy & Politics*, **43**(2), 155–162.

Giljam, R. A. (2016). Towards a holistic approach in EU biomass regulation. *Journal of Environmental Law*, **28**(1), 95–123.

Glazer, A. and Rothenberg, L. (2005). *Why Government Succeeds and Why It Fails*. Cambridge: Harvard University Press.

Goldthau, A., Westphal, K., Bazilian, M. and Bradshaw, M. (2019). How the energy transition will reshape geopolitics. *Nature*, **569**(7754), 29–31.

Goodin, R. (1996). Institutions and their design. In *The Theory of Institutional Design*, ed. R. Goodin. Cambridge: Cambridge University Press, pp. 1–53.

Graichen, V., Cludius, J. and Gores, S. (2017). *Estimate of 2005–2012 Emissions for Stationary Installations to Reflect the Current Scope (2013–2020) of the EU ETS*. ETC/ACM Technical Paper 2017/11. Bilthoven: European Topic Centre on Air Pollution and Climate Change Mitigation.

Gravey, V. and Jordan, A. J. (2016). Does the European Union have a reverse gear? Policy dismantling in a hyperconsensual polity. *Journal of European Public Policy*, **23**(8), 1180–1198.

Gravey, V. and Jordan, A. J. (2019). Policy dismantling at EU level: reaching the limits of 'an ever-closer ecological union'? *Public Administration* (online version).

Green Growth Group (2014). Green Growth Group Ministers' statement on climate and energy framework for 2030.

Greeuw, S. C. H., van Asselt, M. B. A., Grosskurth, J. et al. (2000). *Cloudy Crystal Balls: An Assessment of Recent European and Global Scenario Studies and Methods*. Environmental Issue Report 17/2000. Copenhagen: European Environment Agency.

Greif, A. and Laitin, D. (2004). A theory of endogenous institutional change. *American Political Science Review*, **98**(4), 633–652.

Grzymala-Busse, A. (2011). Time will tell? Temporality and the analysis of causal mechanisms and processes. *Comparative Political Studies*, **44**(9), 1267–1297.

Gulbrandsen, L. and Christensen, A. R. (2014). EU legislation to reduce carbon emissions from cars. *Review of Policy Research*, **31**(6), 503–528.

Gunningham, N., Grabosky, P. and Sinclair, D. (1998). *Smart Regulation: Designing Environmental Policy*. Oxford: Oxford University Press.

Gürtler, K., Postpischil, R., and Quitzow, R. (2019). The dismantling of renewable energy policies: the cases of Spain and the Czech Republic. *Energy Policy*, **133**, 110881, 1–11.

Gyekye, L. (2018a). Biofuels industry gives thumbs up to EP's RED vote. *ENDS Europe*, 18 January
Gyekye, L. (2018b). MEPs back 45% CO_2 cut for cars and vans. *ENDS Europe*, 11 September.
Hacker, J. (1998). The historical logic of national health insurance: structure and sequence in the development of British, Canadian, and US medical policy. *Studies in American Political Development*, **12**(1), 57–130.
Hacker, J. (2002). *The Divided Welfare State: The Battle over Public and Private Social Benefits in the United States*. Yale: Yale University Press.
Hacker, J. (2004). Privatising risk without privatising the welfare state: the hidden politics of social policy retrenchment in the United States. *American Political Science Review*, **98**(2), 243–260.
Hacker, J. and Pierson, P. (2014). After the 'master theory': Downs, Schattschneider, and the rebirth of policy-focused analysis. *Perspectives of Politics*, **12**(3), 643–662.
Hacker, J., Pierson, P. and Thelen, K. A. (2015). Drift and conversion: hidden faces of institutional change. In *Advances in Comparative-Historical Analysis*, eds. J. Mahoney and K. A. Thelen. Cambridge: Cambridge University Press, pp. 180–208.
Haigh, N. (1996). Climate change policies and politics in the EC. In *Politics of Climate Change: A European Perspective*, eds. T. O'Riordan and J. Jäger. London: Routledge, pp. 155–185.
Haigh, N. (2009). *Manual of Environmental Policy: The EU and Britain*. Leeds: Maney Publishing.
Hall, P. (1993). Policy paradigms, social learning and the state: the case of economic policymaking in Britain. *Comparative Politics*, **25**(3), 275–296.
Hansjürgens, B. (2011). Markets for SO_2 and NO_X – what can we learn for carbon trading? *Wiley Interdisciplinary Reviews: Climate Change*, **2**(4), 635–646.
Heclo, H. (1974). *Social Policy in Britain and Sweden: From Relief to Income Maintenance*. Yale: Yale University Press.
Heidenheimer, A., Heclo, H. and Adam, C. (1990). *Comparative Public Policy*. 3rd ed. New York: St Martin's Press: Palgrave MacMillan.
Hepburn, C., Grubb, M., Neuhoff, K., Matthes, F. and Tse, M. (2006). Auctioning of EU ETS Phase II allowances: how and why? *Climate Policy*, **6**(1), 137–160.
Heritier, A. (1999). *Policy Making and Diversity in Europe*. Cambridge: Cambridge University Press.
Hess, D. (2014). Sustainability transitions: a political coalition perspective. *Research Policy*, **43**(2), 278–283.
Hey, C. (2010). The German paradox: climate leader and green car laggard. In *The New Climate Policies of the European Union*, eds. S. Oberthur and M. Pallemaerts. Brussels: VUB Press, pp. 211–230.
High Level Panel of Experts on Food Security and Nutrition (HLPE). (2013). *Biofuels and Food Security*. HLPE Report 5. Rome: Committee on Word Food Security.
Hilden, M., Jordan, A. J. and Rayner, T. (2014). Climate policy innovation: developing an evaluation perspective. *Environmental Politics* **23**(5), 884–905
Hix, S. (2007) The European Union as a polity (I). In *The Sage Handbook of European Union Politics*, eds. K. Joergensen, M. Pollack and B. Rosamond. London: Sage, pp. 141–158.
HM Government (2013). *Driving Success: UK Automotive Strategy for Growth and Sustainability*. London: HM Government.
Hodgson, R. (2017a). MEPs adopt tighter rules on crop-based biofuels. *ENDS Europe*, 24 October.

Hodgson, R. (2017b). 'Clean mobility' package calls for 30% car emissions cut. *ENDS Europe*, 8 November.
Hodgson, R. (2017c). Coal support set to continue under EU ETS reform deal. *ENDS Europe*, 9 November.
Hodgson, R. (2017d). EU governments settle for 27% renewables target. *ENDS Europe*, 19 December.
Hodgson, R. (2018a). Governments deeply divided over EU car emission limits. *ENDS Europe*, 25 June.
Hodgson, R. (2018b). Parliament demands 40% cut in car CO_2 emissions. *ENDS Europe*, 3 October.
Holzinger, K., Knill, C. and Schäfer, A. (2006). Rhetoric or reality? 'New Governance' in EU environmental policy. *European Law Journal,* **12**(3), 403–420.
Hooghe, L. and Marks, G. (2003). Unraveling the central state, but how? Types of multi-level governance. *American Political Science Review*, **97**(2), 233–243.
Hovi, J., Sprinz, D. F. and Underdal, A. (2009). Implementing long-term climate policy: time inconsistency, domestic politics, international anarchy. *Global Environmental Politics*, **9**(3), 20–39.
Howes, T. (2010). The EU's new renewable energy directive. In *The New Climate Policies of the European Union: Internal Legislation and Climate Diplomacy*, eds. S. Oberthür and M. Pallemaerts. Brussels: VUB Press, pp. 117–150.
Howlett, M. (2009a). Process sequencing policy dynamics: beyond homeostasis and path dependency. *Journal of Public Policy*, **29**(3), 241–262.
Howlett, M. (2009b). Governance modes, policy regimes and operational plans: a multi-level nested model of policy instrument choice and policy design. *Policy Sciences*, **42**(1), 73–89.
Howlett, M. (2011). *Designing Public Policies: Principles and Instruments*. London: Routledge.
Howlett, M. (2014). From the 'old' to the 'new' policy design: design thinking beyond markets and collaborative governance. *Policy Sciences*, **47**(3), 187–207.
Howlett, M. (2019). *The Policy Design Primer: Choosing the Right Tools for the Job*. London: Routledge.
Howlett, M. and Cashore, B. (2009). The dependent variable problem in the study of policy change: understanding policy change as a methodological problem. *Journal of Comparative Policy Analysis*, **11**(1), 33–46.
Howlett, M. and del Rio, P. (2015). The parameters of policy portfolios: verticality and horizontality in design spaces and their consequences for policy mix formulation. *Environment and Planning C,* **33**(5), 1233–1245.
Howlett, M. and Lejano, R. (2013). Tales from the crypt: the rise and fall (and rebirth?) of policy design. *Administration and Society*, **45**(3), 357–381.
Howlett, M. and Rayner, J. (2013). Patching vs packaging in policy formulation: assessing policy portfolio design. *Politics and Governance*, **1**(2), 170–182.
Howlett, M., Mukherjee, I. and Rayner, J. (2017). The elements of effective program design: a two-level analysis. In *Handbook of Policy Formulation*, eds. M. Howlett and I. Mukherjee. Cheltenham: Edward Elgar, pp. 129–146.
Howlett, M., Ramesh, M. and Perl, A. P. (2009). *Studying Public Policy*. 3rd ed. Oxford: Oxford University Press.
Huberty, M. and Zysman, J. (2013). Preface. In *Can Green Sustain Growth? From the Religion to the Reality of Sustainable Prosperity*, eds. J. Zysman and M. Huberty. Stanford: Stanford University Press, pp. xi–xiv.

Huberty, M., Kelsey, N. and Zysman, J. (2013). Can 'green' sustain growth? In *Can Green Sustain Growth? From the Religion to the Reality of Sustainable Prosperity*, eds. J. Zysman and M. Huberty. Stanford: Stanford University Press, pp. 247–256.

Huitema, D., Jordan, A., Massey, E. *et al.* (2011). The evaluation of climate policy: theory and emerging practice in Europe. *Policy Sciences*, **44**(2), 179–198.

Iacobuta, G., Dubash, N. K., Upadyaya, P. *et al.* (2018). National climate change mitigation legislation, strategy and targets: a global update. *Climate Policy*, **18**(9), 1114–1132.

Ingram, H. and Schneider, A. (1990). Improving implementation through framing smarter statutes. *Journal of Public Policy*, **10**(1), 67–88.

Institute for European Environmental Policy (2014). *Re-examining EU Biofuels Policy*. London: IEEP.

Intergovernmental Panel on Climate Change (IPCC). (2018). *Summary for Policymakers of IPCC Special Report on Global Warming of 1.5°C approved by governments*. IPCC Press Release 2018/24/PR, 8 October 2018.

International Carbon Action Partnership (2019). *Emissions Trading Worldwide: Status Report 2019*. Berlin: ICAP.

International Emissions Trading Association (IETA) (2012). *Options to Reform the EU ETS: An Analysis by IETA*. Brussels: IETA.

International Energy Agency (IEA) (2011). *Technology Roadmap: Biofuels for Transport*. Paris: IEA.

International Energy Agency (IEA) (2017). *Tracking Clean Energy Progress 2017*. Paris: IEA.

International Energy Agency (IEA) (2019). *Tracking Clean Energy Progress 2019*. Paris: IEA.

International Institute for Sustainable Development (IISD) (2008). *Biofuels: At What Cost?* Geneva: IISD.

Jackson, T., Begg, K. and Parkinson, S. (eds.). (2000). *Flexibility in Global Climate Policy: Beyond Joint Implementation*. London: Earthscan.

Jacobs, A. (2009). Policymaking as political constraint: institutional development in the U.S. Social Security Program. In *Explaining Institutional Change: Ambiguity, Agency, and Power*, eds. J. Mahoney and K. Thelen. Cambridge: Cambridge University Press, pp. 94–131.

Jacobs, A. M. (2011). *Governing for the Long Term: Democracy and the Politics of Investment*. Cambridge: Cambridge University Press.

Jacobs, A. M. and Weaver, R. K. (2015). When policies undo themselves: self-undermining feedback as a source of policy change. *Governance*, **28**(4), 441–57.

Jacobs, L. and Mettler, S. (2018). When and how new policy creates new politics: examining the feedback effects of the Affordable Care Act on public opinion. *Perspectives on Politics*, **16**(2), 345–363.

Jenkins, J. A. and Patashnik, E. M. (2012). Living legislation and American politics. In *Living Legislation: Durability, Change, and the Politics of American Lawmaking*, eds. J. A. Jenkins and E. M. Patashnik. Chicago: University of Chicago Press, pp. 3–19.

Jervis, R. (1997). *System Effects: Complexity in Political and Social Life*. Princeton: Princeton University Press.

Johnson, F. X. (2011). Regional-global linkages in the energy-climate-development policy nexus: the case of biofuels in the EU Renewable Energy Directive. *Renewable Energy Law and Policy Review*, **2**(2), 91–106.

Jordan, A. and Adelle, C. (2013). EU environmental policy at 40. In *Environmental Policy in the EU: Actors, Institutions and Processes*, eds. A. Jordan and C. Adelle. 3rd ed. London: Routledge, pp. 369–386.

Jordan, A. and Adelle, C. (eds.). (2013). *Environmental Policy in the EU: Actors, Institutions and Processes*. 3rd ed. London: Routledge.

Jordan, A. and Matt, E. (2014). Designing policies that intentionally stick: policy feedback in a changing climate. *Policy Sciences,* **47**, 227–247.

Jordan, A., Rayner, T., Schroeder, H. *et al.* (2013) Going beyond two degrees? The risks and opportunities of alternative options. *Climate Policy* **13**(6), 738–750.

Jordan, A. and Turnpenny, J. R. (eds.). (2015). *The Tools of Policy Formulation: Actors, Capacities, Venues and Effects*. Edward Elgar: Cheltenham.

Jordan, A., Wurzel, R. and Zito, A. (2003). 'New' instruments of environmental governance: patterns and pathways of change. *Environmental Politics*, **12**(1), 3–24.

Jordan, A., Wurzel, R. and Zito, A. (2005). The rise of 'new' policy instruments in comparative perspective: has governance eclipsed government? *Political Studies,* **53**(3), 477–496.

Jordan, A., Benson, D., Wurzel, R. and Zito, A. (2012). Environmental policy. In *Constructing a Policy-Making State? Policy Dynamics in the EU*, ed. J. Richardson. Oxford: Oxford University Press, pp. 104–124.

Jordan, A., Huitema, D., van Asselt, H. *et al.* (eds.). (2010). *Climate Change Policy in the European Union: Confronting the Dilemmas of Mitigation and Adaptation?* Cambridge: Cambridge University Press.

Kaufman, H. (1976). *Are Government Organisations Immortal?* Washington, D.C.: Brookings Institution.

Kay, A. (2005). A critique of the use of path dependency in policy studies. *Public Administration*, **83**(3), 553–571

Kay, A. (2012). Policy trajectories and legacies: path dependency revisited. In *Routledge Handbook of Public Policy*, ed. E. Araral *et al.* London: Routledge, pp. 462–472.

Keating, D. (2012a). Germany fights against Italy over car emissions. *European Voice*, 27 June.

Keating, D. (2012b) Commission proposes vehicle emissions limits for 2020. *European Voice*, 11 July.

Keating, D. (2012c). On the right road? Commission pushes for lower CO_2 emissions. *European Voice*, 19 July.

Keating, D. (2012d). Commission compromise on biofuel impact. *European Voice*, 11 September.

Keating, D. (2012e). Second thoughts on biofuel. *European Voice*, 26 September.

Keating, D. (2013a). MEPs on collision course over emissions. *European Voice*, 30 April.

Keating, D. (2013b). Emissions impossible? *European Voice*, 3 July.

Keating, D. (2013c). MEPs back biofuel cap, but fail to secure a mandate for talks. *European Voice*, 11 September.

Keating, D. (2013d). Car CO_2 showdown at environment council. *European Voice*, 9 October.

Keating, D. (2013e). Member states assess German damage to institutional trust. *European Voice*, 16 October.

Keating, D. (2013f). Lithuania seeks deal on car emissions. *European Voice*, 30 October.

Keating, D. (2013g). Council rejects biofuel compromise. *European Voice*, 12 December.

Keating, D. (2014a). Commission's climate course. *European Voice*, 22 January.

Keating, D. (2014b). Targets: the end of the road? *European Voice*, 19 February.

Keating, D. (2014c). Ministers to clash over biofuel. *European Voice*, 26 February.

Keating, D. (2014d). Climate debate pits west against east. *European Voice*, 5 March.
Keating, D. (2014e). A new regime on emissions for 2030. *European Voice*, 9 October.
Keating, D. (2014f). EU adopts 2030 climate targets. *European Voice*, 24 October.
Keating, D. (2015). Lawmakers gear up for battle on ETS reform. *ENDS Europe*, 18 September.
Keay-Bright, S. (2000). *A Critical Analysis of the Voluntary Fuel Economy Agreements Established between the Automobile Industry and the European Commission*. Brussels: European Environmental Bureau.
Kelsey, N. (2018). Industry type and environmental policy: industry characteristics shape the potential for policy making success in energy and the environment. *Business and Politics*, **20**(4), 615–642.
Kelsey, N. and Zysman, J. (2013). The green spiral. In *Can Green Sustain Growth? From the Religion to the Reality of Sustainable Prosperity*, eds. J. Zysman and M. Huberty. Stanford: Stanford University Press, pp. 79–88.
Kemp, R. and Potoglio, S. (2011). The innovation effects of environmental policy instruments – a typical case of the blind men and the elephant? *Ecological Economics*, **72**(C), 28–36.
Keohane, R. (2015). The global politics of climate change: challenge for political science. *PS: Political Science and Politics*, **48**(1), 19–26.
Keohane, R. O. and Victor, D. G. (2011). The regime complex for climate change. *Perspectives on Politics*, **9**(1), 7–23.
Keppler, J. H. and Cruciani, M. (2010). Rents in the European power sector due to carbon trading. *Energy Policy*, **38**(8), 4280–4290.
Keyes, J. M. (1996). Power tools: the form and function of legal instruments for government action. *Canadian Journal of Administrative Law and Practice*, **10**, 133–174.
Kleine, M., and Pollack, M. (2018). Liberal Intergovernmentalism and its critics. *Journal of Common Market Studies*, **56**(7), 1493–1509.
Kline, D. (2001). Positive feedback, lock in and environmental policy. *Policy Sciences*, **34**, 95–107.
Knothe, G. (2001). Historical perspectives on vegetable oil-based diesel fuels. *Inform*, **12**, 1103–1107.
Kooiman, J. (2003). *Governing as Governance*. London: Sage.
Kość, W. (2014). Member states split on ETS reform start date. *ENDS Europe*, 29 September.
Krasner, S. (1988). Sovereignty: an institutional perspective. *Comparative Political Studies*, **21**(1), 66–94.
Kumlin, S. and Stadelmann-Steffen, I. (eds.). (2014). *How Welfare States Shape the Democratic Public: Policy Feedback, Participation, Voting, and Attitudes*. Cheltenham: Edward Elgar.
Laing, T., Sato, M., Grubb, M. and Comberti, C. (2014). The effects and side-effects of the EU emissions trading scheme. *Wiley Interdisciplinary Reviews: Climate Change*, **5**(4), 509–519.
Lazarus, R. (2009). Super wicked problems and climate change: restraining the present to liberate the future. *Cornell Law Review*, **94**, 1153–1234.
Le Goff, F. (2011). EU faces uphill battle to cut transport emissions. *ENDS Europe*, 10 November.
Lenschow, A. and Rottmann K. (2005). *Privatising EU Governance: Emergence and Characteristics of Voluntary Agreements in European Environmental Policy*. Paper presented at 'Soft Modes of Governance and the Private Sector' CONNEX workshop, 1–3 December.

Levidow, L. and Papaioannou, T. (2014). UK biofuel policy. *Environment and Planning A*, **46**(2), 280–298.

Levin, K., Cashore, B., Bernstein, S. and Auld, G. (2012). Overcoming the tragedy of super wicked problems: constraining our future selves to ameliorate global climate change. *Policy Sciences*, **45**, 123–152.

Liang, J. and Fiorino, D. (2013). The implications of policy stability for renewable energy innovation in the United States, 1974–2009. *Policy Studies Journal*, **41**(1), 97–118.

Lise, W., Sijm, J. and Hobbs, B. F. (2010). The impact of the EU ETS on prices, profits and emissions in the power sector: simulation results with the COMPETES EU20 model. *Environmental and Resource Economics*, **47**(1), 23–44.

Londo, H. M., Deurwaarder, E. P. and van Thuijl, E. (2006). *Review of EU Biofuels Directive Public Consultation Exercise*. Amsterdam: ECN.

Low Carbon Vehicle Partnership (2005). *Coalition Launches Biofuels Declaration to Boost to Biofuels.* 15 June.

Lowi, T. (1972). Four systems of policy, politics and choice. *Public Administration Review*, **32**, July/August, 298–310.

Mahoney, J. (2000). Path dependence in historical sociology. *Theory and Society*, **29**(4), 507–548.

Mahoney, J. (2015). Process tracing and historical explanation. *Security Studies*, **24**(2), 200–218.

Mahoney, J. and Thelen, K. (2009). A theory of gradual institutional change. In *Explaining Institutional Change: Ambiguity, Agency, and Power*, eds. J. Mahoney and K. Thelen. Cambridge: Cambridge University Press, pp. 1–37.

Mahoney, J. and Thelen, K. (eds.). (2010). *Explaining Institutional Change: Ambiguity, Agency, and Power*. Cambridge: Cambridge University Press.

Majone, G. (1994). The rise of the regulatory state in Europe. *West European Politics*, **17**(3), 77–101.

Marcu, A., Alberola, E. Caneill, J.-V. et al. (2019). *2019 State of the EU ETS Report*. Paris: Institute for Climate Economics.

Marier, P. (2012). Policy feedback and learning. In *Routledge Handbook of Public Policy*, ed. E. Araral *et al.* London: Routledge, pp. 401–414.

Marshall, A. (2014). UK wins as EU plumps for 40% carbon target for 2030. *The ENDS Report*, 28 January.

Matt, E. (2012). *The Political Economy of EU Environmental Governance: The Case of the Voluntary Agreement to Reduce Carbon Dioxide Emissions from New Cars*. PhD Thesis, University of East Anglia, Norwich.

May, P. and Jochim, A. (2013). Policy regime perspectives: policies, politics, and governing. *Policy Studies Journal*, **41**(3), 426–452.

McGee, P. (2017). How VW's cheating on emission was exposed. *Financial Times*, 11 January.

Meadowcroft, J. (2009). What about the politics? Sustainable development, transition management, and long term energy transitions. *Policy Sciences*, **42**, 323–340.

Meadowcroft, J. (2011). Engaging with the politics of sustainability transitions. *Environmental Innovation and Societal Transitions*, **1**(1), 70–75.

Meckling, J. (2011a). The globalization of carbon trading: transnational business coalitions in climate politics. *Global Environmental Politics*, **11**(2), 26–50.

Meckling, J. (2011b). *Carbon Coalitions: Business, Climate Politics, and the Rise of Emissions Trading*. Cambridge: MIT Press.

Meckling, J. (2019). Governing renewables: policy feedback in a global energy transition. *Environment and Planning C*, **37**(2), 317–338.

Meckling, J. and Nahm, J. (2018). The power of process: state capacity and climate policy. *Governance*, **31**(4), 741–757.

Meckling, J., Sterner, T. and Wagner, G. (2017). Policy sequencing toward decarbonisation. *Nature Energy*, **2**, 918–922.

Meckling, J., Kelsey, N., Biber, E., and Zysman, J. (2015). Winning coalitions for climate policy. *Science*, **349**(6253), 1170–1171.

Mettler, S. (2011). *The Submerged State: How Invisible Government Policies Undermine American Democracy*. Chicago: University of Chicago Press.

Mettler, S. (2015). Twenty years on: Paul Pierson's *Dismantling the Welfare State? PS: Political Science and Politics*, **48**(2), 270–273.

Mettler, S. and SoRelle, M. (2014). Policy feedback theory. In *Theories of the Policy Process*, eds. P. Sabatier and C. Weible. 3rd ed. New York: Westview Press, pp. 151–181.

Mettler, S. and Soss, J. (2004). The consequences of public policy for democratic citizenship: bridging policy studies and mass politics. *Perspectives on Politics*, **2**(1), 55–73.

Michaelowa, A., Allen, M. and Sha, F. (2018). Policy instruments for limiting global temperature rise to 1.5°C – can humanity rise to the challenge? *Climate Policy*, **18**(3), 275–286.

Mickwitz, P., Hyvättinen, H. and Kivimaa, P. (2008). The role of policy instruments in the innovation and diffusion of environmentally friendly technologies. *Journal of Cleaner Production*, **16**(1) S1, S162–S170.

Mikler, J. (2009). *Greening the Car Industry*. Cheltenham: Edward Elgar.

Mol, A. (2006) Environmental governance in the Information Age: the emergence of informational governance. *Environment and Planning C*, **24**(4), 497–514.

Moore, B. (2018). *The Political Effects of Climate Policy: Policy Feedback from the European Union Emissions Trading System*. PhD Thesis, University of East Anglia, Norwich.

Mukherjee, I. and Giest, S. (2019) Designing policies in uncertain contexts: entrepreneurial capacity and the case of the European Emission Trading Scheme. *Public Policy and Administration*, **34**(3), 262–286.

Müller, P. and Slominski, P. (2013). Agree now – pay later: escaping the joint decision trap in the evolution of the EU emission trading system. *Journal of European Public Policy*, **20**(10), 1425–1442.

North, D. (1990). *Institutions, Institutional Change and Economic Performance*. Cambridge: Cambridge University Press.

Nowotny, H. (1994). *Time: The Modern and Postmodern Experience*. Cambridge: Polity Press.

Ntziachristos, L. and Dilara, P. (2012). *Sustainability Assessment of Road Transport Technologies*. Ispra: European Commission Joint Research Centre.

Oberlander, J. and Weaver, R. K. (2015). Unravelling from within? The Affordable Care Act and self-undermining policy feedbacks. *The Forum*, **13**(1), 37–62.

Oberthür, S. and Dupont, C. (eds.). (2015). *Decarbonization in the European Union: Internal Policies and External Strategies*. Basingstoke: Palgrave MacMillan.

Oberthür, S. and Ott, H. (eds.). (1999). *The Kyoto Protocol: International Climate Policy for the 21st Century*. Berlin: Springer Verlag.

Oberthür, S. and Pallemaerts, M. (2010). The EU's external and internal climate policies. In *The New Climate Policies of the European Union: Internal Legislation and Climate Diplomacy*, eds. S. Oberthür and M. Pallemaerts. Brussels: VUB Press, pp. 27–64.

Oberthür, S. and Roche Kelly, C. (2008). EU leadership in international climate policy: achievements and challenges. *The International Spectator*, **43**(3), 35–50.

Oliver, C. (2014). Biofuels: wasted energy. *Financial Times*, 15 April.
Oosterhuis, F. (2006). *Innovation Dynamics Induced by Environmental Policy*. Amsterdam: IVM, Vrije University.
Organisation for Economic Co-operation and Development (OECD) (1980). *Pollution Charges in Practice*. Paris: OECD.
Organisation for Economic Co-operation and Development (OECD) (1994). *Managing the Environment: The Role of Economic Instruments*. Paris: OECD.
Orren, K. and Skowronek, S. (2002). The study of American Political Development. In *Political Science: State of the Discipline*, eds. I. Katznelson and H. Milner. New York: W. W. Norton & Company, pp. 722–754.
Pahl, S., Sheppard, S., Boomsma, C. and Groves, C. (2014). Perceptions of time in relation to climate change. *Wiley Interdisciplinary Reviews: Climate Change*, **5**(3), 375–388.
Pahle, M. Burtraw, D., Flachsland, C. *et al.* (2018). Sequencing to ratchet up climate policy stringency. *Nature Climate Change*, **8**, 861–867.
Pallemaerts, M. and Williams, R. (2006). Climate change: the international and European policy framework. In *EU Climate Change Policy: The Challenge of New Regulatory Initiatives*, eds. M. Peeters and K. Deketelaere. Cheltenham: Edward Elgar, pp. 22–50.
Palmer, J. R. (2014). Biofuels and the politics of land-use change: tracing the interactions of discourse and place in European policy making. *Environment and Planning A: Economy and Space*, **46**(2), 337–352.
Palmer, J. R. (2015). How do policy entrepreneurs influence policy change? Framing and boundary work in EU transport biofuels policy. *Environmental Politics*, **24**(2), 270–287.
Parson, E. A. and Karwat, D. (2011). Sequential climate change policy. *WIREs Climate Change*, **2**(5), 744–756.
Patashnik, E. M. (2000). *Putting Trust in the Federal Budget*. Cambridge: Cambridge University Press.
Patashnik, E. M. (2003). After the public interest prevails: the political sustainability of policy reform. *Governance*, **16**(2), 203–234.
Patashnik, E. M. (2008). *Reforms at Risk: What Happens after Major Policy Changes Are Enacted*. Princeton: Princeton University Press.
Patashnik, E. M. and Zelizer, J. (2010). When policy does not remake politics: the limits of policy feedback. Paper presented at the Republic of Statutes Conference, Yale Law School, 10–11 December 2010.
Patashnik, E. M. and Zelizer, J. (2013). The struggle to remake politics: liberal reform and the limits of policy feedback in the contemporary American state. *Perspectives on Politics*, **11**(4), 1071–1087.
Patt, A. G. and Weber, E. U. (2014). Perceptions and communication strategies for the many uncertainties relevant for climate policy. *Wiley Interdisciplinary Reviews: Climate Change*, **5**(2), 219–232.
Pearse, R. (2017). *Pricing Carbon in Australia: Contestation, the State and Market Failure*. London: Routledge.
Pechmann, P. (2018). *Architectural Policy Design: How Policy Makers Try to Shape Policy Feedback Effects When Designing Policies*. Unpublished PhD Thesis, Aarhus University, Denmark.
Peters, B. G. (1999). *Institutional Theory in Political Science*. London: Pinter.
Peters, B. G. (2018) *Policy Problems and Policy Design*. Cheltenham: Edward Elgar.
Peters, B. G., Pierre, J. and King, D. S. (2005). The politics of path dependency: political conflict in historical institutionalism. *The Journal of Politics*, **67**(4), 1275–1300.

Peters, D., Alberici, S., Passmore, J. and Malins, C. (2015). *How to Advance Cellulosic Biofuels: Assessment of Costs, Investment Options and Policy Support.* Utrecht: Ecofys and the Passmore Group.

Pickstone, S. (2019). European leaders fail to endorse net-zero climate goal. *ENDS Europe*, 22 March.

Pierre, J. and Peters B. G. (2005). *Governing Complex Societies: Trajectories and Scenarios.* Basingstoke: Palgrave MacMillan.

Pierson, P. (1993). When effect becomes cause: policy feedback and political change. *World Politics*, **45**(4), 595–628.

Pierson, P. (1994). *Dismantling the Welfare State? Reagan, Thatcher and the Politics of Retrenchment.* Cambridge: Cambridge University Press.

Pierson, P. (1996). The path to European integration: a historical institutionalist analysis. *Comparative Political Studies*, **29**(2), 123–163.

Pierson, P. (2000a). Increasing returns, path dependence, and the study of politics. *American Political Science Review*, **94**(2), 251–267.

Pierson, P. (2000b). The limits of design: explaining institutional origins and change. *Governance*, **13**(4), 475–499

Pierson, P. (2004). *Politics in Time: History, Institutions, and Social Analysis.* Princeton: Princeton University Press.

Pierson, P. (2005). The study of policy development. *The Journal of Policy History*, **17**(1), 34–51.

Pierson, P. (2006). Public policies as institutions. In *Rethinking Political Institutions: The Art of the State,* eds. S. Shapiro, S. Skowronek and D. Galvin. New York: New York University Press, pp. 114–134.

Pierson, P. (2015). Reflections of the evolution of a research program. *PS: Political Science & Politics*, **48**(2), 292–294.

Pierson, P. and Skocpol, T. (2002). Historical institutionalism in contemporary political science. In *Political Science: State of the Discipline,* eds. I. Katznelson and H. Milner. New York: W. W. Norton & Company, pp. 693–721.

Point Carbon (2008). *Carbon 2008 – Post-2012 Is Now.* Oslo: Point Carbon.

Ponte, S. and Daugbjerg, C. (2015). Biofuel sustainability and the formation of transnational hybrid governance. *Environmental Politics*, **24**(1), 96–114.

Princen, T. (2009). Long-term decision-making: biological and psychological evidence. *Global Environmental Politics*, **9**(3), 9–19.

Putnam, R. (1988). Diplomacy and domestic politics: the logic of two-level games. *International Organisation*, **42**(3), 427–60.

Rabe, B. G. (2016). The durability of carbon cap-and-trade policy. *Governance*, **29**(1), 103–119.

Raval, A. (2019). Oil majors work to carve out a greater role for greener biofuels. *Financial Times*, 12 March.

Rennings, K., Brockmann, K. L. and Bergmann, H. (1997). Voluntary agreements in environmental protection: experiences in Germany and future perspectives. *Business Strategy and the Environment*, **6**(5), 245–263.

Richardson, G. (1991). *Feedback Thought in Social Science and Systems Theory.* Philadelphia: University Pennsylvania Press.

Rietig, K. (2018). The links among contested knowledge, beliefs, and learning in European climate governance: from consensus to conflict in reforming biofuels policy. *Policy Studies Journal*, **46**(1), 137–159.

Rietig, K. and Laing, T. (2017). Policy stability in climate governance: the case of the United Kingdom. *Environmental Policy and Governance*, **27**(6), 575–587.

Rip, A. and Kemp, R. (1998). Technological change. In *Human Choice and Climate Change, Vol. II (Resources and Technology)*, eds. S. Rayner and E. Malone. Columbus, OH: Battelle Press, pp. 327–367.

Roach, S. (2015). VW emissions scandal spreads. *ENDS Report*, 4 November.

Roberts, C., Geels, F. W., Lockwood, M. *et al.* (2018). The politics of accelerating low-carbon transitions: towards a new research agenda. *Energy Research and Social Science*, **44**, 304–311.

Rojo, J. (2017a). Court action prompts diesel ban in Munich. *ENDS Europe*, 16 June.

Rojo, J. (2017b). France to ban sales of petrol and diesel cars by 2040. *ENDS Europe*, 7 July.

Rose, R. (1990). Inheritance before choice in public policy. *Journal of Theoretical Politics*, **2**(3), 263–291.

Rosenbloom, D., Meadowcroft, J. and Cashore, B. (2019). Stability and climate policy? Harnessing insights on path dependence, policy feedback, and transition pathways. *Energy Research & Social Science*, **50**, 168–178.

Ross, F. (2000). Beyond left and right: the new partisan politics of welfare. *Governance*, **13**(2), 155–183.

Roth, R., Clark, J. and Kelkar, A. (2001). Automobile bodies: can aluminium be an economical alternative to steel? *JOM*, **53**(8), 28–32.

Rothstein, B. (1992). Labor-market institutions and working-class strength. In *Structuring Politics: Historical Institutionalism in Comparative Analysis*, eds. S. Steinmo, K. Thelen, and F. Longstreth. Cambridge: Cambridge University Press, pp. 33–56.

Royal Academy of Engineering (2017). *Sustainability of Liquid Biofuels*. London: Royal Academy of Engineering.

Sabatier, P. and Jenkins-Smith, H. (1999). The advocacy coalition framework. In *Theories of the Policy Process*, ed. P. A. Sabatier. 2nd ed. Boulder: Westview Press, pp. 117–168.

Salamon, L. M. (2002). The new governance and the tools of public action. In *The Tools of Government: A Guide to the New Governance*, ed. L. M. Salamon. Oxford: Oxford University Press, pp. 1–47.

Salvidge, R. (2012). Carmakers on track to hit CO_2 targets for 2020. *ENDS Europe*, 5 December.

Sandbag (2019). *Carbon Price Viewer*. Available at: https://sandbag.org.uk/carbon-price-viewer/ [Accessed 23 August 2019]

Schattschneider, E. E. (1935). *Politics, Pressures and the Tariff: A Study of Free Private Enterprise in Pressure Politics, as Shown in the 1929–1930 Revision of the Tariff*. New York: Prentice-Hall.

Schmidt, T. S. and Sewerin, S. (2017). Technology as a driver of climate and energy politics. *Nature Energy*, **2**(6), 17084.

Schmidt, T. S. and Sewerin, S. (2018). Measuring the temporal dynamics of policy mixes. *Research Policy* (online version).

Schmidt, T., Sewerin, S. and Bateson, B. (2018). *Does policy design predict a policy mix's future?* Paper presented at the IWPPP1 workshops (Policy Feedback and Policy Dynamics, Topic 1, Workshop 8), Pittsburgh, 26–28 June.

Schneider, A. L. (2013). Policy design and transfer. In *Routledge Handbook of Public Policy*, ed. E. Araral *et al.* London: Routledge, pp. 217–228.

Schneider, A. L. and Ingram, H. (1997). *Policy Design for Democracy*. Lawrence, KS: University Press of Kansas.

Schneider, A. L. and Ingram, H. M. (2019). Social constructions, anticipatory feedback strategies, and deceptive public policy. *Policy Studies Journal*, **47**(2), 206–236.

Schneider, A. L. and Sidney, M. (2009). What is next for policy design and social construction theory? *Policy Studies Journal*, **37**(1), 103–119.

Schreurs, M. A. and Tiberghien, Y. (2007). Multi-level reinforcement: explaining European Union leadership in climate change mitigation. *Global Environmental Politics*, **7**(4), 19–46.

Scott, J. (2011). The multi-level governance of climate change. In *The Evolution of EU Law*, eds. P. Craig and G. de Burca. 2nd ed. Oxford: Oxford University Press, pp. 805–836.

Searchinger, T., Heimlich, R., Houghton, R. A. *et al.* (2008). Use of U.S. croplands for biofuels increases greenhouse gases through emissions from land-use change. *Science*, **319**(5867), 1238–1240.

Seto, K. C., Davis, S. J., Mitchell, R. B. *et al.* (2016). Carbon lock-in: types, causes and policy implications. *Annual Review of Environmental Resources*, **41**, 425–452.

Sharham, A. (2015). European car sales on growth road for first time since crisis. *Financial Times*, 17–18 January.

Sharman, A. and Holmes, J. (2010). Evidence-based policy or policy-based evidence gathering? Biofuels, the EU and the 10% target. *Environmental Policy and Governance*, **20**(5), 309–321.

Sheingate, A. D. (2003). Political entrepreneurship, institutional change, and American political development. *Studies in American Political Development*, **17**(2), 185–203.

Sidney, M. S. (2005). Policy formulation: design and tools. In *Handbook of Public Policy Analysis: Theory, Politics and Methods*, eds. F. Fischer, G. J. Miller and M. S. Sidney. London: CRC Press, pp. 79–87.

Sijm, J., Neuhoff, K. and Chen, Y. (2006). CO_2 cost pass-through and windfall profits in the power sector. *Climate Policy*, **6**(1), 49–72.

Simkins, G. (2012). Barroso calls for 'balanced' ILUC proposal. *ENDS Europe*, 21 May.

Simkins, G. (2013). EP committee calls for 2025 CO_2 target for cars. *ENDS Europe*, 24 April.

Simkins, G. and Roach, S. (2015). VW emissions scandal raises prospect of tighter regulation. *ENDS Report*, 26 October.

Skjærseth, J. B. (1994). The climate policy of the EC: too hot to handle? *Journal of Common Market Studies*, **32**(1), 25–45.

Skjærseth, J. B. (2010). EU emissions trading: legitimacy and stringency. *Environmental Policy and Governance*, **20**(5), 295–308.

Skjærseth, J. B. (2013). Governance by EU emissions trading: resistance or innovation in the oil industry? *International Environmental Agreements: Politics, Law and Economics*, **13**(1), 31–48.

Skjærseth, J. B. (2015). EU climate and energy policy: demanded or supplied? In *The Domestic Politics of Climate Change: Key Actors in International Climate Cooperation*, eds. G. Bang, A. Underdal, and S. Andresen. Cheltenham: Edward Elgar, pp. 71–94.

Skjærseth, J. B. (2016). Linking EU climate and energy policies: policy-making, implementation and reform. *International Environmental Agreements: Politics, Law and Economics*, **16**(4), 509–523.

Skjærseth, J. B. (2018). Implementing EU climate and energy policies in Poland: policy feedback and reform. *Environmental Politics*, **27**(3), 498–518.

Skjærseth, J. B. and Wettestad, J. (2008). *EU Emissions Trading: Initiation, Decision-Making and Implementation*. Aldershot: Ashgate.

Skjærseth, J. B. and Wettestad, J. (2009). The origin, evolution and consequences of the EU Emissions Trading System. *Global Environmental Politics*, **9**(2), 101–122.

Skjærseth, J. B. and Wettestad, J. (2010a). Fixing the EU Emissions Trading System? Understanding the post-2012 changes. *Global Environmental Politics*, **10**(4), 101–123.

Skjærseth, J. B. and Wettestad, J. (2010b). The EU Emissions Trading System revised. In *The New Climate Policies of the European Union: Internal Legislation and Climate Diplomacy*, eds. S. Oberthür and M. Pallemaerts. Brussels: VUB Press, pp. 65–92.

Skocpol, T. (1992). *Protecting Soldiers and Mothers: The Political Origins of Social Policy in the United States*. Cambridge: Harvard University Press.

Skocpol, T. (2013). *Naming the Problem: What It Will Take to Counter Extremism and Engage Americans in the Fight against Global Warming*. Paper prepared for the symposium on The Politics of America's Fight against Global Warming, 4 February.

Skodvin, T., Gullberg, A. T. and Aakre, S. (2010). Target-group influence and political feasibility: the case of climate policy design in Europe. *Journal of European Public Policy*, **17**(6), 854–873.

Skogstad, G. (2017). Policy feedback and self-reinforcing and self-undermining processes in EU biofuels policy. *Journal of European Public Policy*, **24**(1), 21–41.

Skovgaard, J. (2013). The limits of entrapment: the negotiations on EU reduction targets, 2007–11. *Journal of Common Market Studies*, **51**(6), 1141–1157.

Skovgaard, J. (2014). EU climate policy after the crisis. *Environmental Politics*, **23**(1), 1–17.

Skovgaard, J. (2017). The role of finance ministries in environmental policy making: the case of European Union Emissions Trading System reform in Denmark, Germany and the Netherlands. *Environmental Policy and Governance*, **27**(4), 351–364.

Skovgaard, J. and van Asselt, H. (eds.). (2018). *The Politics of Fossil Fuel Subsidies and Their Reform*. Cambridge: Cambridge University Press.

Smith, A., Voss, J.-P. and Grin, J. (2010). Innovation studies and sustainability transitions: the allure of the multi-level perspective and its challenges. *Research Policy*, **39**(4), 435–448.

Solmeyer, A. R. and Constance, N. (2015). Unpacking the 'black box' of social programs and policies: introduction. *American Journal of Evaluation*, **36**(4), 470–474.

Soss, J. and Schram, S. F. (2007). A public transformed? Welfare reform as policy feedback. *American Political Science Review*, **101**(1), 111–127.

Stern, N. (2006). *The Economics of Climate Change: The Stern Review*. Cambridge: Cambridge University Press.

Stern, N. (2015). *Why Are We Waiting? The Logic, Urgency, and Promise of Tackling Climate Change*. London: MIT Press.

Stokes, L. C. and Breetz, H. L. (2018). Politics in the U.S. energy transition: case studies of solar, wind, biofuels and electric vehicles policy. *Energy Policy*, **113**, 76–86.

Taminiau, Y., Molenkamp, G. and Tashchilova, S. (2006). The pendulum: The Auto-Oil Programmes revisited. *Energy and Environment*, **17**(2), 243–262.

Taschner, T. (1998). Environmental management systems: the European regulation. In *New Instruments for Environmental Policy in the EU*, ed. J. Golub. London: Routledge, pp. 215–241.

Taylor, C., Pollard, S., Rocks, S. and Angus, A. (2012). Selecting policy instruments for better environmental regulation. *Environmental Policy and Governance*, **22**(4), 268–92.

ten Brink, P. (2010). Mitigating CO_2 emissions from cars in the EU. In *The New Climate Policies of the European Union* eds. S. Oberthur and M. Pallemaerts. Brussels: VUB Press, pp. 179–210.

Tetlock, P. E. and Belkin, A. (eds.). (1996). *Counterfactual Thought Experiments in World Politics: Logical, Methodological, and Psychological Perspectives.* Princeton: Princeton University Press.

Thelen, K. (1999). Historical institutionalism in comparative politics. *Annual Review of Political Science*, **2**, 369–404.

Thelen, K. (2003). How institutions evolve. In *Comparative Historical Analysis in the Social Sciences*, eds. J. Mahoney and D. Rueschemeyer. Cambridge: Cambridge University Press, pp. 208–240.

Thelen, K. (2006). Institutions and social change. In *Rethinking Political Institutions: The Art of the State*, eds. S. Shapiro, S. Skowronek and D. Galvin. New York: New York University Press, pp. 135–170.

Thompson, F. (2012). *Medicaid Politics: Federalism, Policy Durability, and Health Reform.* Washington, DC: Georgetown University Press.

Thompson, G., Joseph, S., Juniper, T. *et al.* (2004). Brown should stand firm on rising fuel prices. *The Guardian*, 4 June.

Timilsina, G. (2014). Biofuels in the long-run global energy supply mix for transportation. *Philosophical Transactions of the Royal Society A*, **372**, 1–19.

Toplensky, R. and McGee, P. (2018). EU launches probe into BMW, Daimler and VW over cartel claims. *Financial Times*, 18 September.

Transport & Environment (T&E) (2012). *How Clean Are Europe's Cars? An Analysis of Carmaker Progress towards EU CO_2 targets in 2011.* Brussels: European Federation for Transport and the Environment.

Transport & Environment (T&E) (2013). Germany and its luxury carmakers force drivers to spend more on fuel. T&E press release, 29 November.

True, J., Jones, B. and Baumgartner, F. (2007). Punctuated equilibrium theory. In *Theories of the Policy Process*, ed. P. A. Sabatier. 2nd ed. New York: Routledge, pp. 155–188.

UK Government (2014). *UK Analysis: Impacts of the Market Stability Reserve on the EU ETS.* London: UK Government.

United Nations Environment Programme (UNEP) (2015). *Emissions Gap Report 2015: A UN Synthesis Report.* Nairobi: UNEP.

United Nations Environment Programme (UNEP) (2018). *Emissions Gap Report 2018.* Nairobi: UNEP.

United Nations Framework Convention on Climate Change (UNFCCC) (2012). *Decision 1/CP.17: Establishment of an Ad Hoc Working Group on the Durban Platform for Enhanced Action.* Bonn: UNFCCC.

United Nations Framework Convention on Climate Change (UNFCCC) (2015). *Decision 1/CP.21: Adoption of the Paris Agreement.* Bonn: UNFCCC.

United States Department of Agriculture (2018). *EU Biofuels Annual 2018.* Global Agricultural Information Network Report NL8027. Washington, DC: USDA.

Unruh, G. C. (2000). Understanding carbon lock-in. *Energy Policy*, **28**(12), 817–830.

Unruh, G. C. (2002). Escaping carbon lock-in. *Energy Policy*, **30**(4), 317–325.

Unruh, G. C. and Carrillo-Hermosilla, J. (2006). Globalizing carbon lock-in. *Energy Policy*, **34**(10), 1185–1197.

Urry, J. (2008). *Mobilities.* Malden: Polity Press.

van Apeldoorn, B. (2002). *Transnational Capitalism and the Struggle over European integration.* London: Routledge.

van Asselt, H. (2010). Emissions trading: the enthusiastic adoption of an 'alien' instrument. In *Climate Change Policy in the European Union: Confronting the Dilemmas of Mitigation and Adaptation?* eds. A. Jordan *et al.* Cambridge: Cambridge University Press, pp. 125–144.

van der Heijden, J. (2011). Institutional layering: a review of the use of the concept. *Politics*, **31**(1), 9–18.
van Noorden, R. (2013). EU debates U-turn on biofuels policy. *Nature*, **499**(7456), 13–14.
van Renssen, S. (2012). Commission aims to fix EU ETS by year-end. *ENDS Europe*, 19 April 2012.
van Renssen, S. (2018). The inconvenient truth of failed climate policies. *Nature Climate Change*, **8**, 355–358.
Vereinigung Deutscher Elektrizitätswerke (VDEW) (2000). *VDEW Comments on 'Green Paper on Greenhouse Gas Emissions Trading in the European Union'* (in German). Brussels: VDEW.
Victor, D. (2011). *Global Warming Gridlock: Creating More Effective Strategies for Protecting the Planet*. Cambridge: Cambridge University Press.
Vis, P. (2006). The first allocation round: a brief history. In *EU Energy Law: The EU Greenhouse Gas Emissions Trading Scheme*, eds. J. Delbeke, O. Hartridge, J. G. Lefevere et al. Deventer, Netherlands: Claeys & Casteels, pp. 187–212.
Volpi, G. and Singer, S. (2002). EU level agreements: a successful tool? Lessons from the agreement with the automotive industry. In *Voluntary Environmental Agreements: Process, Practice and Future Use*, ed. P. ten Brink. Sheffield: Greenleaf Publishing, pp. 142–154.
Voss, J.-P. (2007). Innovation processes in governance: the development of 'emissions trading' as a new policy instrument. *Science and Public Policy*, **34**(5), 329–343.
Voss, J.-P. and Simons, A. (2014). Instrument constituencies and the supply side of policy innovation. *Environmental Politics*, **23**(5), 735–754.
Walker, J. (1983). The origins and maintenance of interest groups in the USA. *American Political Science Review*, **77**(2), 390–406.
Ward, A. and Toplensky, R. (2017). EU emissions reforms send a strong smoke signal. *Financial Times*, 17 November.
Weale, A., Pridham, W., Cini, M. et al. (2000). *Environmental Governance in Europe: An Ever Closer Ecological Union?* Oxford: Oxford University Press.
Weaver, R. K. (1988). *Automatic Government: The Politics of Indexation*. Washington, DC: Brookings Institution.
Weaver, R. K. (2006). Government institutions, policy cartels and policy change. In *Rethinking Political Institutions: The Art of the State*, eds. S. Shapiro, S. Skowronek and D. Galvin. New York: New York University Press, pp. 216–237.
Weaver, R. K. (2010). Paths and forks or chutes and ladders? Negative feedbacks and policy regime change. *Journal of Public Policy*, **30**(2), 137–162.
Weaver, R. K. and Rockman, B. (eds.). (1993). *Do Institutions Matter? Government Capabilities in the United States and Abroad*. Washington, DC: Brookings Institution.
Webster, M. (2008). Incorporating path dependency into decision analytic methods. *Decision Analysis*, **5**(2), 60–75.
Weir, M. (2006). When does politics create policy? The organizational politics of change. In *Rethinking Political Institutions: The Art of the State*, eds. S. Shapiro, S. Skowronek and D. Galvin. New York: New York University Press, pp. 171–186.
Wells, P. (2010). *The Automotive Industry in an Era of Eco-austerity*. Cheltenham: Edward Elgar.
Wettestad, J. (2000). The complicated development of EU climate policy. In *Climate Change and European Leadership*, eds. M. Grubb and J. Gupta. Dordrecht: Kluwer, pp. 25–47.

Wettestad, J. (2005). The making of the 2003 EU Emissions Trading Directive: an ultra-quick process due to entrepreneurial proficiency? *Global Environmental Politics*, **5**(1), 1–23.

Wettestad, J. (2009a). European climate policy: toward centralized governance? *Review of Policy Research*, **26**(3), 311–328.

Wettestad, J. (2009b). EU energy-intensive industries and emission trading: losers becoming winners? *Environmental Policy and Governance*, **19**(5), 309–320.

Wettestad, J. (2014). Rescuing EU emissions trading: mission impossible? *Global Environmental Change*, **14**(2), 64–81.

Wettestad, J. and Jevnaker, T. (2016). *Rescuing EU Emissions Trading: The Climate Policy Flagship*. London: Palgrave Macmillan.

Wettestad, J. and Jevnaker, T. (2019). Smokescreen politics? Ratcheting up EU emissions trading in 2017. *Review of Policy Research*, 1–25 (online version).

Wettestad, J., Eikeland, P. O. and Nilsson, M. (2012). EU climate and energy policy: a hesitant supranational turn? *Global Environmental Politics*, **12**(2), 67–86.

Williams, S. (2014). Last ditch protest against 'weak' biofuel reform. *ENDS Europe*, 9 December.

Williams, S. (2015). Unused allowances 'will thwart ETS reform'. *ENDS Europe*, 17 February.

Wilson, J. Q. (1980). The politics of regulation. In *The Politics of Regulation*, ed. J. Q. Wilson. New York: Basic Books, pp. 357–394.

Wilson, J. Q. (1989). *Bureaucracy*. New York: Basic Books.

Woerdman, E., Roggenkamp, M. and Holwerda, M. (2015). *Essential EU Climate Law*. Cheltenham: Edward Elgar.

World Bank (2010). *World Development Report 2010*. Washington, DC: World Bank.

Wurzel, R. K. (2002). *Environmental Policy Making in Britain, Germany and the EU*. Manchester: Manchester University Press.

Wurzel, R. K., Zito, A. R. and Jordan, A. J. (2013). *Environmental Governance in Europe: A Comparative Analysis of New Environmental Policy Instruments*. Cheltenham: Edward Elgar.

Wynne, B. (1993). Implementation of greenhouse gas emissions reduction in the EC. *Global Environmental Change*, **3**(1), 101–128.

Zysman, J. and Huberty, M. (eds.). (2013). *Can Green Sustain Growth? From the Religion to the Reality of Sustainable Prosperity*. Stanford: Stanford University Press.

Index

Actors
    capacities of 12, 23, 49, 181, 188, 206, 214, 218, 220, 240
    identities of 12, 188, 206, 214, 220, 240
    preferences of 12, 22–3, 32, 49, 52, 181, 188, 206–7, 213–15, 218, 220, 240, 242
Adaptation (to climate change) policy 27
Agriculture policy 10, 31
    of the EU 34, 86, 108, 110, 123
Air pollution (local) 176, 179–80, 238
Alliance of Energy Intensive Industries 92, 142, 150, 202, 215
Automatic 47–8
    policy changes 47–8, 52, 233
    policy devices 47–8, 52
    see also, manual
Auto-Oil Programme 100, 162–3, 166
Aviation 71, 85, 90, 190
    and the EU Emissions Trading System 71, 90, 97, 104

Backloading 149–53, 193, 204, 226
    see also emissions trading
Biodiesel 81, 189
Bioethanol 81, 189
Biofuel 24, 30, 50, 67, 69–70
    as a 'dirty fuel' 202
    as a policy panacea 115, 189, 202
    backlash against 117
    definition of 80
    Directive on (2003) 80, 83–7, 106, 112, 131, 189, 199ff, 201–2, 208, 217, 221–2, 224
    emergence of EU policies on 83
    EU production trends 84–5, 115, 119, 125, 189
    feedstocks 84, 117
    global production trends 82, 84–5, 115, 125, 189
    opposition to 115–17
    policies on 82, 86
    supply chains 118, 126, 191, 202, 237
    sustainability criteria for 107, 112, 115–16, 119, 121–4, 129
    types of 81
    see also, biodiesel
    see also, bioethanol
    see also, biofuel types
    see also, Indirect Land Use Change (ILUC)
Biofuel types 81–2
    first generation 81, 107, 115, 118–19, 123–9, 132, 190, 200, 206, 221, 224
    second generation 82, 107, 113, 115, 119, 121, 123–5, 129, 132, 190, 201, 221, 224
    third generation 82, 107, 115, 119, 121, 124–5, 129, 190, 201, 221, 224
    see also biodiesel
    see also bioethanol
Brazil 83–6, 119, 217

Canada 5, 71
Car emissions 97, 158, 168–9, 171, 175–6, 179–80, 183
    in the EU 97, 158, 238
    Recommendation on (1999) 102, 163, 166, 182
    Regulation on (2009) 103, 158–9, 172–3, 176–7, 182, 196, 204, 225
    Regulation on (2014) 103, 178, 181–2, 225
    Regulation on (2019) 104, 182–3, 208, 225
    voluntary agreement on (1999) 101–3, 158, 163, 182, 195, 204, 225
    see also, air pollution (local)
Car industry 59, 64, 99–100, 106, 160, 162, 179–80
Car production 99–100
    trends in the EU 99–100
Carbon lock-in 10
Central and Eastern European Member States 70, 72–3, 96, 146–7, 149, 155, 157, 178, 203, 227
China 227
Climate change xi, xiii, 3, 5–7
    defining characteristics of 58
Climate change policy xii, 4, 6–10, 12, 16, 19, 23, 26–7
    main instruments of in the EU 62, 64, 78

origins in the EU 64
see also, adaptation policy
see also, deep decarbonisation
see also, net zero greenhouse gas emissions
Comitology 61, 94
   and EU climate policy 94, 132, 138, 147, 151, 175, 233
Conference of the Parties to the UNFCCC 67
   Berlin (1995) 67, 162, 237
   Copenhagen (2009) 70–3, 120, 144, 147–8, 227, 243
   Katowice (2018) 75
   Paris (2015) 73–4, 129, 154, 179, 243
   see also, United Nations Framework Convention on Climate Change
Council of Ministers 61, 63
Counterfactual analysis 52, 216–17
   method of 52–3
   as a means to understand climate policy durability 52–3, 216–17
Court of Justice of the EU 153

Deep decarbonisation xi–xii, 3–5, 8, 10, 12, 21, 23, 74
   policy of the EU 71–3, 230–1, 233, 237–8, 241
   see also, net zero greenhouse gas emissions
Delbeke, Jos 135, 151, 233
Depoliticisation 14, 48
DG Climate Action 71, 126, 148
DG Energy 110, 126, 132
DG Environment 63, 65, 76, 133, 135–8, 145, 148, 160, 163–5, 170–1, 175, 192–4, 197, 203, 206, 214
DG Industry 160, 163–5
Dieselgate 103, 180, 196, 205, 219, 238, 241, 243
   see also, car emissions
'Dirty' biofuels 107, 119, 202, 215, 219, 243
   see also, biofuel
Drop-in technologies 106
   and biofuel 110–11, 190, 199, 201
   and car emissions 165, 168, 195
   in the car sector 106, 110
Durable politics 35
   see also, policy durability
   see also, durability
   see also, flexibility
   see also, policy flexibility
Durability (of policy) xii, 4, 32
   characteristics of 32
   definitions of xii, 4
   main dimensions of 7–8, 235
   see also, flexibility

Electricity generation industry 90–1, 97
   see also, Eurelectric
Emissions trading 92–3
   adoption by the EU 92–3
   and EU allowance prices 140, 142, 144–5, 148–51, 157, 195, 202–3, 226, 237
   Decision on the Market Stability Reserve (2015), 153
   Directive on (2003) 92, 96–7, 133–4, 138–9, 145, 156, 191, 202, 208, 217, 223, 233
   Directive on (2009) 95–6, 143, 145–7, 156, 191, 223
   Directive on (2018) 95–6, 153, 155–6, 210, 223, 226–7
   emergence of in the US 134
Endogenous (policy) change 52
   see also, exogenous factors
Energy efficiency 64, 69–70, 73, 75, 142, 149
   of cars 160–1, 167–8, 179
   policies of the EU 64
Energy-intensive industries 91–2
   see also, Alliance of Energy Intensive Industries
Energy security 83, 108, 110, 114, 126
Eurelectric 91, 136, 145, 150, 152, 181
European Automobile Manufacturers' Association (ACEA) 64, 99–102, 158, 160, 164–72, 174, 176–7, 183
   see also, car industry
European Biodiesel Board (EBB) 85, 112, 119, 125, 128, 190
European Bioethanol Fuel Association (eBIO) 85, 119, 190
European Biofuels Technology Platform (EBTP) 85, 190
European Climate Change Programme (ECCP) 68–9, 171
   ECCP1 69, 77, 137, 140, 143
   ECCP2 69, 77, 141, 143–4
European Commission 25, 50, 61, 63
   see also, DG Climate Action
   see also, DG Energy
   see also, DG Environment
   see also, DG Industry
European Council 61
European Environment Agency (EEA) 61, 66, 75, 77
   and biofuels 84, 200, 202
European Environmental Bureau (EEB) 86, 111, 116, 118, 129, 167, 199–200
European Parliament 61, 63–4, 70, 224, 226, 228
   Committee on the Environment, Public Health and Food Safety 173
   Committee on Industry, Research and Energy 173
European Petroleum Industry Association (EUROPIA) 86, 112
European Union xii, 9, 18, 24
   climate policy (development of) 9, 27, 37, 76
   hyperconsensual nature of 61, 76, 234
   policy design spaces in 61
   policy dismantling in 61
   policy instrument preferences of 27, 60, 62, 231
European Union Emissions Trading System (EU ETS). *See*, emissions trading
European Vegetable Oil and Proteinmeal Industry (FEDIOL) 85
Exogenous factors 42–3, 219, 221, 226–7, 231, 241
   interaction with endogenous factors 134, 216–17, 228, 239, 241

Feedback
    loops 42, 188, 206, 213, 219, 228
    negative 36, 198–206ff
    positive 30, 188–98ff
    see also, policy feedback
Feed-in tariffs 34, 45, 48, 198
Financial crisis 71, 90, 96, 124, 146, 148, 157, 176, 179, 227
Flexibility 7, 10, 21–2, 29, 230, 232, 234–6, 238, 241
    clauses 22, 42, 46–7, 219–20, 228
    devices 11, 22–3, 27, 29–30, 42, 45–7, 51–4, 220, 228
    in policy design 44, 46, 50–1, 57, 60–2, 64
Focusing events 13, 38, 41, 69, 118, 142, 193, 199, 202, 219, 228, 243
    see also, political agendas
France 60, 73, 75, 85, 108, 123, 126, 151–2, 155, 160, 164, 172, 180–1
Friends of the Earth 132

Gazprom 69
Germany 5, 48, 63, 65, 67, 73, 79, 85, 108, 115, 139–40, 145–6, 151–2, 160, 162–5, 169, 171–2, 178, 203–4
Green Growth Group 72, 154
Greenpeace 178

Heatwaves xi
High Ambition Coalition 74
High Level Group of the European Commission 143, 171
    on Automotive Regulatory Systems (CARS 21) 171
    on Competitiveness, Energy and Environment 143, 202, 204
Historical institutionalism 19, 32, 59, 188, 197

Indirect land use change (ILUC) 84, 89, 118
    Directive on (2015) 89, 107–8, 118, 128–31, 191, 201–2, 208, 210, 221–2
    EU policy on 118, 121, 123–8, 201–2
    science of 84, 108
Intentional policy design xii, 8–10, 14, 16, 20, 24–5, 27, 29, 42–3, 53, 60, 188, 229–30, 233
    see also, policy design
Interest groups 5, 12–13, 16–18, 22, 26, 38, 40–1, 58–60, 80, 84, 90, 99–100, 152, 160, 188, 190, 193, 195–6, 199, 206–7, 212, 214–16, 221, 231
Intergovernmental Panel on Climate Change (IPCC) 3–4, 64, 67
International Emissions Trading Association (IETA) 134, 193, 203
Interpretive feedback mechanisms 13, 14–15, 18, 26, 29, 38, 41–2, 66, 104, 144, 187ff, 193, 199, 201–3, 205–7, 215–17, 219, 224, 232
    see also, policy feedback mechanisms
    see also, resource/incentive feedback mechanisms

Kyoto Protocol 67–72, 74, 93, 236
    and car emissions from the EU 165, 171
    and the EU Emissions Trading System 93, 133–6, 138–9, 141–2, 144

Manual 47–8, 52, 61, 96, 138, 233
    policy changes 47, 52
    policy change devices 47, 52
    see also automatic
Market-based instruments 24, 63
    definition of 50
    in the EU 63
    main types of 9, 23–4, 27, 48–52, 63, 78, 195, 207–8
Market Stability Reserve (MSR) 134, 149, 151–3, 156, 204, 208, 226, 233
    see also, emissions trading
Merkel, Angela 172, 178
Monitoring 22, 42, 45–7, 62, 66, 68, 77, 87, 94, 194, 196, 220, 236
    clauses 45, 232
    in the EU Emissions Trading System 215
    of biofuel production 150
    of car emissions 168–9
Motor Vehicle Emissions Group (MVEG) 160–1

National Allocation Plan (NAP) 94–5, 138, 145, 192, 203
    see also, emissions trading
Negative feedback 36, 198–206ff
    in policy 14, 19, 21, 26, 36
    in politics 36
    see also, positive feedback
Negative learning 13, 38, 194, 197, 205, 215
    see also, policy learning
Negative policy feedback 8, 14, 19, 36–7, 198–206ff, 217–18, 220, 243
    characteristics of 36–9
    definition of 19, 37
    explanations of 36–9, 229
    see also, positive policy feedback
Netherlands 63, 65, 73, 75, 79, 119, 127, 132, 135, 149, 155, 159–60, 164
Net zero greenhouse gas emissions xi, 3, 8, 74–5, 237–8, 243
    see also, deep decarbonisation

Obama, Barack 71, 75
Organisation for Economic Co-operation and Development (OECD) 50, 81–2, 117, 202
Oxfam 86, 117

Paris Agreement xi, 73–5, 129, 155, 227
Path dependence 16, 25, 28, 30–2, 52–3, 230, 242
    see also, policy lock-ins
    see also, positive policy feedback
Pensions policy 6, 22, 28
    in the US 14, 16, 33, 37, 58
Poland 70, 72–3, 75, 126–7, 140, 149–53, 155, 178, 203

Policy 20
  definition of 20
  different sub-levels of 20, 23
Policy adoption 4, 8, 16
Policy alarms 240
Policy change xii, 36
  broader theories of 241
Policy design xii, 8, 27, 43–4, 241
  challenges of 4, 16
  game of 76
  intentionality of 8, 14–15, 43, 230
  intentions 43
  meanings of 44, 230
  processes of 48, 232
  scope of 26
  space 24, 27, 233
  stringency 26
Policy dismantling 5, 14, 21, 32, 40, 54, 61, 230
Policy drift xiii, 7, 10, 14, 20, 22, 28, 47, 52, 61, 235, 238, 241, 244
Policy durability 5, 210, 212, 234–6, 238
  active forms of 239
  and flexibility 10–11, 235–6, 238, 241
  definition of 4, 6, 213, 238
  devices 11, 22, 45, 47, 51, 77, 232, 241
  dimensions of 7, 10
  see also, automatic
  see also, manual
  see also, policy flexibility
Policy entrepreneurs 16, 41–3, 58, 65, 136, 221, 227–8
Policy evaluation 11, 181, 202
Policy feedback xii, 5, 211, 213, 219, 228, 240
  definition of 5, 11–12, 17, 213
  directions of 11–12
  effects 11–12, 17, 27, 188, 213, 219
  existing literature on 5–6, 214
  first-order effects 17, 27
  loops 17, 32, 188, 206, 213, 219, 228
  mechanisms of 11, 13
  sequences 27, 220
  syncretic approach to 41
Policy feedback mechanisms 11, 13
  see also, interpretive feedback mechanisms
  see also, resource/incentive feedback mechanisms
Policy flexibility 7, 46, 234
  definition of 22
  devices 22, 46–7, 51, 77, 220, 232
  see also, automatic
  see also, manual
  see also, policy durability
Policy formulation xii, 16, 38–9, 42, 87, 91, 94, 114, 122, 125, 135, 137, 140, 197, 199–200, 219, 234
Policy fragility 187, 213, 226
Policy innovation 72, 78, 92, 101
Policy instruments xii, 7, 9, 17, 23, 44
  definition of 49
  main sub-types of 9, 19, 23–4, 27, 49

sequences 80, 104, 207–8, 210–11, 213, 219, 231
  stringency of 24
  toolbox of 49, 54
  typology of 49, 51
Policy layering 20, 28, 241
Policy learning 13, 34, 41, 187, 194
  see also, negative learning
Policy lock-ins 22, 35, 60, 99, 125, 218, 220, 228, 230, 238
  and policy durability 35
  see also, path dependence
Policy outcomes 7, 9
  see also, policy drift
Policy packages xii, 9, 23, 212
Policy paradigm 23, 25, 38, 42, 229, 232, 239
  definition of 23, 244
  of EU climate policy 23, 65, 70–1, 73–4, 239–40
Policy programme 20, 22
  definition of 20
  goals of 20, 22
Policy regimes 19, 28, 31–2
  in climate policy 31
Policy reporting 22, 201–2
  in EU policy 68, 87, 89, 94, 110, 114, 121, 129, 143, 175, 190–1, 194, 201
  see also, monitoring
Policy scope 26
Policy stringency 6
Political agendas 99–100, 161, 171, 180
  and focusing events 38, 69, 193, 199, 202, 219, 228, 243
  and windows of opportunity 123, 135, 163, 227, 237
Polity 45–8, 60–1, 66, 74, 77, 138, 228
Positive feedback 30, 188
  in policy 32
  in politics 31
  see also, negative feedback
Positive policy feedback xii, 6, 8, 14, 32, 188–98ff, 215, 217–19, 243
  characteristics of xii, 43
  explanations of 32–3, 229
  see also, negative policy feedback
Process tracing 8–9, 19, 21, 188, 207, 214, 231
  and forward tracing 16, 18, 25, 188, 217–19, 231, 234–6, 238, 241
  and policy feedback research 19, 21, 188, 207, 214, 231
  backward tracing 12, 32
  definition of 52
  method of 52–4

Regulatory instruments 24, 62
  definition of 62
  main types of 24, 62
  smarter forms of 54
Regulatory policy 6, 14, 16, 18
Relational contracts 46–7, 54
  use in EU climate policy 73, 76–7, 88, 165, 174, 232

Renewable energy 89
  Directive on (2009) 89, 106, 109, 119–22, 131, 190, 201, 222, 233
  Directive on (2018) 89, 130–1, 221–2
  Directive on Indirect Land Use Change (2015) 89, 107
  policy in the EU 108
Renewable Ethanol Association (ePure) 85, 128, 130, 226
Resource/incentive feedback mechanisms 13
  see also, policy feedback mechanisms
Revert clauses 46–7
  in EU climate policy 73, 76–7, 79, 236
Russia 69, 79

Scientific complexity 58
Smart regulation 54
  see also, regulatory instruments
Subsidies 34, 45, 62, 83, 86, 110, 121, 126, 132, 190, 198, 211, 216, 243
Sunset clauses 46–7, 77
  see also, regulatory instruments
Sweden 34, 114–15
Systems analysis 30, 36, 188, 197–8
  and feedback 188, 197–8

Target groups 6, 8, 10, 12, 22, 24–6, 32–4, 40–1, 43, 45, 47, 51–2, 59, 187–95, 198–204, 206, 214–15, 220, 231
  see also, interest groups
Technology 59, 78, 242
  and policy change 242
  drop-in types of 99, 106, 110–11, 165, 190, 195, 201
  radical innovations 99–100
Transport and Environment (T&E) 112, 169, 174–6, 178–9, 200, 227

Transitions approaches 242
Trump, Donald 75

Unemployment policy 6, 34
United Kingdom 60, 65, 67, 73, 79, 92–3, 95, 126, 135, 148–9, 151–2, 155, 160–1, 170, 178
United Nations Framework Convention on Climate Change (UNFCCC) 66–7, 74, 76, 80, 142, 144, 147, 161–2, 173, 175
United States 9, 14–17, 26, 33, 39, 46, 58, 67–8, 75, 103, 119, 134–5, 142, 161, 169, 171, 180, 215, 217, 236

Veto players 60–2, 76, 136
Veto points 47, 234
Voluntary agreement 29, 49, 51, 63–4
  EU agreement on car emissions (1999) 101–3, 158, 163, 182, 195, 204, 225
  see also car emissions
Voluntary instruments 24, 63
  definition of 50
Volkswagen 103, 179
  and Dieselgate 103, 180, 196, 205, 219, 238, 241, 243

Welfare state 20
  in the US 16, 39
  policies on 5–7, 15, 19, 57–8, 62, 78, 206, 242
  reform of 32, 230
Wicked policy problems 3, 8, 188, 212
World Bank 4
World Trade Organisation (WTO) 111
World Wildlife Fund for Nature (WWF) 86, 167

CPSIA information can be obtained
at www.ICGtesting.com
Printed in the USA
LVHW060825280721
693842LV00007BA/576